GRAMMATICAL METAPHOR

AMSTERDAM STUDIES IN THE THEORY AND HISTORY OF LINGUISTIC SCIENCE

General Editor

E. F. KONRAD KOERNER

(Zentrum für Allgemeine Sprachwissenschaft, Typologie und Universalienforschung, Berlin)

Series IV – CURRENT ISSUES IN LINGUISTIC THEORY

Volume 236

Anne-Marie Simon-Vandenbergen, Miriam Taverniers
and Louise Ravelli (eds.)

Grammatical Metaphor: Views from systemic functional linguistics

GRAMMATICAL METAPHOR

VIEWS FROM SYSTEMIC FUNCTIONAL LINGUISTICS

Edited by

ANNE-MARIE SIMON-VANDENBERGEN

MIRIAM TAVERNIERS
University of Gent

LOUISE RAVELLI
University of New South Wales

JOHN BENJAMINS PUBLISHING COMPANY
AMSTERDAM/PHILADELPHIA

TM The paper used in this publication meets the minimum requirements of American National Standard for Information Sciences — Permanence of Paper for Printed Library Materials, ANSI Z39.48-1984.

Library of Congress Cataloging-in-Publication Data

Grammatical metaphor: views from systemic functional linguistics / edited by Anne-Marie Simon-Vandenbergen, Mirjam Taverniers, Louise Ravelli.

    p.   cm. -- (Amsterdam studies in the theory and history of linguistic science. Series IV, Current issues in linguistic theory, ISSN 0304-0763 ; v. 236)

    Includes bibliographical references and index.

    1. Metaphor. 2. Systemic grammar. 3. Language acquisition. I. Simon-Vandenbergen, A. M. II. Taverniers, Miriam. III. Ravelli, Louise. IV. Series.

P301.5.M48G69 2003

415'.01--dc22   2003062592

ISBN 90 272 4748 X (Eur.) / 1 58811 368 X (US) (Hb; alk. paper)

John Benjamins Publishing Co. • P.O.Box 36224 • 1020 ME Amsterdam · The Netherlands
John Benjamins North America • P.O.Box 27519 • Philadelphia PA 19118-0519 • USA

Contents

Preface

James R. Martin
University of Sydney

It goes without saying that Michael Halliday is the most extravagant grammarian of his generation, elaborating his descriptions of English and Chinese above and beyond the call of duty. And alongside this descriptive largesse, Halliday also ranks as one of the most extroverted linguists of the 20th century – continually enriching the gaze of his discipline in the manner of Saussure, Sapir, Whorf, Hjelmslev and like-minded seers. In my experience, the key concept which has operationalised this extroversion is grammatical metaphor, which makes this volume a timely one as a new generation of functional linguists recontextualises linguistics for a new millennium.

I had the personal good fortune of working with Halliday in the Linguistics Department he founded at the University of Sydney, and so was able to work with drafts of papers and chapters and listen to talks and lectures as his presentations of grammatical metaphor evolved from the early 80s. I was of course at the time overwhelmed by the richness of Halliday's emerging functional grammar of English, and struggling to learn to use it to analyse English texts and explore Tagalog grammar in comparable terms. But as a discourse analyst, the ideas that really excited me had to do with interpersonal and ideational metaphor – since they opened up a pathway from grammar to discourse semantics, and from discourse semantics to context that had not been available before.

As far as discourse semantics was concerned, my colleagues and I drew heavily on Halliday's work on mood, speech function and interpersonal metaphor to develop models of dialogue; and we were inspired by Halliday's outline of ideational metaphor to develop our understanding of information flow ('hierarchy of periodicity' as it came to be known). As for context, grammatical metaphor gave us some essential tools we needed for analysing tenor (metaphors of modality and mood in relation to power and solidarity), field (ideational metaphor in relation to taxonomising and reasoning) and mode (congruent and metaphorical textures of information flow across modalities). Halliday's genetic perspective on all of this, as a text unfolds, as language develops in the individual and as a culture evolves further enriched our understanding of discourse – including those varieties we were unpacking with a view to intervening in language education programs.

These were heady days, and all of this was tremendously exciting – for description, theory and a range of applications. In retrospect I have no doubt that Halliday's concept of grammatical metaphor mobilised the rest of his linguistics in ways that could not otherwise have been enacted. Indeed, as early as 1990 in draft of *English Text* I was waxing poetically about grammatical metaphor, in an arguably imprudent lapse of style, as "the key to understanding text in context – to contextualising the ineffable ... the meta-process behind a text... (the co-ordinator of) the synoptic systems and dynamic processes that give rise to text ... the technology that lets the modules harmonise ... their medium, their catalyst, the groove of their symbiosis, their mediator ... the re/source of texture" (Martin 1992: 490-491). Over the top perhaps; but it registers the positive affect charging the previous decade of research, and the politics of making that work relevant to the world outside.

I think the present volume both symbolises and enacts comparable feelings; and I'm sure it will spread some comparable excitement around. Like everything in linguistics, grammatical metaphor is an unfinished project through the lens of which we catch a glimpse of language as it instantiates around us moment by moment, in the meanings through which we live our lives. The papers included here open up this window in ways it has not been opened before. Many conversations will ensue, from which we will learn more about what it means to engage extravagantly with language – so that we can dialogue across the disciplinary boundaries of modernity in more extroverted ways. For this prospect I commend the editors for their thoughtful collection of papers, which push productively at the edge of knowledge along one very very fruitful frontier.

J R Martin
Department of Linguistics, University of Sydney

Reference

Martin, J.R. (1992) *English Text: System and structure*. Amsterdam: Benjamins.

Grammatical metaphor in SFL
A historiography of
the introduction and initial study of the concept

Miriam Taverniers
University of Ghent

This paper presents the concept of 'grammatical metaphor' as it has been introduced and developed within the theory of SFL. Its purpose is purely historiographic, i.e. it merely *presents* the emergence of a framework for exploring grammatical metaphor in the 1980s, paying special attention to the theoretical context which formed the background for the introduction of this new concept in SFL.[1]

1. Halliday 1985

The concept of grammatical metaphor was introduced in Halliday's *Introduction to Functional Grammar* (1985), in a separate chapter on this subject: "Beyond the clause: Metaphorical modes of expression". In this chapter, the term 'grammatical metaphor' is launched as a type of metaphor complementing the more commonly known lexical metaphor, and two types are distinguished: ideational and interpersonal grammatical metaphors.

1.1. Grammatical metaphor and the lexicogrammar continuum

Halliday places his introduction of the term grammatical metaphor in a more general framework outlining traditionally recognized types of 'rhetorical trans-ference' or 'figures of speech': metaphor, metonymy and synecdoche. Focussing on metaphor, he expands the traditional definition in a number of steps, thus making room for a newly-identified type, grammatical metaphor.

First, a different type of perspective on metaphor is introduced. Traditionally, metaphor is viewed as variation in the use of words, i.e. variation in *meaning*: "a word is said to be used with a transferred meaning" (Halliday 1985: 321). In this sense, a lexeme with a certain *literal* meaning can have *metaphorical*, transferred uses or meanings. In terms of three general types of perspectives which are distinguished in SFL (cf., e.g. Halliday 1996: 16), this is a view 'from below', taking the words as starting point, and then saying something about the meanings these words realize.

This view can be complemented by a perspective 'from above', as Halliday shows. Here, the starting point is a particular meaning and the relevant question is: which are the different ways in which this meaning can be expressed or realized? Looked at from this angle, metaphor is defined as "variation in the *expression* of meanings" (ibid., emphasis MT). The two alternative perspectives are visually represented in Figure 1 (based on Halliday's figure (1994/1985: 342)).

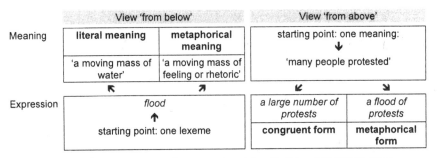

Figure 1: Two perspectives on metaphor (after Halliday 1994/1985: 342)

Taking this view 'from above', it is argued, "we recognize that lexical selection is just one aspect of lexicogrammatical selection, or 'wording'; and that metaphorical variation is lexicogrammatical rather than simply lexical" (1994/1985: 342). In this perspective, different expressions of one meaning are compared. In general, it is hard to find alternative expressions of a given meaning which only differ from each other in one lexeme. Halliday gives the following example: the expression *protests flooded in* can be linked to *protests came in in large quantities, protests were received in large quantities* or *very many people protested*. In none of these is the variation purely lexical; there is also a difference in the grammatical configuration: in *protests came in in large quantities*, a prepositional phrase is added, in *very many people protested* the noun *protests* is now represented by a verb. This brings Halliday (1985: 320, 1994/1985: 342) to grammatical metaphor:

There is a strong grammatical element in rhetorical transference; and once we have recognized this we find that there is also such a thing as grammatical metaphor, where the variation is essentially in the grammatical forms although often entailing some lexical variation as well.

In the area of grammatical metaphor, Halliday claims, the term 'literal' is no longer appropriate. The variation between the different expressions of the same meaning is defined in terms of *markedness*: certain forms can be recognized as unmarked expressions of the given meaning, conforming to the "*typical* ways of saying things" (ibid.: 321, emphasis MT) – these forms are the non-metaphorical variants, which are called 'congruent' realizations.

Before we turn to the more detailed description of types of grammatical metaphor which Halliday gives further on in this chapter, it is useful to point out some general aspects of the shift in perspective – from a focus on lexical variation to a focus on grammatical variation – which lies at the basis of Halliday's introduction of the concept 'grammatical metaphor'.

Crucially, the very recognition of a 'grammatical' type of metaphor is a consequence of the 'view from above', which is introduced as an alternative to the traditional view on metaphor – and the nature of this perspective determines the major aspects of Halliday's further characterization of grammatical metaphor in this chapter. Since these aspects also form a central motif through the various explorations of grammatical metaphor in later work, it is important to explicitly explain them against the background of this general 'perspective from above'.

As Halliday indicates, the main feature of the view 'from above' is that it defines metaphor as variation in the *expression* of a given meaning, rather than variation in the *meaning* of a given expression. This has important consequences which are not explicitly pointed at by Halliday (see the summary in Table 1):

(i)   What comes to be compared are grammatical *configurations*, whereas in the traditional perspective, the focus is on meanings of a single lexeme. It is exactly this feature which brings in grammatical variation, which can then be interpreted in terms of metaphor.

(ii) *Various* different types of configurations can be compared as expressions of the same meaning. This means that, whereas in the traditional perspective, there is a simple opposition between literal and metaphorical, there is now a *scale of congruency*: some expressions are typical realizations of the given meaning, and are defined as congruent; others are more or less incongruent, as compared to the congruent realization(s). This feature will be important in the *description* of various types of metaphors in later work.

(iii) The concept of *realization* comes to play an important role: what is compared, in this view, is different realizations of the same meaning. This aspect will be important in the *theoretical* characterization of grammatical metaphor in later work.

Traditional view: 'from below'	New view: 'from above'
focus on lexical metaphor	focus on grammatical metaphor
metaphor as variation in the *meaning* of a given expression	metaphor as variation in the *expression* of a given meaning
comparison of the meanings of one *lexeme* (in different collocational contexts)	comparison of various grammatical *configurations* as expressions of the same meaning
literal versus metaphorical (transferred) meanings of a given lexeme	*degrees of (in)congruency*: congruent and less congruent expressions of a given meaning
(realization inherently plays a role in lexical metaphor, but the concept is not used in the traditional view on metaphor)	the feature of congruency applies to *realizations* of the same meaning

Table 1: Two perspectives on metaphorical variation

1.2. *Ideational grammatical metaphor*

Ideational grammatical metaphors are called **metaphors of transitivity**. The grammatical variation between congruent and incongruent forms here applies to transitivity configurations, and can be analysed in terms of the functional structure of these configurations. In order to bring out the metaphorical nature of an incongruent expression, it is compared to an equivalent congruent realization. The functional analyses of the two expressions are combined into a single diagram with a congruent and incongruent layer, so that grammatical contrasts between the constituents are shown in the vertical dimension: "(t)he technique here is to match the elements vertically as closely as possible" (Halliday 1985: 325, 1994/1985: 346). In this way also variations pertaining to lexical metaphor become clear, and suggestions can be made as to the reasons (e.g. in terms of Theme-Rheme distribution) why a metaphorical construal was chosen. Examples[2] given by Halliday are ›*Mary came upon a wonderful sight*‹ and ›*a wonderful sight met Mary's eyes*‹ as metaphorical variants of *Mary saw something wonderful*. In Figure 2, these are analysed according to the type of representation which Halliday proposes. Another of Halliday's oft-cited examples is ›*the fifth day saw them at the summit*‹ (congruent: *they arrived at the summit on the fifth day*).

Congruent	Mary	saw	something wonderful.		Mary	saw	something wonderful.
	participant: Senser	process: mental:perceptive	participant: Phenomenon		participant: Senser	process: mental:perceptive	participant: Phenomenon

Incongruent	A wonderful sight	met	Mary's eyes.		Mary	came	upon a w. sight.
	participant: Actor	process: material	participant: Actor		participant: Actor	process: material	Circumstance: location

Figure 2: Analysis of transitivity metaphors

In the analysis of more complex types of transitivity metaphors, it is possible to indicate a *"chain of metaphorical interpretations"* (Halliday 1985: 328, 1994/1985: 349) as steps in between the metaphorical form under analysis and a (completely) congruent expression. An illustration of such a chain given by Halliday is included below as example (1) (with (e) representing the most congruent form).

(1) a. ›Advances in technology are speeding up the writing of business programs.

b. ›Advances in technology are making the writing of business programs faster.

c. ›Advances in technology are enabling people to write business programs faster.

d. ›Because technology is advancing, people are (becoming) able to write business programs faster.

e. Because technology is getting better, people are able to write business programs faster.   (Halliday 1994/1985)

A number of aspects are mentioned about the distribution of transitivity metaphors. Ideational metaphors are found in all types of adult discourse. Complete congruency and complete incongruency are rare (Halliday 1985: 328, 1994/1985: 349):

> It seems that, in most types of discourse, both spoken and written, we tend to operate somewhere in between these two extremes. Something which is totally congruent is likely to sound a bit flat; whereas the totally in-congruent often seems artificial and contrived.

In general, Halliday argues, written language has more ideational meta-phors than spoken discourse. This is attributed to a more general difference in types of complexity: written language is said to be "lexically dense", whereas spoken language is "grammatically intricate". In written language, various lexical meanings are often 'packed' into one single nominal group. This is the context in which ideational metaphor occurs. (Halliday does not further explain this aspect of the distribution of metaphor.)

Throughout the history of language, demetaphorization occurs: grammatical metaphors gradually lose their metaphorical nature, and in this way become "domesticated" (ibid.). Halliday gives three types of what he regards as 'domesticated' transitivitiy metaphors in English:

(i) expressions of the type ›*have a bath*‹, ›*do a dance*‹, ›*make a mistake*‹: in these forms, the meaning of the process is expressed in the Range rather than the verb;

(ii) examples such as ›*she has brown eyes*‹ (congruent: *her eyes are brown*) or ›*he has a broken wrist*‹ (congruent: *his wrist is broken*);

(iii) expressions such as ›*he writes good books*‹ (congruent: *he writes books, which are good*) or ›*we sell bargains*‹ (congruent: *the things we sell are cheap*).

1.3. Interpersonal grammatical metaphor

Since interpersonal grammar in general is organized in two systems, viz. of MOOD and MODALITY, two types of interpersonal grammatical metaphor can be distinguished.

In **metaphors of modality**, the grammatical variation which occurs is based on the logico-semantic relationship of projection. Whereas modal meanings are congruently realized in modal elements in the clause (i.e. modal operators, modal adjuncts or mood adjuncts), interpersonal metaphors are defined by Halliday as expressing modal meanings *outside the clause*, for instance by means of an additional projecting clause, as is illustrated in example (2). In this way, metaphors of modality are *explicit* realizations of modal meanings. Speakers can express their opinions in separate clauses in various ways. Some further possibilities given by Halliday are illustrated in (3).

(2) a. *I think* ↪ *it's going to rain.*
   b. Congruent: *It is **probably** going to rain.*   (Halliday 1985)

(3) *it is obvious that* ↪ ...
   everyone admits that ↪ ...
   the conclusion can hardly be avoided that ↪ ...
   no sane person would pretend that ↪ ... *not* ...
   commonsense determines that ↪ ...
   you can't seriously doubt that ↪ ...   (Halliday 1985)

Because of the great diversity in explicit expressions of modal meanings, Halliday states, "(i)t is not always possible to say exactly what is and what is not a metaphorical representation of modality" (1985: 334; 1994/1985: 355). Typical examples of interpersonal metaphor (involving projection) are characterized by two features (it is these features which suggest that these expressions are metaphorical):

(i)   The proposition is expressed in the projected clause, rather than the projecting one. This is shown by the fact that the tag represents the projected clause, as in *I think* ➔ *it's going to rain, isn't it?* (not: *don't I?*).

(ii)   When the proposition is negative, the negation can either be expressed in the proposition itself, or in the projecting clause. This is illustrated in (4), where (a) and (b) (with transferred polarity feature) are said to have the same 'meaning'.

(4)   a. *I think* ➔ *Jane doesn't know.*
         b. *I don't think* ➔ *Jane knows*

Halliday describes **metaphors of mood** in a similar way as metaphors of modality: in this type of interpersonal metaphor, a mood meaning is not expressed in the clause, but rather as an explicit element outside the clause. Typical examples of mood metaphors are "speech-functional formulae" (1994/1985: 365), of which Halliday gives the following examples:

(5)   'Command' functioning as a 'warning':
         a. *I wouldn't* ➔ *... if I were you.*
         b. Congruent: *don't ...!*

(6)   Modalized 'offer', typically functioning as 'threat':
         a. *I've a good mind to* ➔ *...*
         b. Congruent: *Maybe I'll ...*

(7)   Modulated 'command', typically functioning as 'advice':
         a. *She'd better* ➔ *...*
         b. Congruent: *She should ...*

The possible explicit expressions of mood meanings are very diverse, and it is not easy to decide whether a given expression should be interpreted as a mood metaphor.

1.4. Ideational and interpersonal metaphors: General aspects

In the final paragraphs of his chapter, Halliday points to the interaction between ideational and interpersonal metaphors, and mentions some general aspects which characterize both types.

Some expressions contain both interpersonal and ideational metaphors. Halliday illustrates this with the example *look at ›the way they cheated before‹*. As an expression of a 'request' with the meaning *'consider the fact that they cheated before'*, this form is metaphorical in the ideational sense only. However, when taken as an incongruent realization of the meaning *'the evidence is (the fact) that they cheated before'*, both interpersonal and ideational metaphors are involved (*look at ➔ ›the way they cheated before‹*).[3]

Halliday finally suggests that the concept of grammatical metaphor "enables us to bring together a number of features of discourse which at first sight look rather different from each other" (1985: 343, 1994/1985: 366). In this sense, interpersonal and ideational metaphors are "really instances of the same phenomenon arising in these two different contexts (ideational and interpersonal, MT)". All the instances of grammatical metaphor which are analysed can be linked to the same general features:

> In all the instances that we are treating as grammatical metaphor, some aspect of the structural configuration of the clause, whether in its ideational or in its interpersonal function or in both, is in some way different from that which would be arrived at by the shortest route – it is not, or was not originally, the most straightforward coding of the meanings selected. (Halliday 1985: 343, 1994/1985: 366)

1.5. Conclusion

In this section, we have looked at the first presentation of grammatical metaphor as offered by Halliday in his *Introduction to Functional Grammar* (1985). Halliday introduces the concept as an equivalent of lexical metaphor on the opposite end of the lexicogrammatical continuum. We have seen that the recognition of this type of metaphor depends on a shift in perspective – starting from the semantics rather than the lexicogrammar, which redefines metaphor as variation in the expression of a given meaning. I have argued that the nature of this new perspective determines the main features of the framework in which grammatical metaphor is understood: *various configurations* are compared as alternative *realizations* of the same meaning; their variation is analysed in terms of their *functional structures*; and they can be placed on a scale of *congruency*, the metaphorical variants being termed 'incongruent'.

The notion of congruency is characterized in terms of *markedness*: congruent expressions are the unmarked, typical realizations of the given meaning. In this initial description, the new concepts of grammatical metaphoricity and incongruency are characterized in relation to intuitive notions: what is congruent conforms to 'the typical ways of saying things', it is the form of coding 'arrived at by the shortest route', 'the most straightforward coding of the meanings selected'. No explicit definition of grammatical metaphor is given, and while the intuitive explanations seem plausible in the descriptions of ideational and interpersonal metaphors, it is not clear *why exactly* the analysed expressions are metaphors. More specifically, it is difficult to see why exactly the different types of expressions mentioned (metaphors of transitivity, metaphors of modality and of mood) are all metaphorical, i.e. what is common in their structure.

2.   The theme of congruence in earlier work

In his *Introduction to Functional Grammar* (1985), Halliday introduces grammatical metaphor as a specific phenomenon which has to be accounted for in a grammar, and characterizes it in general in terms of congruence. Although the term 'grammatical metaphor' first appears in this context, the concept of incongruence (and even metaphor in a broad sense) turns up at different points in earlier work by Halliday and by Robin Fawcett. This section aims to outline the various meanings of 'congruence' in these different contexts. Because of the role of 'congruence' in the characterization of grammatical metaphor, these meanings can be seen as the general background against which the concept of grammatical metaphor emerged.

2.1.   The concept of congruence in early work by Halliday

2.1.1.   Congruence, markedness and probability value

Halliday's "Grammatical categories in Modern Chinese" (Halliday 1976/1956) is the first publication in which the term 'congruent' appears. In this article, Halliday describes different types of grammatical structures in Chinese. In cases where alternative forms exist of a basic structure (differing, for example, in word order), the likelihood of occurrence of each form is expressed as a probability value (such as "'+", meaning 'is likely to occur'; "'−", meaning 'may occur'). In this context, "a grammatical structure which reflects a contextual structure (by matching it with maximum probability)" (Halliday 1976: 42) is termed *'congruent'*. In language, this is indicated in the *unmarked* phonological reflection of that form. Halliday gives an example of Given–New structures:

Here the congruent grammatical form is that in which given precedes new; in the congruent form, stress is facultative (that is, there is no stress system at this point), while in the incongruent form the formal mark of incongruence is the phonological reflection of the new by stress. The use of the concept here, and the choice of the phonologically unmarked member as the congruent term, are justified by the probability function taken together with the stress marking of the one form and not the other. (ibid.)

2.1.2. Congruence and social varieties of language

The theme of congruence turns up in two studies of language in social contexts (a major theme in SFL in the 1970s). In the article on "Language in urban society", Halliday (1978b) deals with the use of different social varieties of language in different contexts. The use of high varieties of language in formal contexts and low varieties in informal contexts is called "the congruent pattern" (Halliday 1978b: 156). It is the pattern in which a language variety is used in that context by which it is defined as the *norm*. A speaker can also use a language variety incongruently, i.e. in a context where it is not the norm. This incongruent use of language is meaningful, Halliday stresses, because it creates a *foregrounding* effect.

Congruence is linked to the idea of metaphor in an article devoted to "Anti-languages" (Halliday 1978c). An antilanguage is a type of language created by and maintaining an antisociety, which is set up within an existing society as a form or resistance. As a conscious alternative to standard language, an antilangue has its own types of codings, which are variants of the standard ones. This can be seen at various levels in the antilanguage, especially phonology and morphology, but also lexicogrammar and semantics (Halliday illustrates these variants with expressions from the Calcutta underworld language):

(i)   Phonological variants are formed through processes such as metathesis, back formation, consonantal change, syllabic insertion.

(ii)   Morphological variants differ from standard language through derivational processes: suffixing, compounding, shift of word class.

(iii)   Lexical variants involve lexical borrowing or alternation (i.e. lexical metaphorical transfers).

(iv)   Syntactic variants are formed through expansions.[4]

(v)   Semantic variants are new forms which have no 'semantic' equivalent in the standard language.

The term *variants* is used here as in Labov's (1969) variation theory, in the sense of "alternative ways of 'saying the same thing'" (Labov 1969, quoted by Halliday, quotation marks WL). Halliday points out that each of these (types of) variants can be described in more general terms as "an *alternative realization* of an element on the next, or on some, higher stratum" (Halliday 1978c: 173, emphasis MT). Morphological, lexical and syntactic variants are alternative lexicogrammatical realizations of the same meaning, phonological variants are alternative realizations of the same word (and hence, also, the same meaning). In general, "(a)ssuming the semantic stratum to be the highest within the linguistic system, *all* sets of variants have the property of being identical semantically; *some* have the property of being identical lexicogrammatically as well" (Halliday 1978c: 173, emphasis MAKH). This is a general way in which the variants can be understood. On the other hand, Halliday observes:

> Now the significant thing about the items that are phonologically or morphologically distinctive in the underworld language is that many of them are not, in fact, variants at all; they have no semantic equivalent in standard Bengali. This does not mean that they cannot be *translated* into standard Bengali (or standard English, or standard anything else): they can. But they do not function as *coded* elements in the semantic system of everyday language. (Halliday 1978c: 173, emphasis MAKH)

Halliday dismisses this issue of whether variants have the same meaning or not by calling them "metaphorical variants":

> There is no way of deciding whether such metaphorical representations 'have the same meaning' as everyday forms or not, i.e. whether they are or are not variants in Labov's definition. [...] Nor is there any need to decide. We can call them all 'metaphorical variants', since it is helpful to relate them to variation theory; what is most important is the fact that they are metaphorical. (Halliday 1978c: 175)

However, Halliday keeps the general idea that variants are alternative realizations of an element at the next higher stratum – and in this vein, he recognizes a fifth type of variant: semantic variants. Semantic variants realize the same element in the stratum of the cultural context: they "'come together' (i.e. are interpretable) at the higher level, that of the culture as an information system" (ibid.: 177).

The variants are referred to as *phonological metaphors*, *grammatical metaphors* (which are morphological, lexical or syntactic) and *semantic metaphors*. As alternative realizations, the variant expressions in an antilanguage can generally be defined as new ways of *coding* which do not occur in the system of everyday language.

The stratum of the context of culture is important in an understanding of antilanguage in general. Halliday explains this by using Lévi-Strauss's (1966) interpretation of social systems in terms of metaphor and metonymy: an anti-society is a metonymic extension of (mainstream) society, and its realizations (both in its social structure and in its language: in an antilanguage) can be regarded as metaphorical to the mainstream realization (mainstream society and everyday language). The metaphorical nature of the antilinguistic variant forms, Halliday argues, is precisely what sets off an antilanguage from the standard language against which it is created as a conscious alternative. Therefore, an antilanguage in general can be seen as "a metaphor for everyday language" (ibid.: 175).

Because an antilanguage as a whole is a metaphor for everyday language, it is only with reference to everyday language that the antilinguistic variants can be called metaphorical. Within the antilanguage as such, these expressions are the *norm*, they are "the *regular* patterns of realization" (ibid.: 177, emphasis MT).

Whereas antilanguage as a whole is a metaphor of everyday language, metaphorical expressions naturally occur *within* everday language as well. Halliday explains the phenomenon of metaphor as a natural feature of language in terms of coding:

> Conversation [...] depends for its reality-generating power on being casual; that is to say, it *typically* makes use of *highly coded* areas of the *system* to produce *text* that is *congruent* – though once coding and congruence have been established as the norm, it can tolerate and indeed thrives on a reasonable quantity of matter that is incongruent or uncoded. 'Uncoded' means 'not (yet) fully incorporated into the system'; 'incongruent' means 'not expressed through the most typical (and highly coded) form of representation'; and both concepts are of a 'more or less' kind, not 'all or nothing'. (Halliday 1978c: 180, emphasis MAKH).

In certain types of social context, the coding process itself is important, and through this the aspect of (in)congruence comes to be foregrounded. This is the case in the language of young children, where a system is still emerging; or in what Halliday calls "verbal contest and display", where the coding is fore-grounded because of a particular function of the system, for example, as a form of resistance. An antilanguage is such a type of 'verbal context and display'.

2.2. Congruence in the interpersonal component: Halliday 1984

In the article "Language as code and language as behaviour: A systemic-functional interpretation of the nature and ontogenesis of dialogue", Halliday (1984) deals with the relationship between system (language as code, as a potential) and process (language as actual behaviour) in the interpersonal component. The general aim of this paper is to show how systems are actualized in dialogue, and how an analysis of dialogue leads to a refinement of the systems. Halliday illustrates this system-process interaction with examples from the ontogenesis of language, setting up interpersonal systems for various stages in the development of one child's language.

The concept of incongruence plays a role in the relationship between system and process. Halliday first indicates this for the adult interpersonal systems, and then turns to the ontogenetic development of language. In this summary, we will only focus on the first part of the paper.

After a description of basic interpersonal systems at the levels of context (move), semantics (speech function) and lexicogrammar (mood), the question is how these strata are linked to one another through realization, and here the concept of congruence comes in. Options from the system of the move (NEGOTIATION)[5] have congruent realizations in the system of SPEECH FUNCTION; options in the SPEECH FUNCTION network have congruent realizations in the MOOD system. A congruent realization is defined as "that one which can be regarded as *typical* – which will be selected in the absence of any good reason for selecting another one", a realization which is "*unmarked*" (Halliday 1984: 14, emphasis MT).

Focussing on the relations between semantics and lexicogrammar, the relevant system networks are given in Figures 3 and 4. Congruent mappings between selections in the two systems are represented in Table 2 (based on Halliday 1984: 16).

Table 2 only shows the typical, congruent mappings between semantics and lexicogrammar. When turning to language as behaviour, as it actually occurs in dialogue, this basic matrix has to be extended: more delicate options can be indicated, and, more importantly, in this process, incongruent realizations have to be taken into account. As Halliday indicates, there is a link between incongruency and increased delicacy: "*many of the more delicate distinctions within any system depend for their expression on what in the first instance appear as non-congruent forms*" (Halliday 1984: 14; emphasis MAKH).

MIRIAM TAVERNIERS

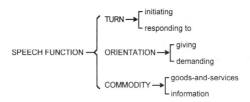

Figure 3: SPEECH FUNCTION: primary options

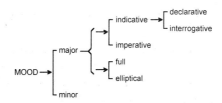

Figure 4: MOOD: primary options

		goods-&-services		information	
		semantic option	congruent realization	semantic option	congruent realization
initiating	give	**'offer'**	*(various)*	'statement'	*full declarative*
	demand	'command'	*full imperative*	'question'	*full interrogative*
respond-ing	give on demand	**'compliance'** **(response offer)**	*(various)*	'answer' (response statement)	*elliptical declarative; minor*
	accept	'acceptance' (response command)	*elliptical imperative; minor*	'acknowledgement' (response question	*elliptical interrogative; minor*

Table 2: Basic options in the SPEECH FUNCTION system and their congruent realizations
(after Halliday 1984: 16)

In the realization relationships between SPEECH FUNCTION and MOOD, incongruent types of expressions are especially important in particular areas. In general, Halliday notes, there is a greater tendency to incongruence in the exchange of 'goods-&-services'. According to him, this is "hardly surprising": since information is inherently linguistic, it is only natural that language has clear categories, declarative and interrogative, to express different types of exchange of 'information'. The exchange of 'goods-&-services', by contrast, takes place outside the system of language: as such it is not dependent on an expression in language. As a result, language does not have a clearly defined type of pattern which is specialized for the expression of exchanges of 'goods-&-services'.

This can be seen most clearly in the area of 'offers': there is no single type of expression in English which can be regarded as a congruent realization of an 'offer' – various possible patterns can be used as verbalizations of 'proposals'. Halliday gives the following examples: *here you are!, would you like a newspaper?, shall I hold the door open for you?*. For 'commands', the imperative can be regarded as the unmarked, congruent realization, but, Halliday argues, non-congruent forms are more often used to express the 'command' function.

In the second part of this paper, Halliday illustrates the emergence of incongruence in the ontogenesis of language. He shows how a child's language gradually evolves from an initial system in which there is a small number of clear-cut, congruent options, into a more elaborate adult system, which heavily relies on incongruent realizations as well, and where indeed, in some areas (especially 'commands' and 'offers'), there is no clearly-defined congruent option.

2.3. Congruence in the ideational component: Fawcett 1980

Before the term 'grammatical metaphor' had been introduced into SFL, Fawcett (1980) proposed a general 'congruence network', in which nominalized types of construal (which, as we have seen above, in Halliday's later account form the principal type of experiential metaphor), are systemically represented, in general, as less typical variants of other, 'straightforward' construals.

Fawcett's "congruence network" is proposed in order to "handle the complex range of possible relationships between the referent as a raw input to the linguistic system and the input to the various system networks" (Fawcett 1980: 91). The congruence network does not belong to any functional component: it is regarded as the "first system network in the semantics",[6] the network which specifies the possible entry conditions for further systems.

The entry condition of the congruence network, which is represented here as Figure 5, is the input to linguistic processing in general, termed the 'referent'. The network then indicates the various ways in which this referent may be processed. At the primary level of delicacy, the referent may be processed in three ways: regarded as situation, regarded as thing, and regarded as quality. For each of these general options, more delicate further possibilities are specified. At this point the concept of 'congruence' comes in, interpreted in Halliday's sense:

> The term congruence [...] provides an apt label for the system network in which we decide whether or not to use the typical set of semantic options – and so the typical syntactic unit – for a referent. (Fawcett 1980: 92)

For example, for the option referent regarded as situation, three further possibilities are available, of which one is congruent (termed 'straightforward' and marked with an asterisk), as realized in, for example *Ivy quickly refused his offer*. Other types of construals of this same referent regarded as situation, are (1) a construal as 'possessed' situation ('gerund'), as in *Ivy's quickly refusing his offer*, and (2) a construal as quasi-thing (nominalization or 'mixed nominal'), as in *Ivy's quick refusing of his offer*.

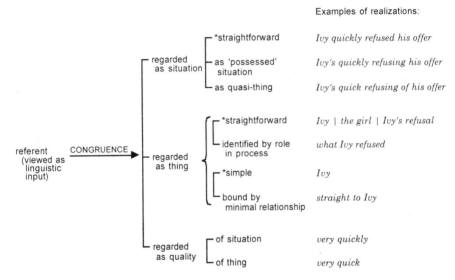

Figure 5: Congruence network proposed by Fawcett (1980: 93)

A selection from the congruence network, rather than a 'syntactic' label, such as 'clause', then forms the input (the entry condition) for further functionally-specific system networks. For example, the point of origin of the illocutionary force network is the following selection from the congruence network: referent > regarded as situation > straightforward (Fawcett 1980: 201ff.).

3.   An initial framework for ideational grammatical metaphor: Ravelli 1985, 1988

In "Grammatical metaphor: An initial analysis", Louise Ravelli (1988)[7] presents a framework for the study of ideational metaphor. She focusses on three main aspects: general *models* explaining the phenomenon of grammatical metaphor; different *types* of ideational grammatical metaphor and how they can be recognized; and ways in which grammatical metaphor influences the *complexity* of a text.

As we saw in Section 1 above, Halliday compared two different views on the phenomenon of metaphor in general and took a 'view from above' in order to introduce 'grammatical metaphor'. Ravelli takes the same 'view from above' as a starting point – defining grammatical metaphor in terms of alternative lexicogrammatical realizations of the same meaning. However, following a suggestion by Halliday, she proposes a refinement of this model which takes into account the fact that metaphor also involves 'semantic' *variation*. It is not completely accurate to say that two alternative lexicogrammatical realizations (a congruent one and a metaphorical one) have 'the same meaning'. Instead, the incongruent form "has a feedback effect into the semantics" (Ravelli 1988: 137, cp. 1999: 104), and this is especially so because a metaphorical expression may select or omit different aspects of the meaning configuration which is realized by an equivalent congruent expression. In general, Ravelli argues, "(e)ach expression thus shares some semantic content, but differs in detail" (1988: 137). In this view, grammatical metaphor is interpreted as "a combination of semantic features" or a "semantic compound" (Ravelli 1988: 137). This new model, indicating the 'semantic' feedback effect of metaphor, is visually presented by Ravelli as in Figure 6.

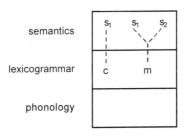

s – semantic choice
c – congruent choice
m – metaphorical form

Figure 6: Ravelli's alternative model of grammatical metaphor as a 'semantic' compound (from Ravelli 1988: 137, 1999: 104)

What is crucial in this refined model, is that the starting point is no longer one single meaning: it is recognized that metaphor also involves a *meaning difference*. However, Ravelli indicates, in the present state of systemic theory it is not yet possible to bring out the exact nature of the 'semantic' difference, since in order to achieve this, "it would be necessary to represent the level of semantics with system networks as for the lexicogrammar" (ibid.: 138). Therefore, although this model is theoretically more powerful, it can not yet be used in descriptions of metaphor. For this reason Ravelli takes Halliday's general view 'from above', with 'one meaning – different realizations', as the underlying framework in the rest of her paper.

On the basis of an exploration of metaphors in different texts, Ravelli proposes a classification of ideational metaphors into nine general types. These types are summarized in Table 3. With reference to the problem of modelling mentioned above (viz. the absence of system networks for the semantics), she notes that the 'semantic' choice which forms the basis of each type of metaphor is here represented in terms of grammatical labels, which are "terms with which we are familiar" (ibid.: 139), such as 'material process, circumstance, participant'.

Semantic choice	Metaphorical realization		Congruent realization	Example
	Function	Class	Class	
1a material process	Thing	nominal group	verbal group	the appointment of an ambassador
1b mental process	Thing	nominal group	verbal group	it changed our perception of the situation
1c relational process	Thing	nominal group	verbal group	the sheer cost of it
1d verbal process	Thing	nominal group	verbal group	we had no talks last year
1e behavioural process	Thing	nominal group	verbal group	its continuation
2 process	Epithet, Classifier	nominal group	verbal group	incoming soviet missiles
3a quality of a Thing	Thing	nominal group	adjective	peace through strength
3b quality of process	Thing	nominal group	adverb	a sense of security
3c quality of a process	Epithet, Classifier	adjective	adverb	its intrinsic worth
4a modality	Epithet	adjective	(modal) adverb	the possible outcome
4b modality, modulation	Thing	nominal group	adjective, passive verb	first strike capability
5a logical connection	Thing	nominal group	conjunction	for that reason
5b logical connection	Process	verbal group	conjunction	the arms race contains the threat
6 circumstance	Process	verbal group	prepositional phrase	night follows day
7a participant	Classifier	adjective	nominal group	economic development
7b participant	Thing	nominal group	nominal group	the art of generalship
8a expansion	Relative Act, Clause	embedded clause	ranking clause	WWII is more likely than [[peace breaking out]]
8b projection	Fact	embedded clause	ranking clause	[[all it can do]] is [[to retaliate]]
9 circumstance	Epithet, Classifier	adjective	prepositional clause	historical experience

Table 3: Ideational metaphor types in Ravelli 1988

Specific aspects pertaining to particular types of metaphor are commented on:

(i)   **Nominalization** is claimed to be the type of ideational metaphor "of which there is the greatest awareness" (ibid.: 140), and Ravelli links this to the first type in the classification, which is found to account for 35% of all examples of metaphors in the analysed texts.

(ii)   There is a relationship of **metaphorical dependence** between categories 1 and 3b: when a process is metaphorically expressed as a Thing, a constituent qualifying the process must be realized as an Epithet modifying the metaphorical Thing.

(iii) Of the fourth type, Ravelli writes that it "takes some account of inter-personal metaphor", since the congruent realization here is a modal adverb (4a: *it will possibly turn out that*) or "an adjective or a passive verb" (4b: *they are capable of striking first*). The effect of these metaphors is an objectifying and backgrounding of the opinion expressed by the speaker.

(iv)   Types 3c, 4b and 7b show a general feature characteristic of ideational metaphor, which Ravelli calls **paradigmatic plurality**, or **paradigmatic recursion**: "a metaphorical realization can pass through the network a second time, again being realized metaphorically" (ibid.: 140). Ravelli shows that two steps of metaphorical realizations are exemplified in these types, for example: *they feel secure* (congruent realization) → *‹their secure feeling‹* (1st metaphorical realization) → *‹their feeling of security‹* (2nd metaphorical realization). Although this feature of recursion is only illustrated here in types 3c, 4b and 7b, it is argued that "it is possible that recursion is general to all categories of metaphor" (ibid.: 141).

Ravelli explores the possibility of representing grammatical metaphor in a *system network*, which would be especially valuable for two reasons: (1) in general this would explain grammatical metaphor in terms of a *choice* in a system where also other, congruent options are available; (2) more specifically, a system network could account for different types of *recursion* effects found in metaphor.

Paradigmatic plurality, it is argued, is a type of recursion which is not systemic as such, and therefore cannot be represented as an option in a network:[8] it is simply a "rewiring mechanism" (Ravelli 1988: 141, 1999: 62), an extra possibility for a metaphorical realization, to enter *again* at a different point in the system.

When "more than one item of a clause may be a metaphorical realization", this is accounted for in terms of "**syntagmatic plurality**": in such cases one occurrence of grammatical metaphor is syntagmatically dependent[9] on another process of metaphor (Ravelli 1999: 66, 99). In this type of recursion, the recursive option has to be prepresented as a network feature (Ravelli 1988: 141).

The feature of syntagmatic plurality leads Ravelli to make a distinction between two levels at which ideational metaphors can be analysed. Simple metaphors can be distinguished from other types of expressions, in which

various instances of metaphorical realizations interact with each other. All the
simple types of metaphors outlined in Table 3 are referred to as metaphors which
occur at a **micro level**, whereas metaphors involving syntagmatic plurality are
called metaphors at a **macro level** (Ravelli 1988: 142, 1999: 66–67). In this
sense, macro-level metaphors are _clusters of micro-level metaphors. Ravelli
illustrates this difference with the following example:

> (8)   ... (it) will have a real impact on political thinking   (Ravelli 1988, 1999)

This clause contains four micro-level metaphors: ›real‹, ›impact‹, ›political‹
and ›thinking‹, which are grouped into two macro-level metaphors: ›real impact‹
and ›political thinking‹.

Ideally then, both micro- and macro-level metaphors could be represented
in a system network allowing recursion – a feature which, Ravelli states, is
usually indicated in a network by means of simultaneous systems.[10] Ravelli
refers to Fawcett's (1980, cf. Section 2.3 above) 'congruence network' as a
possible model. However, she notes, because it is based in Fawcett's general
cognitive-functional theory of language, this network represents "the speaker's
'knowledge of the world'" rather than "observable systems of semiotics" which
provide the "context for language" in a systemic-functional theory. By
'observable systems of semiotics', Ravelli means the strata of semantics and
lexicogrammar.

A systemic-functional representation of grammatical metaphor has to take
into account a 'semantic' and lexicogrammatical level. Ravelli offers an initial
schematic representation which is reproduced here as Figure 7.

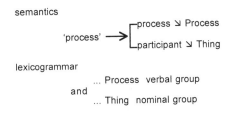

Figure 7: Levels in a network representation of grammatical metaphor
(from Ravelli 1988: 137; 1999: 101)

Ravelli (1999: 101) indicates that Fawcett's network is useful in that it can
be modified to serve as a network at the level of the semantics. The 'semantic'
network would indicate the common meaning realized by different expressions:
in this example, this is the initial choice 'process', represented as the entry

condition for a system. The meaning difference (cf. above) arising from a congruent vs. incongruent realization of this initial choice would be represented as a system, i.e. as a further step in delicacy within the 'semantic' network (in this case: the options "process" and "participant"). The realizations of these further choices "would then carry through to the lexicogrammar" (Ravelli 1999: 101). However, the level of lexicogrammar poses many problems. In order to represent grammatical metaphor in the network, and to make recursion possible, there must be a clearly defined entry condition for the systems containing metaphorical options, i.e. "the rank or delicacy at which grammatical metaphor becomes an option must be determined" (ibid.: 99). It is precisely this determination which is problematic:

> Grammatical metaphor cannot be a feature at the rank of clause, because although the entire clause *may* be metaphorical, often only parts of a clause are metaphorical. Thus grammatical metaphor would appear to be a feature at the rank of group/phrase – the constituents of the clause. Yet it is not the case that *groups* – such as nominal groups, for example – may be realised metaphorically: the group *is* the metaphorical realisation of something else. (Ravelli 1999: 99, emphasis LR)

Ravelli concludes: "Thus it is extremely difficult to capture any descriptive generalisations about grammatical metaphor at the level of lexicogrammar" (ibid.).

As to the recognition of grammatical metaphor, Ravelli proposes two devices which can be useful in determining whether a given expression is incongruent or not:

(i)   **Derivation**. Many metaphors are formed through derivational processes. However, it is noted that this is not a reliable recognition criterion, since "many metaphorical examples are found without any derivational suffixes, and [...] not every suffix indicates a metaphorical form" (Ravelli 1988: 141).

(ii) **Agnation**. Any metaphorical expression has (an) agnate form(s) which show(s) its (more) congruent realization(s). The rewording of a meta-phorical expression into a (more) congruent one is referred to as "*unpacking*" the grammatical metaphor (Ravelli 1999: 77). Although a comparison between different agnates is very useful in recognizing metaphorical realizations, it becomes difficult or impossible in cases where lexical metaphor is also involved. (ibid.).

Ravelli's study also involves an investigation of the relationship between grammatical metaphor, mode and complexity. The hypothesis formulated by Halliday (1985, cf. Section 1 above) that written versus spoken varieties of language exhibit a different type of complexity, viz. lexical density versus grammatical intricacy, is borne out in Ravelli's analysis. Moreover, she found that a high frequency of grammatical metaphor corelates with a high level of lexical density and a low level of grammatical intricacy (cf. Ravelli 1988: 144–145, 1999: 73–75). Ravelli offers the following explanation for this correlation: in congruent grammar, process meanings are related to each other through clause complexing (i.e. using the logical resources of taxis and logico-semantic relations), and in this way, a text which is largely congruent is grammatically intricate. Grammatical metaphor, which construes processes as nominal groups, makes it possible for two process meanings to be linked to each other *within* a clause; this type of incongruent construal leads to a higher lexical density (more lexical words in the same clause) and a lower grammatical intricacy (the systems of clause complexing are avoided).

Finally, Ravelli also points out another major effect of grammatical metaphor which she found in the analysis of texts. When process meanings are metaphorically construed as Things, this creates new possibilities for the textual organization of a clause: a process meaning can now function as the Theme of the clause (whereas in the congruent pattern, the Theme function is restricted to participants and circumstances (Ravelli 1988: 145)), and it can also become the unmarked focus of information (in the Given/New structure). It is argued that a recognition of such textual effects is essential to an understanding of grammatical metaphor, since it provides a functional explanation of the phenomenon.

4.   Review: Leading motifs in the initial studies of grammatical metaphor

In this paper, we have considered the first studies in which 'grammatical metaphor' and 'incongruence' appear within SFL. We have focussed on the introduction of the concept grammatical metaphor by Halliday in 1985; the theme of congruence in earlier studies (probability values and social variation in Halliday's early work, incongruence in the interpersonal component (Halliday) and incongruence in the ideational component (Fawcett)); and the framework of ideational metaphor proposed by Ravelli.

The initial accounts of metaphor and incongruence which we have considered in this paper involve three general types of issues: a *theoretical characterization* and analysis of the phenomenon 'grammatical metaphor' in general, a *classification* of *types* of metaphor, and a *functional explanation* of the effects of metaphor in texts:

(i) *The analysis of grammatical metaphor.* A metaphorical realization is analyzed by rewording – or *unpacking* – it into a (more) congruent agnate form, and by comparing its structure to the congruent structure. Halliday presents this analysis in diagrams showing the functional structure of each expression as a separate layer, so that metaphorical shifts become visible in the vertical dimension of the diagram. With complex (especially ideational) metaphors, it is sometimes necessary to unpack them in various steps, so that a 'chain of metaphorical realizations' (cf. Halliday) can be set up.

(ii) *Types of metaphor.* In the initial studies of grammatical metaphor, two general types are distinguised pertaining to the ideational and interpersonal metafunctions. Halliday subdivides interpersonal metaphor into two sub-types, according to the primary interpersonal systems at the level of lexicogrammar: mood and modality. Ravelli proposes a classification of ideational metaphors into a larger number of types, distinguished in terms of grammatical class and function.

(iii) *Functions of metaphor.* Ravelli indicates two general effects of ideational metaphor, which, as she states, are important in the functional explanation of the phenomenon. These effects pertain to the textual metafunction: ideational grammatical metaphor can be used to organise a text into a particular thematic or information structure, for example it enables a 'process' to function as Theme or to get an unmarked information focus.

The keynote motif in the initial studies of grammatical metaphor is the characterization of metaphor in terms of **'alternative realizations'**. This basic idea is theoretically expanded in two ways: on the one hand, it is linked to the motif of *incongruence*, which was already used before the concept of grammatical metaphor was introduced; on the other hand, the idea of 'alternative realizations' is explored in relation to two important theoretical dimensions in SFL: the notion of *stratification* (and the semiotic relationship of realization) and the *system-structure* relation (including the system network as a linguistic tool). In the remainder of this section, these various aspects are looked at in turn.

4.1. Incongruence

The general characterization of grammatical metaphor in terms of 'alternative realizations' naturally leads to the concept of 'congruence': in general, when there is variation among types of expressions, some realizations are congruent, whereas others are incongruent – as was already recognized in very early work by Halliday (1976/1956). The concept of congruence is described in various ways. It is most often associated with *markedness* (Halliday 1976/1956, 1984, 1985) or *typicality* (Halliday 1984, 1985): congruent expressions are typical, unmarked ways of realizing a feature. A number of expressions used to describe the distinction between congruence and incongruence are summarized in Table 4.

Congruence	
• congruent form = "**unmarked**" form	Halliday 1976/1956: 42
• "a grammatical structure which **reflects a contextual structure** (by matching it with **maximum probability**)"	Halliday 1976/1956: 42
• "the **regular** patterns of realization"	Halliday 1978c: 177
• "he (the speaker) may also use the forms (variants of language) incongruently: that is, **outside the contexts which define them as the norm**"	Halliday 1978b: 156
• a congruent realization = "that one which can be regarded as **typical** – which **will be selected in absence of any good reason for selecting another one**"	Halliday 1984: 14
• "the **typical** ways of saying things"	Halliday 1985: 321
• "that (structure) which would be **arrived at by the shortest route**"	Halliday 1985: 321
• "the **most straightforward** coding of the meanings selected"	Halliday 1985: 321
Incongruence	
• "'incongruent' means '**not** expressed through the most **typical** (and **highly coded**) form of representation"	Halliday 1978c: 180

Table 4: Expressions used by Halliday to characterize congruence and incongruence

In the context of the systemic representation of variation (i.e. in system networks), the concept of congruence is linked to two fundamental scales in SFL: instantiation and delicacy.

4.2. *Metaphor and realization*

The general characterization of grammatical metaphor in terms of 'alternative realizations' is stated more precisely as 'alternative *lexicogrammatical* realizations of a choice in the *semantics'* (cf. Ravelli 1988: 135). The concept of realization, and especially the interstratal coding relationship between semantics and lexicogrammar play an important role in the recognition and understanding of grammatical metaphor as a specific phenomenon of language. The early studies of metaphor show two lines of thinking on this subject. On the one hand, Halliday's (1985) 'view from above', which is proposed as an alternative to the traditional conception of (mostly lexical) metaphor, leads to a recognition of grammatical metaphor in a framework of 'alternative realizations of the *same* meaning' (cf. Section 1.5 above). On the other hand, as Ravelli (1988, 1999) indicates, it is not true that an incongruent expression has 'the same meaning' as the congruent realization with which it is compared. Instead, the incongruent variant has its own feedback effect into the semantics, leading to 'semantic' *variation*. We have seen that the issue of whether or not metaphorical variant expressions have the same meaning as their non-metaphorical counterparts was recognized but dismissed in Halliday's (1978c) study of antilanguage. The two lines of thinking which characterize the early studies of grammatical metaphor – i.e. 'same meaning, different forms' versus 'semantic variation as well as lexico-grammatical variation' – will lead to different conceptions about the networking of metaphor, as we will see in the following section.

4.3. Metaphor and system network representations

The idea of '*alternative* realizations' inherently implies a conception of metaphor in terms of *choice*, a fundamental concept in SFL which is formalized by means of *system networks*. The concept of choice is the general motivation behind the exploration of how metaphor can be represented in system networks: to show that a metaphorical expression is a meaningful choice, an option which has been selected in contrast to more congruent realizations. In the ideational component, there are two more specific, structural motivations for exploring how metaphor can be networked: a network representation of metaphor would indicate the systemic relationship between congruent expressions and their incongruent *agnates* which are used in the analysis to determine their metaphorical structure; and a network could also contain an option of *recursion*, which is found to be important in the structure of ideational metaphors (Ravelli 1988).

In the studies of metaphor and incongruency which we have considered, the possibility of incorporating grammatical metaphor in system networks has been approached in different ways. In one type of approach, the feature of congruence is directly indicated in the options in a system network. This is exemplified in Fawcett's (1980) '*congruence network*', where congruent and incongruent options are represented as systemic features within a system, the congruent ones being indicated by an asterisk. Although in his early description of Chinese, Halliday (1976/1956) did not yet use the system network as a formal representation, whenever different types of expressions are possible for the same basic form, they are assigned a *probability value*, which indicates whether they are congruent or not within the set of possibilities. In these early proposals, incongruency is built into the description as an aspect of variation at a certain level: in Halliday's study, this is the level of lexicogrammar, in Fawcett's it is the level of 'the speaker's knowledge of the world'.

Later studies (Halliday 1984, Ravelli 1988) take into account the stratified model of language, and conceptualize metaphor in terms of the coding relationship of realization between a 'semantic' and a 'lexicogrammatical' stratum. Here, the question is how the idea of 'alternative lexicogrammatical realizations of a choice in the semantics' can be represented in a system network. Halliday (1984) and Ravelli (1988) make different proposals for interpersonal and ideational metaphor.

˗   Halliday (1984) explains *interpersonal metaphors of mood* in terms of mappings between the 'semantic' system of SPEECH FUNCTION and the lexicogrammatical system of MOOD. Congruent coding relationships are indicated between the primary options of both systems, for example the 'semantic' choice 'statement' (initiating–giving–information) is congruently realized in the lexico-grammatical choice major mood > free > indicative > declarative. When looking at the instantiation of both systems in actual texts, we have to take into account incongruent expressions. An incongruent realization of a 'semantic' (speech functional) choice is then indicated as a more delicate option in the MOOD network (i.e. taking into account simultaneous or more delicate systems, such as MOOD PERSON, MODALITY): for example a modulated interrogative with interactant > addressee as MOOD PERSON (e.g. *Could you ...?*) is an incongruent realization of the 'semantic' option 'command'.[11]

Ravelli (1988) explores how metaphor can be represented in *ideational* system networks. In keeping with her important observation that an incongruent lexicogrammatical realization does not have exactly the same meaning as its congruent equivalent(s), but rather has a feedback effect into the semantics (cf. above), she makes an initial proposal for a network presentation in which a variation between congruent and incongruent alternatives is also shown at the level of the semantics (cf. Figure 7 above). However, Ravelli does not actually set up a network for ideational metaphor, because of two problems:

(i)   There is not yet a system network representation of the stratum of semantics, although, Ravelli notes, Fawcett's 'knowledge' network can be modified for this purpose. (It should be added here that this remark only applies to the ideational component, with which Ravelli is concerned.)

(ii)   The level of lexicogrammar is problematic because it is difficult to represent an option for a metaphorical expression in terms of the rank scale, i.e. it cannot be determined which grammatical unit serves as an entry condition for a system in which grammatical metaphor is an option.

As Ravelli presents it (Ravelli 1999: 99; see the quote on p. 25 above), the difficulty lies in determining the rank at which grammatical metaphor is an option (i.e. is a systemic feature). However, the exact way in which 'grammatical metaphor' is a feature in a system is not defined, and is stated in contradictory ways: when grammatical metaphor 'is a feature at a certain rank', does this mean (1) that units of this rank are metaphorical realizations, or (2) that the meanings of units of this rank are realized metaphorically? This contradiction is revealed when Ravelli argues that, on the one hand, the clause cannot be the rank at which grammatical metaphor appears as a feature, because the clause as such is not a metaphorical realization (i.e. only parts of the clause may be metaphorical), and on the other hand, the group/phrase cannot be an entry condition for the feature grammatical metaphor, because "it is not the case that groups [...] may be realized metaphorically".

Notes

1. For an elaborate evaluation of the notion of 'grammatical metaphor' in SFL and a proposal for an alternative model, see Taverniers (2002).

2. Throughout this paper, the signs " ▸ ◂ " indicates an example of experiential metaphor, while instances of interpersonal metaphor are marked by the sign " ⇒ ".

3. Although the specific contribution of the interpersonal and ideational metaphors is not explicitly described by Halliday, it can be assumed that the imperative mood is an interpersonal metaphor (since the meaning is not 'request' but 'statement'), whereas the realization of the proposition *they cheated before* as an embedded expansion in the nominal group ▸*the way* ^{x}*((they cheated before))*◂ can be interpreted as an ideational metaphor (compared to the ideationally congruent realization as an embedded projection: *consider (the fact)* "*((that they cheated before)))*).

4. Although it is clear that 'expansion' is not to be read here in its technical sense as a type of logico-semantic relation (expansion as opposed to projection), Halliday does not explain the type of syntactic variety.

5. The 'move' is not the name of a system, but rather an entry condition. "NEGOTIATION" is the label which Martin (1992: 50) uses to refer to the system which is referred to by Halliday.

6. In Fawett's linguistic theory, the stratal relationship between semantics and lexicogrammar is mapped onto the relationship between system and structure: the system networks form the semantics, while the structural realization rules form the lexicogrammar.

7. This article is based on a 1985 BA dissertation (University of Sydney), which is published in the *Monographs in Systemic Linguistics* series, see Ravelli 1999.

8. By "an option in a network", Ravelli means an option in a *system of* RECURSION (with two features: 'stop' and 'go on'). A system of recursion occurs in the logical system network for complex units (simultaneous with two other systems: TAXIS (hypo/para) and TYPE OF INTERDEPENDENCY (expansion/projection)). Ravelli refers to the logical system network in the full version of her study (1999: 62; 34).

9. From the description and the example which is given (cf. below, example (14)), it is clear that this is the type of dependence which Ravelli referred to earlier with reference to the relationship between types 1 and 3b in the classification of metaphors.

10. That is, a system of RECURSION is represented as simultaneous with other systems in a network.

Ravelli does not explain the *systemic* nature of paradigmatic and syntagmatic recursion. In describing the two types of recursion, she refers to a difference in terms of their role in a system network representation:

Note that the recursive option as described here (re. paradigmatic plurality, MT) is not an option in the network, but a rewiring mechanism at a point of realization, to bring a realization of the network back into the system at a less delicate point. Apart from paradigmatic plurality, grammatical metaphor also exhibits the feature of syntagmatic plurality, where the recursive option IS the network feature. (Ravelli 1988: 141, emphasis LR; cp. Ravelli 1999: 62)

On the other hand, when focussing on the possibility of representing grammatical grammatical metaphor in the ideational networks, Ravelli writes:

A recursive option is needed in the network to account for both syntagmatic plurality (where more than one item of a clause may be a metaphorical realisation) and paradigmatic plurality (where one item, itself a metaphorical realisation, may re-enter the network with the potential for a subsequent metaphorical realisation.) (Ravelli 1999: 99)

11. I give this example to make clear the basic distinction between Halliday's and Ravelli's proposals for networking incongruence. Halliday (1984) does not give specific examples of incongruent realizations in the adult system, and in his ontogenetic study in the second part of the paper, most examples illustrate the relationship between the levels of context (NEGOTIATION) and semantics (SPEECH FUNCTION).

References

Fawcett, Robin P. (1980) *Cognitive Linguistics and Social Interaction: Towards an integrated model of a systemic functional grammar and the other components of a communicating mind.* Heidelberg: Groos.

Halliday, M.A.K. (1976/1956) Grammatical categories in modern Chinese: An early sketch of the theory. In: Kress, Gunther (ed.) *Halliday: System and Function in Language.* London: Oxford UP. 36–51. Extract from: Grammatical categories in modern Chinese, *Transactions of the Philological Society* 1956: 180–202.

Halliday, M.A.K. (1978a) *Language as Social Semiotic: The social interpretation of language and meaning.* London: Arnold.

Halliday, M.A.K. (1978b) Language in urban society. In: Halliday, M.A.K. (1978a). 154–163.

Halliday, M.A.K. (1978c) Antilanguages. In: Halliday, M.A.K. (1978a). 164–182.

Halliday, M.A.K. (1984) Language as code and language as behaviour: A systemic-functional interpretation of the nature and ontogenesis of dialogue. In: Fawcett, Robin P., M.A.K. Halliday, Sydney Lamb & Adam Makkai (eds.) *The Semiotics of Culture and Language*. Vol. 1: Language as Social Semiotic. (Open Linguistics Series.) London: Pinter. 3–35.

Halliday, M.A.K. (1985) *Introduction to Functional Grammar*. London: Arnold.

Halliday, M.A.K. (1994/1985) *Introduction to Functional Grammar*. 2nd edition. London: Arnold.

Halliday, M.A.K. (1996) On grammar and grammatics. In: Hasan, Ruqaiya, Carmel Cloran & David Butt (eds.) *Functional Descriptions. Theory in practice*. (Current Issues in Linguistic Theory, 121.) Amsterdam: Benjamins. 1–38.

Labov, William (1969) Contraction, deletion, and inherent variation of the English copula. *Language* 45: 715–762.

Lévi-Strauss, Claude (1966) *The Savage Mind*. London: Weidenfeld & Nicolson. Translation of French original: La pensée sauvage, Paris: Plon, 1962.

Martin, J.R. (1992) *English Text: System and structure*. Amsterdam: Benjamins.

Ravelli, Louise (1985) *Metaphor, Mode and Complexity: An exploration of co-varying patterns*. BA Dissertation, University of Sydney.

Ravelli, Louise (1988) Grammatical metaphor: An initial analysis. In: Steiner, Erich H. & Robert Veltman (eds.) *Pragmatics, Discourse and Text. Some systemically oriented approaches*. London: Pinter. 133–147.

Ravelli, Louise (1999) *Metaphor, Mode and Complexity: An exploration of co-varying patterns*. (Monographs in Systemic Linguistics, 12.) Nottingham: Department of English and Media Studies, Nottingham Trent University.

Taverniers, Miriam (2002) *Systemic-Functional Linguistics and the Notion of Grammatical Metaphor. A theoretical study and a proposal for a semiotic-functional integrative model*. PhD dissertation, University of Ghent.

Part I

Grammatical metaphor:
Clarification and application

Renewal of connection
Integrating theory and practice
in an understanding of grammatical metaphor

Louise J. Ravelli
University of New South Wales, Sydney

1. Introduction

In the first edition of Halliday's *An Introduction to Functional Grammar* (1985), Halliday expands the traditional notion of metaphor, essentially a lexical phenomenon, to include metaphorical processes in the grammar. Both, he notes, involve processes of rhetorical transference, the most familiar instances of lexical metaphor – metaphor, metonymy and synecdoche – all involving lexical transference of some kind. Halliday gives the example 'a flood of protests poured in' (1985: 319), where the verb 'flood', usually associated with rivers, is transferred to refer to 'protests'. However, as Halliday also explains, "lexical selection is just one aspect of lexicogrammatical selection, or 'wording'; and (that) metaphorical variation is lexicogrammatical rather than simply lexical" (1985: 320). So-called lexical metaphors also involve grammatical variation, thus for a more literal version of 'protests flooded in':

> ... we should have to say *protests came in in large quantities*, or *protests were received in large quantities*; or even *very many people protested*. There is a strong grammatical element in rhetorical transference; and once we have recognized this we find that there is also such a thing as grammatical metaphor, where the variation is essentially in the grammatical forms although often entailing some lexical variation as well. (ibid.)

An example of variation in grammatical forms might be 'He *cut* the material' versus 'The *cut* of the dress was very elegant' (Jespersen 1933: 73, in a discussion of what he called 'grammatical homophones'). In this case the same lexical item appears in both a verbal and nominal form. In other examples, lexical variation may also be involved, thus in 'we had no *inkling* of the problem', '*inkling*' encompasses both grammatical variation, from verb to noun, and lexical variation, from something like 'could not imagine' to 'inkling' (there is no semantically equivalent verb 'to ink'). The verbal to nominal transfer is the most prototypical form of grammatical metaphor, and, although there are a range of other types, it has long been recognised as an important phenomenon in English (cf. Jespersen 1933; Gowers 1954; Halliday 1967; Quirk and Greenbaum 1973).

Accounting for this variation as grammatical metaphor has been an important step forward in systemic-functional linguistics. It challenges the descriptive framework, to define and account for the phenomenon theoretically. It connects with fundamental concerns of this and related schools with questions of social context. It enables important insights into areas of practical application: textual studies, questions of language development and literacy, the processes of semiosis. There has been much research which has followed Halliday 1985, and this volume represents some of the most recent developments. The diversity of questions, issues and applications represented here suggests that, to borrow a phrase from Firth (1957), it is timely to renew connection both with the fundamentals of this theory, and with its most recent instantiations.

This paper 'touches base' with a number of fundamental points which recur as issues of concern in the papers in this volume, contrasting early and later theoretical formulations. In particular, we contrast some early definitions of grammatical metaphor with more recent formulations, and consider some of the practical ramifications of the shift, on teaching practice, for instance, and on expanded understandings of metaphor in broader processes of semiosis. In addition, we revisit some of the difficulties in analysing grammatical metaphor – deciding what is and is not metaphorical – and in a consideration of academic writing, suggest that the fuzziness of this boundary is not just an analytical difficulty, but is a productive linguistic feature.

2.   Renewing definitions

Let me attempt to explain metaphor with an analogy; dare I say a 'visual metaphor': think of a contemporary museum exhibition, where there are interactive displays, with buttons to push, wheels to turn, things to listen to and observe. Have you noticed how children use these? They push the buttons and turn the wheels, and rush off to the next exhibit. Adults linger; they listen and observe, and learn. They may be able to interpret the exhibit for the child, explaining the principles at stake and what the interactive illustrates. Adults have learned that the interactive 'stands for' something, namely knowledge, or at least, the opportunity to learn about and generate knowledge. Children begin by taking these opportunities literally, as a chance to play, and somewhere along the line, they learn that the 'play' actually also stands for something else, and that is learning or knowing.

Thus, museum interactives are a kind of metaphor, standing for two things at the same time, playing and learning. There is definitely some kind of 'transfer' going on, but to what extent is this analogy useful for understanding language? As Halliday has explicated so clearly and rigorously in his paper "Things and Relations" (1998), the lexico-grammatical metaphor which we refer to in this volume is a very particular process. In reference to language as a stratified system, Halliday says that:

> Of course, the initial categorising of experience is already a kind of metaphorical process, since it involves transforming the material into the semiotic. But having said that, I will go on to use the term 'metaphor' just in its canonical sense, that of transformation within the semiotic mode. (Halliday 1998: 190–191)

Thus, Halliday suggests that lexico-grammatical metaphor is a somewhat special process, requiring its own definition. And of course, *defining* lexico-grammatical metaphor, producing a workable, replicable definition, is a recurring issue for this volume. Let me review some of the available definitions. The following discussion will refer primarily to *grammatical* metaphor, but as emphasised by Simon-Vandenbergen in this volume, it is essential to understand that this also applies to the 'lexical' side of 'lexico-grammatical'.

2.1. Early definitions of grammatical metaphor

As noted in the introduction, Halliday identifies processes of rhetorical transference as central to an understanding of metaphor. While lexical metaphor is the most familiar, he identifies *lexicogrammatical* variation as being a feature of all linguistic metaphor, thus opening up the possibility for grammatical, as well as lexical, metaphor. Halliday then goes on to further explain the grammatical side:

If something is said to be metaphorical, there must also be something that is not; and the assumption is that to any metaphorical expression corresponds another, or perhaps more than one, that is 'literal' – or, as we shall prefer to call it, CONGRUENT. In other words, *for any given semantic configuration there is (at least) one congruent realization in the lexicogrammar. There may then be others that are in some respect transferred, or METAPHORICAL.* (Halliday 1985: 321. Emphasis added.)

Thus, to continue with Halliday's example, if one wanted to represent 'what Mary saw', the speaker might use a structure of Senser + Process + Phenomenon, something like 'Mary saw something wonderful'. However, we may choose to 'encode things differently', saying for instance, 'Mary came upon a wonderful sight' or a 'wonderful sight met Mary's eyes'. Importantly, these examples:

...are not synonymous. The different encodings all contribute something to the total meaning. But they are potentially co-representational, and in that respect form a set of metaphoric variants (of an ideational kind). (Halliday 1985: 322)

Halliday's definition is taken up by Ravelli 1985, in a thesis which explores the role of grammatical metaphor in written discourse, and which provides one of the first attempts at categorising types of grammatical metaphor (see also Ravelli 1988). At the heart of Ravelli's definitions are the following: "[...] one choice in the semantics may have two (or more) lexicogrammatical realisations" (1985: 3) and grammatical metaphor is "an alternative lexicogrammatical realisation of a semantic choice." (1985: 55).

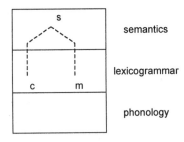

s – semantic choice
c – congruent form
m – metaphorical form

Figure 1: Grammatical metaphor interpreted as realisation choice
(Ravelli 1985: 104)

Visually, the definition of grammatical metaphor as an alternative lexico-grammatical realisation was represented as in Figure 1. Thus, at stake here is the understanding that two instances in the lexicogrammar can be seen to be, somehow, semantically equivalent. Note that in this representation, there is no 'explanation' of the phenomenon of metaphor as such; it is an assertion that the alternative realisations form a semantically equivalent paradigm.

In addition to the notion of 'alternative lexicogrammatical realisation', is the associated feature that "[a] grammatical metaphor is a realisation of a meaning in an atypical lexicogrammatical form." (Ravelli 1985: 4). That is, one of the alternative realisations is the typical/expected/congruent one; the other is incongruent/not typical/ grammatically metaphorical. However, this conflation of 'congruence' with 'typicality' and of 'incongruence' with 'markedness' is potentially misleading. Halliday clearly suggests that metaphorical variants are somehow semantically more complex than non-metaphorical, or congruent, variants, and equally clearly, he notes that "Part of knowing a language is to know what is the most typical 'unmarked' way of saying a thing." (1985: 322; see also 1994: 343). That is, in any language there is a 'most direct route' for the realisation of particular semantic figures. However, 'incongruence' and 'markedness' are not in fact the same; it is possible for a metaphorical choice to be the unmarked one – in a particular register, for instance. Nevertheless, while a metaphorical variant may be the unmarked choice within a particular text type, it remains a marked variant in terms of semantic organisation and realisation. Many papers in this volume revisit this issue, and it is not the purpose of this paper to provide a definitive answer here. What is at stake is the foregrounding of 'alternative lexicogrammatical realisation' in this early definition and explanation of grammatical metaphor.

2.2. Metaphor as simple versus compound semantic choice

Even at the time, as acknowledged in the thesis, other definitions of grammatical metaphor were available, and preferable in terms of their theoretical explanation. Halliday proposed (personal communication) that grammatical metaphor was not an alternative lexicogrammatical realisation, but the result of a compound semantic choice, as opposed to a simple semantic choice (see also Derewianka, this volume, and 1995: 4). This relationship was presented as in Figure 2.

From this point of view, grammatical metaphor is in fact more like a pun; theoretically it is a much more productive definition, as the semantic junctions can be described through system networks [two or more semantic choices combining to form the entry condition for another, that is, metaphorical, choice]. Most importantly, this definition enables the key defining motif of grammatical metaphor to be captured, namely the *stratal tension* between the semantics and the lexicogrammar (Martin 1997: 33). To quote again from Halliday:

> [...] since the grammar has the power of construing, by the same token (that is, by virtue of being stratified) it can also deconstrue, and reconstrue along different lines. [...] A stratified system has inherent metaphoric power. (Halliday 1998: 190)

> [...] grammatical metaphor [...] is a realignment between a pair of strata: a remapping of the semantics on to the lexicogrammar; [...] there could be no metaphor without stratification, and once the content plane has become stratified, such transformation automatically becomes possible. (Halliday 1998: 192)

To put it simply, metaphorical processes depend on a kind of play between the two strata, a sense of two things happening at once, or a tension between the form and its meaning. It is the stratified nature of language as a semiotic system which gives rise to the potential for metaphorical processes, as also discussed by Derewianka (1995: 77; this volume).

Therefore, central to the definition of grammatical metaphor is the understanding of stratal tension, and semantic compounding. The definition and explanation of grammatical metaphor presented by Ravelli 1985 does not include this stratal tension; there, the 'business' of metaphor is played out in the lexicogrammar alone. It is important to recognise that an explanation of metaphor which incorporates semantic compounding and stratal tension represents a significant shift in the field.

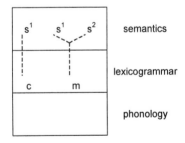

s – semantic choice
c – congruent form
m – metaphorical form

Figure 2: Grammatical metaphor interpreted as semantic compound
(Ravelli 1985: 104)

2.3. Pushing the (definitional) boundaries

There are, then, a number of features which are central to the definition of grammatical metaphor, including at the very least, transformation within the semiotic mode, semantic compound and stratal tension. Elsewhere in this volume, it becomes clear that 'unpacking' metaphors, and finding agnate forms, are also central.

At the same time, however, it would also seem productive to broaden the definition, to seek echoes of grammatical metaphor in other semiotic processes. My opening analogy with the museum interactives was not just for curiosity's sake. While there are many reasons for being interested in processes of grammatical metaphor, one central reason is in terms of its relation to an understanding of written texts, and thus to processes of literacy. It is unarguably the case that today, in technologised societies, notions of literacy are changing. Visual literacy and multi-modal literacy, for instance, are becoming more and more important, and it is worth considering if we have something equivalent to the processes of grammatical metaphor in these domains.

Clearly, while it is not the grammar as such which is central in these other semiotic domains, processes of semiosis are nevertheless at stake. As mentioned, for museum displays and interactives to function successfully, they have to be more than just 'play'. The semantic junction is that playing is also a form of learning or knowing; the stratal tension is that these two possibilities co-occur: playing must be goal-directed, and learning must be fun, in order for the educational objectives of the museum to be achieved. If the stratal tension is lost, then going to the museum becomes just hard work, another chore to be accomplised at school. Or alternatively, it becomes just another form of entertainment, no different to a theme park. Contemporary museum practices include a wide range of exhibition devices, which can (perhaps) be seen to be graded with respect to playing and learning; some, such as the games for very young children, foreground the 'play' aspects, while retaining educational goals; others, such as didactic text panels aimed at adults, foreground learning, but nevertheless within a framework which is supposed to be interesting and engaging.

O'Halloran and Veltman (this volume) argue for broader conceptualizations of metaphor, in terms of other modes of semiosis, and other linguistic levels, specifically the phonological. It would be surprising if other semiotic systems (visual images, sound, layout, ...), do *not* manifest processes equivalent to what we know as metaphor in the grammar. As Halliday argues, grammatical metaphor is absolutely central to a stratified communication system; therefore other stratified systems must be similar. The fact that other semiotics, such as images and architecture, are stratified is evidenced by the work of Kress and van Leeuwen (1996), and O'Toole (1992), who both develop explanations of visual and other semiotic systems as metafunctionally complex, stratified systems. This is not to suggest that we will find an exact transference of the phenomenon of metaphor; we should not, necessarily, expect to find the equivalent of 'nominalisations' in images (although we might find just that). What we should seek are parallel phenomena and processes, as with the museum interactives, which function in two ways, creating a kind of tension between the two ways in which such an interactive can mean. That these interactives form part of a stratified system, can be seen in the way that 'play' itself interfaces below with the micro-level of sensory-motor processes, in a way that is unstratified in an infant's exploration of bodily movement (Thibault 1999).

It seems more than appropriate to pursue this line of reasoning in relation to changing literacy practices. We need to know more about the nature and function of other semiotic systems, such as the visual, as well as about multi-modal texts, that is, those texts which deploy a number of constituent semiotic systems. While interactive museum exhibits are a very particular kind of text, other multi-modal texts, like CD-Roms, web pages and so on, are becoming commonplace for technologised societies, again, with significant implications for questions of literacy. Thus, as well as continuing to explore metaphor in the lexicogrammar, and metaphor in the grammatics, as the various papers in this volume do, it is also important to consider metaphor in semiosis generally, both in other semiotic systems, and in complex, multi-modal texts.[1]

3.   From theory to practice: Metaphors in the teaching of metaphor

While the theory and definitions of metaphor are intrinsically interesting, it must also be remembered that 'A theory is a means of action' (Halliday 1994: xxix). That is, the theory must have some purpose, and serve some practical application. (And equally, any practical application should have some theoretical validity.) Firth (1957), in exploring the relations between analytical categories and textual data, emphasised the need to constantly re-visit this process, or as he called it, to develop a 'renewal of connection' between categories and data. As many of the papers in this volume demonstrate, it is in the exploration of actual instances of data that the need to augment or adjust the theory of metaphor becomes evident. From a Firthian perspective , theory and application – far from being separate pursuits – are simply two sides of the same coin. However it is never a case of examining data in any decontextualised way; the Firthian and Hallidayan emphasis on context ensures that data is always socio-culturally situated, and thus the renewal of connection is also between theories of context, and social-linguistic practice.

Certainly, as already mentioned, one of the typical domains to which an understanding of lexicogrammatical metaphor is applied is that of education, in terms of the development of literacy processes. In my own practice, I teach about grammatical metaphor to a range of audiences, including undergraduate students who are trying to master the nuances of academic writing, or specialist scientists and educators in museum contexts, who want to move away from highly metaphorised texts to something more accessible to the general public, or people in business contexts, who also want to move away from highly metaphorised texts, to something which generally goes by the (problematic) name of 'plain English'.

In example (1), we can see an example of student writing that would benefit from further metaphorisation. The student is in first year University, in a course in Management.

(1)   A manager may have the best workers available, but if the manager is not able to tell them what he/she wants then they are a wasted expensive resource.

This student is stuck in a congruent and simplistic representation, unable to achieve the technicality and abstraction required of their discipline. In contrast, examples (2), (3) and (4), from a natural history museum, an art gallery, and a government office, respectively, all exhibit a saturation of lexicogrammatical metaphor, to an extent which is generally agreed to be inappropriate if the audience is non-specialised.

(2)   Nutrient enrichment through organic discharges, agricultural run-off and the use of phosphorous-based cleaning products affects the distribution and abundance of fisheries resources.

(3)   The sensual morphology of this leonine figure's breast and penis forms collapses mundane separations between organic states and genders.

(4)   Early advising is required by the department as to our decision.

These highly metaphorised styles are generally 'out of favour' in public contexts, and writers thus need to learn to control a more congruent style. The teaching context here is not one of linguistics, but of language, that is, teaching different groups of people about writing. In these teaching contexts, I would not foreground the term 'grammatical metaphor', but nevertheless, it is the pheno-menon which is being taught.

Teaching about grammatical metaphor may be in terms of moving 'to' or 'away from' metaphorisation. Interestingly, however, the 1985 definition of grammatical metaphor, as explained above, has had a particular impact on my teaching practice.

3.1. Grasping at nominal straws: 'Translation' as a metaphor for metaphor

In teaching about grammatical metaphor, a common way of explaining the phenomenon is to adopt another metaphor, that of translation. I have certainly done this in my own practice. For instance, a student might be told to take a spoken-like text, and make it 'more written', or vice versa. The notion of 'translating' between the spoken and written modes is, in one way, a useful starting point, because it is in understanding the different and complementary natures of the two modes that students begin to grasp what it is that is required of them in academic or other contexts (see, for example, Halliday 1985 on some of the differences between spoken and written language).

However, the notion of 'translation' is an inappropriate metaphor; it suggests a simple process of transference, an exact relationship, and as is common knowledge from experience of translation between languages, there is never such a thing as exact transference. More specifically, it is in the nature of metaphor, as Goatly observes (1997: 2–3), to 'highlight and suppress' various aspects of experience, so exact transference is extremely unlikely.

Using the translation metaphor in teaching leads to at least two problems: firstly, those students trying to move from the spoken end of the mode continuum to the written end, especially those who are from a non-English speaking background, tend to grasp at nominal straws in their efforts to find appropriate nominalisations. They use their (implicit) knowledge of derivational suffixes to produce nominal forms which may or may not be in use in the language, and which may or may not be appropriate in their field. Thus, a student writing about problems in international relations developed the phrase 'widening cleavages' (Droga 1998). The same phenomenon is found in ontogenesis, as all parents would know, and as is illustrated by Derewianka, when her son invented nominalisations such as 'increasement' in 'an increasement of friction' (between two characters in a play) and 'stopness' in 'the computer shuts itself down after a period of 'stopness'' (Derewianka 1995: 118). While making mistakes is clearly part of the learning process, it would seem that, for apprentice writers, the 'translation' metaphor tends to encourage these mistakes.

In addition, the translation metaphor creates a problem for those students trying to move from the written end to the spoken. In these cases, it encourages a search for the one correct 'unpacking' of the nominalisation at hand, and students become unduly concerned about finding the correct answer, or unduly perturbed at the range of other resources which are affected when the metaphor is unpacked. In fact, the whole point of unpacking grammatical metaphor is to reveal the non-exact relationship between the two processes, and to learn to understand the syndrome of features which are implicated in processes of metaphor (see, for example, Halliday 1998, for some discussion of this). Heyvaert (this volume) and Arus (this volume) suggest why, indeed, unpacking to a singular agnate is so unsatisfying. Once again, however, the translation metaphor tends to discourage such an understanding.

Translation, therefore, is a problematic metaphor, and it arises *because of* the theoretical understanding explained in 2.1, as illustrated in Figure 1. If there is one meaning with two realisational forms, why not 'translate' between them? Here we see just one instance of the impact of theory on practice, where the conceptualisaton of the theory has bled into the hidden assumptions of practice. What, then, might be a more effective way of explaining the process to students, and perhaps of understanding it ourselves?

3.2. Metaphor as a resource in its own right

Metaphor does, of course, have to be understood as *a resource in its own right*. Derewianka notes that grammatical metaphor is not a 'component' of the linguistic system as such, but a mechanism or a process (1995: 73). It is a way of meaning; students being apprenticed into academic modes of writing need to learn what counts as being meaningful in their field; what constitutes 'writtenness' in texts, what ways of positioning themselves are valued. Control and understanding of grammatical metaphor will be one of the resources the student needs to master this task.

Similarly, in other contexts such as museums or business, the move away from highly metaphorical texts is motivated by a desire to move away from certain ways of meaning; namely the depersonalized and highly autocratic modes of meaning which are familiar in traditional institutional contexts. As these institutions reposition themselves in more globalised, more competitive and (sometimes) more democratic worlds, they seek to adopt meaning-making practices which are commensurate with these shifts. The 'old' ways of meaning, emphasising elitist forms of discourse, are no longer appropriate. As ever, theory and practice are inextricably linked, and the ability to reflect on metaphors in and of the grammatics, suggests that more appropriate ways of teaching about metaphor need to be found, ways which reflect a more appropriate theoretical explanation of the phenomenon.

4.   **Motivating metaphor:**
     Metafunctional and contextual considerations

As well as defining metaphor and reflecting on the links between theory and
practice, the papers in this volume also contribute to an understanding of the
metafunctional and contextual motivations which give rise to the lexicogrammatical metaphor. Martin, in *English Text* (1992: 490) is rather effusive in
the importance he accords to grammatical metaphor, noting that:

> it is the meta-process behind a text [and that] it is linguistics' most
> important tool for understanding discourse semantics [...] and for
> understanding the relationship between texture and context. It is thus the
> key to understanding text in context – to contextualising the ineffable.

Martin argues that the relationship of metaphor to context is crucial, and that
therefore, the phenomenon is central to a theory of language. This is confirmed
by Halliday, as in the quotes above on stratification, pointing again to the
significance of the phenomenon. In systemic-functional linguistics, then,
metaphor, especially grammatical metaphor, holds an unusually prominent place
in our theory of language. It is not, as Goatly suggests, marginalized within
systemic-functional linguistics because it 'complicates the elegance of the
functional theory' (Goatly 1997: 4) Rather, it is central to an understanding of
language, and to an understanding of the relationship between language and
context.

The relationship of metaphor to the metafunctions, and thus to register
variation, is the first step in understanding its contextual significance. To return
again to the position of Ravelli (1985), one of the main points of that thesis was
to explore the relationship with the contextual variable of *Mode*, noting for
instance:

> the contextual variable of Mode influences the choice between realising
> meanings congruently or metaphorically, and the consequence of this
> choice is reflected in the complexity of the text (Ravelli 1985: 12–13)
>
> and the motivation is "to achieve a particular organisation in the text"....
> "to achieve a particular Thematic structure or information focus of the
> message" (Ravelli 1985: 95–96).

Ravelli established, through analysis and measurement of lexical density,
grammatical intricacy and grammatical metaphor, that mode and metaphor did
indeed co-vary, as Halliday had hypothesized.

Grammatical metaphor is indeed very much at the heart of written language, particularly the hitherto privileged discourses of scientific and academic reasoning. It lies equally at the heart of the backlashes against these, in movements away from privileged institutional positions, towards such discourses as 'plain' English or accessible texts. It is a kind of 'linguistic magic': for struggling writers, successful mastery of grammatical metaphor is the fastest way to progress in the written mode (cf. Cox 1994).

However it is not, of course, grammatical metaphors in isolation which hold the secret; a few nominalisations here and there don't make a good written text. Rather, it is the management of the Theme and Information systems which is at stake; in the words of Halliday, (1998: 203): 'The management of these two systems is one of the factors that contributes most to the overall effectiveness of the text.' This connection was asserted in Ravelli 1985, but that work was necessarily limited in the extent to which it could explain the connection. However, it has since been explicated in great depth, by, for instance, Halliday (e.g. 1998), and Martin (1992; see also Martin 1999 for an effective and accessible explanation).

Spoken and written modes organise themselves differently, creating different textual meanings, as realised by Theme and Information. Grammatical metaphor is the resource which facilitates this. Hence, variation in mode, co-varying with grammatical metaphor, impacts upon the textual metafunction.

This impact arises from what Halliday (1998: 195) identifies as the two key motifs of a stratified system: the potential to refer, and the potential to expand. In the scientific discourses which Halliday reviews, grammatical metaphor exploits the power of referring 'so as to create *technical taxonomies*'. In this way, a particular picture of the world can be built up. In addition, grammatical metaphor exploits the power to expand "[...] – relating one process to another by a logical-semantic relation such as time – [...] so as to create *chains of reasoning* [...] construing a line of argument leading on from one step to the next." (ibid.) Thus, grammatical metaphor enables 'technicalising' and 'rationalising', and these processes are dependent on the clausal to nominal shift which most strongly characterises grammatical metaphor; this "knight's move within the grammar: down in rank, and sideways in class and function". This 'knight's move' leads to distillation and compression, enabling the creation of technical terms, and a move forward in the argument (Halliday ibid.).

Importantly, Halliday adds (1998: 201) that "technicality by itself would be of little value unless accompanied by a discourse of reasoning", hence, while the processes of distillation and compression are necessary resources for theory building, the components of theory must be reasoned about, and connected logically, hence the significance of the management of the textual metafunction.

While the relationship between metaphor, mode and the textual meta-function is one area which has been vigorously pursued, there remains the potential to explore further here, particularly because of the link to literacy. While there may be some backlash against traditional modes of literacy, written texts still hold sway in most examinable contexts. In addition, most western academic communities are experiencing a sea-change in the demographic profile of the typical student. In Australia for instance, the tertiary student body has increased dramatically, from about 160 000 in 1978, to about 658000 in 1997 (ABS 1978, 1998). This student body is no longer a largely homogenous group from a middle-class, native-English speaking background, but rather is a very diverse population, including many students from working class backgrounds, who may well be the first in their families to attend University; many students from non-English-speaking backgrounds, including Indigenous cultures, and international students who speak English as a second or foreign language. In Britain, similar demographic changes have also taken place (Hewings 1999). While entry criteria must still be met in order to gain entrance to University, institutions can no longer presume that students will have the literacy skills required to succeed at a tertiary level, and thus it is now imperative that explicit deconstructions of otherwise implicit modes of meaning takes place. Thus knowledge of and about literacy processes, and questions of access to literacy in a range of contexts, are issues which must continue to be pursued.

Yet equally clearly, mode is not the only contextual variable relevant to an understanding of lexicogrammatical metaphor. As always, the three metafunctions are intertwined, and to quote Halliday again, he summarises the impact of grammatical metaphor within scientific discourses as follows:

> Ideationally, the nominalising grammar creates a universe of things, bounded, stable and determinate; and (in place of processes) of relations between things. Interpersonally, it sets itself apart as a discourse of ... the expert, readily becoming a language of power and technocratic control. (Halliday 1998: 228)

Thus, a full understanding of grammatical metaphor requires exploration of the ideational and interpersonal metafunctions, linked to the register variables of Field and Tenor, and these domains are also pursued in this volume, including but also going beyond scientific texts. It seems, however, that there is the potential for some disquiet in dealing with co-variation across the metafunctions, and across the register variables. That is, if an instance of lexicogrammatical metaphor is explained as a result of variation in Mode and textual meaning, but if it also has an impact on Field/ideational meaning, and Tenor/interpersonal meaning, then how is it that that is explained? The answer, of course, is in the metafunctional hypothesis of systemic-functional linguistics. The three meta-functions are inextricably intertwined; they are separated for analytical and explanatory purposes, but linguistically, always operate together. As Martin notes (1999: 296): "Halliday's metafunctions are the most powerful technology we have for factoring out the complementary meanings of a text and relating them systematically to their social context." But the theory also has to "address the integration of different kinds of meaning in text" (Martin, ibid.).

Consider example (1) again, and a rewritten version in (5), the latter demonstrating a shift in the meanings being made (note that (5) is just one suggested re-wording of (1); many versions would be possible):

(1)   A manager may have the best workers available, but if the manager is not able to tell them what he/she wants then they are a wasted expensive resource.

(5)   Successful management requires effective communication in order to maximise the potential of the workforce.

Example (5) definitely exhibits a shift in mode towards the more 'written' end of the continuum, with an increase in lexical density from about 3 lexical items per clause in (1), to eight in (5). There is a corresponding decrease in grammatical intricacy (see again, Halliday 1985; Ravelli 1985, 1988). The textual orientation has also changed: the departure point of the message is no longer the manager, as an individual, but a more abstract process of 'management'. Along with these changes in Mode and textual meaning, however, are concomitant changes across all the metafunctions. The Field has changed, being now more technical and abstract: the ideational meanings are no longer about people and what they do, but about management, communication, workforce potential and their logical dependence on each other. Tenor and interpersonal meanings have also changed: instead of a personal, human focus, the focus is abstract and impersonal (management, rather than managers), and the explicit evaluation of people (*best* workers) is replaced by an evaluation of things (*successful* management), or else reconstrued entirely as a nominal element (workforce *potential*), all of which are choices more appropriate to the formality associated with written texts.

Any instance of lexicogrammatical metaphor thereby encompasses and impacts upon all the metafunctions. To focus on the core of a metaphor, such as 'management', and to say it 'is' an ideational metaphor, or it 'is' an interpersonal metaphor, is inappropriate. Such metaphors, or at least, the syndrome of features with which they are associated, can be categorised as either, or both, depending on the needs and focus of analysis. At the same time, concern about this interaction points to the need for clearer accounts of the interdependence and intersection of the metafunctions, whether realised metaphorically or otherwise.

4.1. Broader contextual considerations

The full contextualisation of metaphorical processes is found beyond register, in the broadest explanations of the social and cultural contexts which motivate our communication. It is in these processes that we should seek the motivations for grammatical metaphor, in ideology, as explicated in Melrose's paper, this volume, or following earlier work by Thibault, through intertextuality. In his 1991 paper, Thibault takes up Kress's observation that the notion of grammatical metaphor does not in itself provide "an account of the social and political motivations which 'drive' the metaphorical process" (Kress 1989: 455, as cited by Thibault 1991: 301). This observation is very apposite; while it is possible to establish important links between grammatical metaphor and register variables, this on its own is not sufficient to provide a 'motivation' for the phenomenon. As already discussed above, the motivation for shifts in writing practices, either to or away from metaphorised styles, is not 'in order to' make the text appear 'more' or 'less' written, but in order to participate in a certain way of meaning which is valued. Another perspective on the driving forces behind metpahor is provided by Thibault , who suggests that the intertextual dimension can provide just such a motivation. He argues (ibid.) that: "A given metaphorical variant always appears so from the point of view of multiple intertexual (and other) criteria."

The relationship with intertextuality can be illustrated by returning to the example of children in the museum, discussed in the opening of this paper. As we have seen, museum interactives represent a kind of semantic junction; the child learns that the interactive stands for two things: playing/doing and learning/knowing. (And as mentioned earlier, knowing that you can 'play' with something is already a developmental step.) From Thibault's point of view, it is intertextuality which drives metaphorical processes, and it is in the processes of socialisation, at home, at school, in the community and in the peer group, that the child comes across other experiences in which playing/doing becomes a form of learning/knowing.

Such processes happen naturally, a child learns by experimenting: the first stage of transforming the material into the semiotic. And in Western society, these processes are reified through formal educational practices (in other cultures, for example Indigenous communities in Australia, experimentation is highly privileged as a form of knowledge, without being reified as a formal educational practice; cf. Christie 1985). Thus it is in the *intersection* of intertextual experiences that the museum interactive takes its intended place. The many textual experiences of both playing and learning overlap and intersect in such ways, that a particular text, such as a museum interactive, can play on the overlapping spaces between them.

An understanding of intertextuality, then, is one way of facilitating our understanding of the contextualisation and contingency of metaphorical processes, and hence, of the motivations relevant to the phenomenon. It also suggests why the 'congruent' is inherently problematic to define, because there are multiple, intersecting criteria at stake. In exploring motivations, however, it is useful to remember the three possible development perspectives on linguistic semiosis, referred to frequently throughout this volume, namely the ontogenetic, logogenetic and phylogenetic perspectives, reflecting development in the individual, the unfolding of a text, and the evolution of a system, respectively (cf. Martin 1997).

An additional dimension to the possible motivations of metaphor can be found in the growing curiosity about the interpersonal domain, mentioned above, reflecting a concern with Tenor, and hence with social relations. In connection with the interpersonal metafunction, there is a realignment of social relationships taking place, reflected in the backlash against traditional discourses mentioned previously. This backlash is associated with a number of developments in globalisation, access to mass media, and the distribution of technology, which change the social relationships between institutions and those who participate in those institutions, either from 'within' or from 'without', these changing relationships being reflected in texts. To use the example of museums again, museums today no longer want to represent themselves as being the omniscient and elite 'knowledge holders' of the past, but rather as being accessible and equitable institutions, with the role of provoking interest in challenging issues, rather than simply disseminating 'correct' information. As a result, all their semiotic practices change, from the nature of the language used in texts for visitors, to the very design of exhibitions themselves. Many workplaces and public institutions manifest similar changes, as with 'plain English' movements, for example.

The second process which seems to be associated with this, and which represents significant phylogenetic change, is that of changing visual literacies, as mentioned previously. In particular, it seems that the visual representation of textual information, through the systems of Theme and Information, is undergoing significant change. Many texts today deliberately 'mis-manage' the visual highlighting of these systems: it is now commonplace to see ads, posters, and magazines which use highlighting, colour, bolding and so on to foreground otherwise un-marked aspects of Theme and Information systems.

So, for instance, to use a fabricated example, a more traditional written text may make no special use of visual semiotics to highlight important points, relying on unmarked values of Theme and Information to add appropriate weight. Thus in example (6), the highlights of Gent – the Cathedral, Castle, Museum and waterways – are accumulated as News in the unmarked, final position of the clause:

(6)   The highlights of Gent include St Bavo's Cathedral, The Castle of the Counts, and The Museum of Fine Arts. While you are in Gent, be sure to enjoy a boat excursion on the Gent waterways.

A slightly more modern text might use some feature of visual semiotics to further emphasise the informational weight of these items, using a different colour, font size or bolding for instance. Example (7) uses underlining.

(7)   The highlights of Gent include <u>St Bavo's Cathedral</u>, <u>The Castle of the Counts</u>, and <u>The Museum of Fine Arts</u>. While you are in Gent, be sure to enjoy a boat excursion on the <u>Gent waterways</u>.

An even more contemporary text might highlight content in a seemingly random way, as exemplified in example (8), making use of different fonts, font sizes, italicisation and bolding to replicate such processes.

(8)   The highlights OF Gent include **St Bavo's** *Cathedral*, The **Castle of the** Counts, and THE Museum of Fine Arts. While you are in Gent, be sure to **enjoy a boat** *excursion* on the Gent waterways.

If traditional written texts focus so much effort on the management of Theme and Information systems, and if this is so important to the key motifs of technicalising and rationalising, why do we now see texts which deliberately 'mis-manage' these systems? While it is not possible to provide any answers here, such answers may lie in the 'driving forces' discussed above, the intertextual play with contemporary processes of visual representation, the dynamic and multiple texts and communicative acts accessible via new technologies, and a realignment of values towards the popular, and away from the traditional and elite. The phylogenesis of our most privileged discourses has been in order to manage and intersect the processes of technicalising and rationalising, and these processes are central to ideologies of specialised knowledge and expert relations. In the context of backlashes against these discourses, it is not entirely surprising to see such processes being unravelled. The example and the questions it raises suggest a fruitful direction for the 'bigger questions' which motivate our work, a need to examine the cutting edge of these new texts, and a need to explore the relevant functional motivations.

5. Difficult nuts to crack: The hoary chestnuts of metaphor

Always with grammatical metaphor, there seem to be a number of recurring descriptive difficulties; ineffable phenomena, and things on which we do not, as a community, have a clear agreement. Many of these problems were brushed over in Ravelli 1985/1999, including the competing definitions of grammatical metaphor and the difficulties in accounting systematically for various unpackings, as mentioned in Section 1. In addition, a number of items which are related to grammatical metaphor, but which are nevertheless somewhat different, were excluded, namely those items which were taxonomised (such as 'government'), abstract and general (such as 'warfare'), or technical.

The reason for excluding these at the time was because they become fixed realisations in the language; the stratal tension is lost and it is either not possible or appropriate to unpack them. (Although as Simon-Vandenbergen points out in this volume, they do become available for further metaphorisation).

However, is the position as clear as that? When do we agree that a metaphor is dead, that it no longer deploys stratal tension? How clear is the criterion of unpacking as a test for these as metaphors or otherwise? Halliday, Thibault and others have indicated that grammatical metaphor is a gradable phenomenon, a continuum rather than a case of 'either/or'. Thus, there are bound to be some grey areas, some fuzzy boundaries.

Let me take up just one of these grey areas, that of abstraction, and examine the consequences of this boundary, and whether we should be calling it grammatical metaphor or not, and whether it matters.

There are a particular set of abstract terms which are variously called Vocabulary 3 items (Winter 1977); A-nouns (Francis 1985, 1994) or lexical signals (Hoey *passim*). These overlapping categories are exemplified by words like 'factor', 'example', and 'similarity'. There are quite contradictory positions on whether the Vocabulary 3 and A-nouns should be classified as metaphorical or not, and sometimes the contradictions are made by the same writer. Martin, for instance, in a 1997 paper, clearly differentiates abstract things from grammatical metaphor. He (p. 30) identifies abstract terms like 'fact' as semiotic abstractions, separating them out from grammatical metaphor, and notes (personal communication) that developmentally, children grasp these before they grasp grammatical metaphor. Most importantly, he adds that these kinds of terms can't be unpacked, and that would seem to be a defining feature of grammatical metaphor.

Yet on the other hand, Martin argues elsewhere (1992) that Francis' A-nouns, words like 'argument' or 'example' *are* grammatical metaphors, because they "organise text, not field". Martin thus argues for textual grammatical metaphor, in a somewhat more liberal position than Halliday (1994), Matthiessen (1995), or Halliday and Matthiessen (1999), who do not include it. Martin says (1992: 416):

> [...] discourse systems can be used to construe text as 'material' social reality. From the point of view of lexical relations, Winter's (1977) Vocabulary 3 items and Francis's 1985 A-nouns (e.g. *reason, example, point, factor*) organise text, not field. Similarly, text reference [e.g. *this*; LR] identifies facts, not participants, and internal conjunction [e.g. *finally*, LR] orchestrates textual not activity sequences.

In other words, Martin suggests that there are congruent ways of using textual resources, namely to organise [the representation of] Field, identify participants in an unfolding text, and organise activity sequences [congruent with Field]. The metaphorical use of these resources arises when they are deployed for different effects, as Martin says, to make the text itself the social object. (And of course this is exactly what we admire in great writers or great rhetoricians, their facility with *text*.)

If we accept Martin's position, we would definitely want to include Vocabulary 3 items and A-nouns as metaphorical, particularly because they "organise text, not field". But extending the definition this far means that a number of abstract items, such as 'fact' would be netted in to the definition.. And elsewhere, as I've just pointed out, Martin draws a dividing line between abstract and metaphorical things.

Yet it is nevertheless the case that these semiotic things, occurring developmentally prior to grammatical metaphor, do facilitate the organisation of text, rather than field, and they don't refer to participants, but to stretches of text. From an ontogenetic perspective, Derewianka (1995, this volume) has established their importance as a step in the child's overall development of metaphorical potential, but after careful consideration of the arguments for and against, decides to call them *meta-comments* rather than grammatical metaphor as such, again primarily because of the difficulty in unpacking them.

Nevertheless, they are clearly a step on the way towards grammatical metaphor, and I suggest that the fuzziness of the boundary between the two is there for productive reasons. Halliday argues that such fuzziness, or indeterminacy, is an inherent feature of a grammar, allowing it to accommodate multiple and sometimes conflicting complexities, and enabling the grammar to grow by "moving into new domains", or by "increasing the delicacy in their construction of existing domains" (Halliday 1996: 13). In other words, there must be some purpose to this fuzzy boundary between abstraction and grammatical metaphor, and, as is suggested by ontogenetic studies, it is to act as a step towards metaphor 'proper'.

Let me illustrate this in relation to one particular context, that of hyper-Themes or topic sentences in undergraduate academic writing, that is, those sentences which foreground the essay's organisation and development, often, but not always, in first position in the paragraph. Elsewhere, I have argued for a more delicate description of hyper-Themes, according to the logico-semantic relation encoded by the hyper-Theme in relation to an unfolding taxonomy of ideas in the essays (Ravelli & Milionis 1998; Ravelli 2000b).

That is, in an unfolding essay, the writer builds up a picture or taxonomy of key points, and needs to connect these together. The hyper-Theme provides those connections by realising logico-semantic relations between paragraphs. In other words, hyper-Themes function as a nexus point for the intersection of the technicalising and rationalising processes which Halliday identifies as the cornerstones of scientific (and academic) reasoning. Most importantly, they are a *metaphorical realisation* of the intersection of these motifs, via the metaphorical realization of logico-semantic relations between paragraphs, and the use of abstraction and metaphor to name significant points in the argument. Consider the following example:

(9) A further similarity is that both systems have relied ultimately on force.

This example is from a first year History essay, which argues that the collapse of the Dutch empire, rather than Dutch colonialism per se, led to the development of the present Indonesian ruling class. The student has already established a number of similarities between the 'old' system, namely Dutch rule, and the 'new' system, namely the New Order. These similarities are in terms of administration (paragraph 5) and policies of economic and technical advancement – with corresponding political suppression (paragraph 6). In the paragraph which this sentence begins, the student discusses reliance on force. This paragraph is thus in an extending relation to those which have come before; it extends a particular branch of the unfolding taxonomy of ideas in this essay, by adding a new point, at the same level of abstraction as some of the preceding points (cf. Halliday 1994, Chapter 7). These relations are illustrated in Figure 3.

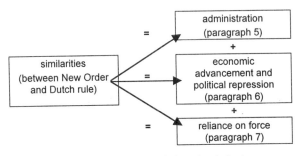

Figure 3: Basic taxonomic relations in student essay

The clause structure of the hyper-Theme itself embodies the metaphorical realisation of the expansion relationship between paragraphs, in this case, a relationship of extension.

The hyper-Theme in the extending paragraph is of the identifying clause type, with a Value/Token relationship (see analysis of example (9) below):

(9)

A further similarity	is	that both systems have relied ultimately on force
Value	Pr: rel	Token

Bearing in mind the difficulties associated with unpacking, a more congruent version of this clause might be as in Example (10):

(10) Another two things are similar and they are (the fact) that both systems have relied ultimately on force.

As with the other familiar instances of metaphor, the hyper-Theme enables the distillation and compression of meanings present in the congruent, agnate form. Importantly, it points backwards and forwards at the same time; creating links to what has come before, and suggesting ways forward, as illustrated in Figure 4.

Here, 'similarity' is at the same time an A-noun, and a grammatical metaphor, type 1 in terms of Halliday's 1998 categorisation, representing a shift from a congruent quality (similar) to a metaphorical entity (similarity) (Halliday 1998: 209). It constitutes a *retrospective* link; retrospective in relation to the preceding text and existing lexical strings, providing an abstract encapsulation of the parallelism between preceding points; they are linked by this common thread. 'Further' explicitly marks that an additional point is being made.

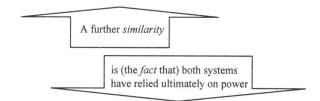

A further *similarity*

is (the *fact* that) both systems
have relied ultimately on power

Figure 4: Advance and retrospective links in a hyper-Theme

In Rheme position (of the hyper-Theme), we find an *advance* label; in the case of this particular example, the label has to be inferred [i.e. ... is *the fact that* both systems ...], but in other examples, it is present. It is an advance label because it is yet to be lexicalised. Note that it is not the word (e.g. *fact*) as such which will be lexicalised, but the whole phrase or group of which it is part, and even more specifically, it is that which *follows* the item which is 'filled out' in the remainder of the paragraph, viz, the Qualifier in the nominal group: [the fact] *that both systems have relied ultimately on force.* Or, in another example, 'the way *countries tend to be focussed*'.

By providing abstract names to the points being made in the essay, and by providing logical connections between these points, the student achieves the two key motifs which Halliday has identified as central to academic discourses, namely technicalising and rationalising. Hyper-themes are not the only resource for achieving this, but in combination with grammatical metaphor and abstraction, they distill a sequence of clause relations into a clause, and provide links forwards and backwards to significant points of the argument. The hyper-Theme thus functions as a significant nexus point for the intersection of the processes of rationalising and technicalising.

While the hyper-Theme as a whole is a metaphorical encapsulation of these processes, the deployment of Vocabulary 3 items, A-nouns, (or in Hoey's terms, lexical signals), whether we want to call them abstractions or metaphors proper, is crucial. These terms facilitate the potential to refer to key points in a text, and so to move from a congruent representation of content, to a metaphorical encapsulation of significant steps in an argument. Consider the following hyper-Theme, this time from a first year essay in management:

(11) A particular example of a manager's perception of employees in an
international organisation compared to that in the domestic context is
demonstrated by comparing the ideology of Japanese and American
management.

This hyper-Theme embodies an elaborating relationship in terms of the
unfolding taxonomy of the essay; the student has already argued that
management practices differ on domestic and international fronts, and now
wishes to illustrate that with a comparison of Japanese and American practices.
The word 'example' is central to the realisation of the hyper-Theme here,
as illustrated in Figure 5:

Theme			Rheme
(a) particular	*example*	*of a manager's perception … domestic context*	*is demonstrated by comparing the ideology of Japanese and American management*
Pre-Modifier	Head	Post-Modifier	
textual connection	advance label, relexicalised in Rheme	recoverable from preceding text	

Figure 5: Realisation of a hyper-Theme

Here, the word 'example' is the Head of the nominal group in topical Theme
position; in Francis' terms, it is an *advance* label, and is about to be
relexicalised. On its own it has little lexical content, but that content is about to
be supplied. In fact, the content is supplied (in this case) in the Rheme
(comparing the ideology of Japanese and American management), as well as in
the remainder of the paragraph, which elaborates the point. What it is an
example *of* is supplied in the Qualifier position of the topical Theme, namely 'a
manager's perception …' and this Qualifier is recoverable from preceding text,
that is, it reiterates previously established information. Thus the word 'example'
has an important role to play, creating the nexus between pointing forward and
pointing back, and enabling the student to connect different points, by creating
an abstract relation between them.

Thus, without a grasp of abstraction, it would be impossible to construct
effective hyper-Themes, because abstractions, as well as more readily identified
grammatical metaphors (such as 'similarity') function as the lynch-pin of the
hyper-Theme, facilitating forward and backward connections. It is not, therefore,
surprising that a fuzzy boundary exists between abstractions and grammatical
metaphor, as one is a step towards the other (as confirmed ontogenetically, see
again Derewianka). Certainly the position of Ravelli 1985/1999, simply

excluding them from analysis, is too simplistic, and the various existing positions on this, and other such problematic categories, suggest that more work needs to be done in these areas.

Again I reiterate links here between theory and practice, and between the grammar and the grammatics. Students often manage to get a handle on abstract items like 'factor', but they don't necessarily use them very effectively. Many teachers would be familiar with essays which discuss 'the first factor', 'the second factor', 'the final factor' and so on. They thus appear to reflect an element of organisation but in fact are ineffective, because the abstract terms are used as if they are just (general) names of things; headings in a list which has no breadth and little depth. Abstract items ought, to use another metaphor, be more like gates in a lock, facilitating movement between levels. Understanding this function is just one more way of improving understanding of, and teaching about, academic discourse, especially in terms of facilitating access to these discourses. It requires a move away from simplistic teaching about the resource itself (e.g. lists of appropriate vocabulary), and towards a more contextualised understanding of the resource, especially its role in contributing to important features and qualities of academic discourse.

6. Conclusions

This paper has ranged over a wide domain, from early definitions of metaphor, to questions about its role in modes of semiosis other than language, to a practical reflection on the role of (some aspects of) metaphor in academic discourse. Linking these is a concern with a constant renewal of connection between theory and practice: each is made relevant by the other, each is extended by the other. My own early definitions and understandings of metaphor, clearly inadequate in comparison with more recent understandings, can be seen to have had a negative impact on some aspects of my own pedagogical practices in relation to the teaching of writing in various contexts. Other aspects of practice, exploring some of the finer details of academic writing, can be seen to impact in turn on theory, requiring extensions and revisions in domains which may have previously been brushed over. This constant cycle of travelling between theory and practice, between category and data, between context and text, can also be seen in the exploration of the driving forces behind metaphor, and in the exploration of the metaphoric potential of semiotic systems beyond language. This renewal of connection may raise more questions than answers, but it is clear that the grey areas of the theory simply point to rich areas of meaning potential.

Note

1. For relatively recent work in these areas, see for example Kress & Van Leeuwen 1996, O'Toole 1994, Van Leeuwen 2000, Martinec 1998, Baldry 2000; Ravelli 2000.

References

Australian Bureau of Statistics (1978) *University Statistics 1978: Part 1, Students.* Canberra: ABS (Catalogue No. 4208.0).

Australian Bureau of Statistics (1998) *Education and Training in Australia.* Canberra: ABS (Catalogue No. 4224.0).

Baldry, Anthony (ed.) (2000) *Multimodality and Multimediality in the Distance Learning Age.* Campobasso: Palladino Editore.

Carter, Ronald (1996/1987) *Vocabulary: Applied linguistic perspectives.* London: Routledge.

Christie, Michael J. (1985) *Aboriginal Perspectives on Experience and Learning: The role of language in Aboriginal education.* Deakin: Deakin UP.

Cox, Kathy (1994) Tertiary Level Writing by Magic – Presto! Nominalisation. *Elicos Association of Australia Journal* 12.1: 8–23.

Derewianka, Beverly (1995) *Language Development in the Transition from Childhood to Adolescence: The role of grammatical metaphor.* Unpublished PhD Thesis, Department of English and Linguistics, Macquarie University.

Droga, Louise (1998) Successful writing at university: What do international students need to know? Paper presented to the 1998 ASFLA Conference, University of South Australia, Adelaide.

Firth, J.R. (1957) A synopsis of linguistic theory, 1930-1955. In: *Studies in Linguistic Analysis (special volume of the Philological Society).* London: Blackwell. 1–31. (Reprinted in F.R. Palmer (ed.) (1968) *Selected Papers of J.R. Firth 1952-1959.* London: Longman. 168–205.)

Francis, Gill (1985) *Anaphoric Nouns* (ELR Monographs.) University of Birmingham.

Francis, Gill (1994) Labelling Discourse. In: M. Coulthard (ed.) *Advances in Written Text Analysis.* London: Routledge. 83–101.

Goatly, Andrew (1997) *The Language of Metaphors.* London: Routledge.

Gowers, Ernest (1954) *The Complete Plain Words.* London: HM Stationary Office.

Halliday, M.A.K. (1967) Aspects of Varieties Differentiation. *Journal of Linguistics* 3.2: 177–274.

Halliday, M.A.K. (1985/1994) *An Introduction to Functional Grammar.* London: Arnold.

Halliday, M.A.K. (1996) On grammar and grammatics. In: R. Hasan, C. Cloran & D. Butt (eds.) *Functional Descriptions: Theory in Practice.* Amsterdam: Benjamins. 1–38.

Halliday, M.A.K. (1998) Things and relations: Regrammaticising experience as technical knowledge. In: Martin & Veel (eds.) (1998). 185–235.

Halliday, M.A.K. & Matthiessen, C.M.I.M. (1999) *Construing Experience Through Meaning: A language-based approach to cognition*. London: Cassell.

Hewings, Ann (1999) *Disciplinary Engagement in Undergraduate Writing: An investigation of clause-initial elements in Geography essays*. Unpublished PhD Thesis, University of Birmingham.

Hoey, Michael (1979) *Signalling in Discourse* (Discourse Analysis Monographs (Birmingham), 6.) Birmingham: English Language Research, University of Birmingham.

Hoey, Michael (1983) *On the Surface of Discourse*. London: Allen & Unwin.

Hoey, Michael (1994) Signalling in Discourse: A functional analysis of a common discourse pattern in written and spoken English. In: M. Coulthard (ed.) *Advances in Written Text Analysis*. London: Routledge. 26–45.

Hoey, Michael (1997) The interaction of textual and lexical factors in the identification of paragraph boundaries. In: M. Reinhardt & W. Thiele (eds.) *Grammar and Text in Synchrony and Diachrony: In honour of Gottfried Graustein*. Vervuert: Iberoamericana. 141–167.

Hoey, Michael (1998a) Some text properties of certain nouns. Forthcoming in: *Proceedings of the Colloquium on Discourse Anaphora and Reference Resolution, Lancaster 1998*.

Hoey, Michael (1998b) The hidden lexical clues of textual organisation: A preliminary investigation into an unusual text from a corpus perspective. Forthcoming in *Proceedings of the 3rd International Conference on Teaching and Learning Corpora, Keble College, Oxford, July 1998*.

Hoey, Michael (2000) *Textual Interaction: An introduction to written discourse analysis*. London: Routledge.

Jespersen, Otto (1933) *Essentials of English Grammar*. London: Allen & Unwin.

Kress, G. (1989) History and language: Towards a social account of linguistic change. *Journal of Pragmatics* 13: 445–466.

Kress, G. & van Leeuwen, T. (1996) *Reading Images: The grammar of visual design*. London: Routledge.

Martin, J.R. (1992) *English Text: System and structure*. Amsterdam: Benjamins.

Martin, J.R. (1993) Life as a noun: Arresting the universe in science and humanities. In: M.A.K. Halliday & J.R. Martin (eds.) *Writing Science: Literacy and discursive power*. London: The Falmer Press. 221–267.

Martin, J.R. (1997) Analysing genre: Functional parameters. In: F. Christie & J.R. Martin (eds.) *Genre and Institutions: Social processes in the workplace and school*. London: Cassell. 3–39.

Martin, J.R. (1999) Close reading: Functional linguistics as a tool for critical discourse analysis. In: Len Unsworth (ed.) *Researching Language in Schools and Communities: Functional Linguistic Perspectives*. Cassell: London. 275–303.

Martin, J.R. & Robert Veel (eds.) (1998) *Reading Science: Critical and functional perspectives on discourses of science*. London: Routledge.

Martinec, R. (1998) Cohesion in action. *Semiotica* 120.1/2: 161–180.

Matthiessen, Christian M.I.M. (1995) *Lexicogrammatical Cartography: English Systems*. Tokyo: International Language Science Publishers.

Nwogu, Kevin & Thomas Bloor (1991) Thematic progression in professional and popular medical texts. In: E. Ventola (ed.) *Functional and Systemic Linguistics: Approaches and uses.* Berlin: Mouton de Gruyter. 369–384.

O'Toole, M. (1992) *The Language of Displayed Art.* London: Leicester UP.

Quirk, R. & S. Greenbaum (1973) *A University Grammar of English.* London: Longman.

Ravelli, L.J. (1985/1999) *Metaphor, Mode and Complexity: An exploration of co-varying patterns.* BA Honours Thesis, University of Sydney. (Published 1999, in: *Monographs in Systemic Linguistics,* 12. Nottingham: Department of English and Media Studies, Nottingham Trent University,.)

Ravelli, L.J. (1988) Grammatical metaphor: An initial analysis. In: E. Steiner & R. Veltman (eds.) *Pragmatics, Discourse and Text: Some systemically-inspired approaches.* London: Pinter. 133–147.

Ravelli, L.J. & A. Milionis (1998) Successful management of academic writing through the intersection of textual and taxonomic structure (or what really makes a good topic sentence). Paper presented to ASFLA 98, University of South Australia, Adelaide.

Ravelli, L.J. (2000a) Beyond shopping: Constructing the Sydney olympics in three-dimensional text. *Text* 20: 4.1–27.

Ravelli L.J. (2000b) Familiar territory, shifting grounds: Aspects of organisation in written texts. Plenary Address at the 27th International Systemic-Functional Congress, University of Melbourne, July 2000.

Thibault, Paul J. (1991) Grammar, technocracy and the noun: Technocratic values and cognitive linguistics. In: Ventola (ed.) (1991). 281–305.

Thibault, Paul J. (1999) Metaphor in word, image, movement: Building bridges between mind, body and world. Plenary Address, 11th Euro-International Systemic Functional Workshop, University of Ghent, Belgium, 14-17 July 1999.

van Leeuwen, Theo (2000) *Speech, Music, Sound.* London: MacMillan.

Ventola, Eija (ed.) (1991) *Functional and Systemic Linguistics: Approaches and uses.* Berlin: Mouton de Gruyter.

Wignell, Peter (1998) Technicality and abstraction in social science. In: J.R. Martin & R. Veel (eds.) *Reading Science: Critical and functional perspectives on discourses of science.* London: Routledge. 297–326.

Winter, Eugene (1977) A clause-relational approach to English texts: A study of some predictive lexical items in written discourse. *Instructional Science* 6: 1–92.

Nominalization as grammatical metaphor
On the need for a radically systemic and metafunctional approach

Liesbet Heyvaert
University of Leuven

1. Introduction[1]

The systemic-functional perspective on nominalizations is closely tied up with the concept of grammatical metaphor: nominalization is presented as a major resource for the creation of 'metaphorical' rather than 'typical' or 'congruent' lexicogrammatical realizations of semantic categories. A nominalized structure like *the cast's brilliant acting*, for instance, is thus viewed as the metaphorical counterpart of the clause *the cast acted brilliantly* (Halliday & Matthiessen 1999: 229). Most noteworthy about the systemic-functional approach to nominalizations, and in line with its *systemic* concern, is the central role that it assigns to a nominalization's *paradigmatic* features: one of the most important tenets of the metaphorical interpretation of nominalizations is that, to fully grasp the meaning of a nominalization, the identification and analysis of both the metaphorical and the congruent realization are essential. Or, as Halliday puts it, "a piece of wording that is metaphorical has as it were an additional dimension of meaning: it 'means' both metaphorically and congruently" (1994: 353). The nominalization *alcohol impairment*, for instance, is thus said to realize the meaning of Thing (the metaphor *impairment*), as well as that of Process (the congruent paradigmatic variant *impair*) (Halliday 1994: 353).

To describe the relationship between paradigmatic variants like *the cast's brilliant acting* and *the cast acted brilliantly*, the concept of 'agnation' (Gleason 1965) is used: it is claimed that every metaphorical structure has "an agnate form corresponding to its congruent realization" (Ravelli 1988: 141). A closer look at how exactly agnation is used in the metaphorical analysis of nominalizations reveals the following tendencies: to start with, much emphasis is put on finding one construction that can be considered as the congruent agnate of the nominalization and that is itself, syntagmatically speaking, a good English structure, e.g.:

(1)   her sailing out of the room/ she sailed out of the room
        (Ravelli 1988: 134)

(2)   the writing of business programs/ people can write business programs
        (Halliday 1994: 349)

(3)   him preparing dinner/ he prepared dinner (Matthiessen 1995: 356–357)
        the cast's brilliant acting/ the cast acted brilliantly
        (Halliday & Matthiessen 1999: 229)

The congruent agnate of a deverbal nominalization (to be distinguished from de-adjectival nominalizations like *long/length*) is, moreover, typically *clausal*: "nominal groups may serve as metaphorical realizations of process configurations in alternate with congruent clauses" (Matthiessen 1995: 678). Some examples, in addition to those in (1) to (4), are:

(5)   the allocation of an extra packer/ they allocate an extra packer
        (Halliday 1994: 353)

(6)   the government's decision/ the government decided
        (Halliday & Matthiessen 1999: 244)

For the actual analysis of nominalizations, their congruent agnates and the relationship between them, systemic-functional linguistics, finally, draws on its *functional* insights. Especially the comparison of how *ideational* functions are realized in clauses and their metaphorical equivalents is singled out as interesting: nominalizations are described as 'ideational' metaphors. They are, in other words, primarily seen as a resource for reconstruing experience along *experiential* and *logical* lines: "The semantic process is represented congruently as the Process in the transitivity structure of the clause; but through grammatical metaphor it may be nominalized and represented as if it were a participant or circumstance, possibly together with other elements of clause structure (...)" (Matthiessen 1995: 356).

    This article confronts the systemic-functional, metaphorical perspective on nominalizations with a descriptive analysis of two types of nominalizations: the first type is generally called 'gerundive nominalization' (Lees 1960/1968: 71) and covers structures like (examples drawn from the COBUILD Corpus, henceforth CB):

(7)   You were to keep quiet about *his having been here.*

(8)   Vice President Quayle announces that *his being dropped from the ticket* is a closed issue, as though the decision is his to make.

(In Halliday's framework, these would be analyzed as embedded projections or Facts (1994: 264–269)).

The second type of nominalization under scrutiny is that formed by adding the suffix *-er* to a verb stem. The so-called 'agentive' *-er* suffix gives rise to agentive nominals (see (9)), but also to non-agentive nominals like those in (10):

(9)   *baker, can opener, computer...*

(10)   *bestseller*   'a book or other item that sells well'
       reader   'a coursebook consisting of a compilation of literature'
       cooker   'an apple for cooking'

The systemic-functional interpretation of grammatical metaphor, as it has been presented in the literature so far, proves to be inadequate to describe the systems of *-ing* and *-er* nominalization satisfactorily. I believe this to be due to the fact that systemic-functionalism does not fully play its trump cards in the analysis of nominalization-as-metaphor, namely its paradigmatic and meta-functional view on language. More particularly, instead of using agnation to elucidate the lexicogrammatical features of nominalizations and thus clarify their meaning, it focuses too much on finding a grammatically correct congruent clause. Some nominalizations, however, can hardly be related to a good clausal agnate. What's more, the analysis of gerundive nominalization makes clear that it does not suffice to relate a nominalization to one congruent agnate only: in particular, one thus fails to identify different types of nominalizations and the systemic choices behind each type. To take an example, both the nominal-izations *Tom's cleaning of the kitchen* and *Tom's cleaning the kitchen* can be said to agnate with *Tom cleans the kitchen.* As will be shown, however, their semantic and syntactic features differ significantly, which can only be revealed by considering the nominalizations' paradigmatic relations more closely.

I will argue that each nominalization should be viewed as the metaphorical counterpart of not one congruent agnate, but of a *network of agnate structures,* clausal and other. Such a network is formed when agnation is used heuristically: an essential prerequisite for uncovering the system network behind each type of

nominalization is the identification and interpretation of the different structural units that it consists of. *Identifying* these units is, I will show, necessarily based on the paradigmatic structures or agnates they relate to: agnation is then used to demarcate the unit boundaries. I will, for instance, use agnation to identify *cleaning the kitchen* as the Head unit in the nominalization *Tom's cleaning the kitchen*, while in *Tom's cleaning of the kitchen*, the central unit is *cleaning* only. In addition to identifying the relevant units in each nominalization type, agnation also helps to *interpret* their meaning: in spite of the fact that they are superficially identical, the units *Tom's* and *cleaning* in *Tom's cleaning the kitchen* and *Tom's cleaning of the kitchen* will thus be shown to belong to different agnation networks and have distinct meanings. Using agnation to mark off and interpret the units of a nominalization thus leads to the nominalization being embedded in a unique network of agnates: each of the agnates highlights a specific grammatico-semantic feature of the nominal, and together, they define the nominalization. An agnation network is, moreover, essential to situate each particular nominalization within its natural habitat: an aspect of agnation which has been largely ignored in the metaphorical approach to nominalizations is that agnation can also help to identify *enate* relations, i.e. structurally identical nominalizations.

The system of *-er* nominalization, in addition, illustrates that the description of a nominalization's agnation network should be *multifunctional*, rather than being reduced to ideational categories only. The experiential resemblances and differences between metaphorical *-er* and its congruent agnates may be the most obvious ones to notice, it is *interpersonal* categories which turn out to be the driving motive behind *-er* nominalization: only when you map interpersonal categories like Subject and Finite onto the experiential roles that are designated by the suffix (e.g. Agent, Patient), can the true semantic import of *-er* be revealed.

In a first part, systemic-functional linguistics will be shown to rightly characterize the relationship between a nominalization and its non-nominal counterpart as an instance of 'agnation': I will look into the notions of 'agnation' and 'enation' as defined by Gleason (1965) and compare Gleason's view with the metaphorical description of nominalizations. I will then zoom in on the systemic-functional idea that each deverbal nominalization can be related to one congruent, preferably clausal agnate: various analyses found in Halliday (1994) and in Halliday & Matthiessen (1999) will be critically examined in terms of the use that they make of agnation. Subsequently, the more radically paradigmatic notion of agnation networks as heuristic tool for the identification and interpretation of structural units will be presented as essential for the analysis of

nominalizations: it is only a network of agnate structures that can help to establish the semantics of a nominalized structure, reveal the system behind it, and relate it to its enate constructions. Gerundive nominalization will provide evidence in favour of this claim.

In a second section, I will focus on -*er* nominalization and how it elucidates the importance of interpersonal categories for the description of agnation networks. Finally, in a last part, I will briefly take up the issue of whether the concept of metaphor is appropriate to refer to the process of nominalization: is the relationship between a nominalized structure and its non-nominal counterpart one of resemblance, and, if so, how far does that resemblance go? It will be argued that the discussion of nominalization has focused too much on representational issues and on the textual consequences of construing clauses as nominal groups: equally important to understand the motives behind nominalization are the interpersonal resemblances between clausal and nominal structure.

2. The role of agnation in the analysis of nominalizations

2.1. Nominalization

Nominalization can be defined as the process by which non-nominal structural elements are made to function as nominal elements.[2] A nominalization is then either an item that has been 'transcategorized' from, for instance, verb to noun class (Matthiessen 1995: 101; e.g. *die* becomes *death*), or it is a clause, finite or non-finite, that comes to function at nominal rank, e.g.:

(11) I regret *the role of mother isn't generally more highly regarded by everyone.* (CB)

(12) *Merely getting a piece of fabric evenly damp but not wet* required endless care. (CB)

2.2. Agnation as systematic grammatico-semantic relationship between structures

How does systemic-functional linguistics describe the relation between a nominalized structure and its non-nominal alternative? Halliday (1994) points out that, while a nominalization like, for instance, *his death* and its variant *he died* are not synonymous, they are nonetheless systematically related in meaning: they are "plausible representations of one and the same non-linguistic 'state of affairs'" (1994: 344). Or, as Ravelli puts it, they are close in meaning

"primarily because of shared experiential content" (1988: 134). At the same time, however, their meaning differs, because of the impact of distinct structural features: Halliday & Matthiessen (1999) describe a metaphor as 'junctional' because "it embodies semantic features deriving from its own lexicogrammatical properties" (1999: 283). Less explicitly stated in the literature on nominalizations, though implied in some of the analyses found in Matthiessen (1995) and Halliday & Matthiessen (1999), is the idea that the structural differences between nominalized and non-nominalized variants are just as well systematic and can be described in general terms. In the pair *he died/ his death*, for instance, a combination of Subject and Finite (Actor and Process) is turned into a possessively premodified noun, expressing a Thing.

To capture the fact that there exist non-nominal structures that are systematically related to nominalizations in terms of meaning and structure, systemic-functional linguistics rightly uses the term *agnation*. It was first introduced by Gleason (1965) to describe structures "with the same major vocabulary items, but with different structures", of which "the relation in structure is regular and systematic, that is, (...) it can be stated in terms of general rules" (1965: 202). McGregor (1997) speaks of "minimal and near minimal grammatical pairs" (1997: 11). Gleason further specifies that agnate structures need not be "on the same grammatical level" (1965: 211), and he gives the example of a nominalization: the clause *the boy runs* and the nominalized equivalent *the boy's running*, he argues, are instances of agnation (1965: 212). In short, nominalizations and their non-nominal alternatives seem to meet the conditions of agnation as they were set out in Gleason (1965). The actual systemic-functional use of agnation in the context of grammatical metaphor will, however, be shown to deviate from Gleason's view in a number of ways.

2.3. Agnation and enation are mutually defining

To Gleason, the identification of agnate relations necessarily also involves the concept of *enation*: he argues that, ideally, structures are analyzed by means of a "two-dimensional set of frames" which he defines as "a set related in one direction by enation and in the other by agnation" (Gleason 1965: 201). What does he mean by 'enate' structures? Constructions can be said to 'enate' with each other when they have identical structures: the units which they consist of are of the same classes, and they are arranged in identical constructions (Gleason 1965: 199). An example of an enate relationship is, for instance, that between the clauses *he heard it*, *he felt it* and *he saw it*: their units have been organized into structurally identical combinations (Gleason 1965: 202).

Important is that relations of agnation and enation cannot be stated clearly without one another: as Davidse (1998: 283) puts it, "the systematicity of an agnation pattern should be confirmed by enate examples displaying the same agnation relation", while "for examples to be enate, they should have identical sets of agnates". The structures *he heard it, he felt it* and *he saw it* can, in other words, only be identified as enate because they share certain agnates: all of them can, for instance, be passivized (*it was heard by him, it was felt by him* and *it was seen by him*, Gleason 1965: 202). Constructions like *the man saw a stranger* and *the man seemed a stranger*, in contrast, are not enate, because they belong to different agnation networks: *a stranger was seen by the man* is possible, while *a stranger was seemed by the man* is not. *The man seemed to be a stranger*, on the other hand, is acceptable, while *the man saw to be a stranger* isn't. To conclude, enate relations guarantee that the agnates that are identified are based on "the pervading patterns of the language" (Gleason 1965: 202), rather than being unique relations between isolated structural pairs.

In the existing systemic-functional literature on nominalization-as-meta-phor the concept of enation is absent: the metaphorical view on nominalization is almost exclusively aimed at unpacking individual syntagms into congruent agnates, rather than on elucidating the choices behind nominalized structures and linking them up with enate nominalizations. Because the congruent agnates that are thus identified are not themselves systematically informed by enate nominalizations with similar agnates, they fail to fulfill the role which Gleason had intended them for: they do not contribute to the linguistic analysis of the nominalized structure, but merely function as *paraphrases*. Agnates that are not based on enate regularities do not go beyond the particular features of the individual structure they are claimed to agnate with: they fail to pick up on the more fundamental, *systemic* choices that are realized by the lexicogrammar of a construction. Take, for instance, the nominalization *the writing of business programs* (Halliday 1994: 349). Its congruent agnate is said to be *people can write business programs*. This agnate, however, does not clarify the linguistic features of the nominalization type to which this particular instance belongs, neither does it distinguish it from other, non-enate types of *-ing* nominalizations (e.g. *writing business programs*, which in Halliday (1994) would be classified as an 'Act' nominalization, and the structure *people's writing business programs*, which can be grouped among the 'Fact' nominalizations). In brief, the present systemic-functional use of agnation in the discussion of grammatical metaphor deviates from Gleason (1965) in that it is not systematically inspired by enate structures, nor is the congruent agnate itself used to define enate relations. As a result, the congruent agnates do not reflect recurrent structural patterns and, ultimately, fail to contribute to the linguistic analysis of the nominalized structure in question.

2.4.   Agnation networks vs. the systemic-functional focus on one clausal agnate

For congruent agnates to be of help with the analysis of nominalizations and the identification of types of them more is needed than the addition of the enate dimension. It is clearly implied in Gleason (1965) that agnates are always part of agnation *networks*: one agnate structure cannot uniquely identify the structure it agnates with. It only highlights a particular grammatico-semantic feature of it. Together with the other agnate structures in the network, however, it provides a detailed picture of the grammatico-semantic choices that are realized by a particular structure. An example of such an agnation network in Gleason (1965) is the following: to distinguish *the new house* from *the school house*, Gleason discusses three agnates of the former construction that do not relate to the latter: *the new school house* vs. **the school new house*, *the very new house* vs. **the very school house*, and, finally, *the house which is new* vs. **the house which is school* (Gleason 1965: 204). These three agnate structures can be said to form a small network of agnation that helps to characterize *the new house* and distinguish it from the non-enate structure *the school house*.

A closer look at the use of agnation in the metaphorical analysis of nominalizations reveals the tendency to view a deverbal nominalization as the metaphorical realization of one structure, which is preferably clausal in nature. The search for this congruent agnate clause dominates the analysis of nominal-ization-as-metaphor. Some examples of nominalizations and their clausal agnates are (examples drawn from Halliday & Matthiessen 1999: 251; see also the examples (1) to (6)):

(13)   his arrest by the police/ he was arrested by the police

(14)   yesterday's decision by the group/ the group decided yesterday

In the case of nominalized structures that are ambiguous, each of the meanings is related to one congruent agnate: a nominalization like *alcohol impairment*, for instance, is thus said to agnate with *alcohol impairs*, as well as with *alcohol is impaired* (Halliday 1994: 353).[3]

Some nominalizations, however, cannot be associated with a good clausal agnate, unless one adds lexicogrammatical items that do not function in the nominalized structure. Consider, for instance, the following example of a congruent agnate given in Halliday & Matthiessen (1999: 255):

(15)   the development of our understanding/ [the way] we understand develops[4]

In the urge to find a good congruent equivalent for each nominalization, even constructions that are no longer agnates in the Gleasonian interpretation are suggested. The following metaphorically related constructions are not based on identical lexical items.

(16)   prolonged exposure/ the item is exposed for a long time (1999: 256)

The examples in (15) and (16) also make clear that systemic-functional research on deverbal nominalizations does its utmost to find agnates that are *clausal* in nature. Gleason, however, explicitly points out that "any construction can be agnate to another of the same kind, provided only that it is large enough to have some internal structure" (1965: 211). Particularly relevant for nominalization is thus, for instance, that morphologically complex words like -*ing* formations in gerundive nominals can be related to non-clausal agnate constructions. In fact, the discussion of gerundive nominalization will make clear that the linguistic analysis of a nominalized group can benefit greatly from the use of non-clausal agnates.

By pointing at the present systemic-functional focus on finding a good clausal agnate, I do not wish to say that the metaphorical system is conceived of as being necessarily *binary*. Many nominalizations, it is argued in Halliday & Matthiessen (1999), require 'intermediate' levels of analysis: "Paradigmatically, there will typically be other wordings intermediate between an instance of grammatical metaphor and its 'most congruent' agnate variant" (1999: 249). The nominalizations in (17) and (18), for instance, illustrate this principle of multiple unpackings:

(17)   the development of our understanding/ our understanding develops/ [the way] we understand develops (Halliday & Matthiessen 1999: 255)

(18)   prolonged exposure/ exposure is prolonged/ the item is exposed for a long time (1999: 256)

Rather than being presented as a *network* of interrelated agnate structures forming a tool to elucidate the grammatico-semantic features of the nominalization, however, these levels of unpacking are especially looked at from the perspectives of language development, language acquisition and textual development, according to which they form a *continuum*: "the metaphorical relationship is not a symmetrical one: there is a definite directionality to it, such that one end of the continuum is metaphorical and the other is what we shall call congruent" (Halliday & Matthiessen 1999: 235). More specifically, the metaphorical variants turn out to evolve after the congruent structure.[5] In short, in the present systemic-functional analysis of grammatical metaphor, sets of agnate constructions are primarily conceived of as forming 'intermediate' levels on a temporal continuum linking up metaphors and their congruent agnates. They are hardly considered as parts of a network of linguistic analysis.

2.5. Agnation as heuristic: The interplay between a syntagm and its paradigms

Inspired by the analysis of gerundive nominalization, I want to formulate a complementary way of looking at sets of agnation. More particularly, I claim that agnation can fulfill a crucial role in the linguistic analysis of nominalization-as-metaphor, if only one adheres more closely to Gleason's interpretation of it: agnates can adduce the paradigmatic evidence that is needed to recognize and interpret the syntagmatic features of a nominalization and distinguish it from other types. Notice that these syntagmatic patterns are mostly taken for granted in research on nominalization: it is never seriously taken into account that a nominalization's syntagmatic organization and division into units itself might have to be looked into more closely before one can establish its meaning. Consider Halliday and Matthiessen's (1999) discussion of 'syndromes': the notion of 'syndrome' is meant to capture the fact that grammatical metaphors are typically "clusterings of metaphorical effects among which there is some kind of interdependence" (1999: 244; for elaborate analyses of such syndromes, see Halliday & Matthiessen 1999: 250–255). The internal syntagmatic structure of a nominalization is thus described as a series of elements, each of which contributes to the general metaphorical import of the syntagm. The nominalization *the government's decision* illustrates such interdependent clustering of metaphorical effects: it is argued to consist of two metaphorical effects, among which there exists a relation of interdependency. In particular, the trans-categorization of *decide* into *decision* gives rise to the possessive form of *government* (Halliday & Matthiessen 1999: 244).

While for many nominalizations it is indeed fairly easy to identify the units which they consist of and uncover the grammatico-semantic functions which they fulfill in the nominalized syntagm, that is not true for all nominalizations: the analysis of gerundive nominalization, for instance, makes clear that it is sometimes difficult to recognize exactly which metaphorical effects or elements a nominalization is construed of in the first place. A nominalization like *the writing of business programs* (Halliday 1994: 349), for instance, has metaphorical effects that differ from those in *writing business programs*: not only do these nominalizations consist of distinct syntagmatic units, the metaphorical effects realized by them are also substantially different. As will be argued later, the metaphorical effect of the nominalization *writing business programs* lies in the fact that it downranks a processual unit (*writing business programs*) as Head/Thing of the nominal group. In the structure *the writing of business programs*, in contrast, one metaphorical effect is created by the transcategorization of the verb *write* into the noun *writing*, and this is then accompanied by the metaphorical effect of turning the Range of the process into a nominal, postmodifying *of*-structure. In short, gerundive nominalization forces us to bear in mind that the syntagmatic organization of metaphorical elements can not always be taken for granted.

Then how should nominalizations be analyzed and which role can agnation play in the analysis? I claim that the 'metaphorical effects' which Halliday and Matthiessen (1999) distinguish in nominalizations should be given a sound lexicogrammatical basis by reinterpreting them as 'values' in the Saussurean sense: the elements that carry metaphorical effects should be considered as linguistic units with certain metaphorical values. Establishing the units of a nominalization and identifying their value then becomes a precondition for identifying the nominalization's overall metaphorical import. This Saussurean approach to nominalization-as-metaphor draws on McGregor's (1997) view on linguistic units: in his *Semiotic Grammar*, McGregor reinterprets Saussure's 'sign' or 'concept-sound' entity into a 'form-function' unit, i.e. a unit of which the value is created by the systematic association of a particular form with a particular function. The exact value of such linguistic units is then created through their relation with other form-function correlations.

In line with Saussure's view, McGregor (1997: 46) argues that it is the combination of syntagmatic and paradigmatic relations of a unit that defines its function and ultimately, its value in the system: "Paradigmatic and syntagmatic relations, as Saussure rightly appreciated, are (...) mutually dependent and defining. The syntagm (and any of its parts) is only identifiable in terms of the paradigmatic relations which the syntagmatically related units attract with entities outside of it". In other words, if we are to identify the metaphorical value of a nominalization, we have to describe the syntagmatic and paradigmatic relations of its units in detail. In what follows, I will show that Gleason's concept of agnation can form an ideal tool for uncovering the paradigmatic and indirectly also the syntagmatic relations of the linguistic units in gerundive nominals.

3.   The system of gerundive nominalization

3.1.   Lees's (1960) network of related structures

In his *Grammar of English Nominalizations*, Robert B. Lees (1960) discusses various types of *-ing* nominalizations, among which a type which he calls 'gerundive'. Some examples of gerundive nominals are:

(19)   his eating vegetables   (1960/1968: 71)

(20)   his drawing the picture   (1960/1968: 65)

Another type of *-ing* nominalization is called 'action' nominalization (1960/1968: 64) and is illustrated in (21) and (22) (Lees 1960/1968: 65):

(21)   his bringing up of the box

(22)   his drawing of the picture

If we interpret these nominals as metaphorical counterparts of a clausal construction, the following agnation pairs are possible:

(23)   his eating vegetables / he ate vegetables

(24)   his drawing the picture/ he drew the picture

(25)   his bringing up of the box/ he brought up the box

(26)   his drawing of the picture/ he drew the picture

As can be deduced from the pairs in (24) and (26), both the nominalization *his drawing the picture* and *his drawing of the picture* are related to the clausal structure *he drew the picture*. In other words, relating gerundive and action nominals to one clausal agnate illustrates their commonality. It does not, however, clarify their differences. In his analysis, Lees (1960) recognizes that gerundives and action nominalizations can be related to the same clausal structure, but he also points to the lexicogrammatical peculiarities of each type by means of series of constructions that relate to only one of them. These structures are, in fact, nothing but instances of agnation: indeed, most of the 'tests' used by mainstream linguistics to analyze constructions are actually testing the syntagm's relation to other structures or agnates (see Davidse 1998: 284).

Lees argues that gerundive nominals agnate with structures that contain auxiliaries, witness the following pair:

(27) his bringing up the box/ his having brought up the box
      (Lees 1960/1968: 65)

Secondly, gerundive nominals also systematically relate to structures that have adverbial modification, e.g.

(28) his drawing the picture/ his drawing the picture rapidly
      (Lees 1960/1968: 65)

Finally, it is pointed out that the possessive premodifier in gerundive nominals may be replaced by an oblique: in other words, possessively premodified gerundives can be systematically related to gerundives that are premodified by an oblique:[6]

(29) I don't approve of *his going there*/ I don't approve of *him going there*
      (Lees 1960/1968: 72)

Again by pointing at a number of related constructions, Lees identifies gerundive and action -*ing* nominals as constituting two different nominalization systems, or, to put it in agnation terms, as being non-enate: firstly, action nominals are non-enate to gerundives because they do not agnate with the paradigms in (27), (28) and (29):

(30) his bringing up of the box/ *his having brought up of the box
      (Lees 1960/1968: 65)

(31) his drawing of the picture/ *his drawing of the picture rapidly
      (Lees 1960/1968: 65)

(32) his drawing of the picture/ *him drawing of the picture

At the same time, gerundives are non-enate to action nominals for several reasons: firstly, gerundives do not systematically relate to structures with adjectival modification, while action nominals do:

(33) his drawing of the picture/ his rapid drawing of the picture, but *his rapid drawing the picture (Lees 1960/1968: 65)

Secondly, gerundives do not relate to structures that use an article rather than a possessive premodifier:

(34)   his rapid drawing of the picture/ the rapid drawing of the picture, but *the drawing the picture rapidly (Lees 1960/1968: 65–66)

Finally, as is pointed out by Lees (1960/1968: 66), action nominals can be systematically related to derived nominals with suffixes other than -*ing*, while gerundives can't, e.g.:

(35)   his strong objecting/ his strong objection, but his objecting strongly/ *his objection strongly

In short, gerundive nominals and action nominals may look very much alike, they differ significantly. Linking them to one congruent agnate only does not help us much further in accounting for these differences. It is only when both types of nominalization are situated within their own network of agnate structures, that their unique grammatico-semantic features are foregrounded.

On the basis of the network of agnate constructions thus established, Lees (1960) distinguishes also semantically between gerundive and action -*ing* nominals, and he ascribes them the following properties: a nominalization like *his drawing of the picture*, he argues, designates an action, a 'doing'. A gerundive nominal like *his drawing the picture*, on the other hand, has what he calls a 'factive' meaning (Lees 1960/1968: 65): the factivity of gerundive nominals makes possible the following syntagms:

(36)   *His eating vegetables* is surprising.   (Lees 1960/1968: 71)

(37)   John didn't like *Mary's drinking*.   (Lees 1960/1968: 105)

(38)   *His having gone* pleased us.   (Lees 1960/1968: 106)

In all of these clauses, Lees claims, the nominalized group can be systematically replaced by and thus related to a nominal group with a postmodified, downranked clause, i.e. *(the fact) that ...* . In addition, the nominalizations in (36) and (38) can also be said to agnate with *to*-infinitive structures: *for him to eat vegetables is surprising* and *for him to have gone pleased us* (Lees 1960/1968: 71).

What exactly is meant by 'factive' has been much debated ever since: Kiparsky and Kiparsky (1971: 348) claim that a fact is "presupposed true by the speaker"; Halliday (1994: 264) views factive nominals as projections that come "as it were ready packaged in projected form", i.e. they are metaphenomena or representations of linguistic representations, of which the projecting verbal or mental process clause is not given. Striking about all of these approaches – including that of Lees – is, however, that they never attempt to make the link between the metaphorical, 'factive' interpretation of the nominalization and its *internal* grammatico-semantic features. Why is it that, when realizing a congruent clause like *Sam cleaned the windows* as a gerundive nominalization *Sam's cleaning the windows*, the nominalized structure acquires a 'factive' meaning, while the nominalization *Sam's cleaning of the windows* will mostly be associated with an 'action' meaning (e.g. *Sam's cleaning of the windows lasted three hours*)?

In what follows, I will show that, to fully account for the overall metaphorical import of the gerundive nominal *Sam's cleaning the windows* and distinguish it from the action nominal *Sam's cleaning of the windows*, one should link it up with the metaphorical effects that are realized by its component parts: the analysis of the metaphorical or nominalized features of the units which gerundive nominals are composed of constitutes an integral part of the general analysis of gerundive nominalization, and may well contribute to a motivation for its 'factive' meaning. Establishing the metaphorical value of the form-function units in gerundive nominals will require an extension of the network of agnate structures as described in Lees (1960). I will discuss in detail two units that are typical of gerundive nominalization, i.e. the possessive premodifier and the *-ing* unit followed by an Object-like constituent. In particular, I will show that it is essential to establish *their* metaphorical value, because, I will argue, their value determines the overall factive value of the gerundive nominal and helps to distinguish gerundive from action nominalization.

3.2. Agnation as a tool for establishing and interpreting units

3.2.1. The units cleaning *and* the windows *constitute a form-function unit*
Various agnates suggest that *cleaning* and *the windows* make up a form-function unit within the nominalization *Sam's cleaning the windows*: comparable units of verb and Object(s) can be found in a series of structures other than the factive - *ing* nominal. A first structure in which we find a unit which can be systematically related to the nominalized unit *cleaning the windows* consists of the use of the combination of verb and Object in a *clause*: there is formal and semantic evidence that, also within a clause, a verb (minus the grounding elements of tense and modality) and its Objects form a unit (Halliday 1994; Davidse 1997). More precisely, a fundamental structural split seems to exist between the Subject and the Finite (and polarity) on the one hand (Halliday's

'Mood' category) and the rest of the clause on the other hand (Halliday's 'Residue'). Semantically speaking, the Mood is argued to relate what is expressed in the Residue to the context of the here-and-now of the speech event (Halliday 1994). Formal evidence for the unit-status of the Predicator and its Objects is provided by

• tags, which can isolate Subject and Finite:

(39)   You will clean the windows, won't you?

• Mood ellipsis (the Mood is left out and the Residue retained):

(40)   What will you do? [I will] Clean the windows.

• Residue ellipsis (which drops the non-grounding verb and its Object):

(41)   I will clean the windows. Will you [clean the windows]?
        Yes, I will [clean the windows].

Another type of structure which can be said to agnate with units like *cleaning the windows* itself constitutes a *clause*: units comparable to *cleaning the windows* can themselves function as clauses, as can be witnessed in the following clauses:

(42)   There his father lived the life of a recluse, *conscientiously tending the woods he loved*. (CB)

(43)   Last Friday, he sent a telegram to the annual meeting of Quebec's independence party, *openly endorsing their separatist demands*. (CB)

In addition, a unit similar to *cleaning the windows* can function as *nominal group*, without being preceded by a possessive pronoun (i.e. Halliday's 'Act' category, 1994: 248):

(44)   (…) young children may tire their parents out so badly that *hitting the pillow* is more important than *melting in your spouse's arms with passionate abandon*. (CB)

(45)   At first glance, *managing time* seems to mean *being better organized, working faster or more efficiently* and *wasting less time*. (CB)

To conclude, gerundive nominals contain a unit that agnates with various verb-Object combinations, each constituting a formal and functional unit in their respective syntagms. Especially relevant then for the discussion of gerundive nominalization is the way in which the value of the nominalized unit *cleaning the windows* in *Sam's cleaning the windows* differs from its agnates in other syntagmatic contexts: which is the unique, metaphorical value of the unit *cleaning the windows* in gerundive nominalizations? To find out more about it, however, two other units have to be looked into first: the *-ing* suffix in *cleaning* can elucidate the internal features of the unit *cleaning the windows*, while the possessive preceding *cleaning the windows* can tell us more about its external functioning within the nominal group.

3.2.2. *-ing as an alternative to tense/modality*
Which network of related structures can *-ing* be situated in? In gerundive nominals, *-ing* turns out to function as an alternative to grounding: it cannot be added to an already grounded structure (e.g. **shoulding clean; *hading been cleaned*), neither can one ground an *-ing* form (**should cleaning*). Rather, the *-ing* suffix of gerundive nominals requires the same base forms as do indicators of tense/modality, i.e. a simple form (a verb stem) or a complex form (verb stem and auxiliaries):

base form	grounding	-ing
clean	cleans/cleaned	cleaning
have cleaned	has cleaned	having cleaned
have been cleaning	has been cleaning	having been cleaning

In other words, the *-ing* form of gerundive nominals relates to base verbal forms like *clean/ have cleaned/ have been cleaning* in the same way as indicators of tense and modality do: *-ing* and tense/modality form mutually exclusive choices in the verb group (see also Halliday 1994: 202–203), with *-ing* realizing a *non-finite* profile.[7] Some examples of gerundive nominals in which *-ing* is attached to a complex verb group are (source: CB):

(46) One of those individuals who is unaccountably gifted as a contemplative, she knew nonetheless that her discovery of that hidden track inward, and *her having been able to follow it into full, ecstatic awareness of God*, was sheer grace. (perfect aspect)

(47) Its volume alone would be impressive, but its originality and sheer brilliance vindicate completely *her having been declared Doctor of the Church*. (perfect aspect and passive voice)

It follows from the analysis of the *-ing* suffix that the unit *cleaning* in *cleaning the windows* has not been transcategorized into a noun: instead of being a nominalizing suffix, *-ing* preserves the verbal nature of the process *clean* and imposes a non-finite perspective on it. The verbal properties of *cleaning* account for the fact that the Patient of the process is construed as Object and that gerundive nominals can take an adverb. They also constitute the most significant difference with action nominals, in which the *-ing* form is transcategorizing: rather than forming an alternative to tense or modality, it relates to other derivational suffixes like *-ment* (as in *appointment*), *-al* (as in *arrival*), and others (see also Lees 1960/1968: 66).[8] If the *-ing* in gerundive nominals is verbal rather than nominalizing, however, we are still left with the question of how gerundive nominals realize the category of *nominalization*, and, more particularly, the metaphorical value of 'factiveness'. To answer that question, the 'nominal' nature of gerundive nominalizations has to be analyzed. The most important overt indicator of their nominality is the possessive premodifier.

3.2.3. The possessive as premodifier of the nominal Head
As was pointed out by Lees (1960), most gerundive nominals have a possessor in initial position. Traditionally, the possessive is said to indicate how 'nominal' the unit *cleaning the windows* has become (e.g., among others, Jespersen 1914-1929, part IV; Schachter 1976; Pullum 1991). And indeed, the possessive forms a convincing argument in favour of viewing the latter unit as Head of the gerundive nominalization, the possessive being a typical way of premodifying a noun. More in general, gerundive nominalization thus turns out to support Halliday's claim that clausal structures can be embedded in nominal groups and function as their Heads (1994: 248 and 266). Gerundive nominals can then be classified among those nominalizations in which the metaphorical value is created by the fact that the Head is a clausal unit that has been downranked as noun in a nominal group.

To fully understand the import of the metaphor, however, the exact nature of the possessive unit and of the noun-status of the nominal Head have to be looked into as well. Once again, agnate relations may be of help here. To start with, as was shown before, the possessive of gerundive nominalization is not an ordinary nominal premodifier: *Sam's cleaning the windows* does not, for instance, agnate with structures like **the cleaning the windows; *that cleaning the windows*. Rather, the possessive relates to an oblique form (as in (48) and (49)) and to a zero-determiner (see (50) and (51); all examples have been drawn from the Cobuild corpus):

(48)   Many Germans say the foreigners are fleeing economic, not political,
       hardship and resent *the government paying for the refugees' food and*
       shelter.

(49)   Meanwhile, there has been another explosion at an office of the ruling
       National Party, with evidence pointing to *it having been the work of white*
       extremists.

(50)   I think my only regret, as I say, was *not being able to train for the job I*
       wanted to do.

(51)   I think I was most appalled at *having been gloriously turned on by a*
       tussle with John Major.

Equally important is that the possessive premodifier necessarily coincides
with what would have been the congruent Subject of the processual unit
functioning as Head. Any experiential role that may be conflated with a clausal
Subject can just as well be mapped onto the premodifier in a gerundive nominal:
the premodifier may be an Agent (e.g. *his having rendered himself up*) or a
Patient (e.g. *his being dropped from the ticket*); even existential 'there' is
possible (e.g. No one would have dreamed of *there being such a place*, Jespersen
1914-1929, part IV: 137).

As far as the analysis of the nominal features of the Head-unit is
concerned, I would like to refer to Langacker (1991). Langacker points out that
transcategorized *-ing* nouns as in *McTavish always does a lot of complaining* are
systematically related in meaning and structure to *mass* nouns (1991: 25): like
mass nouns, and unlike count nouns, they designate uncountable Things that are
internally homogeneous, or, as Halliday puts it, "continuous" (1994: 190).
Structurally speaking, they resemble mass nouns in that they do not tolerate
pluralization, they take quantifiers that occur only with mass nouns (e.g. *a lot*
of), and they can function in a nominal group without an overt Deictic (compare,
for instance, the mass noun *electricity* with the nominalization *complaining*)
(Langacker 1991: 26). I claim that the function which non-finite Heads fulfill in
gerundive nominals can just as well be compared to that of mass nouns: the
verbal *-ing* suffix imposes a profile on the process whereby its component states
are construed "at a level of abstraction that neutralizes their differences"
(Langacker 1991: 26). The process is, in other words, conceived of as an
internally homogeneous continuity. As such, it can be interpreted as a mass noun
functioning as Thing in the nominal group.

Functioning as a mass noun, a unit like *cleaning the windows* can then
either be explicitly related to a Subject, or the Subject can be implied, in which

case no overt Deictic is used, as in *I don't regret having gone to bury myself in the provinces* (CB). It should be noted, however, that factive gerundive nominals always *imply* a Subject, even when it is not explicitly realized: the entity to whom the speaker-now relates the Thing and which is at the same time also the Agent or Patient of the process expressed by the Head, is necessarily explicitly realized in the nominal's syntagmatic environment (see (52) and (53), as well as the examples of non-specific gerundive nominals given before).

(52)   Do you resent *being called Bumbles*? We all do behind your back you know.

(53)   Last year, Mgr. Jacques Gaillot (…) was ousted by the Vatican for *openly promoting the use of condoms to prevent the spread of Aids.*

Factive gerundive nominalization differs in this respect from another type of gerundive nominals, which Halliday terms 'Acts' (1994: 248):[9] unlike factives, Acts are not necessarily related to a specific Subject and they can be generic in meaning, e.g.:

(54)   (…) *talking openly about your anxieties* often helps to cut them down to size.

(55)   *Being a pit orchestra conductor in a big musical production* these days is a little like *standing astride two worlds.*

The fact that, if specific, the Deictic is necessarily possessive, is, I claim, due to the obligatory Subject-like status of the premodifier in gerundive nominalization: its premodifier fulfills the Subject function of the process expressed in the Head-unit and possessive premodifiers are best suited for serving that role. Most importantly, the Subject turns the *-ing* structure and its Objects into an event which is conceived of as an *instance*, related to a specific, Subject-like entity. The temporal or modal 'location' of that instance in the speech event, however, is left inexplicit, due to the non-finite status of the process (for a more elaborate analysis, see Heyvaert 2001). In factive *that*-nominalizations, the instance is also temporally or modally grounded, e.g.:

(56)   He may regret *that he didn't live up earlier tax-cuts promises and other pledges* (…). (CB)

(57)   It was a pity *that the judge, Laurence Waters, was unable to be present.* (CB)

3.3. Gerundive nominalization: Conclusion

The discussion of gerundive nominalization illustrates that the analysis of nominalized structures can greatly benefit from the concept of agnation, provided agnation is used in a more strictly Gleasonian way: the systemic choices that are realized in gerundive nominals can only be fully understood if we situate them against a network of agnate structures, clausal and other. A significant part of this agnation network of gerundive nominals turns out to have already been outlined in the traditional literature on gerundives: Lees (1960), for instance, makes elaborate use of agnates to describe the gerundive nominalization system and distinguish it from non-enate structures such as action nominals. The existing literature fails, however, to bridge the gap between the overall, factive meaning of the nominal and the internal organization of its component parts.

Based on the assumption that the metaphorical value of a nominalization depends on the values of its parts, I therefore suggested to extend the agnation network given in Lees (1960) and use agnation to systematically identify and interpret the constituent parts of gerundive nominals. In particular, I identified the unit *cleaning* as being verbal in nature; I pointed at the unit-status of *cleaning the windows* and interpreted it as a processual unit, downranked as Head of the nominal group, and, finally, I described the paradigmatic features of the possessive premodifier in detail. By carefully analyzing the constituent units of gerundive nominals, the nominal-like functional division into premodifier and Head was put into perspective and the distinctive internal features of the system of gerundive nominalization were revealed: gerundive nominals construe processual units as instances that are tied to a Subject, either explicitly, by means of the possessive premodifier, or with the Subject implied and retrievable from the context. Note that the necessarily 'instantiated' nature of factive gerundives which is revealed by the analysis of their internal lexicogrammatical features ties in well with the overall meaning attributed to them in Kiparsky and Kiparsky (1971) and Halliday (1994): factive gerundives designate processes which the speaker projects as being instances, as being 'true propositions'. Langacker (1991: 34) already pointed out that "the construal of the reified process as representing a particular instance renders it compatible with contexts that presuppose its factuality". Because the speaker prefers to leave the projecting clause unrealized, the instantiated process is downranked within the nominal group, as a nominalization. It is, I claim, this unique combination of being a nominalized, metaphenomenal instance that characterizes factive gerundive nominalizations.

4. On the importance of the interpersonal metafunction to grammatical metaphor

4.1. A metafunctional approach to grammatical metaphor?

Halliday & Matthiessen (1999) argue that grammatical metaphors and their congruent agnates differ in terms of their textual, experiential and interpersonal meaning. More particularly, (ideational) metaphors are claimed to essentially involve a reconstrual of experience, which has textual and interpersonal consequences. Experientially speaking, nominalization can be characterized as a drift towards 'thinginess', whereby clauses are realized as nominal groups, which, through the univariate structure of modification, allow almost indefinite expansion (1999: 265). The textual effect of nominalization is that it creates "a textual 'package', a packed and compacted quantum of information ready to take on its role in the unfolding of the argument" (1999: 239): in other words, nominalization creates a "vast potential for distributing and redistributing information in the clause" (Halliday and Martin 1993: 39). The other side of the coin, however, is what Halliday and Martin call "the interpersonal price of decreasing negotiability" (1993: 41): nominalizations are less negotiable than clauses. While clauses can be enacted interpersonally as propositions that are open to negotiation, nominal groups are taken for granted in the discourse (Halliday & Matthiessen 1999: 242). In addition, nominalizations tend to leave information about the configurational relations unexpressed, as a result of which they contribute to a language that is obscure and elitist, because only accessible to the expert. Nominalizations therefore also have ideological consequences.

While systemic-functional linguistics advocates a metafunctional approach to nominalization-as-metaphor, in actual linguistic practice, it focuses almost exclusively on the ideational (i.e. experiential and logical) similarities and differences between a nominalization and its congruent agnate: elaborate ideational analyses can thus be found in Matthiessen (1995: 356–359) and Halliday & Matthiessen (1999: 228–229; 250–255; 287–288). Descriptions of the textual consequences of nominalization are given far less systematically, and the interpersonal features of ideational metaphors and their agnates are said to be most clearly found "at the macroscopic level, in the overall pattern of interpersonal relationships, and the ideological orientation, that emerge over the course of the text" (Halliday & Matthiessen 1999: 242). Interpersonal analyses of the actual lexicogrammatical properties of nominalizations are therefore never given. The description of gerundive nominalization already showed, however, that the nominal and clausal means of relating a wording to the speech event form an essential part of the linguistic analysis of nominalizations: the paradigmatic status of the possessive and the non-finite status of the *-ing* unit turned out to provide crucial information about the overall metaphorical import of gerundive nominals. In what follows, I will discuss *-er* nominalization and show that, here also, the interpersonal features of the nominalization and of its agnates elucidate the nominalization system.

4.2. A case in point: -er nominalization

4.2.1. Introduction

Most puzzling about *-er* nominalization is the occurrence of nominals that do not profile the Agent of the underlying process, the *-er* suffix being prototypically agentive, e.g.:

(58) *baker*   'a food (meat, fruit or vegetable) that is suitable for baking'
     bestseller   'a book or other item that sells well'
     boiler   'a chicken suitable for boiling'
     broiler   'a young chicken suitable for broiling'
     cooker   'an apple for cooking'
     fryer   'a young chicken or rabbit suitable for frying'
     reader   'a coursebook consisting of a compilation of literature'
     roaster   'a kind of meat suitable for roasting'
     scratcher   'a lottery ticket that one should scratch to reveal the winning patterns'
     steamer   'an edible clam'
     waders   'boots reaching above the knees, used for wading'

I will argue that, to understand the system of *-er* nominalization, the relationship between the units it consists of has to be focused on: e.g. *bake+er; cook+er; teach+er*. That relationship can, however, only be fully clarified when it is not reduced to particular *experiential* functions like Agent or Patient: it will be shown that a motivation for the system's features has to be sought in the mapping of particular experiential functions onto *interpersonal* categories. I will start by describing some of the agnate constructions which *-er* nominals can be related to. One of them turns out to be the middle construction (e.g. *His novels read well*). The middle agnates of non-agentive *-er* nominals will then be shown to highlight the fact that non-agentive *-er* nominals, like middles, map non-agentive roles onto the interpersonal Subject-function. Finally, in a last part, I will briefly look into the relevance of the properties of non-agentive *-er* nominals to the *system* of *-er* nominalization.[10]

4.2.2. -er nominals are systematically related to Subject-verb constellations
-er is a morphological means to label types of people and things in terms of a particular process in which they are characteristically involved as participants. By relating entities to a specific process, *-er* provides information about those entities (e.g. *teacher* informs us that 'he/she teaches'). On the clausal level, information is normally provided in the form of an indicative:declarative link between Subject and verb (e.g. *he/she teaches*). The suffix *-er* might therefore be argued to relate to the combination of a Subject and a verb in indicative:declarative clauses: e.g. *teacher* agnates with the units *he/she teaches*. It does not, however, suffice to relate *teacher* to the agnate clause *he/she teaches* to fully explain its features, nor does this account for the internal variety among *-er* nominals. An issue that has to be tackled in addition is what *kinds* of Subject-verb combinations can be said to relate to *-er* nominals.

Most *-er* nominals agnate with a declarative Subject-verb combination in which the Subject is the Agent or causer of the process: more particularly, *-er* can designate a prototypical *first-order* Agent as in *teacher, baker* or *murderer*, or it can profile a *second-order* type of Agent (see Halliday 1994: 172 for this term), as in the following example:

(59)   King's latest novel is, once again, a *page-turner*: I was so obsessed by the story that I couldn't eat, drink or sleep before I'd finished reading it.

The nominal *page-turner* profiles a second-order Agent and denotes 'a *book* that is so good that it almost forces the *reader* to turn the pages': the *book* is designated by the nominal, but the actual, first-order Agent of the process of *turning the pages* is the implied *reader*. In other words, the *-er* nominal relates to a structure in which two moments of causality are implied: the book *makes* the reader *turn* the pages. Other examples of *-er* nominals that designate second-order Agents are *weeper* ('a *movie/book* that makes the *audience/reader* weep') and *laugher* ('*movie/book* that makes the *audience/reader* laugh') (Ryder 1991).

4.2.3. Non-agentive -er nominals and middle formation
The Subject-verb configuration which agnates most systematically with non-agentive *-er* nominalization in English turns out to be the middle construction. Prototypical examples of middles are:

(60)   Broiler rack removes easily. (CB)

(61)   And it's latex paint, so it cleans up quickly and easily with soap and water. (CB)

I claim that the key to understanding the exact nature of the system of -er nominalization lies in this link between non-agentives and middles. To show it, I will briefly describe those features of middle formation that are most pertinent to -er nominalization.

Characteristic of *prototypical* middle constructions is that they construe a Patient as Subject of an active verb form, and express how easy or difficult it is to carry out the action of the verb on the Patient/Subject: Fawcett (1980: 148, as cited in Davidse 1991: 42) calls the construction for that reason 'facility-oriented'. The link between a nominal like *bestseller* and this prototypical, facility-oriented type of middle (*this book/item sells well*) is quite obvious (Levin and Rappaport 1988). If *less prototypical* types of middle constructions are considered, many other -er nominals turn out to be systematically related to middles. Two non-prototypical types of middles are especially interesting in this respect: those that refer to the *result* or outcome of carrying out the process, and those that have *Circumstances* rather than Patients for Subject.

Consider the following patientive middles:

(62)   She does not photograph well, and the portraits of her pinched features snatched outside the High Court only added to the picture of a shrew.
        (CB)

(63)   This fabric washes well. (Fellbaum 1986: 10)

These structures do not point to the ease or difficulty with which the process can be performed on the Subject. Rather, they stress that the result of carrying out the process is good: the photos are beautiful, the fabric retains the shape and colours it had before being washed. They may contain the same adverb that is used in many facility-oriented middles (e.g. *that car drives well*; *this book sells well*), but it is clear that they are not facility-oriented:

(64)   *This car drives well* means that *it drives easily, smoothly* and not that *the result of driving it is good*

        This book sells well means that *it sells easily*, and not that *the result of selling it is good*

        She photographs well means that *the result of photographing her is good*

        This fabric washes well means that *the result of washing it is good*

I claim that patientive nominals like *cooker, boiler, broiler, fryer, steamer, roaster* and *baker* agnate with this result-oriented type of middle: they all designate items of food which, if submitted to a certain process, become particularly tasty or are prepared in the best possible way (*boiler*). They inform us on how to prepare or eat a particular kind of food or drink, on how to achieve the most delicious result. For instance:

> (65)   this chicken boils/broils well
> this kind of apple cooks well
> this type of clam steams well

A second, less prototypical type of middle is that in which the Subject position is not taken in by a patientive participant, but by a Circumstance:

> (66) This music dances better than the other one. (Van Oosten 1986: 84)

> (67) That pitch bowls well.

These structures can be paraphrased as *to this music you can dance better than to the other one* and *on that pitch you can bowl well*: the entity construed as Subject of the middle is actually a Circumstance, rather than an agentive or patientive participant. Even though this type of middle construction is much more frequently used in Dutch than in English (see Heyvaert 1998), it does exist in English, and its existence has interesting implications. Circumstantial middles make clear that the voice relationship between a middle's Subject and its verb cannot be a passive one, as has often been claimed in the literature (e.g. Sweet 1891, Jespersen 1914-1929, Halliday 1967, Keyser and Roeper 1984): the intransitive processes that figure in circumstantial middles cannot have a passive meaning. A middle like *this novel reads well* could still be interpreted as being passive (*this book can be read well*), but circumstantial middles no longer allow such a passive paraphrase (**that pitch can be bowled well; *rock music can be danced better*) (see Davidse and Heyvaert, in press). In short, circumstantial middles suggest that the relation between the Subject and the active verb in middle constructions is not a passive one.

Instead, the distinctive feature of circumstantial middles, and, indeed, of all middles, turns out to be the constructional link that is established between a non-agentive Subject and an active verb. As is claimed in Davidse and Heyvaert (in press), the middle construction does not profile the Agent or *source* of the energy flow expressed by the verb (as happens in ordinary active clauses), nor does it profile a passive relationship between a non-agentive Subject and a process (as happens in passive clauses). Rather, the emphasis lies on the degree to which the non-agentive participant that is construed as Subject is *conducive* to the implied Agent carrying out the action: the Subject is presented as 'letting' the implied Agent function as energy source (e.g. *that pitch bowls well* 'the properties of that pitch are such that it enables you to bowl well on it'; *his novel reads easily* 'the properties of his novel are such that it enables you to read it easily'). In Dutch, the middle construction can even be systematically related to a construction which explicitly realizes the verb 'let', as in *dat bier laat zich drinken* 'that beer lets itself drink' (see also Heyvaert 1998)

4.2.4. The system of -er nominalization

What is the relevance of these middle agnates to *-er* nominalization? One could argue that a nominal like *waders*, for instance, relates to a middle of the circumstantial type (*these boots wade easily*). Even the largest group of *-er* nominals, namely the instrumentals (e.g. *grinder, peeler, toaster, computer, parser, printer*) can, in one interpretation, be related to middles of the circumstantial type: the ambiguity that characterizes a structure like

(68) this peeler peels well

reflects the fact that instruments can be conceived of as tools *with which* a process can be carried out (circumstantial) or as *Agent-like* entities which act themselves. If the instrument is considered to be circumstantial, the structure *this peeler peels well* has to be interpreted as a middle structure ('this tool is such that it enables you to peel well with it'). If, on the other hand, viewed as agentive, *this peeler peels well* is not a middle construction, but an ordinary declarative structure with an Agent as Subject.

More important than trying to relate particular *-er* nominals to middle constructions, however, is to consider the specific kind of relationship which middles establish between a non-agentive Subject and an active verb form: does the fact that a significant number of *-er* nominals relate to middle structures add anything to our analysis of the combination of *-er* and a verbal unit? I believe it does. To start with, middle constructions form a perfect illustration of Halliday's claim that the Subject is not an empty, purely syntactic category, and that it cannot be reduced to the 'causally' responsible entity of a clause either: middles construe an entity as Subject which does not itself form the energy source of the action, but which is identified as being responsible for letting an implied Agent carry out the action (see also Heyvaert 2002: 114–118; 179–181). In other words, the Subject is identified by the speaker as the entity in respect of which the assertion is claimed to be valid (Halliday 1994: 76): the validity of the proposition *this novel reads well*, for instance, depends on *this novel*. Yet, the *novel* does not perform the act of reading.

Saying that all *-er* nominals profile a Subject therefore boils down to claiming that *-er* focuses on an entity which the speaker identifies as being responsible for whether the information provided in the nominal is correct: call someone a *murderer*, and the validity of the proposition *he murders* rests with the *he*-person. Call something a *scratcher*, and it depends on the lottery ticket whether scratching is indeed necessary to reveal the winning patterns. This *speech functional* rather than *causal* notion of Subject responsibility is what relates all *-er* nominals: as in clausal structures, it can be mapped onto a variety of experiential functions, ranging from Agents to Patients to even Circumstances. The relationship between the metaphorical *-er* structure and its congruent agnates should therefore not only be judged in terms of its experiential features: more important is to see how these functions are mapped onto an *interpersonal* category like Subject. In the case of *-er* nominalization, the relationship between non-agentive *-er* nominals and middle formation helps to focus on the fact that this is the distinctive feature of *-er* nominalization: all *-er* nominals ascribe a process to an entity, identifying that entity within the speech event as being responsible for the validity of the proposition.

To summarize, the discussion of *-er* nominals not only provides more evidence in favour of the importance of agnation to the linguistic analysis of nominalization: it also illustrates that each unit's agnates should be carefully described in experiential as well as in interpersonal terms. In a last part, I want to briefly look at the notion of 'metaphor' and how it is used in the context of nominalization. In particular, I will try to find out whether the term 'ideational metaphor' aptly describes the lexicogrammatical processes that take place when a construction is nominalized.

5.   Nominalization as ideational metaphor?

The term 'metaphor' is commonly used to refer to a figure of speech which involves using a word "for something resembling that which it usually refers to" (Halliday 1994: 340), e.g. the metaphor *flood* is used for *a large quantity* in the following clause:

(69) a flood of protests poured in following the announcement
      (Halliday 1994: 340)

The alternative or metaphorical realization of *a large quantity* by *flood* is possible because a *large quantity (of protests)* resembles a *large amount of water*. Halliday, however, rightly points out that such variation of lexical selection is mostly accompanied by lexicogrammatical variation, and that, in fact, any "metaphorical variation is lexicogrammatical rather than simply lexical" (1994: 341). The metaphor *protests flooded in*, for instance, alternates with constructions like *protests came in in large quantities* or with *very many people protested*, which are lexicogrammatical rather than simply lexical variants (1994: 341–342).

In addition to lexical metaphors with lexicogrammatical side-effects, Halliday argues, there also exists variation which is essentially grammatical in nature: a meaning may be realized by different structural configurations. A nominalization, for instance, realizes a processual configuration within the structure of a nominal group. This mapping of different grammatico-semantic domains onto each other is what in systemic-functional linguistics is referred to as 'grammatical metaphor'. But is 'metaphor' a suitable concept to refer to alternative lexicogrammatical realizations in general, and to deverbal nominalizations in particular? If we pursue the comparison with lexical metaphor further, nominalization-as-metaphor can be described as follows: a nominal group or noun is used instead of a processual configuration resembling that which the nominal group structure normally refers to: the metaphor/ nominalization is, in other words, only possible because the 'common' meaning of the nominal group resembles that of the processual unit. I will show that it is this feature of 'resemblance' which lies at the heart of the issue of whether the term 'metaphor' adequately describes nominalization.

As I argued before, the common systemic-functional perspective on the resemblances between a nominalization and its processual variant is ideational. Nominalizations are thus not only classified among what is called the 'ideational' type of grammatical metaphors, they are also primarily described in terms of how they map clausal ideational functions onto nominal ones: processes typically become Things functioning as Head, participants and circumstances are turned into modifiers. Also in terms of their overall meaning, nominalizations are said to especially resemble their processual counterparts with respect to their experiential 'content' (Ravelli 1988: 134). As was shown in the analysis of *-ing* and *-er* nominalizations, however, experiential resemblances are accompanied by ingenious mappings of interpersonal clausal categories onto nominal ones: in factive gerundive nominalization, for instance, the Subject is mapped onto possessive premodification, and the non-finite processual unit is mapped onto a Thing with mass noun status, which still has to be related to the speech event.

The suffix in -er nominals, in addition, was shown to systematically designate Subjects. What's more, these interpersonal categories even seemed to constitute the driving force behind the processes of -ing and -er nominalization: the overall 'factive' meaning of gerundive nominals was contributed to by the instantiated nature of the processual unit functioning as Head, while the Subject-profile turned out to be the distinctive feature of all -er nominals.

The implications of these observations for a general theory of nominalization-as-metaphor are many. To start with, the (interpersonal) description of how nominal and clausal structures can be related to the speech event should be systematically included in any analysis of nominalization (Langacker (1991) gives an elaborate analysis of the resemblances between the clausal and nominal means of grounding). I claim that it is precisely because the nominal group's *common* interpersonal categories resemble those of the clause that a clausal structure can be exchanged so easily for a nominal one, resulting in a nominalization. To put it differently, comparable to what lexical metaphors do with words, nominal groups can replace processual units because they resemble them, not only experientially, but especially with regard to the fundamental interpersonal categories that they realize. It should, however, also be kept in mind that the nominal and clausal ways of grounding a wording in the speech event may be essentially identical, when they are mapped onto each other in a nominalization, a new and unique way of grounding is created: a nominalization means both metaphorically and congruently (Halliday 1994: 353). It might, for instance, be interesting to check whether the possessive realization of the Subject in gerundive nominals foregrounds certain features of the Subject which remain implicit when it is realized clausally.[11]

Finally, the present distinction between 'ideational' and 'interpersonal' metaphor may have to be reconsidered. Nominalizations have always been characterized as 'ideational' metaphors, i.e. metaphors in which "the resources of transitivity" have been "shifted from the metafunctional environments of the clause to those of the nominal group" (Matthiessen 1995: 103). The interpersonal type of metaphor is especially concerned with pairs like

(70)   Probably, that pudding will never be cooked/ I don't believe that pudding will ever be cooked (Halliday 1994: 354)

(71)   You shouldn't say such a thing/ How could you say such a thing? (Halliday 1994: 367)

In (70), the metaphorical variation lies in the second clause realizing the speaker's opinion not as a modal element (*probably*), but as a "separate, projecting clause in a hypotactic clause complex" (1994: 354), i.e. *I don't believe that*. This is called the 'modality' type of interpersonal metaphor. The pair in (71) illustrates another type of interpersonal metaphor, in which a declarative clause (which itself might be conceived of as the metaphorical realization of the imperative *don't say such a thing*) is metaphorically realized by an interrogative. Metaphors like these are called 'mood' metaphors. I claim that the division into ideational and interpersonal metaphors wrongly suggests that the so-called ideational metaphors are exclusively concerned with experiential and logical shifts. Interpersonal categories, however, play a crucial role in *all* types of metaphorical realizations, ideational as well as interpersonal. It might therefore be better to consider all metaphors as essentially 'interpersonal': indeed, the extension of the semantic potential of language might well have to be primarily defined as an extension of the potential to situate a piece of wording in the speech event. Depending on the particular focus of each type of grammatical metaphor, one may then want to distinguish further between, on the one hand, 'ideational' metaphors, and, on the other hand, metaphors of 'modality' and of 'mood'.

6. Conclusion

Summarizing, Halliday's suggestion to view nominalizations as instances of a structural kind of metaphor opens up a number of interesting possibilities: it provides a general theoretical framework within which to situate the concrete linguistic analysis of nominalizations; it encourages us to focus on the paradigmatic relations between nominal and clausal units; and it forces us to bear in mind that the nominalized or metaphorical structure forms a unique combination of linguistic categories. To give the concept of 'metaphor' a linguistic 'raison d'être', however, the present systemic-functional interpretation of it has to be adjusted in several ways: first of all, the concept of agnation should be fully exploited and used to set up agnation networks of nominalizations and of the units they consist of. Secondly, the enate dimension or the systemic choices behind each nominalization should be included in the metaphorical picture. And, last but not least, the relation between the metaphor and its agnates should not be restricted to ideational categories only: the analysis of a nominalization's ideational features should be complemented with an interpersonal perspective. It is only by looking into the way in which nominalizations and metaphors in general realize interpersonal categories, that concrete instances of nominalizations can be fully understood and that the commonality of grammatical metaphors is revealed.

Notes

1. I wish to thank Anne-Marie Simon-Vandenbergen and Miriam Taverniers for the enthusiastic way in which they co-ordinated the 11th Euro-International Systemic Functional Workshop in Ghent in the summer of 1999. Special thanks go to Kristin Davidse, for her unfailing support and for the numerous discussions we've had about a wide range of linguistic and other topics.

2. In his review article of Halliday (1985), Huddleston (1988) points to some of the problems related to viewing a clause as Head of a nominal group. His arguments break down into two main claims: firstly, clauses embedded in nominal groups do not behave like ordinary nominal groups externally, i.e. within the clause (e.g. extraposition is possible, witness *It is not enough [[that you're sorry]]*, but interrogative formation is difficult, e.g. *?Is [[that you're sorry]] not enough?*). A second argument against viewing embedded clauses as Head of a nominal group is that, also internally, they fail to behave like ordinary nominal Heads: they cannot take pre- or postmodifiers (e.g. *[[Why she did it]] remains a mystery*). Huddleston therefore suggests to view embedded clauses as functioning immediately within the clause, without the intermediate analysis of embedding in the nominal group. While it is indeed true that nominal groups with embedded finite clauses behave differently from nominal groups with a common noun head, the analysis of gerundive nominalization will adduce evidence in favour of Halliday's claim that clauses can function as Head: it will be shown that premodification is possible when *non-finite* clauses are embedded within the structure of a nominal group (see also Heyvaert 2001 and 2002).

3. Ambiguity is claimed to be characteristic of many nominalizations: "The principle would seem to be that, where the members of a pair of agnate wordings differ in *rank*, the wording that is *lower* in rank will contain less information" (Halliday & Matthiessen 1999: 231).

4. The clause *we understand* is downranked within the nominal group, as defining relative clause, postmodifying the Head noun *way*. While it cannot be said to be nominalized, it can still be considered as a non-congruent or metaphorical way of realizing a clausal structure. The suggested congruent agnate *[the way] we understand develops* is, in other words, still not fully congruent.

5. The congruent agnate "evolved earlier in the language (phylogenesis); it is learnt earlier by children (ontogenesis); and it typically comes earlier in the text (logogenesis)" (Halliday & Matthiessen 1999: 235).

6. Lees, in fact, restricts this relationship of agnation to a specific subgroup of gerundive nominals, i.e. those that occur "as object of a verb or preposition", and then only if the premodifier "is a pronoun or is very short" (Lees 1960/1968: 72). In addition, he claims that the use of the oblique is only well established in colloquial English. The restrictions which Lees imposes on the relation between the possessive and the oblique in gerundive nominals are, however, not fully confirmed in other research on gerundives: both Jespersen (1914-1929, part IV: 124–140) and Poutsma (1929: 832–837) indicate that, while it is indeed not possible to replace *all* possessives by oblique variants, it is not restricted to nominals occurring as object of a verb or preposition.

7. Also relevant to the status of the *-ing* form in gerundives is that the suffix does not systematically relate to progressive *-ing*: gerundive nominals allow for verbs like *know* and *be* to combine with *-ing* (e.g. *John's knowing the answer surprised us all; Lucy's being late worried her father*). These verbs, however, cannot function in a progressive construction **John is knowing the answer; *Lucy is being late*. In other words, the structures that can

undergo gerundive nominalization do not systematically allow for a progressive agnate form. For a more elaborate treatment of the features of *-ing* in gerundive nominals, I refer to Heyvaert (2000).

8. The transcategorized nature of *cleaning* in the action nominal *Sam's cleaning of the windows* probably explains why the nominal can be used in factive, as well as in action contexts: Langacker (1991: 33) claims that, as with ordinary nouns or nominal heads, various aspects of an action nominal's head can be highlighted in the appropriate context. He gives the example of the noun 'party' and compares that with the action nominal *Harvey's taunting of the bear* (1991: 32–33):

Harvey's taunting of the bear was merciless.	//	The party was boisterous.
Harvey's taunting of the bear lasted three hours.	//	The party lasted three hours.
Harvey's taunting of the bear came as a big surprise.	//	The party came as a big surprise.

9. The 'Act' type of gerundive nominalization can thus not only be distinguished from factive gerundives on the basis of the fact that it realizes a (macro-)phenomenon rather than a metaphenomenon or projection and that it requires other syntagmatic contexts than factives; it also differs from factives in terms of how its nominal Head functions in the nominal group: unlike a factive nominal's Head, the Head of an Act nominalization can behave like a mass noun with generic reading, i.e. with no link at all to the concrete speech event.

10. For more elaborate analyses of *-er* nominals in English and in Dutch, I refer to Heyvaert (1997) and Heyvaert (1998).

11. I am thinking here in particular of the 'contrastive' flavour of the possessive in gerundives: the item which is speech functionally responsible for the gerundive process (i.e. the possessively realized Subject) seems to be distinguished from other items more explicitly than the Subject is in clausal contexts.

References

Collins COBUILD Corpus: Birmingham.

Davidse, K. (1991) *Categories of Experiential Grammar*. PhD Dissertation, Department of Linguistics, Catholic University of Leuven.

Davidse, K. (1997) The Subject-Object versus the Agent-Patient asymmetry. *Leuven Contributions in Linguistics and Philology* 86.4: 413–431.

Davidse, K. (1998) The dative as participant role versus the indirect object: On the need to distinguish two layers of organization. In: W. Van Langendonck & W. Van Belle (eds.) *The Dative*. Volume 2: Theoretical and Contrastive Studies . Amsterdam: Benjamins. 143–184.

Davidse, K. (1998) Agnates, verb classes and the meaning of construals. The case of ditransitivity in English. *Leuven Contributions in Linguistics and Philology* 87.3/4: 281–313.

Davidse, K. & L. Heyvaert (in press) On the so-called middle construction in English and Dutch. To appear in: S. Granger, J. Lerot & S. Petch-Tyson (eds.) *Contrastive Linguistics and Translation Studies: Empirical Approaches*.

Fellbaum, C. (1986) *On the Middle Construction in English*. Indiana: Indiana University Linguistics Club.

Gleason, H.A. (1965) *Linguistics and English Grammar*. New York: Holt, Rinehart and Winston.

Halliday, M.A.K. (1967) Notes on transitivity and theme in English. *Journal of Linguistics* 3.1:37–81.

Halliday, M.A.K. (1994) *An Introduction to Functional Grammar*. 2nd edition. London: Arnold.

Halliday, M.A.K. & J.R. Martin (1993) *Writing Science. Literacy and Discursive Power*. London, Washington D.C.: The Falmer Press.

Halliday, M.A.K. & C.M.I.M. Matthiessen (1999) *Construing Experience Through Meaning. A language-based approach to cognition*. London: Cassell.

Heyvaert, L. (1997) Patientive *-er* Nominals. *Leuven Contributions in Linguistics and Philology* 86.4: 433–456.

Heyvaert, L. (1998) Non-agentive Deverbal *-er* Nominalization in English and Dutch: a contrastive analysis. *Languages in Contrast* 1.2: 211–243.

Heyvaert, L. (2000) Gerundive nominalization: From type specification to grounded instance. In: A. Foolen & F. van der Leek (eds.) *Constructions 'in Cognitive Linguistics*. Amsterdam: Benjamins. 103–121.

Heyvaert, L. (2001) Nominalization as an 'interpersonally-driven' system. *Functions of Language* 8.2: 287–330.

Heyvaert, L. (2002) *A Cognitive-Functional Approach to Nominalization in English*. PhD dissertation, Deptartment of Linguistics, Catholic University of Leuven.

Huddleston, R. (1988) Constituency, multi-functionality and grammaticalization in Halliday's functional grammar. *Journal of Linguistics* 24: 137–174.

Jespersen, O. (1914-1929) *A Modern English Grammar on Historical Principles* (7 volumes). London: Allen & Unwin.

Keyser, S.J. & T. Roeper (1984) On the middle and ergative constructions in English. *Linguistic Inquiry* 15: 381–416.

Kiparsky, P. & C. Kiparsky (1971) Fact. In: D.D. Steinberg & L.A. Jakobovits (eds.) *Semantics: An Interdisciplinary Reader in Philosophy, Linguistics, and Psychology*. Cambridge: Cambridge UP. 345–369.

Langacker, R. (1991) *Foundations of Cognitive Grammar*. Vol. 2: Descriptive application. Stanford: Stanford UP.

Lees, R.B. (1960/1968) *The Grammar of English Nominalizations*. Bloomington: Indiana University; The Hague: Mouton.

Levin, B. & M. Rappaport (1988) Nonevent *-er* nominals: A probe into argument structure. *Linguistics* 26: 1067–1083.

Matthiessen, C.M.I.M. (1995) *Lexicogrammatical Cartography: English Systems*. Tokyo: International Language Sciences Publishers.

McGregor, W.B. (1997) *Semiotic Grammar*. Oxford: Clarendon Press.

Poutsma, H. (1929) *A Grammar of Late Modern English*. Part I. The Sentence. Groningen: P. Noordhoff.

Pullum, G.K. (1991) English nominal gerund phrases as noun phrases with verb-phrase heads. *Linguistics* 29: 763–799.

Ravelli, L.J. (1988) Grammatical metaphor: An initial analysis. In: E.H. Steiner & R. Veltman (eds.) *Pragmatics, Discourse and Text. Some Systemically-inspired Approaches*. London: Pinter Publishers. 133–147.

Ryder, M.E. (1991) Mixers, mufflers and mousers: The extending of the -ER suffix as a case of prototype reanalysis. *Proceedings of the Berkeley Linguistics Society* 17: 299–311.

Schachter, P. (1976) A nontransformational account of gerundive nominals in English. *Linguistic Inquiry* 7.2: 205–241.

Sweet, H. (1891) *A New English Grammar. Logical and Historical*. Oxford: Clarendon Press.

Van Oosten, J. (1986) *The Nature of Subjects, Topics and Agents: A cognitive explanation*. Bloomington, Indiana: Indiana University Linguistics Club.

Ambiguity in grammatical metaphor
One more reason why the distinction transitive/ergative pays off

Jorge Arús Hita
Universidad Complutense de Madrid

1. Introduction

Nominalization is, in the words of Halliday (1994: 352), "the single most powerful resource for creating grammatical metaphor". This fact as well as the high yield that nominalization gives regarding text organization and the subsequent effect on communicative dynamism has turned it into the preferred topic of discussion regarding grammatical metaphor in the Systemic-Functional tradition. Interpersonal grammatical metaphor has also received widespread attention (e.g. Lemke 1998; Butler 1996; Degand 1994; Martin 1995; Thibault 1995; Halliday 1985a, 1994; Ravelli 1988), whereas the systemic literature abounds less in the treatment of the two other kinds of ideational grammatical metaphor, i.e. the one involving a shift in major process type – as in relational (1a) for congruent material (1b):

(1) a. It's under repair.
     b. It's being repaired.

– and that in which the semantic process is represented as if it were a participant (Medium or Range), as in (2a) for congruent (2b) (cf. Matthiessen 1995: 353–6):

(2) a. He did dinner preparations. for congruent.
     b. He prepared dinner.

The important role of nominalization in the textual ordering of discourse has been extensively analysed. Halliday (1985b) has provided a major study on nominalization in written language, which has spurred further works exploring its communicative effects in such fields as science (Halliday & Martin 1993, Halliday 1998), history (Eggins et al. 1993), advertising, poetry (Goatly 1993), etc. Through nominalization, whole experiential representations that would congruently be realized by processes can be reduced to a nominal group serving as the Theme or as the New in the clause, these two elements being the most relevant ones from the point of view of the informative organisation of the text. Matthiessen (1992: 74) points out that ideational decisions are motivated by the textual metafunction, and thus "transitivity selections may be made in such a way that an appropriate textual organisation of a clause is achieved".

Halliday & Martin (1993: 240) show examples like (3), where the nominalization in (3a) allows packing complex meanings into Theme (*The enlargement of Australia's steel making capacity, and of chemicals, rubber, metal goods and motor vehicles*) and New (*the demands of war*). In the congruent versions (3b, c), more typical of spoken language, the unpacking of the grammatical metaphor yields grammatically intricate clause complexes which hamper the backgrounding of the Theme as Given and the foregrounding of part of the Rheme as New.[1]

(3) a. The enlargement of Australia's steel-making capacity, and of chemicals, rubber, metal goods and motor vehicles all owed something to the demands of war

   b. α Australia's steel-making capacity enlarged, alongside that of chemicals, rubber, metal goods and motor vehicles
      β partly because war demanded it

   c. α Australia could make more steel, chemicals, rubber, metal goods and motor vehicles
      β partly because people demanded them
      γ so that they could fight the war

Halliday (1994: 353) points out that, in nominalization, some information is lost with respect to the congruent version. This sometimes creates ambiguity in the interpretation of the nominalization, and metaphorical discourse is thus used as a token of prestige and power which distinguishes the expert from the uninitiated, since the former is expected to be able to understand the intended meaning whereas the latter may not. Halliday uses example (4) to illustrate this point. In the nominalization, the construction does not clearly express the semantic relation between *alcohol* and *impairment*. The two possible readings proposed by Halliday are expressed in (4a, b). In (4a), *alcohol* is Actor, whereas it is Goal in (4b).

(4) alcohol impairment
   a.   alcohol impairs
   b.   alcohol is impaired

In spite of the abundant literature on nominalization, the nature of ambiguities like the one in (4) has not been explored. This paper intends to fill that gap. To do so, I will try to demonstrate the following claims: a) that transitive and ergative processes incorporate into grammatical metaphors their different ways of arranging experience, and b) that the ambiguity seen in (4) can only happen with the nominalization of transitive processes. In Section 2, I will present an overview of the transitivity/ergativity issue for the better understanding of the position taken here. Section 3 will then deal with the concept of ambiguity in nominalization from the point of view of the split transitive/ergative as explained in Section 2, thus supporting the above-made claims. The way in which ambiguous nominalizations are incorporated into discourse will be explained in Section 4, where a corpus-based study of press headlines will allow us to draw interesting conclusions regarding ambiguity.

2.   The transitive/ergative problem

2.1. Different uses of the term 'ergative'

Before dealing with the split into transitive and ergative processes, it is important to clarify what should be understood by ergativity or by ergative processes. Dixon (1979, 1994) and López (1997) raise the issue of the inadequate use of the term 'ergative' by several authors. These include Halliday (1967a, 1970, 1985a), Lyons (1968), Anderson (1968, 1977) and others, who, according to Dixon, use the term 'ergative' in the place of 'causative'.

Ergativity in authors like Dixon (1979) or Hopper & Thompson (1980) is a semantic and morphological issue, which has to do with the semantic identification of S with O in ergative clauses versus the identification of S with A in 'accusative' ones (which I call 'transitive' here). On the other hand, ergativity is reflected purely at syntactic and lexical level for the authors criticized by Dixon. For those, ergative transformations are those in which "a transitive sentence (called effective in this paper, following Halliday 1985a, 1994; Davidse 1992, 1999, Matthiessen 1995, among others) may be derived syntactically from an intransitive (i.e. middle) sentence" (Lyons 1968: 352). This is an interpretation at the syntactic level of the identification of S with O, as in (5a, b), for the ergative paradigm, versus the identification of S with A in the transitive (6). All this, from the point of view of Dixon (1979: 60) is an inaccuracy stemming from failing to distinguish 'pivot', a surface-syntactic category, from 'subject', a deep syntactic/semantic category. Ergativity is thus explained from a syntactic point of view, involving the surface Subject ('Pivot'), when it should be interpreted in terms of the deep Subject ('Subject'), which is a universal category (as opposed to the Pivot, which is language specific).

(5)   a. *The boat* sank
       b. They sank *the boat*

(6)   *Peter* killed Mary

The picture becomes more complex when authors such as Burzio (1981) and Belletti (1987) provide a new view of ergativity based exclusively on the identification of S with O, which, furthermore, has nothing to do with causativity. For both Burzio and Belleti, when S in a middle clause ('intransitive' for those authors) as (7b) matches O in the effective ('transitive' for them) counterpart, as (7a), the verb in those clauses is ergative. Yet, there is a difference with the otherwise similar analysis found in the Systemic-Functional tradition or in Lyons. Both Burzio and Belleti include among ergative verbs, not only those which can generate both middle and effective clauses, but also verbs which are always middle, as *arrivare* in (8a). In the case of middle-only ergative verbs, S is always generated in O position, as we can see in (8a), which is different from (8b) in that S has just been transferred from S position to O position for textual reasons, (8c) being a possible realization too.

(7)   a. *La marina americana ha affondato la nave*
           'The American Navy has sunk the ship.'
       b. *La nave è affondata*
           'The ship has sunk.'

(8)   a. *Arriva Giovanni*
           'Giovanni is arriving.'
       b. *Telefona Giovanni*
           'Giovanni is phoning.'
       c. *Giovanni telefona*

Belleti adds one more feature to ergative constructions, i.e. the assignation of case by the ergative verb to the noun group in object position, although the

:ase assigned by the verb to the noun group functioning as Object is inherent, ı̃ot structural. All this, according to López (1997: 111), leads to the problem of :onsidering the existence of ergative verbs, which are assigned features that ;hould be considered characteristic traits of the constructions in which those ∕erbs participate rather than features of the verbs themselves. Hopper & ſhompson (1980: 266) also warn that "Transitivity² is a relationship which ɔbtains THROUGHOUT THE CLAUSE. It is not restricted to one constituent or ɔair of constituents". Table 1 provides a summary of the differences in :erminology and recognition criteria used by the various sources cited.

Sources	Identification criteria	Status of ergativity
Dixon; Hoper & Thompson	Semantic identification of S/O (ergat.) vs. S/A (transit.)	Ergativity different from Causativity
Lyons; SFG	Syntantic identification of	Ergativity = Causativity
Burzio; Belletti	S/O (ergat.) vs. S/A (transit.)	Ergativity is purely positional

Table 1: Summary of the different interpretations of 'ergativity'

2.2. The transitive/ergative split in Systemic-Functional Grammar

The foregoing brief overview of the different attitudes towards ergativity may serve to illustrate the apparent subtlety of this issue. It should be noted, however, that the differences often seem to be more a problem of terminology, as pointed out by Davidse (1999), than of irreconcilable linguistic disparities. In the Systemic-Functional tradition, within whose frame this paper is written, it is well known that in the Hallidayan model of Transitivity all processes can be analysed both from a transitive and an ergative perspective, as shown in (9) and (10). The ergative interpretation is viewed as cutting across the different process types, and giving a semantic unity to the different analysis that each process type is subject to from the transitive perspective (cf. Halliday 1994: Ch. 5).

(9)	*Mary*	*sailed*	*the boat*	
	Actor	Process	Goal	(transitive interpretation)
	Agent	Process	Medium	(ergative interpretation)

(10)	*The gift*	*pleased*	*Mary*	
	Phenomenon	Process	Senser	(transitive interpretation)
	Agent	Process	Medium	(ergative interpretation)

This dual interpretation of a process is questioned by Davidse (1992, 1999, Davidse & Geyskens 1997), for whom the transitive and the ergative paradigms should be seen as two distinct systems. The process and extension model, transitive, and the instigation of a process model, ergative, have different directionalities that account for processes with a different nature. The former model may extend to the right to include a Goal, as we see in (11), whereas the latter, exemplified by (12) offers the possibility of opening to the left to incorporate an Instigator (cf. Davidse 1992: 108–9).

(11) a. *She   is cycling*   (middle transitive)
        Actor   Prócess
     b. *She is pedalling her bike*   (effective transitive)
        Actor   Process   Goal

(12) a. *The glass   broke*   (middle ergative)
        Medium   Process
     b. *The cat   broke   the glass*   (effective ergative)
        Instigator   Process   Medium

As (11) and (12) show, the main morphological sign of the transitivity or ergativity of a process in English is the fact that the ergative process can have a middle and an effective version, keeping the same lexical verb functioning as Process, whereas transitive processes are *either* middle *or* effective: the same verb *cannot* be the Process both in a middle *and* an effective structure. The most relevant semantic difference is that in an ergative process it is always the same Medium that performs or experiences the action, emotion, etc. in the middle as well as in the effective structure. In (12), it is always *the glass* that breaks, whether we specify the Agent, as in (12b), or not (12a). This, again, is very much related to the identification of S and O used in other approaches, triggering, to a great extent, the disaccord.

Lavid & Arús have applied the transitive/ergative split not only to material processes (1998a), but also to mental (1998b) and relational (1999) ones in both English and Spanish in a contrastive way. Verbal is the only process type without ergative instances in either language, assuming a fourfold process type division into material, mental, verbal and relational. The contrastive study of the systems of Transitivity in both languages shows how the transitive/ergative distinction accounts for important differences between the languages. This is shown in the relational examples (13) and (14). Whereas Spanish (13) is ergative, this is not the case with the same process in English. The effective version (14a) has a perfect match in Spanish (13a), but, since the process is not ergative in English, the literal translation of (13b) as (14b) is incorrect. Therefore a different lexical realization, shown in (14c), is needed to express the same semantic process as middle.

(13) a. *Me llaman Jorge* (relational & effective & ergative)
    b. *Me llamo Jorge* (relational & middle & ergative)

(14) a. *They call me George* (relational & effective & transitive)
    b. **I call George*
    c. *My name is George* (relational & middle & transitive)

Accounting for the transitive/ergative distinction provides therefore important insights for the understanding of the experiential component of language. It can also serve as an important tool, when applied to such fields as translation or second language teaching, since it will help to avoid the generation of incorrect sentences in the target language. This is not the place, though, to deal with these applications, which will be left for a later occasion. As a concluding point to the overview of transitivity/ergativity, Table 2 shows the correspondences between transitive and ergative functions with functions in the general system as they are assumed in the rest of this paper. Since most of the examples examined in the following pages realize material processes, I limit the contents of the table to that process type to avoid a terminological overload (cf. Davidse 1992: 130–1).

Transitive middle	Actor/Medium . Process
Transitive pseudo-effective	Actor/Medium . Process. Range/Range
Transitive effective	Actor/Agent . Process . Goal/Medium
Ergative middle	Affected/Medium . Process
Ergative pseudo-effective	Setting-Subject . Process . Affected
Ergative effective	Instigator/Agent . Process . Affected/Medium

Table 2: Participants in transitive and ergative processes and correspondences with the general system

3.   Ambiguity in grammatical metaphor

3.1. *Ambiguity and vagueness*

It is time now to return to nominalizations such as the one seen in (4) above so as to understand why they are ambiguous while others are not. Let us compare (4) with (15). I said above that in ergative processes it is always the Medium that performs the action both in the middle and the effective. In (4), we saw that the ambiguity stemmed from the impossibility, out of context, of distinguishing interpretation (4a) from (4b). In (15), we obviously still have two possible readings, i.e. (15a) and (15b). The difference lies in the fact that the ambiguity in (4) can seriously hinder the correct interpretation, since reading (4a) implies that it is *alcohol* that does the *impairment*, while reading (4b) is exactly the opposite, i.e. something or somebody impairs *alcohol*, in which case *alcohol* does not *impair* anything. Such ambiguity can prove inextricable in an example like (16). Shared world knowledge may tell us on most occasions that the appropriate reading is (16a), since *impairment* caused by *alcohol* is a much discussed topic. Reading (16b) could, however, be the one intended by the speaker/writer, referring to the debasing of the quality of *alcohol* and its effects on health. In most contexts, the desired reading will be clear, but in a context in which someone is enumerating factors that increase social security spending, (17) would require further clarification. On the other hand, (15) as applied to (17) does not pose a major problem regarding its interpretation: *The ball is bouncing*, and that is *giving me a headache*, no matter whether the reading is (17a) or (17b). At most, there is vagueness[3] as to whether the *bouncing* is instigated or not. Fodor (1970: 429–30) talks about the ambiguity of pronominal references in this kind of processes, as we see in the ergative (18). The demonstrative pronoun may refer to the *glass melting* or to *Floyd melting the glass*, ambiguity which is due to vagueness in agency. Such vagueness is characteristic of middle ergative processes (cf. Davidse 1992: 109), and it has been transferred to the nominalization of the ergative process *bounce* in (15) and (17).

(4)   alcohol impairment
      a. alcohol impairs
      b. alcohol is impaired

(15) the bouncing of the ball
      a. the ball bounces
      b. the ball is bounced = the ball bounces

(16) Alcohol impairment costs the social security a lot of money
      a. Alcohol impairs concentration (on the road/at work), therefore causing accidents and costing the social security a lot of money
      b. Alcohol has been impaired and this is bad for health, therefore costing the social security a lot of money

(17) The bouncing of the ball is giving me a headache
      a. The ball is bouncing and that is giving me a headache
      b. Someone is bouncing the ball and that is giving me a headache

(18) Floyd melted the glass and **that** surprised me

It could be argued that the match between (4) and (15) is inaccurate, since in (4a) we are taking the Modifier, a Participant in the congruent realization, as an Actor/Agent doing something to an implied Goal/Medium, i.e. *Alcohol impairs something*. In (18a), on the other hand, we are taking the Modifier in the nominalization as the Medium, not as the Agent. If we took the Modifier as the Agent doing something to a Medium, the same as in (4a), the reading of (15a) should be *The ball bounces something*.[4] With this reading, (15) would be as ambiguous as (4), thus rendering the transitive/ergative distinction irrelevant. It is at this point that another important difference between transitive and ergative structures springs up.

3.2. Nominalization of transitive processes

According to Fawcett (1980: 140) and Davidse (1992: 113), the ergative paradigm is 'Medium-centred', whereas the transitive paradigm is 'Actor-centred'. This is very much related to the Hallidayan models of extension versus causation; in a transitive structure the issue is whether the Actor (restricting the discussion to material processes) successfully extends its action to another participant. In the material process (19), we see that both the Actor and the Goal can be left out depending on information constraints. The Goal in an effective process is occasionally left out using the active voice, as in (19a), while the Actor is easily, and frequently, left out in the passive voice, as (19c) shows. The difference is that, whereas there must always be an Actor – even if unknown or unimportant, as is often the case in the passive – the Goal is not essential, as we see in (20), since the absence of Goal is what characterizes middle material transitive processes. This is why transitive material processes are Actor-centred. The potential problem arises when we consider that transitive effective processes may leave either the Agent or the Medium unexpressed. This is what creates the ambiguity in nominalization: depending on the nature of the Process and the participants, we may not know whether the expressed participant, in a material process as (4) above, is the Actor, i.e. whether the reading is active, or the Goal, i.e. whether the reading is passive. If ambiguity in transitive nominalizations stems from the role played by the Modifier as a participant in the congruent realization, this ambiguity will be far more unlikely when the nominalization involves a non-ranged middle transitive structure, since middle transitives do not have a Goal. Thus, the middle transitive nominalization (21) has only one possible reading, whereas the effective transitive (22) is ambiguous. It should be noticed that nominalization may sometimes involve not the Goal or the Actor but a Range (23a) or a Circumstance, as in (23b). In that case, the nominalization of a middle transitive may be ambiguous, as in (24).

(19) a. Peter ate
    b. Peter ate the chicken
    c. The chicken was eaten
    d. The chicken was eaten by Peter

(20) Peter is jogging

(21) Peter's arrival was a surprise to everybody
    a. Peter arrived

(22) Peter's invitation was a surprise to everybody
    a. Peter invited
    b. Peter was invited

(23) a. Mountain climbing is Peter's favourite activity
    b. Winter jogging is Peter's favourite activity

(24) Let's talk now about summer arrival
    a. Summer arrives
    b. Someone arrives in summer

3.3. Nominalization of ergative processes

In ergative processes, on the other hand, not only is the Affected/Medium the most nuclear participant, it is also never left unexpressed. The Theme and Subject in both the active and the passive versions of (25) is the same, i.e. *the house*. The difference is that (25a) leaves the feature of agency open, whereas (25b) implies there is an Instigator/Agent. Thus, a nominalization of an ergative process, like (26), taken from Halliday & Martin (1993: 56), can be indeterminate with respect to Agency, which would be more a matter of vagueness than of real ambiguity, as I said above. A reading like *Glass fractures something* seems inappropriate to me, since we tend to think of *glass* as something that typically *fractures* rather than *fracturing* other things. This is because it is the Affected/Medium and not the Instigator/ /Agent that is present in nominalizations of ergative material processes, since it is the Medium and not the Agent that is nuclear to ergative processes in general. If we think of something that can both be the Agent doing something to something else or experience the action as the Medium, as *match* in (27), interpretation (27c) seems problematical. If we wanted to nominalize a process in which *the match* is the Agent, a possibility would be (27d). Notice how a realization like (27e) does not look as natural as (27d), since the Agent, i.e. *the match*, would be occupying a more nuclear position in the nominalization than the Medium, in this case *the house*.

(25) a. The burning of the house
    b. The house burnt
    c. The house was burnt

(26) The fracturing of glass

(27) The burning of the match
    a. The match burned
    b. The match was burned
    c. ?The match burned something
    d. The burning of the house by the match
    e. ?The match burning of the house

Example (21) in Section 3.2 illustrated the nominalization of a middle transitive process. Ergative nominalizations, on the other hand, may refer to both a middle or an effective process, hence their Agency indeterminacy, which, once again in contrast with ambiguity in transitive nominalizations, is always present, although easily surmountable. Transitive and ergative processes, therefore, behave differently with respect to ambiguity in nominalization as a consequence of the intrinsic differences existing between one and the other systems. We have seen that inextricable ambiguity can only affect transitive nominalizations, whereas ergative ones can, at worst, be vague with respect to Agency. Table 3 summarizes the different ways in which transitive and ergative nominalizations are constructed.

Process System	Configuration of nominalization	
Transitive	Modifier/Actor Modifier/Goal Modifier/Circumstance Modifier/Range	+ Head/Process
Ergative	Affected/Modifier + Head/Process	

Table 3: Differences between nominalizations of transitive and ergative material processes including one participant in the metaphor

4. Transitive and ergative nominalizations in discourse

4.1. Ambiguity and vagueness as products of the flow of discourse

Ambiguity has so far in this study been considered as a static phenomenon within nominalizations out of context. It would be problematic to leave the discussion at this point since language is something dynamic, and the flow of discourse will ideally disambiguate those ambiguous nominalizations. In most cases, an otherwise ambiguous nominalization is perfectly understandable due to the fact that the role of the participant functioning as a Modifier in the grammatical metaphor has been clarified in the preceding segments of discourse. As Halliday & Martin (1993: 18) point out, congruent realizations tend to precede metaphorical ones, not only phylogenetically and ontogenetically, but also logogenetically, i.e. in the unfolding of text. Therefore, ambiguous nominalizations may be expected to occur in those cases in which writers or speakers assume too much shared world knowledge between themselves and their readers or listeners. In that case, a new topic introduced by means of a nominalization could temporarily affect the communicative effectiveness[5] of the message, since it would be hard for the message recipient to establish the right schema. If I begin my discourse with (28a), the information will be confusing unless my interlocutor knows beforehand that I am throwing a party, or vice versa, that Mary is throwing a party. However, the problem can easily be solved, as we see in sequence (28b, c). This is possible in spoken discourse, but ambiguity in written discourse does not offer that possibility, so the writer will (or should) always be more careful to avoid such cases.

> (28) a. Mary's invitation has turned out to be a problem.
>   b. Have you invited Mary to something?
>   c. No, she's invited me to a party and her boyfriend is jealous.

While the patterns of metaphor could be expected to be different between spoken and written discourse (cf. Halliday 1985b: 93-ff. for the difference between spoken and written language), for the time being the research is going to be restricted to the scrutiny of written discourse.

4.2. What headlines reveal

4.2.1. The press as a source

The press is a good source for finding nominalizations, and it presents some instances of ambiguous ones. In an issue of *The Financial Times*, headlines (29) and (30) were found, which are arguably unclear until one starts reading the body of the article. The first reading that came to my mind in (29) was (29a), only to find seconds later that the intended one was (29b). In the case of (30) – nominalization of an attributive process and, therefore, ranged – the perusal of the article seems to hint at an interpretation (30b), although not clearly. It could be argued that reading (30a) would prefer a realization with the saxon genitive, *Lawyer's/Lawyers' phobia*. This is contradicted by headline (31), from *The Spectator*, in which the Modifier stands for the Carrier of the congruent possessive process. Once again, it is necessary to start reading the article in order to disambiguate the meaning of the headline. In some other cases, such as (32) from *The Financial Times*, one reading may be ruled out due to the existence of another realization which conveys that intended meaning more successfully. In the case of reading (32b), that meaning is better expressed by the nominalization in (33), due to the presence of the preposition *to*.

(29) Russian investment slumps
  a. Russia invests
  b. Others invest in Russia

(30) Lawyer phobia
  a. Lawyer(s) has/have phobia
  b. Someone has phobia about lawyers

(31) Terrier terror
  a. Terriers have terror of something (badgers)

(32) Staff loyalty in rude health
  a. Staff are loyal
  b. ?The company is loyal to staff

(33) Loyalty **to** staff in rude health = (32b)

Besides the disambiguating effect of the unfolding of discourse, most nominalized transitive processes are disambiguated by the nature of the Modifier, i.e. the participant in the congruent version. Thus, a headline like (34), also from *The Financial Times*, in which the transitive Process *fear* has been nominalized presents no ambiguity since *stability* is an abstract noun, and therefore cannot be the Senser in a mental process, unless we get involved in a very convoluted lexical metaphor. The reading of (34) is therefore clear, with the Modifier as Circumstance in the congruent realization.

(34) Stability fears shake Bovespa
  a. Bovespa fears for stability
  b. *Stability fears something

4.2.2. The rough figures

In order to analyse the reflection of the transitive/ergative split on nominalization, a small corpus of over 800 headlines has been examined. Those headlines come from a variety of sources, including British broadsheets, namely

The Financial Times, The Times, The Daily Telegraph and *The Independent*, and a tabloid, *The Daily Mirror*, as well as American newspapers, *US Today, Chicago Tribune* and *The New York Times.* Some information magazines have also been included in this survey: *The Spectator* and *The Economist* from UK, and *The New Yorker* and *The Atlantic Monthly* from US. The selection was quite random, only trying to include samples of different kinds of press from the points of view of varieties of English and target readers.

As the list of sources reveals, most samples come from the 'quality press', since it is there that a linguistic phenomenon such as nominalization, typically associated with prestige is more likely to come into its own (cf. Downing 1997). The search confirms the expectations, since the only tabloid examined proved to have a lower proportion of nominalizations, compared to the other newspapers. This low proportion is also found in magazines, even though the ones surveyed are prestigious ones.

The following discussion will reflect only findings based on nominalizations of the type addressed in this paper, i.e. those containing not only the process but also one participant of the congruent version.

The first noticeable point is that the immense majority of nominalizations encapsulate transitive processes, with a rough proportion of seventeen to one over ergative processes. Before drawing conclusions, this proportion should be compared with the ratio in congruent processes, which is about ten to one, both in headlines and the main body text of articles. This reveals that transitive processes proliferate in discourse. Although the relative proportion of ergatives is 70% higher in congruent speech than in nominalization (1/10 versus 1/17), both proportions are rather low, and quite close to each other in terms of global percentage (10% versus 6%). The next logical step is to check whether these low percentages simply reflect that there is a lower number of verbal realizations of ergative than of transitive processes in English.

If we count the lexical realizations for material, mental, verbal and relational processes in Matthiessen's (1995) *Lexicogrammatical Cartography*, we find a proportion of about 15% ergative verbs, most of them among material ones, where the percentage rises dramatically to nearly 40% ergative verbs. If we consider that about half of congruently realized processes in the corpus analysed here are material (cf. 51% in Matthiessen 1999: 44), the proportion of ergative processes should have been expected to be significantly higher than just 6%.[6] There are two possible interpretations for these figures. One is that the transitive paradigm might contain those verbs that are most frequently used, in which case figures would not be of much help. This would contradict Halliday's claim that the ergative pattern includes "the majority of those [verbs] which are in common use" (1994: 163). The other, and probably more accurate, interpretation is that, for some reason related to its internal organization, the ergative paradigm needs to meet certain requirements which constrain its realization. The reason will probably be related to Davidse & Geyskens' claim that, whereas the Actor in a transitive process has its own autonómy, "with ergative constructions, specific lexical features not only of the verb, but also of its main participant, can be seen to interlock with the semantics of the constructional paradigm" (1997: 7). This could explain the proportional drop from number of ergative verbs to the actual use of ergative congruent processes and, finally, to ergative nominalizations, where the proportion is lowest.

A third interpretation could make sense of the two previous ones. According to Halliday (1994: 163), English is becoming more and more ergative. A phenomenon like this will most surely happen first in spoken discourse, since it is there that changes in languages typically start. If the ergativization of language is an ongoing process, we should expect it to happen less often in formal written discourse, which adapts to changes more slowly. An interesting follow-up to the research here undertaken will, therefore, be a survey of the frequency of ergative processes in spoken discourse.

4.2.3. Transitive nominalizations in headlines

In view of the established low frequency of ergative nominalizations, it may be helpful to come back to the important distinction established above between the possible ambiguity of transitive nominalizations and the inherent vagueness of ergative ones. As said above, the flow of discourse usually accounts for any possible ambiguity. In a headline, the disambiguation is typically produced by the nature of the Modifier/participant, the background knowledge of the reader or the collocational patterning of the nominalization (cf. Whorf 1964: 247–69 for pattern as a source of meaning). Thus, whenever any one of those three factors enters the picture, the nominalization of a transitive process should present no obstacle for the correct interpretation. Corpus examples (35–38) show two things; first, that the writer of the headline assumes that the reader knows about the topic, and secondly that the Modifier tends to be the Medium from the congruent realization. Thus, the pattern tends to be Modifier/Medium ^ Head/Process. In (35, 36), the Modifier stands for the Goal/Medium of an effective process, whereas in (37) it represents the Actor/Medium of a middle process. In (35, 36), even if the reader has no background knowledge, the headline is disambiguated by the nature of the Goal/Medium, which cannot qualify as an Actor for the process type in which it is involved. The same happens in (38) – the only headline in which the Modifier is not Medium –

where the Modifier is not Sayer/Medium but Verbiage/Range; the fact that *fraud* cannot qualify as a Sayer sorts out the meaning. In 37, on the other hand, a reader not familiar with the exact situation could hesitate between the interpretation (37a), confirmed by the reading of the article, and (37b) with the Modifier encapsulating a Circumstance. In any case, the fact that the prototypical pattern is respected should help the reader.

    (35) Rail repair works continue (The Rail is repaired)

    (36) L2.4 bn offer to buy peace … (Money is offered)

    (37) Milosevic plots party comeback
       a. The party comes back
         (i.e. The party intends to return to power)
       b. ?Milosevic intends to come back to the party

    (38) Lawyer told to pay for fraud claiming (Someone claims fraud)

In the case of middle and Goal-directed transitive nominalizations, a quite frequent alternative to the Medium as Modifier is the Circumstance. In such cases, the semantic pattern Medium ^ Process is outweighed by lexical collocation, which ensures the intended interpretation, as we can see in (39–43). The nominalizations are realized through nouns that collocate so often, at least in the press, that sometimes they can even qualify as lexicalized collocations in the journalistic jargon, as (41). In (40) one more factor is contributing to the correct understanding of the noun group, viz. that verbal processes typically collocate with Circumstance: matter. Some other times, collocation goes hand in hand with background knowledge; in (42, 43), the headlines refer to a piece of news so trite for a period of time – i.e. the weeks after the US presidential elections 2000 – that several ephemeral collocations sprouted around the subject. This happens every time a topic becomes preferred news for a period of time. In (42, 43), in any case, the correct unpacking of the nominalization is guaranteed, once again, by the nature of the Modifier, which refers to a place.

    (39) Internet sales surge (Things are sold through/in internet)

    (40) Minister seeks to resurrect climate talks (They talk about climate)

    (41) Christmas road deaths will rise (People die on the roads)

    (42) Florida recount (They recount [ballots] in Florida)

    (43) Palm Beach count refused by Harris (Harris refused to allow [ballots] to be counted [manually] in Palm Beach)

A favourite candidate to enter nominalizations as a circumstantial Modifier is the fashionable word *online*, which accounts for the correct unpacking of the metaphor by the presence of the preposition *on* as an affix. Examples (44, 45) illustrate this point.

(44) Online purchases jump in third quarter (People purchase on/line)

(45) Robot pricing tool fuels online duel (They duel on/line)

When the pattern Modifier/Medium ^ Head/Process is not respected and the nature of the participant does not help to unpack the grammatical metaphor, the only other way of ensuring the correct transmission of the intended message is through the expression of the Modifier in a prepositional phrase dependent on the Head, as in (46). The preposition, provided it is not *of*, will in these cases clarify the semantic role of the Modifier. Thus, the semantics of the nominalization is again disambiguated here partly through grammar. Yet, the realization through prepositional phrase is sometimes chosen even if the Modifier is the Medium, as in (47).

(46) Payment to football club (football club is paid)

(47) Supreme Court rebuffs appeal by ADM execs (ADM execs appealed)

When none of the requirements so far identified are met, the transitive nominalization may then prove to be ambiguous. In (48), the directionality of the mental process is unclear until one starts reading the article. If just one of the participants were present, it would be interpreted, according to the pattern, as the Senser/Medium, but the inclusion of both participants complicates the interpretation. In (49), the *jet* could arguably be the one escaping, although it actually is a Circumstance. Notice that even the Circumstance may be ambiguous, since we could be talking about an escape **from** the jet, the actual meaning, or a gas escape **in** the jet. The latter kind of ambiguity, though, has nothing to do with the one discussed in this paper.

(48) Dentist fear man hanged (Man feared dentists)

(49) Travel firm cleared of blame over jet escape (someone escapes from jet)

Examples like (48, 49) are the exception. Transitive nominalizations can be handled quite safely in headlines, since several factors account for the correct comprehension of their meaning. As we have seen, these factors are context, background knowledge, pattern of the nominalization and collocational or prepositional disambiguation. Any one of these factors disambiguates the metaphorical realization of a transitive process.

4.2.4. Ergative nominalizations in headlines

All the factors just mentioned will, on the other hand, be irrelevant when we are dealing with ergative nominalizations. As said above, grammatical metaphors of ergative processes will always include the Medium as Modifier of the Head. As we saw, both the verb and the participants in an ergative process must fulfil some conditions that allow them to partake in an ergative process. This will limit the use of ergative constructions, especially in written discourse, where less liberty may be taken than in oral speech. The unavoidable vagueness in agency in the case of ergative nominalizations will restrict their occurrence to those cases in which either the context renders the Agent clear or such Agent is irrelevant. This is tantamount to saying that ergative nominalizations will be primarily used with an intended middle meaning, which is one more restriction on their use. Let us remember that transitive nominalizations tend to favour the inclusion of the Actor/Medium as modifier in middle (material) processes, and Goal/Medium in effective ones; the shift in the conflation of the Medium with one or the other transitive participant permits to convey middle or effective meaning in the grammatical metaphor. In the ergative paradigm, on the other hand, the fact that the Medium is always the Affected in material processes does not allow the expression of the Instigator to the suppression of the Affected. Examples (50–53) are the only instances of nominalization of an ergative process found in my corpus, and they illustrate what is being claimed here about them. Headline (54) poses the problem of realizing a dead lexical metaphor with its own meaning, unrelated in principle to the sea. The article does, however, deal with changes in the sea, thus exploiting both its metaphorical and literal meanings.

(50) Three killed in plane crash (Plane crashed)

(51) Prescott seeks to cool climate change row (Climate changes)

(52) The mysterious affair of the Enigma variation (Enigma varies)

(53) A sea change (Sea changes)

All examples (50–53) have the Medium as Modifier, so the reading is essentially clear. The problem is that, as middle ergative nominalizations, and due to the scant contextual help in the headlines, it is not necessarily clear whether self-instigation or external-instigation should be stressed. Once again, extralinguistic context may help (cf. Davidse 1992: 109), as it does in (50), where, again thanks to a collocation, we know that the news is about what happened to the Medium, and not what an external Instigator brought about in that Medium. In (53), on the other hand, it could be claimed to be unclear beforehand whether the news item is going to be about natural changes in the sea, as it actually is, or, e.g., about the effect of human action on the sea, although the Affected-centredness of ergative processes would favour a middle reading. In any case, given the special nature of this headline, its possible vagueness is overridden by the reading as a dead lexical metaphor. It is only after reading the article that the grammatical metaphor is also felt. At that point, though, the meaning has been unpacked.

In sum, the headlines examined seem to support the claim that transitive and ergative processes carry along their different ways of construing experience when they are expressed metaphorically. The relationships among Process and participants in transitive processes may render nominalizations ambiguous, but this ambiguity is very easily avoided thanks to a number of factors. As a payoff for the avoidance of ambiguity, the resulting nominalization can be completely unpacked. Conversely, ergative nominalizations do not risk conveying a confusing reading, but their agency vagueness is not so easily handled. If we add to this that the semantics of the ergative process constrains not only the choice of verb but also that of Medium, the overwhelming preference for transitive over ergative nominalizations is accounted for.

4.3. Interpretation of the data

The quest for ambiguous nominalizations has provided some insights into the nature of this kind of grammatical metaphor. It is time now to give a more detailed interpretation of the figures yielded by the corpus. Of the 72 nominalizations found (only counting those including a Modifier/participant), 68 were transitive and 4 (examples 50–53, above) ergative. The majority (47, among which all the ergative) represented material processes, whereas 17 were verbal, 5 mental and 3 relational. The patterning Modifier/Medium ^ Head/-Process has been found to be the prevailing one in nominalizations, accounting to a great extent for the correct unpacking of the metaphor. Table 4 shows the times the Modifier in a transitive nominalization conflates with each participant, as well as with Circumstances, from the congruent version. Let us remember that the Modifier is always the Affected/Medium in ergative nominalizations. Relational participants are not reflected, because of their low frequency.

Role of Participant in congruent version	Number of times as Modifier in corpus
Actor (or Senser, or Speaker)/Medium	21
Goal/Medium	16
Actor/Agent	0
Range (or Phenomenon, or Verbiage)/Range	6
Beneficiary	1
Circumstance	23
Total	68

Table 4: Participants and Circumstances as Modifier
in corpus headlines (transitive)

As we can see in the table, participants from different process types having the same role in the general system have been grouped for simplification. The high number of Circumstances are explained not only by collocational patterns as in (41, 44, 45) above, but also by the high number of verbal processes, which usually collocate with Circumstance: matter, as we saw in (40) and as (54, 55) also illustrate.

(54) Compromise proposal debated in climate talks

(55) All sides criticize global warming proposal

An important fact about the corpus shown by Table 4 is that when the Modifier does not conflate with the Medium, it does with any other participant – or Circumstance – except with Agent. This is key to the understanding of ambiguity: when the Modifier in transitive nominalizations encapsulates the Actor, the expected metaphor is middle, thus conflating Actor with Medium in the general system, as we saw in 4.2.1. If the nominalized Actor is Agent, the unpacking will be problematical. Such is the case with the metaphor *alcohol impairment*, where the preferred reading according to common knowledge holds the Modifier as Actor/Agent, i.e. *alcohol impairs*. This clashes with the preferred patterning of nominalizations, which imposes a reading *alcohol is impaired*, with *alcohol* as Goal/Medium. The same can be said about *Mary's invitation* in my example (28) above, with *Mary* as Modifier/Agent in the intended meaning. Therefore, it is no surprise that nominalizations which such pattern should be avoided altogether, as the corpus indicates. The ambiguity could in such cases even be regarded as an oddity, given the meaning/pattern conflict just mentioned. The meaning may eventually be disambiguated, but the oddity persists.

In the light of the findings, and as a final synopsis, Table 5 shows the main effects of transitive and ergative nominalizations.

System	Congruent participant as Modifier in nominalization (Modifier ^ Head)	Typical effect on nominalization (out of context)	Typical effect on nominalization (in context)
Transitive	Actor, Senser, Speaker/ Medium	Potential (but rare) ambiguity	No ambiguity
	Goal/Medium	Potential (but rare) ambiguity	No ambiguity
	Actor/Agent	Ambiguity	Ambiguity/oddity
	Range, Phenomenon, Verbiage/Range	Potential (but rare) ambiguity	No ambiguity
	Circumstance	Potential (but rare) ambiguity	No ambiguity
Ergative	Affected/Medium	Vagueness/no ambiguity	Potential vagueness/no ambiguity

Table 5: Transitive versus ergative nominalizations summarized

5. Concluding remarks

In this paper I have tried to give one more reason for the treatment of the transitive and ergative paradigms as two different ways of reconstructing experience. Transitive and ergative structures show different features not only when representing congruent processes, but also when condensed into nominalizations. The fact that transitive (material) structures are Actor-centred whereas ergative ones are Affected-centred has proved to be the key to the understanding of how the nominalizations of transitive and ergative processes reconvert nuclear participants into Modifiers in different ways. The former may incorporate the Actor, the Goal, the Range, or even a Circumstance, whereas the latter always incorporate the Affected/Medium. All this supports the first claim made in Section 1.

As for the second claim, the Medium has proved to be the key to the understanding of ambiguity. Because the Medium usually partakes in the nominalization, the other most nuclear participant, i.e. the Agent, is not welcome to the nominalization of an effective transitive process, at least in the sequence Modifier ^ Head. An alternative realization could be expected to be in a sequence Head ^ Modifier, with the latter as a *by* prepositional phrase. However, no such instance was found in the corpus either, which suggests that nominalizations with Agent tend to be avoided altogether. This explains the ambiguity, or the "oddity", of the nominalization *alcohol impairment*.

Although the nominalizations in this corpus study come from various process types, the argument has been based on material processes. The reason is twofold. First, material processes are usually taken as the starting point to explain issues of transitivity/ergativity (cf. Halliday 1994: 163-ff; Davidse 1992). Second, it is precisely among material processes, together with some transitive emotive ones, that the tension between Medium and Agent is felt most clearly. Verbal processes are mostly middle and pseudo-effective, whereas effectiveness in relational (identifying) processes, if it really exists (cf. Fawcett 1987), is of a different kind. In any case, the second claim can be safely illustrated referring to functions in the general system (Agent, Medium), as I have done in the previous paragraph, thus allowing for the inclusion of ambiguous nominalizations other than material.

We saw in Section 4.2.2 that a number of factors help overcome the potential ambiguity of most nominalizations of transitive processes. The factors identified were context, background knowledge, pattern of the nominalization and collocational or prepositional disambiguation. When those factors are not enough, unintentional ambiguity is most of the time resolved by the flow of discourse. Yet the assumption of too much world knowledge shared between the speaker/writer and the listener/reader may lead to misinterpretation, which, as seen above, can be promptly overcome in spoken discourse by double checking with the interlocutor, but which could create a bigger communicative problem in written discourse.

The greater semantic restrictions found in ergative constructions have also provided an explanation for the much higher frequency of transitive nominalizations as compared with ergative ones. The latter cover a more limited range of experiential meanings. Being Affected-centred, their use is restricted to headlines about one participant, whereas transitive nominalizations may encapsulate not only single-participant news but also semantically richer fragments of experience, i.e. an effective process, with the Goal/Medium as Modifier. This greater flexibility of transitive nominalizations is enhanced by the possible inclusion of a Circumstance or Range as a Modifier instead of the usual Actor or Goal. The obligatory presence of the Medium helps then to explain why ergative nominalizations are never ambiguous but always vague regarding Agency, which never hampers communication.

The approach in this paper has been to assume that the speaker or writer wants to be clear. Given the importance of grammatical metaphor in discourse, especially written, the findings and discussion in this paper are meant to provide new tools for further study of the uses of this communicative resource. A wider-scope corpus-based research of the potential exploitation of ambiguity and vagueness for ideological reasons would be a reasonable follow-up. Simpson (1993: 104) claims that "the Transitivity model[7] provides one means of investigating how a reader's or listener's perception of the meaning of a text is pushed in a particular direction and how the linguistic structure of a text effectively encodes a particular 'world-view'". It would therefore be interesting to investigate the potential effects of nominalization on the manipulation of reality, since something as important as agency is involved in both ambiguity and vagueness. Corpora for such research should probably be gathered from historical writings or any other areas in which a writer may choose to take sides, such as political essays or columns in newspapers.

Notes

1. For the backgrounding and foregrounding effect of nominalization when expressing relationships between actions, see Halliday & Martin (1993: 60–1).

2. 'Transitivity', in this quotation as well as every time it appears capitalized in this paper, has to be understood in its broadest sense, including transitive and ergative constructions.

3. The concept of vagueness has been used with different senses in semantics. See, e.g., the different uses in Cruse (1986: 51–68) and Kempson (1977: 128–34). For a fuller discussion of vagueness see Alston (1964: Ch. 5).

4. This reading seems absurd only because of the nature of the participant *the ball*, which is inanimate and cannot do an intentional action. If we replace *the ball* with *the juggler* the process loses all oddity. A *juggler* may both *bounce* or *bounce something*.

5. I use the terms 'world knowledge' and 'effectiveness' here as in De Beaugrande & Dressler (1981). For the concept of shared knowledge, other terms have been deemed more appropriate by other scholars, such as Sperber & Wilson's (1986) 'shared cognitive environment'. As for the notion of 'schema', I use it here in Renkema's (1993) and Cook's (1989) sense. The latter (1989: Ch. 6) defines schemata as "mental representations of typical situations, and they are used in discourse processing to predict the contents of the particular situation which the discourse describes".

6. Matthiessen does not make a distinction between transitive and ergative verbs. Nevertheless, the split is perfectly observable in the tables of lexical realizations, since processes are divided in middle and effective. Following from the discussion in section 2, we know that those verbs that appear only as middle or only as effective are transitive, whereas those which appear as potentially middle and effective are ergative.

7. 'Transitivity' has a lower case "t" in the original; I have capitalized it here to abide by the convention established in note 2.

References

Alston, W. (1964) *Philosophy of Language*. Englewood Cliffs, NJ: Prentice-Hall.

Anderson, J.M. (1968) Ergative and nominative in English. *Journal of Linguistics* 4. 1–32.

Anderson, J.M. (1977) *On Case Grammar: Prolegomena to a Theory of Grammatical Relations*. London: Croom Helm.

Belleti, A. (1987) Los verbos inacusativos como asignadores de caso. In: V. Demonte & V. Fernández (eds.) *Sintaxis de las Lenguas Románicas*. Madrid: El Arquero. 167–230.

Burzio, L. (1981) *Intransitive Verbs and Italian Auxiliaries*. Doctoral Thesis, M.I.T. Cambridge, MA.

Butler, C. (1996) On the concept of an interpersonal metafunction in English. In: M. Berry, C. Butler & R.P. Fawcett (eds.) *Meaning and Choice in Language. Studies for Michael Halliday Vol. 2*. Norwood, NJ: Ablex. 151–181.

Cook, G. (1989) *Discourse*. Oxford: Oxford UP.

Cruse, D. (1972) A note on English causatives. *Linguistic Inquiry* 3: 520–528.

Cruse, D. (1973) Some thoughts on agentivity. *Journal of Linguistics* 9: 11–23.

Cruse, D. (1986) *Lexical Semantics*. Cambridge: Cambridge UP.

Davidse, K. (1992) Transitivity/ergativity: The Janus-headed grammar of actions and events". In: M. Davies, J.R. Martin & L. Ravelli (eds.) *Advances in Systemic Linguistics: Recent Theory and Practice*. London & New York: Pinter. 105–135.

Davidse, K. (1999) On transitivity and ergativity in English, or on the need for dialogue between schools. In: J. Van der Auwera & J. Verschueren (eds.) *English as a Human Language*. Lincom: München. 95–108.

Davidse, K. & Geyskens, S. (1997) Have you walked the dog yet? The ergative causativization of intransitives. *Journal of the International Linguistic Association* 49.2: 155–180.

De Beaugrande, R. & Dressler, W. (1981) *Introduction to Text Linguistics*. London & New York: Longman.

Degand, L. (1994) Causation in Dutch and French: Interpersonal aspects". In: R. Hasan, D. Butt & C. Cloran (eds.) *Functional Descriptions. Theory in Practice*. Amsterdam: Benjamins. 207–235.

Dixon, R. (1979) Ergativity. *Language* 55: 59–138.

Dixon, R. (1994) *Ergativity*. Cambridge: Cambridge UP.

Downing, A. (1997) Encapsulating discourse topics. *Estudios Ingleses de la Universidad Complutense* 5: 147–168.

Eggins, S., Wignell, P. & Martin, J.R. (1993) The discourse of history: Distancing the recoverable past. In: M. Ghadessy (ed.) *Register Analysis*. London & New York: Pinter. 75–109.

Fawcett, R.P. (1980) *Cognitive Linguistics and Social Interaction*. Heidelberg: Julius Groos; Exeter: University of Exeter.

Fawcett, R.P. (1987) The semantics of clause and verb for relational processes in English. In: M.A.K. Halliday & R.P. Fawcett (eds.) *New Developments in*

Systemic Linguistics. Volume 1. Theory and Description. London: Pinter. 131–183.

Fodor, T. (1970) Three reasons for not deriving 'kill' from 'cause to die'. *Linguistic Inquiry* 1: 429–438.

Goatly, A. (1993) Species of metaphor in varieties of English. In: M. Ghadessy (ed.) *Register Analysis: Theory and Practice.* London: Pinter. 110–148.

Halliday, M.A.K. (1967a) Notes on transitivity and theme in English, Part 1. *Journal of Linguistics* 3: 37–81.

Halliday, M.A.K. (1967b) Notes on transitivity and theme in English, Part 2. *Journal of Linguistics* 3: 199–244.

Halliday, M.A.K. (1968) Notes on transitivity and theme in English, Part 3. *Journal of Linguistics* 4: 179–215.

Halliday, M.A.K. (1970) Language structure and language function. In: J. Lyons (ed.) *New Horizons in Linguistics.* Harmondsworth: Penguin. 140–165.

Halliday, M.A.K. (1985a) *An Introduction to Functional Grammar.* London: Arnold.

Halliday, M.A.K. (1985b) *Spoken and Written Language.* Victoria: Deakin University

Halliday, M.A.K. (1994) *An Introduction to Functional Grammar.* 2nd edition. London: Arnold.

Halliday, M.A.K. (1998) Things and relations. Regrammaticising experience as technical knowledge. In: J.R. Martin & R. Veel (eds.) *Reading Science.* London: Routledge. 185–235.

Halliday M.A.K. & J.R. Martin (1993) *Writing Science.* London: Falmer.

Hopper, P. & S. Thompson (1980) Transitivity in grammar and discourse. *Language* 56.2: 251–299.

Kempson, R. (1977) *Semantic Theory.* Cambridge: Cambridge UP.

Lavid, J. & J. Arús (1998a) Exploring transitivity/ergativity in English and Spanish: A computational approach. In: M. Martínez (ed.) *Transitivity Revisited.* Huelva: Universidad de Huelva. 259–276.

Lavid, J. & J. Arús (1998b) Aspectos lingüísticos y computacionales de la transitividad mental en inglés y en español. Paper delivered at the XXVIII symposium of the Spanish Society of Linguistics, Madrid, 14-18 December.

Lavid, J. & Arús, J. (1999) The grammar of relational processes in English and Spanish: Implications for machine translation and multilingual generation. Paper delivered at the II International Congress of Translation Studies, Universidade da Coruña, 11-14 February.

Lemke, J. (1998) Resources for attitudinal meaning. *Functions of Language* 5.1: 33–56.

López, B. (1997) *La Posición del Sujeto en la Cláusula Monoactancial en Español.* Santiago de Compostela: Universidad de Santiago de Compostela.

Lyons, J. (1968) *Introduction to Theoretical Linguistics.* Cambridge: Cambridge UP.

Martin, J.R. (1995) Logical meanings in Tagalog. *Functions of Language* 2.2: 189–228.

Matthiessen, C. (1990) *Lexicogrammatical Cartography: English Systems.* Draft 4, University of Sydney.

Matthiessen, C. (1992) Interpreting the textual metafunction. In: M. Davies & L. Ravelli (eds.) *Advances in Systemic Linguistics. Recent Theory and Practice.* London & New York: Pinter. 37–81.

Matthiessen, C. (1995) *Lexicogrammatical Cartography: English Systems.* Tokyo: International Language Science Publishers.

Matthiessen, C. (1999) The system of TRANSITIVITY: An exploratory study of text-based profiles. *Functions of Language* 6.1: 1–51.

Ravelli, L. (1988) Grammatical metaphor: An initial analysis. In: E. Steiner & R. Veltman (eds.) *Pragmatics, Discourse and Text: Some Systemically-Inspired Approaches.* London & New York: Pinter. 133–147.

Renkema, J. (1993) *Discourse Studies: An introductory textbook.* Amsterdam: Benjamins.

Simpson, P. (1993) *Language, Ideology and Point of View.* London: Routledge.

Sperber, D. & D. Wilson (1986) *Relevance.* Oxford: Blackwell.

Thibault, P. (1995) Mood and the ecosocial dynamics of semiotic Exchange. In: R. Hasan & P. Fries (eds.) *On Subject and Theme. A Discourse Functional Perspective.* Amsterdam: Benjamins. 51–90.

Whorf, B. (1964) *Language, Thought and Reality: Selected Writings of Benjamin Lee Whorf.* Edited by J. Carrol, 1ˢᵗ paperback edition. Cambridge, MA.: Massachusetts Institute of Technology.

The evolution of grammatical metaphor in scientific writing

David Banks
Université de Bretagne Occidentale

1. Introduction

The term *grammatical metaphor*[1] has come to be used as a convenient label for the use of non-congruent lexicogrammatical forms. Thompson (1996) describes it as "the expression of meaning through a lexico-grammatical form which originally evolved to express a different kind of meaning" (Thompson 1996: 165). This phenomenon can take many forms (Downing & Locke 1992, Halliday 1994a, Thompson 1996, Martin et al. 1997). Ravelli (1988) lists 19 different types, and Halliday (1998), using a different basis of categorization, gives 13 different types. The form of grammatical metaphor which has received the most attention is the nominalisation of processes, and indeed in some treatments it is the only form discussed (Eggins 1994, Bloor & Bloor 1995). Processes are congruently encoded as verbs; when they are encoded as something else, such as nouns, we have a non-conguent form, and this constitutes a grammatical metaphor. Thus *grammatical metaphor evolved* is congruent, while *the evolution of grammatical metaphor* is non-congruent, and therefore a grammatical metaphor for the congruent form. In Ravelli's classification she gives 5 types of nominalisation of processes, and Halliday in his, gives 3. Ravelli's classification is according to process type: material, mental, relational, verbal, and behavioural (though not existential, of which I did find one example in my corpus). Halliday's classification divides processes into event (the process encoded in the lexical verb), aspect or phase (where this is encoded in a verb such as *try*), and modality. This final category is not, of course, encoded as a lexical verb, and Ravelli deals with this elsewhere in her classification, distinct from the nominalisation of processes as such. This study considers only those cases which are encoded as lexical verbs, including for these purposes those which might be considered phase (cf. Banks in press), and follows Ravelli in distinguishing between different process types. It excludes cases of metaphors of modality, being concerned basically with the ideational metafunction rather than the interpersonal.

The question of analysis is not without its problems. I shall now illustrate some of the difficulties using examples from Krieger & Sigler, one of the contemporary articles in my sample. In this article the word *trawl* is used sometimes for a piece of equipment, and sometimes for the action of trawling. Obviously, it is only the second of these which consitutes a grammatical metaphor. The difficulty arises in cases where it is not immediately evident which meaning is to be taken; it is evident that one trawls with a trawl, so ambiguous cases are bound to occur, giving a rather grey area. The following examples seem to refer clearly to the equipment.

> *... no fish were assumed captured while the trawl was retrieved* (Krieger & Sigler 1996: 283)
>
> *GPS fixes and the rate of cable retrieval were used to determine the speed of the trawl during retrieval.* (Krieger & Sigler 1996: 284)
>
> *On the other hand, the following seems to be fairly clearly a case of the action of trawling.*
>
> *The time between dives and trawls was <4h for 13 of the 16 comparisons.* (Krieger & Sigler 1996: 283)

In the following:

> *Trawl periods ranged from 10 to 18 min, depending on trawl speed and trawl distance needed to intersect the submersible transects.* (Krieger & Sigler 1996: 289)

trawl periods and *trawl distance* also seem to be clearly the action of trawling: the period trawling took and the distance trawled. By assimilation, I would take *trawl speed* to refer to the action too, though it might otherwise have been ambiguous: the speed of trawling or the speed of the trawl. Some cases seem more genuinely ambiguous:

> *The value of comparing in situ observations of groundfish with trawl catches has been documented in other studies.* (Krieger & Sigler 1996: 286)

Is *trawl catches* to be taken as what is caught by trawling, or what is caught by the trawl? A categorical answer does not seem possible. The difficulty is compounded in this particular case by the fact that the authors also use *trawling* as a nominalised process.

> *Submersible dives and bottom trawling were completed during daylight at 180-283 m depths.* (Krieger & Sigler 1996: 283)
>
> *Therefore, rockfish density estimates from submersible counts and from trawling include these three species in addition to Pacific ocean perch.* (Krieger & Sigler 1996: 284)

There is then a grey area in which the analyst has to make decisions. In the present case those decisions have been mainly in the direction of including ambiguous cases in the grammatical metaphor category. Even though this means that the figures are in no sense absolute, I would claim that it does not reduce their indicative value, and that different analytical decisions would not significantly alter the general picture that is emerging.

There are a number of options available in the language for creating nominalised forms of processes, though not all options are necessarily available for an individual verb. These options fall into three basic types: those which are morphologically identical with the agnate verb (e.g. *haul, estimate, change*), those which have no agnate verb, but which nevertheless indicate a process (e.g. *trend, occasion*), and those which have an agnate verb, but are not morphologically identical. This includes the use of suffixes, of which *-ing* (e.g. *tracking, reading*), and *-ion* (e.g. *identification, detection*), are the most common, but there are also examples of *-ment* (e.g. *measurement, movement*), *-ance/-ence* (e.g. *avoidance, preference*), and *-ure* (e.g. *procedure*), as well as those which have no specific suffix (e.g. *growth, analysis*). These morphological distinctions do not seem relevant to the present study, and consequently have not been taken into account here (however, cf. Banks forthcoming).

According to Halliday (1987) the evolution of grammatical metaphor began long ago and is certainly not restricted to English. As far as the West is concerned it began with "the explosion of process nouns in scientific Greek from 550 BC onwards" (Halliday 1987: 146). This led to what he terms an 'attic' style, based on the noun group, and which consequently had a much more static feel than the 'doric' style, which was clause-based and hence more dynamic.

> The doric style, that of everyday, commonsense discourse, is characterized by a high degree of grammatical intricacy – a choreographic type of complexity, as I have described it: it highlights processes, and the

interdependence of one process on another. The attic style, that of emergent languages of science, displays a high degree of lexical density; its complexity is crystalline, and it highlights structure, and the interrelationships of their parts – including, in a critical further develop-ment, *conceptual* structures, the taxonomies that helped to turn knowledge into science. (Halliday 1987: 147)

In what follows I shall outline the development of grammatical metaphor in the form of nominalised processes as a rhetorical resource in scientific discourse. I shall suggest that it has developed differently in the physical and biological sciences, being initially much slower in the latter. This difference seems to have been eliminated by the beginning of the twentieth century, while in the course of the twentieth century the use of this type of grammatical metaphor has been extended from the grammatical function of head to that of modifier in the noun group.

2. The beginnings of English scientific discourse

The earliest known scientific or technical document written in English is Chaucer's *Treatise on the Astrolabe*. This was written in 1391 and Halliday (Halliday 1988, Halliday & Martin 1993) lists among the scientific features of Chaucer's text, the use of technical nouns for parts of the astrolabe, and of abstract nouns for geometrical and mathematical entities. However, as I have previously argued (Banks 1997a, 1997b), one must be clear about the sort of document Chaucer's *Treatise* is. It may well qualify as the earliest known scientific or technical document in English, but that does not mean that it can be directly compared with any type of later scientific document. It is only possible to compare like with like, and so it is important to be clear about the genre we are dealing with here. Chaucer's text is addressed to his ten year old son, Lewis (*Lyte Lowys, my sone*), and in it he explains to him how to use his astrolabe. It therefore cannot possibly be compared to adult experimental scientific writing; it is certainly not a direct forerunner of a sub-genre like the scientific research article. If there is a contemporary parallel to this document, it must be something like the "how it works" type of book written for modern teenagers. When Chaucer's text is compared with this type of document, although obviously there are differences, they are less than would seem to be the case if it is compared with a present-day document which is not appropriate for this purpose. A research article, for example, does not constitute an appropriate document for comparison.

Chaucer's document does display some examples of grammatical metaphor, but, of course, very few texts have none at all. In the Prologue and Part 1, we find the following examples listed in Table 1:

cause	7	arisyng	2
conclusion	16	endityng	2
declinacioun	3	knowing	1
descripcioun	1	moevyng	8
governaunce	1	worchynge	1
mediacioun	1		
praier	2		

Table 1: Examples of grammatical metaphor in Chaucer

Figures in brackets give the number of tokens for each type. We even find examples where Chaucer can be seen moving from the verbal to the nominal form:

And all that moeveth withinne the hevedes of thes Aries and Libra, his moeving is clepid northward: and all that moeveth without these hevedes, his moevyng is clepid southward (Chaucer 1391 [1975]: 548)

Halliday describes Chaucer's *Treatise* as proto-scientific (Halliday 1988, Halliday & Martin 1993), but it is Newton that he singles out as being the initiator of modern scientific discourse. According to Halliday, this discursive sea-change comes about in the *Treatise on Opticks*. This was written in the period 1675-1687, but was not published until 1704, after which it went through several editions until the 4th edition appeared in 1730. The delay in the publication of the first edition was partly due to the fact that the first draft was destroyed in a fire in 1676, but perhaps more importantly to the adverse reactions to his article "A New Theory of Light and Colours" published in the *Philosophical Transactions of the Royal Society* in 1672 (Bazerman 1988, Gross 1990).

Halliday found little grammatical metaphor in those parts of Newton's *Treatise* which are descriptions of experiments, but a good deal in those sections which present arguments and conclusions, while mathematical formulations lead to the use of dense noun groups.

When describing the results of an experiment Newton often uses intricate clause complexes involving both expansion and projection, of the form 'I observed that, when I did *a*, *x* happened'. The mathematical sections, on the other hand, display the complementary type of complexity: a single clause with only three elements, but very long and complex nominal groups [...] (Halliday 1988: 167).

3.   Situating Newton's *Treatise*

I feel however that it is important to understand something of the situation which surrounded the development of Newton's *Treatise*. Newton was not working in an intellectual and social vacuum, and it is valid to consider to what extent the intellectual climate of his time contributed to the development of Newton's scientific style of writing.

The Royal Society had been founded in 1662 and it had adopted rhetorical criteria based on those expounded by Bacon in his *Parasceve ad Historiam Naturalem et Experimentalem*, published in 1620. Here, Bacon advocates that scientific language should have no rhetorical flourishes, no superfluous citations and no verbal ornament, that it should be a simple straightforward account of what was done. These ideas inspired Spratt and underlie his remarks on language in his *History of the Royal Society of London for the Improving of Natural Knowledge*. This was published in 1667, only 5 years after the founding of the Royal Society, so it could hardly be a history, and was in fact much more of a manifesto of the Royal Society (Gross 1990). Among his remarks is the following description of what good scientific language should be like.

> [...] a close, naked, natural way of speaking; positive expression; clear senses; a native easiness: bringing all things as near the Mathematical plainness as they can; and preferring the language of Artizans, Countrymen, and Merchants before that of Wits, or Scholars. (cf. Vickers 1987).

These same ideas were later enshrined in the Statutes of the Royal Society when they came to be written in 1728. There it is said that "in all Reports of experiments to be brought into the Society, the Matter of Fact shall be barely stated, without any Prefaces, Apologies or rhetorical Flourishes [...]" (Vickers 1987).

All of this should be seen against a background of rapidly changing language, and these changes were not always for the better: there was a vogue for a highly florid style, which frequently used a large number of classical or pseudoclassical neologisms, and what critics of the time termed 'inkhorn' terms (Baugh 1959). To a large extent, the members of the Royal Society were reacting against these stylistic fashions; as Gläser (1995) says, Spratt and the

Royal Society wanted to improve scientific language and resist the corruption of English.

Some commentators also find a clash with the philosophical ideas that were current at the time. They claim that for philosophers such as Locke, words represent ideas, whereas for the members of the Royal Society, words represent things, and this is seen as an opposition (e.g. McKinnon 1994). This argument is supported by quotations from Locke such as the following.

> *Man* ... had by nature his organs so fashioned as to be *fit to frame articulate sounds*. ... Besides articulate sounds ... it was further necessary that he should be *able to use these sounds as signs of internal conceptions*, and to make them stand as marks for the *ideas* within his own mind ... (1706, III, I, 1-2)
> ... all words ... signify nothing immediately but the *ideas* in the mind of the speaker ... (1706, III, IV, 1)

This, however, is to lose sight of the fact the Locke was grappling with an epistemological problem, that of how human beings perceive external reality, and subsequently of how that perception can be communicated to other human beings. In other words, it is concerned with the relationships between words, thoughts, and things (Bennett 1971). The problem of the Royal Society was of a different, and rather more pragmatic order. Their problem was the rhetorical one of communicating with clarity and precision, and this at a period when the artifices of florid style were frequently appreciated for their own sake, even when they masked an absence of real content. I do not feel then that there is any real clash between Locke's epistemology and the rhetorical style advocated by the Royal Society; they belong to different spheres.

4.   Scientific writing just before Newton

I would now like to consider two extracts, taken more or less at random, from the period shortly before Newton began writing his *Treatise*. The first of these is by Robert Boyle and is from his *New Experiments Physico-Mechanical, Touching the Spring of the Air, and its Effects: Made for the most part in a New Pneumatical Engine*, published in 1660. This work is cast in the format of a letter addressed to his nephew, the Lord of Dungarvan. It thus bears the dedicatory features of this genre: "And I am not faintly induced to make choice of this subject rather than any of the expected chymical ones to entertain your Lordship upon ..." (Vickers 1987: 48). Nevertheless, the work is mainly a description of experiments, and in the major section of the work the epistolary genre is hardly in evidence at all. If the vocative *my Lord* is omitted from the following, it reads as a straightforward piece of prose.

> By these two differing ways, my Lord, may the springs of the air be explicated. But though the former of them be that which by reason of its seeming somewhat more easy I shall for the most part make use of in the following discourse, yet I am not willing to declare peremptorily for either of them against the other. (Vickers 1987: 53)

The extract analysed contains 2630 words. There are 63 nominalisations of processes, that is an average rate of one per 42 words of running text.[2] In Table 2 these have been categorized according to their transitivity processes. The examples of material processes have been subdivided into those that have a presumed human actor, and those that have a presumed non-human actor.

mental	verbal	material (hum)	material (non-h)	
judgement	account (3)	drawing down	agitation	pressure (5)
observation (2)	answer (2)	experience	bending	protrusion
sight	comparison	experiment (11)	compression (3)	recovery
thought	hypothesis	turning (2)	condensation	refraction
understanding	mention		dilatation (3)	restitution (2)
	objection		endevour	returning
	seconding		expansion (2)	self-dilatation
			exsuction (2)	self-dilation
			motion (5)	
tokens: 6	tokens: 10	tokens: 15	tokens: 32	
types: 5	types: 7	types: 4	types: 17	
9.5%	15.9%	23.8%	50.8%	

Table 2: Examples of grammatical metaphors in Robert Boyle

Since Boyle's work can be situated within the physical sciences, I have taken an extract from the biological sciences, by way of comparison. This extract is from Henry Power's *Experimental Philosophy, in three Books: containing New Experiments, Microscopical, Mercurial, Magnetical, with some Deduction and Probable Hypotheses raised from them, in Avouchment and Illustration of the now famous Atomical Hypothesis.* Although this work is quite clearly scientific, its style is frequently anecdotal.

> One would wonder at the great strength lodged in so small a Receptacle ... Stick a large brass pin through his tayl and he will readily drag it away. I have seen a chain of gold ... of three hundred links, though not above an inch long, both fastened to, and drawn away by a Flea ... Yea, we have heard it credibly reported

... that a Flea hath not onely drawn a gold Chain, but a golden Charriot also with all its harness and accoutrements fixed to it ... (Vickers 1987: 90)[3]

It also bears the hallmarks of the style of the virtuosi, or gentleman scientists, notably of their wonder at what they perceived as the beauty of nature. Of the common fly he says, "it is a very pleasant Insect to behold", and of the horse fly "Her eye is an incomparable pleasant spectacle" (Vickers 1987: 90–91).

The extract from Power's book contains 860 words; there are only 5 examples of nominalised processes, and they are all of the material non-human type: *work, motion, flexure, flea-biting, supportance.* This gives an average rate of one per 175 words of running text.

To the extent that these extracts can be taken to be representative, this shows that there is already a distinction between the physical sciences which have become experimental, and the biological sciences which are still descriptive. Moreover, the extract from Boyle shows that there were precedents for Newton's adoption of grammatical metaphor as a rhetorical strategy, since Boyle already uses this to a considerable extent. Consequently, while Newton's science might be considered to constitute a Kuhnian revolution (Kuhn 1970), providing a new paradigm for scientific thought, the same cannot be said of Newton's writing. This was not a revolution since it fitted into a schema that was already in place, even if he perfected it and carried it to new heights.

5. Development in the biological sciences

Since grammatical metaphor seems not to have been adopted in scientific writing in the biological sciences at the same time as the physical sciences, I have taken two later points in time in an attempt to see how writing developed in the biological sciences. The first of these is the writing of Joseph Banks. Joseph Banks made his name during his circumnavigation of the world with Captain Cook on the *Endeavour,* 1768-1771. The official reason for this journey was to observe the transit of Venus, with the object of improving the accuracy of the calculations necessary for navigation. Ultimately, however, it was to become scientifically important for the botanical and zoological work which Banks accomplished during this voyage. He later established Kew Gardens virtually as we know it today, and at the comparatively early age of 35 he was elected President of the Royal Society. He held this post until his death 42 years later, marking the science of his day with his rather autocratic personality (Cameron 1952, O'Brian 1987, Gascoigne 1994).

Banks wrote virtually nothing in the way of research articles; his main contribution to writing is his *Journal* of the *Endeavour* voyage. Although Banks did not intend this for publication, he undoubtedly expected it to be read by friends and colleagues, so to that extent it is a public document. As I have pointed out in a previous study (Banks 1996), there are at least three different types of discourse in Banks' *Journal*, diary entries, narrative, and scientific description. However, the incidence of nominalised processes is barely more in the sections of scientific description than in the narrative sections. Figures derived from Perrot 1998 indicate that the rate is of the order of one per 150 words of running text.

Perrot (1998) also considers Darwin's *Voyage of the Beagle*, published in 1839 and which has a number of similarities with Banks' *Journal*. This is my second point in time, 70 years after Banks' *Journal*. It too is the journal of a sea voyage, and incorporates a significant amount of scientific description of plants and animals. Perrot shows that in extracts of scientific description totalling 6349 words, there are 106 examples of nominalised process, giving a rate of one per 60 words of running text. Thus although Darwin uses nominalisation to a greater extent than Power and Banks, the rate is still less than that found in Boyle. Perrot describes Darwin's writing as representing an "intermediate stage" in the development of grammatical metaphor (1998: 74).

Halliday has also considered Darwin's writing (Halliday 1994b), but his study is basically a detailed analysis of the two final paragraphs of *The Origin of Species*. Moreover, his analysis is mainly of thematic and information structure, and hence is not directly comparable with what is being studied here.

6.   Faraday: A contemporary of Darwin

In order to have a point of comparison with Darwin, but from the physical sciences, I have taken an extract from the writings of Faraday; the extract is taken from an article published in the *Philosophical Transactions of the Royal Society*, and was published in 1838. This extract of 2980 words has 61 examples of nominalised processes, a rate of one per 49 words of running text.

As shown in Table 3, the rate here is greater than that found in Darwin, but of the same order, indeed slightly less than that found in Boyle. Unless it turns out that the extracts from either Boyle or Faraday are untypical, it would seem that discourse of the physical sciences remained more or less static from this point of view for 150 years. That is, having established nominalisation of processes as a rhetorical strategy, the phenomenon was not extended beyond its original rate of use for a considerable period.

mental	verbal	mat (hum)	mat (non-h)	relational
analysis	description	connection	action (4)	relation (4)
attention	indication	experiment (6)	discharge (26)	
conclusion (2)		introduction	formation	
determination		use	influence (3)	
distinction			occurrence	
investigation			polarization	
observation			propagation	
			variation	
tokens: 8	tokens: 2	tokens: 9	tokens: 38	tokens: 4
types: 7	types: 2	types: 4	types: 8	types: 1
13.1%	3.3%	14.8%	62.3%	6.6%

Table 3: Examples of grammatical metaphor in Faraday

In a more detailed comparison with Boyle, it will be noted that Faraday uses less verbal and material-human nominalisations. In the material-non-human category, Faraday uses more tokens than Boyle (38 as against 32), but Boyle uses considerably more types (17 as against 8). This is largely due to Faraday's extensive use of *discharge* in this particular extract.

7. The early twentieth century

In an attempt to see how things had developed by the early twentieth century, I have taken two research articles from this period. The first, from the field of the physical sciences, is Millikan 1910 (see Table 4). This article of 6530 words has 283 examples of nominalised processes, a rate of one per 23 words of running text.

The second article is Thompson 1913, from the field of the biological sciences (see Table 5). This article was published in *The Proceedings of the Royal Society, Section B – Biological Sciences*, but it is significant that the author's address includes the line *Biochemical Department*. It is the word *biochemical* which I feel is significant, and indicates that an important change has taken place in biological studies. This is confirmed by an even cursory reading of the article, which is quite obviously of an experimental nature. This indicates that the biological sciences have turned the corner, and are no longer simply descriptive, but have joined the experimental field.

This article of 2810 words contains 128 examples of nominalised processes, a rate of one per 22 words of running text, i.e. virtually the same rate as Millikan.

mental	verbal	mat (hum)	mat (non-h)	relational
allowance	question	experiment (14)	action (2)	addition
application	report	measurement (9)	agitation (2)	agreement
assumption (9)		method (26)	approach	appearance
attention		modification (2)	cause	relation (2)
comparison (3)		procedure	change (2)	
conclusion (2)		standardization	communication (2)	
connexion (2)		study	concordance	
consideration (3)		test	condensation	
correction		trial	deflexion (3)	
counting		use	displacement	
determination (24)		work	distortion	
estimate (2)			distribution	
exception			evaporation (11)	
judgement			expansion (22)	
knowledge			fall (16)	
observation (46)			formation	
plan			inonization	
predisposition			lag	
question			movement (3)	
reading			outflow	
solution			passage (4)	
verification (2)			pressure (2)	
view			production	
			ionization	
			motion (6)	
			progress	
			retardation	
			scintillation	
			scattering	
			stroke (2)	
			throwing	
			variation	
			variability	
			velocity (14)	
tokens: 107	tokens: 2	tokens: 58	tokens: 111	tokens: 5
types: 23	types: 2	types: 11	types: 34	types: 4
37.8%	0.7%	20.5%	39.2%	1.8%

Table 4: Examples of grammatical metaphor in Millikan (1910)

Thus it would seem that by the early twentieth century the difference between the physical and biological sciences in relation to nominalised processes had been eliminated, at least in terms of overall use of this strategy. It will however be noticed that there are differences between the two authors in terms of the transitivity distribution. Millikan makes extensive use of nominalised mental processes (37.8%), while Thompson makes comparatively little use of this type (6.3%). On the other hand Millikan makes less use of nominalised material processes (20.5% human and 39.2% non-human) than Thompson (32.8% human and 59.4% non-human). Indeed over 90% of Thompson's nominalised processes are material.

mental	mat (hum)	mat (non-h)		relational
determination (3)	connection	absorption (2)	fluctuation	addition
examination (2)	conservation	action (5)	growth (5)	agreement (3)
observation (2)	distillation	adsorption	incubation (6)	
proof	experiment (23)	aëration	leak	
	filtration	alteration	neutralisation	
	manipulation (2)	change (2)	non-diminution	
	reading (7)	conclusion (2)	non-production	
	sterilization	consumption	occurrence	
	titration (3)	contact	oxidation (8)	
		course (2)	precipitation	
		decomposition (6)	pressure	
		delivery (2)	production (3)	
		distilling	reaction (5)	
		effect	reduction	
		exit	souring	
		extraction	stream	
		fermentation (5)	supply (3)	
tokens: 8	tokens: 40	tokens: 76		tokens: 4
types: 4	types: 9	types: 34		types: 2
6.3%	32.8%	59.4%		3.1%

Table 5: Examples of grammatical metaphor in Thompson (1913)

8.   The late twentieth century

To come up to date with some examples from the late twentieth century, I am going to consider three articles published in 1996. Two of these confirm the general trend, one does not. The exception is Sleigh et al. 1996, which comes from the biological field. This article of 2810 words has 83 examples of nominalised processes (listed in Table 6), a rate of one per 34 words. Hence the global incidence of nominalised processes is less than in either Millikan or Thompson.

On the other hand, Krieger & Sigler 1996 (see Table 7), also from the biological field, has 2930 words and 237 nominalised processes, a rate of one per 12 words of running text.

mental	verbal	mat (hum)	mat (non-h)	existential
aim	description	analysis (3)	activity	existence
belief	recommendation	association	composition (6)	
comparison (2)	report	collection	production (3)	
confidence		conjunction	utilization	
conversion		cruise (9)	variation	
count		effort	change (3)	
estimate (2)		experiment	increase (2)	
examination		fixation	trend (3)	
recognition		input	contribution	
		method	stratification (2)	
		modelling	succession	
		microscopy (2)	depletion	
		occasion (2)	grazing	
		operation	growth	
		passage	bloom	
		sampling (3)	input	
		sequence	concentration	
		study (3)	indication	
		transect	pressure	
			grazing	
			sedimentation	
tokens: 11	tokens: 3	tokens: 35	tokens: 34	tokens: 1
types: 9	types: 3	types: 19	types: 21	types: 1
13.1%	3.6%	42.2%	41.0%	1.2%

Table 6: Examples of grammatical metaphor in Sleigh et al. (1996)

The example from the physical sciences, presented in Table 8, is Lindsay et al. 1996. This has 3870 words and 253 nominalised processes, a rate of one per 15 words of running text.

Thus the overall frequency of nominalised processes in these two articles is of the same order, although Krieger & Sigler use more human (62.0%) than non-human (17.3%) material processes, whereas in Lindsay et al. these percentages are virtually inversed: 63.6% non-human and 22.9% human.

This therefore confirms the general trend towards increased use of nominalised processes, and the fact that the physical and biological sciences now behave in the same way in this respect.

mental	verbal	mat (hum)	mat (non-h)	relational
analysis	overview	catch (20)	ascent	association
approximation		design	avoidance	combination
assessment		detection (2)	escapement	orientation (2)
assumption		dive (5)	behaviour (4)	
comparison (3)		effort	change	
count (12)		fix	completion	
estimate (17)		haul (9)	descent	
identification		measurement (3)	detection	
observation (3)		mensuration (2)	distribution	
reading		method (3)	diving	
regard		process	expansion	
view		readout (2)	formation	
viewing		repeat	growth	
		retrieval (16)	herding (3)	
		sampling	mortality	
		speed (2)	movement	
		strategy	preference	
		study (10)	rooponoo (3)	
		survey (10)	spacing	
		test	speed (7)	
		tracking	spread (6)	
		trawl (49)	tear	
		trawling (5)	travel	
tokens: 44	tokens: 1	tokens: 147	tokens: 41	tokens: 4
types: 13	types: 1	types: 23	types: 23	types: 3
18.5%	0.4%	62.0%	17.3%	1.7%

Table 7: Examples of grammatical metaphor in Krieger & Sigler (1996)

9.   Grammatical function

The rates of nominalisation given for Krieger & Sigler and for Lindsay et al. would seem to be getting close to saturation point, and one might think that this was somewhere near the end of the story. Consideration of the examples indicates however that there has been a further recent development. It is to be expected that nominalisations of processes function as heads in noun groups, and to a large extent this is true. In the more recent texts however, it is noticeable that a considerable number function as modifiers within the noun groups. In the following extracts, nominalised processes are in bold, and those that function as modifiers have been underlined.

> The catchability coefficient estimated in this **study** is based on an increased number of submersible versus **trawl comparisons** and on improved density **estimates** from **trawl catch** rates and submersible **counts**. (Krieger & Sigler 1996, 293)
>
> The **contribution** to the charge-**transfer scattering** from the O_2 and H_2O in the mixture are then subtracted from the total signal using their known charge-**transfer** cross sections. (Lindsay et al. 1996: 215)
>
> To determine the sampling capabilites of the trawl during **retrieval, catch** rates from six "standard **trawl hauls** were compared with **catch** rates from seven **"retrieval" trawl hauls**. (Krieger & Sigler 1996: 284)

This would appear to be a twentieth century development. In the small sample considered here, the earliest examples of nominalised processes functioning as modifiers is in Millikan's 1910 article, and even there, there are only two out of 283 nominalisations. Table 9 shows the percentage of nominalisations which function as modifiers in the five twentieth century texts considered here.

Sleigh et al. use this function no more than Thompson did 8 decades earlier, so once again they seem to correspond to an earlier era. Both of the other two recent articles use it to a considerable extent; indeed in the case of Krieger & Sigler more than a quarter of their nominalised processes are used as modifiers, which on any reckoning must be a surprising figure. A difference between these two is that the majority of the Krieger & Sigler examples functioning as modifiers are in the material-human category, while those to be found in Lindsay are mainly material-non-human.

I take it then that the extension of the use of nominalised processes to the function of modifier in the noun group is a significant development, and one that has taken place in the course of the twentieth century.

10. Closing remarks

While it is evident that nothing in the way of definitive conclusions can be made on the basis of such a small mini-sample, I feel that this study does allow us to set up a number of working hypotheses. These are four in number.

1.   There has been an increasing use of nominalised processes in scientific discourse over the last 250 years.

2.   Initially the physical sciences developed more rapidly than the biological sciences in this respect.

mental	verbal	mat (hum)	mat (non-h)	
analysis (5)	disagreement	approach (4)	acceleration	ionization (8)
consideration (2)	explanation	calibration	behaviour	journey
correction	**relational**	check	collision (8)	measure
count (2)	accord	experiment (5)	combination	mixture
definition	addition (2)	inclusion	composition (2)	neutralization
assessment	agreement	inspection	concentration	opening
determination (5)		investigation (5)	contamination (2)	output (3)
interest (2)		measurement (20)	contribution (2)	oxidation
requirement		method	cooling (2)	dissociation
subtraction (3)		modeling	cycle (2)	pressure (10)
verification		procedures	deflection	process (4)
allowance		production	detection (6)	production
observation		remeasurement	development	contamination
assumption		setting	discharge (15)	reaction (4)
extrapolation		study (9)	displacement (2)	recombination (2)
		success	dissociation (3)	reduction (4)
		test (2)	distribution (2)	reinonization
		work (2)	drift	resolution
			effect (7)	restriction
			emission	saturation
			exchange (6)	scattering (5)
			flow (6)	separation
			flux (8)	stripping
			impact (4)	suppression
			indication (2)	throughput
	verbal		influence (3)	transfer (10)
	tokens: 2		interference	transpiration
	types: 2		invariance	undulation
	0.8%			
mental	**relational**	**material (hum)**	**material (non-h)**	
tokens: 28	tokens: 4	tokens: 58	tokens: 161	
types: 15	types: 3	types: 18	types: 56	
11.1%	1.6%	22.9%	63.6%	

Table 8: Examples of grammatical metaphor in Lindsay et al. (1996)

Text	Nominalisations as modifiers
Millikan 1910	0.7%
Thompson 1913	9.4%
Sleigh et al. 1996	8.4%
Lindsay et al. 1996	15%
Krieger & Sigler 1996	27.4%

Table 9: Use of nominalisations as modifiers in the five 20th century texts

3. The difference between the physical and the biological sciences disappeared by the beginning of the twentieth century, that is about the time when the biological sciences became experimental as opposed to purely descriptive.

4. During the course of the twentieth century there has been an extension of the use of nominalised processes from the function of head in the noun group to that of modifier.[4]

Notes

1. An earlier version of this paper was given at the 11th Euro-International Systemic Functional Workshop at Ghent in 1999.

2. In this study I have opted for a simple frequency rate. Halliday, in discussions of lexical density, advocates using the ranking clause as the unit of measurement (Halliday 1989, 1994). I have used the simpler measure for two reasons. First, it is more likely to be easily understood by those less familiar with Systemic Functional Linguistics; and, secondly and more importantly, over the last three centuries the nature of the clause complex has changed considerably. In Boyle's writing, for example, the complexity of the ranking clause is much greater than one would expect to find in contemporary writing. Use of the ranking clause as a unit would therefore have confused the question with additional parameters and exaggerated the rate of increase of the phenomenon under study.

3. In this respect, it is worth noting that Langacker (1985) refers to the cooperative nature of communicative activity in order to justify the theoretical position that "the speaker and the addressee regard themselves as a collective SELF capable of arriving at a shared conceptualization as the semantic value of a linguistic expression" (1985: 123–4).

4. I would like to thank the editors and an anonymous reviewer for comments on an earlier draft of this paper. Those remarks enabled me to make significant improvements to the earlier draft; it goes without saying, however, that I am solely responsible for any shortcomings that remain.

References

Banks, D. (1996) Joseph Banks and the development of scientific language. In: Gerhard Budin (ed.) *Multilinguism in Specialist Communication, Vol 2*. Vienna: IITF/Infoterm. 697–705.

Banks, D. (1997a) Little Lewis and Chaucer's Astrolabe: Instructions for use in the fourteenth century. In: David Banks & Alain Tsédri (eds.) *Sons et Sens, Mélanges offerts à Jean-François Raoult*. Brest: ERLA, Université de Bretagne Occidentale. 56–72.

Banks, D. (1997b) Your very first ESP text (wherein Chaucer explaineth the astrolabe). *ASp* 15.18: 451–460.

Banks, D. (in press) The range of Range: A transitivity problem for systemic linguistics. *Anglophonia.*

Banks, D. (forthcoming) Vers une taxonomie de la nominalisation en anglais scientifique. In: David Banks (ed.) *Le groupe nominal dans le texte spécialisé.* Paris: L'Harmattan.

Baugh, A.C. (1959) *A History of the English Language.* 2nd edition. London: Routledge & Kegan Paul.

Bazerman, C. (1988) *Shaping Written Knowledge: The genre and activity of the experimental article in science.* Wisconsin: University of Wisconsin Press.

Bennett, J. (1971) *Locke, Berkley, Hume, Central Themes.* Oxford: Oxford UP.

Bloor, T. & M. Bloor (1995) *The Functional Analysis of English: A Hallidayan approach.* London: Arnold.

Cameron, H.C. (1952) *Sir Joseph Banks, K.B., P.R.S.: The autocrat of the philosophers.* London: Batchworth Press.

Downing, A. & P. Locke (1992) *A University Course in English Grammar.* Hemel Hempstead: Prentice Hall International.

Eggins, S. (1994) *An Introduction to Systemic Functional Linguistics.* London: Pinter.

Gascoigne, J. (1994) *Joseph Banks and the English Enlightenment: Useful knowledge and polite culture.* Cambridge: Cambridge UP.

Gläser, R. (1995) *Linguistic Features and Genre Profiles of Scientific English.* Frankfurt am Main: Peter Lang.

Gross, A.G. (1990) *The Rhetoric of Science.* Cambridge, MA: Harvard UP.

Halliday, M.A.K. (1987) Language and the order of nature. In: N. Fabb, D. Attridge, A. Durant & C. MacCabe (eds.) *The Lingusitics of Writing: Arguments between language and literature.* Manchester: Manchester UP. 135–154.

Halliday, M.A.K. (1988) On the language of physical science. In: M. Ghadessy (ed.) *Registers of Written English: Situational factors and linguistic features.* London: Pinter. 162–178.

Halliday, M.A.K. (1989) *Spoken and Written Language.* 2nd edition. Oxford: Oxford UP.

Halliday, M.A.K. (1994a) *An Introduction to Functional Grammar.* 2nd edition. London: Arnold.

Halliday, M.A.K. (1994b) The construction of knowledge and value in the grammar of scientific discourse, with reference to Charles Darwin's *The Origin of Species.* In: M. Coulthard (ed.) *Advances in Written Text Analysis.* London: Routledge. 136–156.

Halliday, M.A.K. (1998) Things and relations: Regrammaticising experience as technical knowledge. In: J.R. Martin & R. Veel (eds.) *Reading Science: Critical and functional perspectives on discourses of science.* London: Routledge. 185–235.

Halliday, M.A.K. & J.R. Martin (1993) *Writing Science: Literacy and Discursive Power.* London: The Falmer Press.

Kuhn, T.S. (1970) *The Structure of Scientific Revolutions.* 2nd edition. Chicago: University of Chicago Press.

Locke, J. (1706) [1965] *An Essay Concerning Human Understanding.* Edited by J.W. Yolton. London: Dent.

Martin, J.R., C. Matthiessen & C. Painter (1997) *Working with Functional Grammar.* London: Arnold.

McKinnon, W.T. (1994) Sprat's *History of the Royal Society:* The dawn of English ESP?. In: M. Brekke, Ø. Andersen, T. Dhal & J. Myking (eds.) *Applications and Implications of Current LSP Research, Vol 1.* Bergen: Fagbokforlaget. 495–501.

O'Brian, P. (1987) *Joseph Banks: A life.* London: Collins Harvill.

Perrot, N. (1998) *The Evolution of Grammatical Metaphor in the Life Sciences.* Unpublished Masters' Dissertation, Université de Bretagne Occidentale, Brest.

Ravelli, L. (1988) Grammatical metaphor: An initial analysis. In: E.H. Steiner & R. Veltman (eds.) *Pragmatics, Discourse and Text: Some systemically inspired approaches.* London: Pinter. 133–147.

Thompson, G. (1996) *Introducing Functional Grammar.* London: Arnold.

Corpus references

Banks, J. (1768-71) [1962]. In: J.C. Beaglehole (ed.) *The* Endeavour *Journal of Joseph Banks,* 2 vols. Sydney: Angus & Robertson.

Chaucer, G. (1391) [1975]. A Treatise on the astrolabe. In: F.N. Robinson (ed.) *The Complete Works of Geoffrey Chaucer.* 2nd edition. Oxford: Oxford UP. 545–563.

Darwin, C. (1839) [1989]. *Voyage of the Beagle.* Edited & abbreviated by J. Browne & M. Neve. Harmondsworth: Penguin.

Darwin, C. (1859) [1968]. *The Origin of Species.* Edited by J.W. Burrow. Harmondsworth: Penguin.

Faraday, M. (1838) Experimental researches in electricity – Thirteenth Series. *Philosophical Transactions of the Royal Society* 128: 125–168.

Krieger, K.J. & M.F. Sigler (1996) Catchability coefficient for rockfish estimated from trawl and submersible surveys. *Fishery Bulletin* 94.2: 282–288.

Lindsay, B.G., D.R. Sieglaff, D.A. Schafer, C.L. Hakes, K.A. Smith & R.F. Stebbings (1996) Change Transfer of 0.5-, 1.5-, and 5-keV Protons with Atomic Oxygen: Absolute differential and integral cross sections. *Physical Review A* 53.1: 212–218.

Millikan, R.A. (1910) A new modification of the cloud method of determining the elementary electrical charge and the most probable value of that charge. *The London, Edinburgh and Dublin Philosophical Magazine and Journal of Science* 6th series 19.110: 209–229.

Newton, I. (1730) [1952]. *Opticks, or A Treatise of the Reflections, Refractions, Inflections & Colours of Light.* 4th edition. New York: Dover.

Sleigh, M.A., E.S. Edwards, A.W.G. John & P.H. Burkill (1996) Microplankton community structure in the North-Eastern Atlantic: Trends with latitude, depth and date, between May and early August. *Journal of the Marine Biological Association of the United Kingdom* 76: 287–296.

Thompson, J. (1913) The chemical action of *Bacillus Cloacæ* (Jordan) on citric and malic acids in the presence and absence of oxygen". *Proceedings of the Royal Society* Section B 86: 1–12.

Vickers, B. (ed.) (1987) *English Science, Bacon to Newton.* Cambridge: Cambridge UP.

Part II

Development of metaphor in children

The use of a metaphorical mode of meaning in early language development

Clare Painter
University of New South Wales, Sydney

1. Introduction

Michael Halliday in *Learning How To Mean* (1975: 137–138) suggested that the aim of the young child learning language is to be "good at meaning" and that one key strategy for this is to exploit a metaphorical mode of meaning. At the broadest level we can think of this as involving some sense of meaning transfer – (some aspect of) the meaning associated with one object or context is transferred to something different; for example, when we refer to someone guzzling food enthusiastically as a *pig*, or we talk about someone being *crushed* by bad news. In such cases, there is a duality in the meaning achieved – since recognising the transfer requires recognising both the original context or referent for the meaning and the different but somehow relatable one. Developing metaphorical meaning, then, must be a way of expanding any meaning system – allowing for the same semiotic resources to create additional meanings – and is therefore of key importance to the developing child.

    In recent years, Halliday has greatly enriched our theoretical ideas about metaphor by applying it to the grammar as well as the lexical aspects of language (see e.g. Halliday 1994: Chapter 10). He argues, for example, that a nominalised clause, such as *panic followed the explosion*, is read in a dual way like lexical metaphors. We interpret the meaning in terms of two processes in a sequence: "people panicked when something exploded", but – because these processes are realised in the grammatical form of nouns (*panic, explosion*) configured with a verb (*followed*), we simultaneously read the meaning as two 'things' in a relationship. Halliday (1989: 96) suggests that learning to deploy metaphor through the grammar is something a child will come to in the late primary years, largely as a response to the functional demands of written language. This paper will consider both the earliest instances of metaphorical meaning in a child's language development and evidence for the origins of the use of the kind of grammatical metaphor just described.

The data to be drawn on here were collected naturalistically from my two sons' learning of their mother tongue, English, using audio and notebook recordings of spontaneously occurring speech. From one child, Hal, I collected speech samples from the age of about 7 months to 2 1/2 years, and from his brother Stephen, conversational data from age 2 1/2 to 5 years. Obviously the nature of making meaning at one year of age is vastly different from what goes on at 4 or 5 years, but what links the different examples to be discussed is the sense that major landmarks in language development either constitute or enable some kind of transferred meaning, increasing the semiotic potential and usually also involving the child in bringing the linguistic system closer to consciousness. The child's learning of language through deployment of the metaphorical mode is therefore also a case of learning *about* language (cf. Halliday 1980).

2.   Protolanguage and first words

Let us begin this exploration with the 'protolanguage', since this is the child's first semiotic system (see Halliday 1975, Painter 1984). During this phase, children work up their own idiosyncratic vocalisations or gestures to create signs with meanings like 'I want that' or 'hello Mum' or 'I like that'. For example, Hal at 12 months used to say [ma] with a reaching gesture when he wanted something, while [ae] (with a rise-fall tone) meant 'I like it'. Even where the vocal expression is actually borrowed from the mother tongue, as when Halliday's son Nigel, at 9 – 10 1/2 months, used the expression [bɸ] to mean 'I want my toy bird', it is axiomatic that a protolanguage sign does not allow for any duality or transference of meaning. The nature of the system is that every new meaning requires a new sign-expression. So 'I want my bird' is construed by a vocalisation which can only mean all of this, and 'hallo my bird' or 'I see my bird' – if such meanings existed – would require distinct vocal expressions. In other words, there is no distinguishable element of 'birdness' that is separately coded in a protolinguistic sign available for use in a variety of speech acts or to be transferred to another referent.

However, despite the fact that metaphor would seem to depend on the possibility of naming, something not possible till the advent of genuine words, it could be argued that some kind of metaphorical mode of meaning-making *is* involved earlier than this in the creation of an 'iconic' protolanguage sign, where some behaviour that displays intention or affect is transformed into a semiotic gesture. In Hal's case, there was only one such example, when at thirteen months, he somewhat self-consciously created a sign to share amusement at some bizarre or 'naughty' behaviour, sometimes using it to deflect adult disapproval from his own behaviour. The expression [ae::haeha] was noted at the time as a 'stage laugh' (Painter 1984: 73), and its creation involved transforming a signal of one kind – the spontaneous expression of laughter – into something related but different – a sign expression to construe amusement. The meaning of laughter as a display of positive affect thus provided a stable meaning which could be 'borrowed' to construct a situation semiotically as funny, whether or not those present found it so. While this is not a case of creating metaphor by providing a sign with an additional less literal meaning, perhaps something analogous can be recognised: one kind of signal was being transformed into a communicative sign of a different order by trading on some shared understanding of the original signal. Since, in the case of Halliday's Nigel, the very earliest systematic signs were iconic ones (Halliday 1975), it may well be that the metaphoric mode can come into play at the inception of our creation of a semiotic system. In Hal's case, he certainly seemed to be more consciously aware of the sign construction process in this instance than with his other signs.

Whatever status is given to protolinguistic communication, the first major milestone of language proper is always taken to be the child's first construal of lexical items with a true naming function, something which in principle allows for metaphor as traditionally conceived. In Hal's case the first construal of a lexical item took place at 14 months with the use of *puss*, which was for several weeks his only word. Its status as a lexeme, rather than as a protolinguistic sign, was evident in the fact that it was used in a number of different functional contexts. In particular its non-literal use in imaginative ways made it conclusive that this was a new developmental stage. The family cat was enormously important in his life and one of her favourite places was on the broad window ledge of the living room nestled behind the curtains. Hal was always delighted when the curtains were drawn or moved and she was discovered there. At 14-15 months of age, Hal several times enacted an imaginative analogy to peeping behind the curtain to discover her. Examples 1a, 1b and 1c (where the child's age is noted in years, months and days) show this kind of use:

(1) a. (1;2;6) H is having a bath, sitting on a rubber non-slip mat. He peels up the corner of the bathmat and mimes peeping under it saying *puss*
     b. (1;2;13) H pulls up living room rug, looking under saying *puss*

c. (1;3;01) M is playing peepbo with H, popping quilt over him to hide him before discovering him. H peeps under quilt himself and says *puss* (absolutely aware she is not there).

In general, the word *puss* was not tied to a given context in the way that protolinguistic signs were, and could vary from being a demand, an observation or an occasion of recall. These examples seem to go further, however, in being independent of any specific occasion of observation or interaction. In effect the meaning of 'there's a cat' or 'I find the cat' remained the same but was transferred into an imaginative context detached from any material cat. So the production of the first word – a recognised milestone in language development – made possible for the first time a transferred use in which the representational or 'ideational' meaning[1] of *puss* was shifted from contexts relevant to the 'literal' cat to imaginatively created ones. And in doing this, perhaps the child was also exploring the naming function of mother tongue words and the independence of words from any given here-and-now context – features that make them of a different order from protolanguage signs.

Another landmark with the use of the first word came when Hal could name a picture as well as a thing. Although rarely discussed, this constitutes a significant move when it first occurs since it requires the child to transfer the verbal symbol for a material referent to a semiotic representation of it. For Hal, this took a little time initially and there was a lag of about 5 weeks before his first few words were used to name pictures as well as objects or actions. The delay can be accounted for by the fact that naming a picture constitutes a slight shift in abstraction since a picture itself 'stands for' an object just as a word does. But once having come to understand this and to use the verbal symbol to name the visual one, most nominal word learning (and certainly most overt adult teaching), actually took place via pictures. It was as if it was easier for the child to focus on learning new symbols through the mediation of an alternative semiotic form, because this kept the task of meaning to the forefront of attention. So, as with the other examples cited so far, symbolising appears to come closer to conscious attention when it involves some aspect of transferred meaning.

The use of a word to construe an imaginative context and the use of a word to name a representation rather than a thing are admittedly not what we first think of as metaphors, but they do share some sense of shifting to the non-literal or non-concrete, and because of this are important in the child's language development. A more obvious example of metaphor, however, would be the phenomenon of 'overextension' of early word meaning, where a child uses a mother tongue word for a referent not included in the word's semantic domain in adult language. This is often assumed to reflect the child's different system of valeur, and in some cases this will certainly be the case. But overextensions in the initial phases are often more plausibly interpreted as metaphorical in nature. For example, Melissa Bowerman (1978) reported her daughter from 15 months using *moon* not only for the moon but for referents as varied as half a grapefruit, a lemon segment and the circular dishwasher dial. I would presume these to be metaphorical overextensions – the child focuses on some point of similarity between unlike things and construes that meaning by pressing into service the only lexical resource at her disposal. What children are probably doing in these situations, then, is not to misunderstand the adult domain of signification but to extend their own possibilities for meaning at a point where their expression systems are very limited.

Where Hal used his first word, *puss*, with a referent other than a cat, it was always where some feature of ideational likeness was transferred from its original context. For example, there were a number of occasions when he used the word to construe either the texture of fur or the action of stroking it, which was familiarly associated with his cat, Katy. This can be seen in examples 2a-d:

(2) a. (1;4;21) H approaches collie dog, saying *doggy*. Then puts hand on dog's coat to stroke, saying *puss.*

b. (1;3;0-1;4;14) H occasionally says *puss* when fondling M's or babyminder's hair

c. (1;5;27) H meets black dog and says *doggy, pussy, Katy* (= this is a dog, soft like a cat and (?black) like Katy)

d. (1;7;13) H points at dog and says *doggy*. Points at its eyes and says *eyes*. Reaches to its coat and says *pussy*

e. (1;9;25)
H: pat doggy (as approaches Pekinese)
M: It's all soft isn't it?
H: (patting) pussy (points at dog) doggy

These examples make it clear that the child was not confused about the denotation of *doggy* and *pussy*. The latter word was used here not in its literal meaning of cat, but to construe a likeness between an aspect of a cat and other creatures. Since at this point Hal had very few quality words, certainly no word for 'soft', 'hairy' or 'furry', he was able to create such meanings through the transferred use of the word *puss*. Once again a minimal lexical resource could be used for multiple meanings.

Later, with the move into structures, likeness across differently categorised phenomena could be made more explicit with an utterance such as *chopsticks;*

they like straws, from Hal at 2;2;14, or – from Halliday's Nigel – *Mummy hair like a railway* (Halliday 1975: 138). Part of being good at meaning at any stage of development, then, is to draw creative links between categories treated by the language as distinct.

Likeness across categories was also construed by Hal in a burst of pretend play at the time of learning his first words at about 16 1/2 months. For example he would say *hat* wearing a leaf or a bowl on his head. Here one material thing was given the meaning of another through re-naming in play. In this case, it was not a matter of making a limited semiotic resource serve to construe multiple meanings, but of semiotically expanding the resources of the material world. There might not be a material hat, but a word could endow some other object with that meaning, metaphorising it into a symbol.

In the period from 16 1/2 to 18 months, Hal made the shift from protolanguage to a transitional mother tongue system in earnest, producing what Bloom (1993) refers to as a 'vocabulary spurt'. A further developmental milestone at this point was the possibility of mis-meaning to create a joke, something achieved through the metaphorical mode. For example, Hal used to say *oh-dear* either as a (literal) expression of dismay or as a call for assistance when something went wrong – such as if his ball rolled out of reach under a chair, or he found a bit broken off a toy. But he also occasionally used the sign teasingly, as when he painstakingly built up a tower of pegs, then swooshed them onto the floor, grinning broadly as he declared emphatically *oh-dear*.

The new meaning seems to have the essence of metaphor in that it depends on a shared understanding of the congruent meaning of *oh-dear* in order for the joke to work. Hal here was meaning not only 'this is fun now', but '(as you know) this is really distressing (when we are being literal rather than playful).' Creating a new ironic meaning by transforming the affective value of the utterance in this way clearly gave Hal great pleasure, as did more ideationally oriented occasions, such as when he would gingerly touch his own plastic cup of juice and withdraw his finger sharply, grinning and saying *hot.* Here Hal was playfully making reference to a regular routine of carefully checking adult coffee mugs to see if they were safe to touch.[2] These 'jokes' thus constituted new representations of the situation (as fun), which not only shared his affect of the moment but also showed and shared a self-awareness concerning his predictable affective and behavioural reactions.

According to the account I have given so far, meaning transfer is not a feature of the protolanguage, although the creation of iconic signs has metaphorical aspects and may for some children be the way into semiosis. Certainly the early move out of protolanguage into the mother tongue involves a number of milestones which one way or another rely on a metaphorical extension of a name for a concrete category. In Hal's language, there was firstly the possibility of construing something imaginary, of naming something semiotic rather than material and of re-naming something material for semiotic purposes. Secondly there was the metaphorical extension of the meaning of a word as a way of investigating ideational likeness, and to allow new meanings to be achieved with limited resources. Finally, there was the possibility of playing with meaning to create humour and perhaps to reflect on feelings and behaviour. The results of the metaphorical mode in general then were to extend the possibilities of meaning, particularly in the following three ways: One was in the direction of greater abstraction (e.g. naming the imagined or semiotic), another was towards reflection on semiotic categories (e.g. on how naming creates a category, on features shared by 'different' categories, on the possibility of mis-meaning) while a third direction was to greater self-consciousness about meaning, affect and behaviour (e.g. how situations affect me, how others are affected by my signs).

3.   Grammatical metaphor

Most of the examples given so far have been from a very early transitional stage in the use of the mother tongue, where the child is using one word at a time or simple two-word structures. However, it is not until children are exchanging information with others using the grammar of mood (imperative, declarative, interrogative forms, etc) and the grammar of transitivity (types of process/participant configurations), that they are accorded full status as language users. And once these grammatical systems are established at about age 2 1/2, then a new possibility for metaphor arises – metaphor that exploits grammatical as well as lexical meaning.

The notion of 'grammatical metaphor' was first put forward by Halliday in his *An Introduction to Functional Grammar,* where he suggests that such metaphor may be in terms of either the interpersonal meaning potential or the ideational. In this discussion of ontogenetic trends, however, constraints of space will require us to restrict the focus to the notion of ideational metaphor – that is, the use of language to create transferred and dual strands of meaning in relation to the representation of experience.

To explain the notion of ideational grammatical metaphor, we can first look at the kind of system a child has evolved early in the third year of life. One aspect is that with the move into structures, different classes of words, such as noun, verb or adjective, are established. Halliday argues that these distinctions

are meaningful, and that through them, the grammatical system construes
experience as involving distinguishable aspects:

> In creating a formal distinction such as that between verb and noun, the
> grammar is theorising about processes; that a distinction can be made, of a
> very general kind, between two facets: the process itself, and entities that
> are involved in it. (Halliday 1998: 190)

Here Halliday implies that through the central unit of grammatical
structure – the clause – language not only construes a distinction between
entities and processes, but sees a meaningful figure of experience as involving
the participation of entities in some process. An example would be the clause
The boy kicked a football, where two nominal groups are configured with a
verbal group. Meanings of location or manner and the like, 'circumstances'
which can also be part of the configuration, are of course typically realised
adverbially or by a prepositional phrase, while sequences of such configurations
will be brought into a grammatical relation with one another through
conjunctions.

Thus, as Halliday (1998: 190) explains, "[Ideational] experience is
construed into meaning in the grammar of English along the [...] lines [of
Table 1]":

	semantic		lexico-grammatical
ranks:	sequence (of figures)	realised by	clause complex
[i.e. hierarchy	figure	"	clause
of units]	element (of figure)	"	group or phrase
types of element	process	"	verbal group
	participating entity	"	nominal group
	circumstance	"	adverbial group or prepositional phrase
	relator	"	conjunction

Table 1: The congruent construal of experience in English
(after Halliday 1998: 190)

The relations shown between ideational semantics and grammar in Table 1
are non-metaphorical: they are the congruent or literal relations that will be
found almost without exception in the speech of two-year-olds and their
caregivers.[3] That is to say, in the language of adults and children speaking
together there is a high consistency between the size of grammatical unit and the
meaning construed, and between the class of word or group and the kind of

meaning construed. However, the consistency is not absolute, and it is worth briefly noting the few early uses of language that disturb this congruent mapping between semantics and grammar, since they provide a model for the child of the possibility of the more creative mis-matching between semantics and grammar which Halliday terms grammatical metaphor. The latter is exemplified in an expression like *The investigation provoked an outcry*, where the nouns construe processes rather than entities, and the verb construes a relation of causality rather than an action. Thus we read the meaning in a double way: we construe processes in a causal sequence – that of people speaking out after someone investigates, but reconstrue them metaphorically as 'things' which can participate in the 'action' of provoking. Such grammatically metaphorical expressions are not found in the speech of two-year-olds.

One exception to the congruent relation between semantics and grammar in early language, however, is the use by the child of everyday English clause structures which have already coded a mismatch between lexical class and grammatical function (see Torr, this volume). In Halliday's (1994: 146) terminology, these are the Process^Range structures of everyday speech, such as *have a bath, have a cuddle, do a pee, make a big mess, do a big laugh, do a big kick,* all of which examples come from the speech of Hal or Stephen between 2 and 2 1/2 years of age. In these structures, the verbal element does not construe the action except in the most general terms. Instead it is the nominal element that actually specifies the nature of the action, construing it grammatically as though it were a thing.

A second situation where the congruent patterns between semantics and grammar are disturbed is in the play between ranks that occurs when one clause is embedded inside another. In my children's conversations, this was first observed in routines with *where?* or with the mental processes of perception *see* and *look,* as in the following examples (where embedded clauses are enclosed in square brackets):

(3) a. (2;0;13) H: (reading book) Where's [[a man shouting]]?
          Where's [[a man eating a biscuit]]?
     b. (2;0;20) H: Where's [[elephants crying]]?
     c. (2;0;4) H: See [[marmalade allgone]]
     d. (2;4;12)
          H: See [[mummy's doing]]
          H: Gonna see [[what's in there]]
          H: Look [[what daddy's done]]
     e. (2;7;7) S: See [[what do my cheeks]]

Early examples with *where?* were in the reading of picture books where Hal anticipated some favourite scene, and are interesting in that what is nominalised is a non-finite clause that construes verbally a visual representation of a 'figure' – that is, a process together with the participants involved in it. Perhaps this is the first context for nominalised clauses because the image itself is already a way of freezing the experience, making it static, observable and tangible and therefore more legitimately construed as a participant. Similarly, it is in the nature of a perceptual process that what is seen – like what is represented as a picture – can involve a scene rather than a single entity.

These examples seem to be the earliest ways in which an English-speaking child gains some experience in the unhinging of ideational semantics and grammar that allows for much more radical metaphorical reconstrual of experience. I can find no evidence, though, of my children having any consciousness at this point about the lack of congruence between semantics and grammar, nor do they appear to use these routinised forms to explore and extend their meaning-making creatively. I would not want therefore to claim that children are engaged in exploiting grammatical metaphor at this point. The significance of these kinds of utterances lies rather in providing the child with some limited early experience which embodies this potential of the semiotic, albeit in a 'frozen' form.

At what point, then, and under what impetus is ideational grammatical metaphor first used by children learning the language? The earliest context for nominalisation that is not entirely routine appears to be the use of Postmodifiers within the nominal group – that is, the use of a Modifier after the Head noun. In Stephen's speech the first use of a Postmodifier was to identify for the addressee some specific referent for which he had no appropriate lexical item. To achieve this goal he used a general word as Head and provided details in a Postmodifying clause or phrase, as in *Where's the thing [[go in there]]?* (2;7;1). Where a more experienced speaker could have specified the thing in question with a noun, Stephen had to define it in terms of its familiar location or function. As a result, an event or 'figure' was construed as a quality of thing, introducing a small disturbance into the congruent patterning in terms of rank. So just as limited vocabulary resources may be initially overcome by metaphorical 'overextensions', a lack of vocabulary put pressure on the child in this case to use grammatical resources to substitute for a lexical meaning, by exploiting the potential for embedding in the nominal group structure.

A more thoroughgoing exploitation of the grammar's potential for non-congruent realisation of semantics did not, however, take place until after age three and was precipitated by the child's use of the grammar to explore the semantics. This involved making use of the self-reflexive capacity of language, its ability to act as its own metalanguage, particularly by means of the relational grammar of classifying and defining clauses.

In the first place, exploring the semantics had meant that as well as classifying observed things with utterances like *That's a dog; That's a tractor* and so on, Stephen began, after age three, to use the grammar to relate one symbolic category to another, in clauses like *Is a platypus an animal?* or *Flood means windy,* exploring linguistic meaning relations without reference to material observation. And having taken this step, metaphor then came into play, as processes, circumstances and figures began to be re-construed as entities for the purposes of exploration. For example, the relevant meaning being explored might be an action just as well as an entity, but in order to produce definitions, it was necessary to construe the action into a participant role in a relational clause, as in examples 4a and 4b:

(4)   a. (3;7;5) (M asking S to put head right into water to get hair wet for champoo)
         M: C'mon. Drown
         S: Not drown!! Drown is [[go down to the bottom and be dead]]

      b. (3;9;30) (S approaching M with precarious duplo structure)
         S: Balance means [[you hold it on your fingers and it doesn't go on the floor]]

It can be argued that the process of identifying one meaning with another, as is done in these clauses, is itself an exercise in metaphorical thinking, but what I am drawing attention to here is the way the multi-level semiotic is exploited to produce new meanings. That is, we read the embedded element simultaneously as participant – the role of a nominal element – and as a figure, an act, a configuration of an event, – the role of a clause.

By the time another year had passed, Stephen was trying to understand the semantic domain of time, a rather more abstract one than that of concrete actions. At age three and a half, he had taken up, without much understanding, expressions from adult speech like *for a long time; we haven't got time* and *next week.* When, at age four and a half, Stephen tried to come to terms with this semantic domain, he constructed time expressions, not in their congruent form as temporal circumstances, but as participants in defining clauses, such as, *Is a week seven sleeps?; Is a week a long time?* (4;5;7). In this way a meaning of extent was transferred from its circumstantial role to become a metaphorical 'thing' that could be brought into a synonymy relation with another thing. Thus

Stephen created metaphorical transformations of circumstances as well as processes, as he packaged meanings in such a way that they could be brought into a relationship for the purpose of better understanding language.

Another move to package meanings to enable metalinguistic reflection involved grammatical metaphor that went further than the nominalisations so far described. It involved the transformation of a logical link and the construal of textual grammatical metaphor (see Martin 1992: 416). The latter includes the metaphorical use of a reference word like *that* which occurs when its 'pointing' function is transferred from indicating a concrete referent or a linguistic thing, to construing a fact, an abstraction created by language. An example of logical and textual grammatical metaphor from Stephen's speech is when he discussed the categorisation of a plane, saying *It's got two wings there and two wings there ... That means [[it's a biplane]]* (3;9;21). A more congruent way to mean this is to say *It's got two wings there and two wings there, so I know it's a biplane.* But in Stephen's text, the logical link of causality which congruently relates two figures has been construed instead as the process *means*[4] which is configured with two metaphorical participants:

That	means	[[it's a biplane]]
participant	process	participant

Moreover, one of the participants here is the reference word *that* standing for the abstraction: 'the fact that it's got two wings there'. This reconstruing of experience so that logical relations are realised as processes, and participants are facts rather than entities, is developmentally significant in that it creates a form of language that is quite abstract in comparison with most preschool talk.

The impetus for these developments, in Stephen's case, was his reflection on the system of meaning he was building. In addition, his exposure to new meaning systems – those of writing and of numbers – took him even further along the path of grammatical metaphor and abstraction. His experience with written text led him at about three and a half to produce nouns like *story* and *joke*[5] and the names of letters and numbers, as in the following kinds of examples:

(5) a. (3;8;16) S: Ireland start with a I
     b. (3;11;07)
        S: Is fifty a number?
        F: Yeah
        S: How does it go?
        F: It comes after forty-nine
        S: A hundred comes after forty-nine

In 5b, the participants are abstract categories like *a number* and the action processes *go* and *come* have been reconstrued metaphorically as relations, allowing numeration to begin to be understood through the metaphor of relative locations.

While all the instances of language use I have given in this section are still a long way from the abstract and sophisticated forms of written language, they are important as early examples of exploiting the semiotic potential to engender additional meanings by reconstruing experience using grammatically metaphorical forms. Any such re-construal allows for new meanings to be created against the background of an earlier pattern of construal – the congruent or 'literal'. The impetus for these new meanings was always the task of using the grammar to explore the semiotic itself, something facilitated by playing about with the established and understood relations between levels of the linguistic system.

4   Interpreting metaphor in the grammar of *saying*

In describing Stephen's entry into grammatical metaphor, I have already mentioned how his encounter with the world of written text during his fifth year was one factor encouraging developments. It was long before this, however, at about age 2 1/2, that Stephen began to explore the relation between spoken and written symbols, very explicitly seeing it as a metaphorical one.

Evidence for this comes from Stephen's behaviour at age 2 1/2 when he began pointing to a printed word and suggesting that it was "the same as" a spoken word. For example:

(6)   (2;7;1) S: That's same as Daddy (pointing to a word in book) that's same as the moon? Where's same as the moon?

A week or two later, however, he was following adult models and using the verb *says* to construe the relation of identity:

(7)   a. (2;7;13) (S and M looking at Peter Rabbit)
        S: (pointing to a random word) That says Peter Rabbit
      b. (2;7;19)
        S: (pointing to shopping bag with an S on) That says Stephen?
        M: No, that's says Food Plus; that's the name of the shop

Using Halliday's (1994) terminology, we can say that *say* up till this point had been familiar in Stephen's language as a verbal process construing speech from a human Sayer, in utterances such as:

Sally	says	there's babies in there
Sayer	Process: verbal	Locution

But in the case of *That says Peter Rabbit, say* functions as a relational process construing a relationship of identity between two participants (having the roles of Token and Value in Halliday's (1994) account of grammar):

That	says	Peter Rabbit
Token	Process: relational	Value

In terms of the evolved and adult grammar, this relational use of *say* is quite congruent, not a case of grammatical metaphor, but from the child's perspective, perhaps the prior meaning of 'giving utterance to/speaking' was transferred to a printed sign in order to construe the written symbol as standing for the spoken one. The metaphor of verbalising implicit in the relational use of *say* was indeed brought to the fore on at least one occasion early on when Stephen appeared to be using the verb as a verbal process by having the spoken word 'quoted' by the written one with distinct intonation:

(8)   a. (2;7;24)
        M: (identifying jar) The blue jar with the yellow label.
        S: Oh there; (points) its got words on; (?that) says "shop"

Certainly, a year later written symbols were again somewhat awkwardly construed as verbal Sayers that quoted speech, as in 8b:

(8)   b. (3;5;7) (S jumps off the side of the pram slope at zoo)
        S: (points at a notice) It's not for Mummies and the word says "For big boys; these things are for jumping for big boys"

Transitional texts like 8a and 8b are important because they show the child explicitly taking the metaphorical relation between spoken and written symbol ('X stands for Y') as itself a metaphor for human speech. And it is only by seeing the metaphorical relation between speaking and communicating in print that a child comes to accept that written texts are semiotic sources equivalent (grammatically) to human speakers. After age four, Stephen routinely viewed texts in this way, as in:

(9)   (4;7;21) (M and S are reading about birds in picture book)
        S: Does it tell what he's doing?

Again, English grammar treats it as a literal fact that books, timetables, clocks and other semiotic artefacts of our world speak to us, since any semiotic source can be comfortably construed into the Sayer role in a verbal process clause. But for the young child developing that grammar it requires seeing the process of information-giving via print as metaphorically related to the human activity of speaking. Only then does the child's grammar distinguish mental processes like *think* from verbal ones like *tell* by requiring a conscious participant only for the former. So the use of *say* as a relational process and the use of non-human Sayers with *say* in a verbal process, neither of which we see as metaphorical in adult language, can only be made sense of by the child by seeing the metaphorical relation between written and spoken symbols and between the speech exchange and written communication.

To sum up, then, on the path of metaphor in the ideational grammar: I have argued that Stephen's explorations of the meaning-making system produced the first embeddings, resulting in nominalised and abstract participants. These explorations produced occasional textual and logical metaphor also, thus exploiting the meaning potential to create a real if very limited degree of grammatical metaphor. Stephen's language development was pushed more quickly in these directions by his exposure to the forms of written symbols, which also led him into the adult construal of semiosis, which adopts the metaphor of written texts and other semiotic artefacts as having the power of speech. All these developments were surely foundational in providing a basis for literacy development, although the development of grammatical metaphor to manage the textual demands of written text organisation would still be several years in the future.

5.   Conclusion

This examination of the child's use of 'transferred meaning' in both the early and later preschool years suggests strongly that metaphor is indeed a fundamental and powerful mode of meaning for the child. It may be involved in the very creation of a communicative sign before the child has access to the meanings and expressions of the mother tongue, and once the learner has embarked upon the shared language of the community, it enables the creation of new meanings – 'referential', imaginative and humorous – by playing with the pre-established or congruent relations between context, meaning and expression. With the move into grammar, similes can be pursued in the exploration of sameness and difference that is fundamental to category formation, and a little later, the first steps are taken in the direction of ideational grammatical metaphor. This involves exploiting the potential for playing with the established, congruent relations between the semantics and its expression in lexico-grammatical form.

Finally, since the essence of metaphor is one thing standing for another, and the referential or ideational function is one of the fundamental raisons d'etre of the semiotic, it is not surprising to find that metaphor is built into the language system itself as well as creatively exploited in its use. In this account we have considered briefly some of the metaphorical relations inherent in the grammar of process types, and how one child gradually adopted these taken-for-granted metaphors into his own meaning system.

Traditionally, we associate metaphor with the language of poetry and literature and with our more consciously crafted symbolic articulations, a fact that also has an echo in this ontogenetic account. From one perspective, it is true that the data suggest that metaphorical transference or transformation is an inevitable, natural and ubiquitous aspect of early language learning and use, motivated by the need to form categories and to communicate with a limited meaning resource. At the same time, however, metaphorical uses of the meaning system did very often seem to be associated with a more conscious reflection by the child on the nature of the semiotic and a desire to explore it and understand it. So while there was no intention on the child's part to produce memorable text, there was frequently an intention to probe or focus on the nature of the linguistic system (and associated semiotics), which resulted in stretching the potential of the language and producing novel forms.

Notes

1. Halliday's term for 'content' meaning, as opposed to illocutionary force.

2. It is not surprising then that experimental work should find that "even children as young as 6 or 7 appear able in principle to execute non-literal comprehension processes in favourable circumstances" (Ackerman 1983: 507).

3. On the other hand, very young children may be exposed to a considerable degree of non-congruence in adult realisations of the interpersonal semantics (e.g. of speech function), and in Hal's own language some limited interpersonal grammatical metaphor was possible as soon as the mood system was established (see Painter 1984: 214–9).

4. Evidence from Stephen's language suggesting that *That means* was a participant + process structure and not simply formulaic expression synonymous with *so* is discussed in Painter (1999: 112–3).
5. Terms like *question* and *order* which refer to spoken language forms were not produced for another year.

References

Ackerman, Brian P. (1983) Form and function in children's understanding of ironic utterances. *Journal of Experimental Child Psychology* 35: 487–508.

Bloom, Lois (1993) *The Transition from Infancy to Language: Acquiring the power of expression.* Cambridge: Cambridge UP.

Bowerman, M. (1978) The acquisition of word meaning. In: N. Waterson & C.E. Snow (eds.) *The Development of Communication.* New York: Wiley. 263–287.

Halliday, M.A.K. (1975) *Learning How to Mean.* London: Arnold.

Halliday, M.A.K. (1980) Three aspects of children's language development: learning language, learning through language, learning about language. In: Y.M. Goodman, M.M. Haussler & D.S. Strickland (eds.) *Oral and Written Language Development. Impact on schools (Proceedings from the 1979-80 Impact conferences.)* N.p.: International Reading Association and National Council of Teachers of English. 7–19.

Halliday, M.AK. (1989) *Spoken and Written Language.* London: Oxford UP.

Halliday, M.A.K. (1994) *Introduction to Functional Grammar.* 2nd edition. London: Arnold.

Halliday, M.A.K. (1998) Things and relations: Regrammaticising experience as technical knowledge. In: J.R. Martin & R. Veel (eds.) *Reading Science: Critical and functional perspectives on discourses of science.* London: Routledge. 185–235.

Martin, J.R. (1992) *English Text: System and structure.* Amsterdam: Benjamins.

Painter, Clare (1984) *Into the Mother Tongue.* London: Pinter.

Painter, Clare (1999) *Learning through Language in Early Childhood.* London: Cassell. [London: Continuum 2000.]

The emergence of grammatical metaphor
Literacy-oriented expressions in the everyday speech of young children

Jane Torr
Macquarie University

Alyson Simpson
Australian Catholic University

1. Introduction

This study has been designed to explore how certain expressions used by preschool children in their spontaneous interactions with caregivers serve to orient the children towards understandings about literacy. It is widely understood that book-sharing sessions with pre-school children can potentially foster book handling skills, understandings about print and concepts of narrative structure (Meek 1988, Snow 1993, Sutherland and Arbuthnot 1991, Vukelich 1993). However, other linguistic expressions which occur during everyday interactions (not necessarily involving literature) may also be significant in terms of later literacy development. Snow, for example, asserts that the following oral language skills are crucial for later literacy learning:

> understanding the lexical and grammatical strategies for adjusting to a nonpresent audience, identifying the perspective of the listener so as to provide sufficient background information, knowing the genre-specific rules for various forms of talk such as narrative and explanation, and so on (Snow 1993: 15).

In order to experience success at school, children must develop the ability to use a range of discipline areas, and this involves the ability to organise knowledge in certain ways, including metaphorical forms (an important aspect of the "genre-specific rules" mentioned by Snow in the quote above).

This study will focus on the development of certain language patterns which appear to orient children towards literacy understandings, particularly the use of range of expressions which Halliday (1993), Martin (1990) and others refer to as *grammatical metaphor*. Grammatical metaphor (particularly nominalisation) is considered relevant to literacy development, as it is a major linguistic resource in the construction of written language and technical registers. It has been suggested that the ability to use language in this way typically begins around nine or ten years of age (Halliday 1994, Derewianka 1995). It is not well understood, however, where this ability originates in the earlier language experiences of children.

The general understanding of preschool children's language is that it is simple, direct and uncomplicated. It has been suggested by Halliday (1994: 342) that metaphorical modes of expression are characteristic of almost all adult speech but not young children's speech. The expectation is that young children's oral language will not contain complicated lexicogrammatical patterns such as grammatical metaphor, as the children have not yet developed the linguistic facility to construct and interpret them. This study seeks to explicate more fully the manner in which these lexicogrammatical patterns develop. Such an exploration may enhance our potential for fostering children's understanding and experience of literacy-related language patterns in the preschool years. The functional-systemic perspective (Halliday 1994) we have adopted in this study enables us to observe closely the grammatical forms with which children communicate and the social semiotic environment in which the interpretation of these forms is grounded. This perspective allows us to relate, within one theoretical framework, several developments which may otherwise appear unconnected, such as the development of linguistic play and metalinguistic understandings.

2.   This study

An investigation into the development of grammatical metaphor as a resource for constructing literacy-oriented meanings in the language of young children must do the following:

a.   determine what kinds of metaphors are used by children at various developmental stages,

b.   determine what kinds of related (non-metaphorical) grammatical develop-
      ments foreshadow such uses, and

c.   explore the contexts in which they typically occur.

For example, there appears to be a link between the use of grammatical
metaphor and the negotiation of needs. In the context of children playing board
games, ideational grammatical metaphors are used mostly to claim space or
rights, as the metaphor which turns a *process* into a *thing* creates an entity which
can be possessed, out of an action which cannot. The two relational statements
it's my turn and *it's my piece* are both providing information and claiming
possession, yet the 'piece' may be held in the child's hand, whereas the 'turn' is
a grammatical creation which has been constructed through words as a
commodity which can be traded, disputed and claimed. Such expressions
provide the child with experience of nominalised language in routine contexts
which are emotionally salient in terms of the child's assertion within the family.
      Specifically, this study has the following aims:

1.   to explore when and in what contexts children begin to develop the ability
      to produce the various kinds of grammatical metaphor, and

2.   to consider the significance of such developments in terms of children's
      literacy understandings and ability to handle abstract concepts of
      increasing complexity.

3.   Interpersonal grammatical metaphor: Ontogenesis in early childhood

Halliday's basic definition of a grammatical metaphor is that it is a kind of
linguistic manoeuvre which involves "variation in the expression of meanings"
(Halliday 1994: 341). He states:

> In all the instances that we are treating as grammatical metaphor, some
> aspect of the structural configuration of the clause, whether in its ideational
> function or its interpersonal function or in both, is in some way different
> from that which would be arrived at by the shortest route – it is not, or was
> not originally, the most straight-forward coding of the meanings selected
> (Halliday 1994: 366).

The whole notion of congruence is a contentious one among linguists;
however, for the purposes of this study we have, following Halliday (1994),
regarded expressions where there is a disparity between semantic and lexicogrammatical strata as a form of interpersonal grammatical metaphor. For

example, *it's my turn* (said by a child) is certain to be understood as an imperative (commanding) utterance, even though it is realised as a declarative form.

For our purposes, we are also interested in other grammatical transformations which may be made by speakers. A more complex form of interpersonal grammatical metaphor occurs when a speaker's opinion is coded, not as a modal element within a clause (for example *it could be a safe move*) but as a separate projecting clause in a hypotactic clause complex (for example *I think that's a safe move*). This example is metaphorical because it represents the expression of modality, *I think*, as being the substantive proposition.

4.   Ideational grammatical metaphor: Ontogenesis in early childhood

Ideational metaphors, such as nominalisation, typically occur in scientific and technical discourse. It has been assumed that ideational metaphors will not be found in the speech of young children and their caregivers because of the level of abstraction which they realise. However, certain nominalised expressions, usually referred to as "dead metaphors", may occur in everyday speech within the home. As the term suggests, these are metaphors which have passed into practice from long overuse, and are no longer read as metaphorical substitutions. Examples include common expressions such as *have dinner* and *take a bath* (see also Derewianka, this volume). The processes of *bathing* or *dining* are treated grammatically as if they are things which can be possessed or taken. Although such examples appear simple, the concept of technicalisation as a discursive practice is relevant here, as well as in more technical fields such as science, as it constructs new entities in language which did not exist before.

Examining grammatical metaphor from an ontogenetic perspective, Halliday suggests that there is a progression in the way that children learn to use metaphorical language (1994: xviii and elsewhere). He proposes that children move through three broad developmental phases, termed *generalisation, abstraction* and *metaphor*. First, at about two years of age the child develops the ability to generalise on the basis of experience, for example *car* may refer to vehicles of different shapes, sizes, colours and capacity. This ability to generalise enables the child to organise his or her experience according to similarities and differences between perceived phenomena.

Secondly, at approximately five to six years of age, the child begins to grapple with abstract concepts. This may become evident when the child questions the adult's use of a term which has a non-concrete referent, as in the following example.

Child (4:11):	You know the car outside, do you think they may be burglars?
Mother:	Oh, I don't think so, but I guess you can never really know for sure.
Child:	Do they only come at night?
Mother:	No, they sometimes come in the day. Their main goal is to come when no-one is home.
Child:	(pause) What's goal?
Mother:	Um ... um ... it means ... what they really want to happen.
Child:	(simultaneously) Is it something they have at their house?

The mother is using the term *goal* with a non-literal meaning. The child's question indicates a beginning recognition that his own (concrete) interpretation is not viable in this context. The recognition is important as the ability to handle abstract concepts is seen as a necessary precursor to literacy development.

Thirdly, at approximately nine to ten years of age, children begin to produce genuine ideational grammatical metaphors (particularly nominalisations) in their oral and written language (Halliday 1993, 1994). Derewianka (1995: 173; this volume) provides the following example:

Father: Yes. What would you say? A lot of ... **we export a lot of**
Child (10:00): We are also **a big exporter of natural gas**.

Concerning the manner in which children move through these developmental phases, it is clear that interpersonal types of metaphor appear much earlier in children's language than ideational types of metaphor. However, the nature of the transition from interpersonal to ideational is not well understood at this stage. This study has been designed to explore in more detail young children's use of grammatical expressions which may be metaphorical in nature, and to provide an overview of the age at which such expressions begin to be used by the child. Given the central role played by language in the learning process, and the importance of ideational grammatical metaphor for the child's later success in formal schooling, the child's ability to develop and use metaphorical forms relates closely to the overall social, intellectual and linguistic development of the child. The child's development of metaphor cannot be dissociated from the sociocultural context in which it occurs.

5.   Analytical framework

This study has drawn on data obtained from extensive longitudinal diary studies of five children; Heather and Toby are siblings from one family, and Carla,

Anna and David are siblings from another family. The data were recorded using audiotape recorders and handwritten observations during everyday spontaneous interactions in the home. The data include conversations between the siblings of each family, their parents and close relatives.

Heather's language was recorded over a 30 month period, from the age of 3 years and 6 months (3:6) to 5 years and 9 months (5:9). Approximately 10 hours of videotape and 40 hours of audiotape were collected.

Toby's language was recorded over a 27 month period, from the age 1 year and 9 months (1:9) to 4 years (4:0). Approximately 10 hours of videotape and 40 hours of audiotape were recorded.

Carla's language was recorded over a 21 month period, from the age of 2 and a half years (2:6) to 4 years and 3 months (4:3). Approximately 98 hours of audiotaped conversation were recorded.

Anna's language was recorded over a 32 month period, from 10 months of age (0:10) until 2 years and 6 months (2:6). Approximately 95 hours of audiotaped conversation were recorded.

David's language was recorded over a 24 month period, from 3 years (3:0) to 5 years and 2 months (5:2). Approximately 48 hours of audiotaped data were recorded.

The data were analysed for the presence of interpersonal and ideational grammatical metaphors in the children's speech. An expression was included in the analysis only if it had appeared in the child's linguistic repertoire on three separate occasions.

Each child is from a middle class social group, and given the significant influence of socioeconomic status on literacy practices (e.g. Bernstein 1996, Brice Heath 1983, Hasan 1991, Williams 1995, Schieffelin & Ochs 1986 and others), we acknowledge that there is limited difference in these terms between the data sets, and that data from other socioeconomic groups might produce different results. The actual interactional contexts included the casual conversations accompanying everyday household activities and routines, story-sharing sessions and the talk surrounding board games. Clearly such registerial differences will have some consequences for the type and frequency of linguistic choices made.

The classification of utterances into different types of metaphor is, of course, interpretive to a degree. An utterance was considered to be a genuine grammatical metaphor if, and only if, corresponding non-metaphorical forms also appeared in the child's system at any particular stage, thus suggesting that the child was indeed making a choice of metaphorical meanings in a particular context. For this study we refer primarily for our criteria for assignment to the analysis in Halliday (1994: Chapter 10).

Two other aspects of linguistic development have been included in the analysis, as they appear to relate closely to the development of metaphor. These are: (1) the child's use of modal expressions (e.g. *can, could, shall, should, may, must, might* etc), and (2) the developing use of *transcategorised* elements (the use of morphemes to change the grammatical class of a word e.g. verb *jog* to noun *jogger*).

These aspects, while not metaphorical themselves, are considered relevant in an exploration of metaphor for the following reasons. Modality in the adult language is a highly elaborated part of the grammar, providing speakers with many choices for the expression of their own opinions as to the probability that an event will occur (in contexts of information-exchange) or their assessment of the degree of obligation involved (in contexts of demand). When a small child expresses a demand *Could you put those back, could you?* as opposed to the more straightforward *Put those back*, there is evidence of a developing awareness of the subjectivity of another — the modality is used to enhance the possibility that the demand will be met. The development of modality allows the child to pack more information into the clause, especially expressions of opinion, doubt and point of view. The awareness of the other as a separate being whose consciousness may only be accessed through verbal processes appears to be an important feature of the development of abstract thinking (see Hasan 1991). In other words, the development of modality involves an ability to think in a certain manner which is fundamental to academic inquiry:

> The various dimensions of modality [...] may be ultimately traced back to the effect of a single fundamental human trait on language and thought. This trait [is] a basic worldview according to which it is possible to conceive of things being otherwise [...] (Perkins 1983: 162).

As the development of prediction is viewed as a key element in literacy, then analysis for modality, which constructs an explicit consideration of social relationships negotiated through obligation and probability in the child's language, is vital to any study of literacy-oriented expressions.

It is suggested that the child's ability to verbalise possibility is a precursor to taking up a point of view necessary in a reader, someone who can predict. For example, in a book such as *Would you rather* by John Burningham, children are presented with varying adventurous contexts to examine, with minimal text but with the key question modulated to allow for imaginative play. This can be seen in the following example: *Would you rather be ... covered in jam, soaked in water or pulled through the mud by a dog?* The child is encouraged to think about what she or he *might* do. *Rosie's Walk* by Pat Hutchins is a book which depends on the child reading the text against illustrations; the child is invited to guess what might happen next. Thus these texts demand a level of literacy which incorporates a sophisticated understanding of modality and the child's use of modality indicates his or her potential orientation to literacy events.

As mentioned earlier, transcategorisations are considered to be relevant in an exploration of the origins of metaphor, because they frequently involve a transformation from a 'process' to a 'thing', and thus may constitute a precursor to later grammatical metaphor (see Derewianka 1995: 115; this volume). In this example from a child (4:11), looking at the sky, *You know the light clouds, are they just the shining of the sun?,* the process *shining* is expressed as a nominal element *the shining*.

6.   Trends evident in the data

Our study indicates that pre-school children are capable of sophisticated levels of linguistic manipulation and that the interpersonal function is indeed a very important one for the child's development of grammatical metaphor. The interpersonal function is crucially involved in the adoption and assignment of speech roles, and the giving and receiving of goods and services and information. An analysis of interpersonal grammatical metaphor in our subjects suggests a developing awareness of the other, particularly in contexts where issues of control, power and possession are at stake. Thus developments here relate to subsequent school and literacy-related abilities such as the ability to assert one's point of view and recognise and interpret alternative viewpoints in argument, analysis and debate.

In terms of ideational grammatical metaphor, no genuinely productive forms of nominalisation were found in the children's language before five years. However, children's use of transcategorised forms increased after the age of three, suggesting a nominalising *orientation* which may foreshadow subsequent development of genuine ideational metaphors in late primary school.

Below we have provided a summary of the key developments which appear to relate, either directly or indirectly, to children's subsequent ability to produce and interpret grammatical metaphor in the later years of primary schooling.

6.1.   Children from 1:8 to 2:0 years

This period in children's linguistic development has been termed Phase II or the Transition period (Halliday 1975). During this period, the child has not developed an adult-like Mood system, so it would seem most unlikely that metaphorical forms of any kind would be discernible at this very early period of development, and indeed this was the case. Yet there were two areas suggestive of some ability to engage in transference of meanings, which is the core feature of subsequent understandings of grammatical metaphor.

(i) *Demands for* goods and services using the processes *want* and *have* contrasted with more direct demands using lexical items for the objects or actions desired. For example, imperative-like forms (e.g. *help! read book! drink!*) alternated with demands using *want* or *have* which were more statement-like (e.g. *want Playschool! want look! have apple!*). Here, in emotionally salient contexts, is the first evidence of what Derewianka terms "unhingeing" of the semantics and the lexicogrammar (Derewianka 1995: 107). In this data, *want* and *have* appeared at approximately the same time as early imperative forms.

In these examples, the child is choosing to express his/her demands in statement-like form. Suprasegmental features such as intonation, loudness and voice quality may also carry an "imperative" meaning in such statements. In other words, like adult forms where there is an apparent mismatch between speech function and grammatical realisation, the child is both providing some information about his/her own subjective desires, and also acting on the addressee in an indirect manner. Although caution must be exercised in attributing adult-like intentions to such utterances, nevertheless they occur in emotionally turbulent contexts and appear to be different from more straight-forward demands for goods and services.

(ii) *Linguistic play*, involving the deliberate mis-naming of objects, was observed during this period, for example: Toby (1:10) and mother are looking at picture book. Toby points to illustration of cheese and says laughingly *butter*. Mother says *No, it's cheese*, to which Toby, smiling broadly, repeats *butter*.

While Crystal (1995) and others have documented the importance of language play, in particular phonetic play, to reading development, this study suggests that language play may also relate to subsequent literacy development in the less direct but crucial sense of orienting children towards the potentiality of language to be used metaphorically, in terms described above. Examples of deliberate misnaming have also been observed in naturalistic studies from related disciplines such as psychology (e.g. Dunn 1988: 19). Such behaviours may be interpreted within functional-systemic theory as an embryonic form of the later transference of meaning which is involved in productive grammatical metaphor and significant in terms of linguistic development in middle childhood. Almost as soon as a grammatical system appears, it may be manipulated for playful and imaginative purposes. Furthermore, the above examples, involving as they do a deliberate distortion, require an understanding of another's viewpoint. The capacity to make such "jokes" relies on an understanding that the mother's point of view is not necessarily shared by the child.

6.2. Children from 2:0 to 3:0 years

By two and a half years, most children have adopted the main features of the mother tongue language. The adult Mood system is now regularly used to convey speech functional meanings, with Subject and Finite systematically used to express declarative, interrogative and imperative Mood.

It is during this period that the interpersonal metaphors involving a mismatch between speech functional meaning and grammatical form, fore-shadowed in the previous period, become more fully established, particularly in demanding contexts involving the process *want*, for example *I want another card* (= Give me another card). The declarative Mood is realising the speech function Command. In Anna's language, *want* forms were used much more frequently than imperative forms, although this may have been an individual strategy on her part, rather than a general developmental trend.

During this period modal forms first appear, usually in contexts involving demands for goods and services, for example *Can you help me?* as an alternative to the direct imperative *Help me,* or in the expression of constraints on behaviour, for example *have [to] blow* (= have to blow to cool hot food). Examining the sophistication of young children's social awareness, Perkins (1983) makes several useful distinctions concerning the use of two specific modal forms, identifying them as examples of the "core of the English modal system" (Perkins 1983: 150). These are the expressions noted in the above examples, *have to* and *can*. According to Perkins, the expression *have to* needs only a very broad understanding of social constraints, and the expression *can* needs only a relatively undifferentiated understanding of the empirical world (Perkins 1983: 126). The use of modals marks an increase in the child's capacity to use language as a resource for intruding his/her own perspective into the speech situation. Systems of modality in adult language are a resource for the expression of point of view in argumentation and academic debate, and it is thus no surprise that they originate in early childhood in contexts involving the negotiation of needs:

Modal auxiliaries allow a tracing of dialogic processes of inscribing 'self' and 'other' within a discursive terrain which is explicitly politicised in the sense that differences in power as well as intertwinings and interdependencies in interests are explicitly marked through the grammar (Lee 1992: 180).

6.3. Children from 3:0 to 4:0 years

Several developments occur during this period which relate to subsequent linguistic and literacy development. Utterances in which there is a disparity between speech function and grammatical form are becoming more common, but still occur mostly in contexts where goods and services are at stake, for example the use of a declarative to realise a command, as in *I'll do it. I don't want it cut* (=don't cut it) (3:7). There are a few examples of declarative Mood used to realise an offer, for example *Mum, perhaps I will move down the end* (3:7), and of declarative Mood to ask an information-seeking question, for example *I wonder if you brought my clothes in that time* (3:9). Congruent and non congruent forms are sometimes juxtaposed:

C: (3:4) Mum, you better wash my face. ... Mum, wash, wash my face.

Systems of modality and modulation are becoming more elaborated, as more delicate distinctions between degrees of probability and obligation are made, for example (3:10) *shouldn't be like that, should it?* and (3:4) *he must be somewhere*. Contexts are no longer confined to demands for goods and services, with some modals constructing hypotheses about the possibility that an event will occur, for example (3:10) *might be still hot* and (3:11) *I thought that she just might like to*. However, contexts still relate closely to the everyday concerns affecting the child personally, rather than to abstract possibilities. Future events are now sometimes expressed grammatically, for example (3:3) *Mummy will roll it, when you go to work*.

The use of clause complexes involving the logical relation of projection is becoming more frequent in the data. Projections are used both in congruent and metaphorical constructions. The following are examples of congruent projections: (3:4) *Mum, you know you have to share* and (3:4) *you said you wanted me to draw a house*. Interpersonal grammatical metaphor now appears in the data, for example (3:4) *I think about seven ... Mum, I think they have that many* and (3:4) *I think it's thirty o'clock*.

Occasionally so-called "dead metaphors" appear in everyday contexts, such as daily routines and board games, for example (3:4) *I better have my medicine* and (3:11) *You are going to have a sleep after your bedtime*.

The first appearance of transcategorised forms was noted in the data, for example (3:11) *That's a dangerous move.*

6.4. Children from 4:0 to 5:0 years

As discussed in the introductory section, this is a period when children develop the ability to deal with more abstract concepts, that is, with ideas which are non-literal and which may be beyond the realm of their own personal experience. It was during this period that children began to use metalinguistic terms, for example (4:1) *That means me and you ... without saying the words, not the tiny little words;* (4:3) *Mummy, "air" means the air in the sky* and child (4:2) (responding to older sister saying the number two) *I know how to spell tutu. It's T U T U tutu.* The children are beginning to recognise and explore language as a symbolic system, which is essential for literacy development. Language itself is now a system which can be reflected upon, and the consciousness of the exploration relates to the development of written language. Meanings are no longer confined to immediate personal experiences. The child is generalising in such a way that "universal" meanings are being constructed which are inherent in the systems of knowledge encountered within the formal education system (see Painter 1993, Bernstein 1996, Hasan 1991 and elsewhere).

Interpersonal metaphors continue to become more elaborated. Choices within systems of modality and modulation continue to expand, to include both positive and negative expressions, across high, median and low values, with explicit subjective options only occurring at this stage (see Halliday 1994: 360, Torr 1998). There are still no examples of genuine ideational grammatical metaphors, but "dead" metaphors are becoming more common, sometimes modified by adjectives, for example:

(4:6) That's a smart move.
(4:3) I'm going to give her [doll] a long feed.

There is an increase in the number of transcategorisations, for example one child, playing at "schools", says *We, schooltime everyone! It's pasting time* (4:8). The child is taking on adult patterns of constructing meanings, in order to move into adult reality. Another example follows: (4:3) *There's so much mucking up I can't even go again.*

Table 1 summarises children's development of key features related to the development of grammatical metaphor:

Age	Congruent : Statement as declarative, Question as interrogative, Command as imperative	Incongruent realisations of speech functions	Modality and modulation	Interpersonal metaphor as clause complex	Transcatego-risation	'dead' metaphor	Grammatical metaphor as nominalisation: verb = noun or process substitution
20mt hs	*						
2-3 yrs	*	*	*				
3-4 yrs	*	*	*	*	rare*	rare*	
4-5 yrs	*	*	*	*	*	*	* rare use no original production

Table 1: Overview of key aspects in the development of grammatical metaphor
* Stands for "is present" in child's system

7.   Issues arising from the study: Significance for teachers

This study has been designed to develop an overview of language development in the preschool years, with a particular focus on *precursors* of grammatical metaphor in children's spontaneous oral language in the home. Grammatical metaphor has been shown to be a significant feature of language and literacy development during middle childhood, yet little research has focused on its origins in early childhood. When children commence formal schooling, many new demands are made on their language resources. The transition to school involves learning new registers, understanding and producing written language and interpreting oral language deployed in new ways. Metaphor is an important part of this learning, because of its central role in the construction of school based systems of knowledge and discourse. Both interpersonal and ideational metaphor needs to develop during the primary school years. Interpersonal metaphor is crucial in terms of the ability to express point of view, argue a position and negotiate with others. Ideational metaphors, particularly nominalisations, are important because of their role in the organisation of knowledge in scientific and technical disciplines.

This study suggests that grammatical metaphor does originate and flourish in interpersonal contexts during the preschool years, particularly in situations where the acquisition of goods and services is at stake. Systems of modality and modulation provide the child with a resource for the expression of his/her opinions and recognition that alternative perspectives are possible, and dexterity with these systems may well enhance the child's potential to achieve certain purposes and desires. As soon as children have a functioning Mood system, they begin to produce utterances where speech function and grammatical form are not in a one-to-one relationship. This realisation paves the way for subsequent developments in grammatical metaphor, all of which have at their core a transformation at the grammatical level.

Preschool children's linguistic development is related to literacy development in many subtle and complex ways. Researchers on emergent literacy have illuminated those interactions and behaviours surrounding books and story which appear to foster and reflect literacy understandings (Meek 1988, Sutherland & Arbuthnot 1991, Vukelich 1993 and many others). This study suggests that other contexts, not directly involving literature, may also be crucial for subsequent literacy development, in terms of the child's ability to use language to achieve a variety of purposes which are valued in school contexts. The negotiation of goods and services in the preschool years appears to be particularly fruitful in terms of fostering children's ability to employ their linguistic resources to recognise another's point of view and, through interaction with caregivers, construct the kinds of universalistic meanings which are fundamental to academic success.

An understanding of these literacy-oriented expressions in the everyday language of small children will enable educators and caregivers to recognise the importance of facilitating a wide range of linguistic experiences. Children need to be encouraged to negotiate with others, verbally express their wishes and needs, interpret the points of view of others, hypothesise about experience and engage in developed conversations with caregivers.

References

Bernstein, B. (1996) *Pedagogy, Symbolic Control and Identity*. London: Taylor & Francis.

Brice Heath, S. (1983) *Ways with Words: Ethnography of communication in communities and classrooms*. New York: Cambridge UP.

Burningham, J. (1978) *Would You Rather?* London: Cape.

Crystal, D. (1995) From babble to scrabble: Integrating language creativity and linguistic intervention. In: J. Murray (ed.) *Celebrating Difference, Confronting Literacies: Conference papers from 21st National Conference of the Australian Reading Association*. Melbourne: ARA.

Derewianka, B. (1995) *Language Development in the Transition from Childhood to Adolescence: The role of grammatical metaphor.* Unpublished PhD thesis, Macquarie University.

Dunn, J. (1988) *The Beginnings of Social Understanding.* London: Blackwell.

Halliday, M.A.K. (1975) *Learning How to Mean: Explorations in the Development of Language.* London: Arnold.

Halliday, M.A.K. (1993) Some grammatical problems in scientific English. In: M.A.K. Halliday & J.R. Martin (eds.) *Writing Science: Literacy and Discursive Power.* London: Falmer. 69–85.

Halliday, M.A.K. (1994) *An Introduction to Functional Grammar.* 2nd edition. London: Arnold.

Hasan, H. (1991) Questions as a mode of learning in everyday talk. In: T. Le & M. McCausland (eds.) *Language Education: Interaction and development: Proceedings of the International Conference, Vietnam.* Launceston: University of Tasmania Press. 70–119.

Hutchins, P. (1969) *Rosie's Walk.* London: Bodley Head.

Lee, A. (1992) *Gender and Geography: Literacy pedagogy and curriculum politics.* Unpublished PhD thesis, Murdoch University.

Martin, J.R. (1990) Literacy in science: Learning to handle text as technology. In: F. Christie (ed.) *Literacy for a Changing World.* Melbourne: Australian Council for Educational Research. 79–117.

Meek, M. (1988) *How Texts Teach What Readers Learn.* Stroud, Glos.: Thimble Press.

Painter, C. (1993) *Learning through Language.* Unpublished PhD thesis, University of Sydney.

Perkins, M.R. (1983) *Modal Expressions in English.* London: Pinter.

Schieffelin, B.B. & E. Ochs (1986) *Language Socialization across Cultures.* New York: Cambridge UP.

Snow, C. (1993) Families as social contexts for literacy development. In: C. Daiute (eds.) *The development of Literacy through Social Interaction* (New Directions for Child Development, 61.) San Francisco: Tossey-Bass.

Sutherland, Z. & M.H. Arbuthnot (1991) *Children and Books.* 8th edition. New York: Harper Collins.

Torr, J. (1998) The development of modality in the preschool years: Language as a vehicle for understanding the possibilities and obligations in everyday life. *Functions of Language* 5.2: 157–178.

Vukelich, C. (1993) Play: A context for exploring the functions, features and meanings of writing with peers. *Language Arts* 70: 386–392.

Williams, G. (1995) *Joint Book Reading and Literacy Pedagogy: A socio-semantic examination.* Unpublished PhD thesis, Macquarie University.

Grammatical metaphor in the transition to adolescence

Beverly Derewianka
University of Wollongong

1.   Introduction

According to Halliday, at around 9–10 years the child is able to comprehend metaphorical modes of expression, and to produce them at around 14–15 years (1986, 1985, 1991). He sees the move into grammatical metaphor as a complex step in the evolution of the child's language system (1985). Instead of expanding simply through elaboration and extension, the system is now enhanced by 'turning back on itself'. It is no longer a matter of constantly adding new subsystems, but of deploying existing subsystems to serve new functions. Any instance of such cross-coding will resonate with the traces of both the 'literal' and the 'transferred' meaning. In order to apprehend the metaphorical meaning, the immanent literal meaning must also be recognised. Halliday refers to this phenomenon as a 'semantic blend'. Whereas in the congruent form, we could say that we are dealing with the realization of a 'semantic simplex', in the metaphorical form, the realization is of a 'semantic complex'. In the transition to grammatical metaphor, the adolescent is able to mean more than one thing at a time in terms of the semantic cross-coding inherent in metaphorical constructions. The effect of this cross-coding is to multiply the potential of the system. The semantic complexity may be further increased when we have instances of recursive grammatical metaphor, where one metaphor is compounded by another, requiring multiple 'loopings' through the system in order to retrieve the congruent.

In order to investigate the nature and development of grammatical metaphor, a study was undertaken of the researcher's son, Nick, in the transition from childhood to adolescence. Between the ages of five and thirteen, all of Nick's available written texts were collected, categorised according to genre, and analysed for instances of grammatical metaphor. These data were supplemented by observations, fieldnotes, interviews, and recordings of oral interaction surrounding the production of his written texts. Where it is of interest, examples from these tapes have been included in this chapter, including contributions by Nick's younger brother, Stefan.[1]

It was decided that in order to quantify the instances of grammatical metaphor at different ages and in relation to different genres, it would be necessary to specify the number of clauses written in each year and each genre. Growth in the use of different types of grammatical metaphor could then be calculated in terms of a percentage of clauses written. Table 1 gives an overview of the number of clauses written in each year, roughly according to genre. (Drafts have been included in the count only where they differed substantially from the final product.)

Age	5	6	7	8	9	10	11	12	13
RECOUNT	65	180	75	36	365	139	425	198	95
HISTORICAL ACCOUNT					177	43		142	89
NARRATIVE		211	67	95	56	100	199	257	141
PROCEDURE		16		51	16	87	14		
REPORT		14	15	9		415	221	375	
EXPLANATION				25	29		15	50	62
EXPOSITION				20	4	416	27	183	
REVIEWS						100	31	365	272
BIOGRAPHY			7	6	37	125		27	271
OTHER	8	20	19	43	10	8		41	36
TOTAL: 6404 clauses	73	441	183	285	694	1433	932	1638	966

Table 1: Number of clauses according to age and genre

Drawing on the taxonomy of grammatical metaphor developed by Halliday and Matthiessen (1999), an analysis of all the core written data was undertaken. Instances of different types of grammatical metaphor were identified and categorised according to the taxonomic categories in order to ascertain ontological trends in the development of different types of grammatical metaphor.

The following section will look at what might be seen as precursors of grammatical metaphor and protometaphorical forms, before moving on to the documentation of more adult instances.

2.   Gateways to grammatical metaphor

This section will begin by looking at certain semantic strategies which do not themselves involve the use of grammatical metaphor, but which encourage the playful 'unhingeing' of the semantics and the lexicogrammar. These could be seen as precursors to grammatical metaphor.

It will then consider the role of certain linguistic strategies – trans-categorisation and particular types of rankshifting – which closely resemble grammatical metaphor and which, in fact, are often mistaken for grammatical metaphor. These strategies are ontogenetically prior to grammatical metaphor, and it will be argued that they could be seen as protometaphorical in the child's language development.

2.1.   Precursors of grammatical metaphor

2.1.1.   Playing with interstratal relationships
In early childhood, children start to play around with language, exploiting its potential for mismatches between perceived reality and linguistic expression. This complex manipulation of the relationship between the lexicogrammatical and semantic strata might be seen as a 'gateway' to grammatical metaphor.

Humour, no longer restricted to visual images such as face-pulling and slapstick, can now be achieved through linguistic means. Puns, for example, are early instances of the child learning to recognise the stratal tension between the semantics and the lexicogrammar:

M: Where would you like to hang the fan?
S: This is a silly suggestion, but it might be cool .... get it? .... cool 'excellent' and cool 'like a breeze'. [age 8]

The use of sarcasm could be seen as another instance of the tension between the meaning and expression:

M: Thankyou Nick *(sarcastic)* – that's very annoying.
S: She said 'thankyou'. *(Recognises the sarcasm but insists on the literal)* [age 9]

Even in the telling of lies the child sees that it is possible to construct an alternative reality linguistically. The following example demonstrates a conscious awareness of what is involved in lying:

S: Mum, this is a lie – 'Let's not and say we did'. Like if Mr. O. *[teacher]* tells us to do something and we say let's not but say we did. [age 9]

2.1.2. Lexical metaphor

In particular, the child's growing awareness of metaphorical modes of expression could be seen as a precursor to grammatical metaphor. In its classical sense, metaphor refers to lexical metaphor, where a particular lexeme is said to have both a 'literal' and a 'transferred' meaning. Grammatical metaphor is similar to lexical metaphor inasmuch as both phenomena involve a semantic category which can be realised congruently or metaphorically. In the case of grammatical metaphor, however, what is varied is not the lexis but the grammar.

The following instances demonstrate early recognition of the nature of lexical metaphor.

> (Tending a blister):
> S: Mum, we should have called blisters 'everlasting teardrops' [age 8]

> (Eating lunch outside):
> M: It's a bit windy out here.
> S: I think it's the gods having a flatulence. [age 8]

> (Editing homework)
> N: You know how a comma means 'have a rest'. Well, 'let's comma' means
>   'let's have a rest'. [age 9]

Lexical metaphors can range from 'faded' to 'innovative'. In his later writing (age 9 onwards) Nick uses a variety of both conventional and original metaphors:

> The Europeans used China as a supermarket
> quietly pickpocketing the land.
> The Dutch, the British, the Spanish and the Americans all looted China. [age 9]

Halliday (1975) describes the development of simile and metaphor as a fundamental semiotic strategy, involving a recognition of likeness between things which are essentially different. We might see the above strategies as part of an emerging awareness of the ability to expand one's meaning potential by 'decoupling' meaning from wording and recoupling them in unexpected ways.

2.2. Protometaphor

2.2.1. Transcategorisation as protometaphor

In considering the evolution of grammatical metaphor, Halliday and Matthiessen (1999) distinguish between two superficially similar phenomena – transcategorisation and grammatical metaphor.

Transcategorisation refers to the shifting of a lexeme from one class to another, allowing for an increase in the lexical stock by transforming nouns into adjectives, verbs into nouns, adjectives into verbs, and so on. Transcategorisation may be effected syntactically, where the 'form' remains the same ('underived') or grammatically through the use of derivational morphemes.

e.g. noun   *fluke*   .   verb *fluke*
      adjective   *awake*   :   verb *awaken*

While grammatical metaphors also make use of derivational morphology, they are different in nature from transcategorisation. When an element is transcategorised, it loses its original status. With grammatical metaphor, however, one element is reconstrued as if it were another, retaining the semantic force of both the elemental categories. In this process the original interpretation is not supplanted; it is combined with the new one into a more complex whole. When a quality or process, for example, is treated metaphorically as a thing, the resultant 'pseudo-thing' embodies a junction of two semantic categories: e.g. 'process thing' or 'quality thing'.

As a probe to distinguish transcategorisations from metaphors, we could say that grammatical metaphor is 'unpackable' (i.e. as a semantic element, it can be traced back to some role it could play within a higher semantic unit) while a transcategorised element is not. For example, in the data we find:

(i)   In the end, Ray is *the only SURVIVOR.*
(ii) ... the Romans believed in *the SURVIVAL of the dead.*

While both these nouns derive from the verb 'survive', *survivor* cannot be unpacked. It could be glossed as 'one who survives', thereby demonstrating its verbal origins, but it remains simply an element in the same clause:

(i)   In the end, Ray is the only ONE WHO SURVIVES.

The second example, however, can be unpacked to a ranking clause, with the elements now playing roles in the transitivity structure of the unpacked clause:

(ii) ... the Romans believed
      that THE DEAD SURVIVE [live on]

Many instances of transcategorisation are often mistaken for grammatical metaphor. Whether an expression is metaphorical or not depends on its context of use. The same word may be an example of transcategorisation in one context and an example of grammatical metaphor in another. There are several such cases in the data, e.g.:

'possession'

a) transcategorised
   after carrying *my POSSESSIONS* for what seems like an endless trek.
   [age 12]

b) metaphorical
   She was sent to gaol for *the POSSESSION of stolen goods.*
   ['... because she possessed stolen goods'] [age 12]

Halliday and Matthiessen (1999) maintain that there is no sharp line between deriving a thing from a process (transcategorisation) and construing a process as a thing (grammatical metaphor), and in fact Halliday (p.c.) suggests that transcategorisation could be seen, both phylogenetically and onto-genetically, as protometaphorical. In this sense, transcategorisation is of interest to this study inasmuch as it might function (as in the case of the tropes above) to provide a precursor/gateway to grammatical metaphor per se.

In the present data, transcategorisation is present even in the earlier written texts and there is a trend towards increasing use of transcategorised elements over the years, with a significant increase around age 9.

2.2.2. Rankshifted embeddings as protometaphor

Another phenomenon which serves to increase the grammatical potential is 'rankshifting', a mechanism whereby a unit may come to serve to realise an element of a unit of the same rank or of a lower rank (Matthiessen 1995). But just as the relationship between grammatical metaphor and transcategorisation is often the source of some confusion, so too is the relationship between grammatical metaphor and the notion of rankshifting. Halliday and Matthiessen (1999: 249) maintain that "rank shift is not inherently metaphorical" (ibid.: 201). While both transcategorisation and rankshift could, in origin, be described as metaphorical semogenic processes through a shift in class or a shift in rank, neither necessarily involves metaphor.

In clarification, Matthiessen (1995) explains that certain effects of rankshift involve grammatical metaphor while others are non-metaphorical. Most instances of grammatical metaphor, in fact, do involve rankshift, where units are "construed not only according to their own location in the system but also as if they were units with a different location in the system" (e.g. a clause construed not only as a clause but also metaphorically as a nominal group – *the gas expanded so the container exploded > the expansion of the gas caused the explosion of the container*). However, rankshift which results in embeddings is considered to be not metaphorical, but simply the translocating of a unit from one rank to another. These embeddings can be either in the form of (i) defining relative clauses (*the place **where angels fear to tread***) or (ii) a clause functioning as the Head of a nominal or adverbial group (***where angels fear to tread** is where I want to be*).

Painter (1992) recognised that examples of rankshifted embeddings from her data hardly qualified as the kind of abstraction characterised by adult grammatically-metaphorical language. Nevertheless, Painter argues that these uses of rankshifting may serve as an entry-point to more abstract language as far as the child in concerned, "in that the structure itself is in a sense 'incongruent' because it violates the canonical constituency pattern whereby larger units are made of smaller (lower rank) units" (p.30). On the grounds that such embeddings may originally have been metaphorical, and following Painter's suggestion that they may serve as a 'gateway' to further abstraction, we might consider rankshifted embeddings to be 'protometaphorical' in the same way as transcategorisation was treated above.

In Nick's early writing, we find a sprinkling of embedded clauses:

YEAR 1 [age 5]
Instead we panted on a role of paper *[the things] that might happen in the future.*

YEAR 2 [age 6]
to thank her for the spicel doller coin *which she gave me*
and I likede the letter *that you gave me*
and the Grand prix was filled with people *waiting.*
"Dad ... d.a.d DAD!! *What I really want* is a story."

YEAR 3 [age 7]
Our class had a race with our boats *that we made out off paper.*
We made two boats one *wich Tom showed us one*
The oasis is a place *were camel cravans come*
and drink water
or camp there.
He was the first *to land.*

YEAR 4 [age 8]
then put the end of it on the terminal *wich hasn't got the sticky tape*

A boy *named John Reagan* started it of
And I also don't want highways *going through the town like the ones
up in Sydney.*

But at age 9, as was the case with transcategorisation, we find an enormous increase in the incidence of embedded clauses with 123 instances. Even conceding that in this year, Nick wrote more than in previous years, the ratio of clauses written to instances of embedded clauses is still significantly high. This trend is continued at age 10, with 212 instances of embedded clauses found in the data

2.2.3. Faded metaphors

As with lexical metaphor, grammatical metaphor can be ranged along a continuum from 'dead' to 'original'. There is no clear line, however, between moribund and living metaphors. As soon as an original metaphor appears and starts to become institutionalised, it begins to lose its power to call up ideas which the words once expressed (Hegel, cited in Cooper 1986). In this study, the term 'faded' will be used (after Derrida) to refer to instances which were in origin metaphorical but which have since become established as the norm.

In terms of the linguistic development of the individual, we can also observe the difference between faded metaphors which are simply 'picked up' from constant exposure and unconsciously replicated and those which involve the more deliberate construction of an 'original' metaphor. While the former play an important role in modelling the nature of grammatical metaphor for the child, the latter serve as evidence of the child's motivated use of metaphor. These 'fresh' metaphors often take the form of a 'clumsy' or 'self-conscious' construction as the child grapples creatively with the phenomenon. Even at age 16, we find Nick writing that

> ... in the interim Martha and George continue their roles of hosting the party with *an INCREASEMENT of friction between them.*

The pressure to metaphorise has led to an over-reaching, resulting in the awkward 'increasement'. In the data, this tends to occur more frequently in the spoken mode, as both boys experiment with what they see as 'adult' language. Stefan, for example, in an attempt to demonstrate his expertise as he explains the workings of a computer monitor, states that:

> It shuts itself off after *a period of STOPNESS.* [age 14]

He obviously had a feel for the sort of language required, but could not yet come up with a stock phrase such as 'a period of inactivity'. Such examples would appear to have greater significance in describing the child's coming to terms with grammatical metaphor.

There are many instances in English that are in origin metaphorical[2] but which have long since lost all sense of their metaphoric nature.

> Much of the history of every language is a history of demetaphorising: of expressions which began as metaphors gradually losing their metaphorical character. (Halliday 1985: 327).

Here we will consider a few instances of 'domesticated' metaphors and argue that in a study of the ontogenetic development of grammatical metaphor in the child, it might be useful to include such cases in the discussion, even though these would normally be discounted as metaphorical in the writing of an adult.

2.2.3.1. Process + Range. Perhaps the most widespread use of a faded grammatical metaphor is the Process + Range construction, where what would be represented congruently as a process (e.g. *dance*) is represented metaphorically as the Range (e.g. *do a dance*) together with a lexically empty verb (see Table 2).

congruent	metaphorical
dine	have dinner
err	make a mistake
bathe	take a bath

Table 2: Process + Range constructions

Phylogenetically, expressions such as 'gave a nod' and 'made a noise' have taken over from the earlier 'nod' and 'sound' (Halliday 1990). These constructions have become entrenched to the extent that they are generally no longer considered to be live metaphors. For the purposes of this study, however, they are worthy of mention inasmuch as they are found in everyday spoken language and occur from a very early age. They could thus be usefully regarded as 'models' of grammatical metaphor, providing early experience of the phenomenon of metaphor without requiring conscious manipulation on the part of the child. In particular, the Process + Range construction models one of the most significant features of grammatical metaphor – the way in which the nominalising of the process makes available the potential of the nominal group through modification. Nick's earliest use of the Process + Range construction in his writing demonstrates precisely this point:

We also went for a bush WALK and horse RIDING.

Congruently, Nick could have written something like:

We also went walking in the bush and we rode horses.

In choosing the Process + Range construction of 'go + a walk', 'go + a ride', where the processes 'walk' and 'ride' have now become nouns ('walk' and 'riding') accompanied by the general verb 'go', he was able to build up the nominal group through the use of classifiers (*a **bush** walk and **horse** riding*). In this way he is developing a strategy typical of the written language he will need to produce in later years.

While this construction has become the unmarked form of encoding these particular types of process, the congruent forms do exist in the language, so the use of an incongruent form does represent a choice, albeit an unmarked one (Halliday 1985). In analysing the data, therefore, Process + Range constructions have been counted as metaphorical whenever a plausible non-metaphorical alternative was available but not chosen, particularly when the choice is motivated by such factors as exploiting the nominal group. Thus, Nick writes:

The pilot aged 20 from Clare in South Australia *was doing a cross-country training flight*. [age 11]

rather than the possible, but more awkward, congruent alternative:

The pilot aged 20 from Clare in South Australia *was flying cross-country for training*.

2.2.3.2. Be/go + Circumstantial element. While the above categories of grammatical metaphor are found in the speech of young children, Halliday identifies another category found in the written language of the primary school. Rather than use the congruent *be* or *go* with a circumstantial element, a simple verb is used (see Table 3).

Halliday and Matthiessen (1999) see these as intermediate between the commonsense language of daily life in the home and the technicalised educational discourse of the secondary school.

congruent	metaphorical
be about	concern
be instead of	replace
be like	resemble
go with	accompany

Table 3: Be/go + Circumstantial element

Examples from the data include:

Emerging from the subway station, [age 12]
Then suddenly the crowd *dispersed.* [age 12]
as the air pressure *decreases* [age 12]
and the general *retreats.* [age 12]
Absconding a second time [age 13]
after I had *recovered* [age 13]
Antonio *regains* some dignity, control, [age 13]

2.2.3.3. Technical terms. One of the functions of technicality is to distill or condense, and this distillation often involves the use of grammatical metaphor in the first instance. In the creation of a technical term, the notion is defined precisely and unambiguously and taxonomised so that there is no room for interpretation. In the process, any stratal tension inherent in the original metaphor disappears and the metaphor is no longer 'in play'. Technical terms, therefore, are generally not analysed as being metaphorical.

As with the above examples of other 'dead' metaphors, however, there is a case in this study for including them in the analysis. Phylogenetically it is often difficult to ascertain the extent to which a technical term has become sufficiently institutionalised to warrant nailing down its coffin. Ontogenetically it is even less clear. While the child is still in the process of defining the parameters of the term and locating it in a relevant field-specific taxonomy, the technical term is still open to ambiguity and 'fuzzy edges'. In this sense, the grammatical metaphor is still in play. For this reason, any technical term which is perceived to be not yet fully under control will be included, while others which are obviously well established will be omitted from the analysis. There is, however, no clearcut way of determining the status of the technical term in relation to the child's grasp of the underlying concept, so the analysis will have to rely on such factors as the accuracy with which the term is used, the child's familiarity with the field, any signs of 'awkward' use of the term, or the coining of 'idiosyncratic' technical terms.

3.   Into the adult system

Having discussed those 'para-metaphorical' categories which are of interest to the present study, the following sections will deal with the classification and analysis of the principal types of mature grammatical metaphor as found in Nick's texts.

Grammatical metaphor typically occurs as a 'syndrome' of features between which there is a high degree of interdependence. Generally, the metaphorising of one element creates a situation which necessitates the metaphorising of related elements:

> On *Macquarie's ARRIVAL in England* he was already a thing of the past.

A congruent version of this could have been:

> When Macquarie arrived in England ....

However, with the nominalising of 'arrived' to 'arrival', an implication sequence is set in train with 'Macquarie' no longer an Actor but a Possessor in the nominal group, and 'in England' changing from a Circumstance to a Qualifier.

In the analysis, each such syndrome will be counted as one instance of metaphor, even though several different metaphorical effects could be identified within one syndrome. There are cases, however, where discrete metaphors are to be found within a syndrome. These will be counted as separate instances.

Following Halliday & Matthiessen (1999), the types of metaphor will be organised in terms of the metafunctional effect of the metaphor. There are thus four major groupings of experiential metaphor:

    I.   shift to 'thing'
    II.   shift to 'quality'
    III. shift to 'process'
    IV. shift to 'circumstance'

Within each of these major groups, there will be a number of sub-groups, according to the nature of the semantic junction (e.g. quality: thing).

3.1.   (I) Shift to 'thing'

By far the largest group of metaphors is that which construes other elements as 'things'. As illustrated in Table 4, this group can be further subdivided, giving a fuller picture of the nature of this type of metaphor:

#	semantic shift	class shift	example
la	quality	adjective	unstable
	> quality: thing	> noun	> instability
lb	process	verb	
	> process: thing	> noun	
	(i) 'doing' process	verb	transform
	> 'doing' process: thing	> noun	> transformation
	(ii) 'sensing' process	verb	imagine
	> 'sensing' process: thing	> noun	> imagining
	(iii) 'saying' process	verb	declare
	> 'saying' process: thing	> noun	> declaration
	(iv) 'relating' process	verb	has
	> 'relating' process: thing	> noun	> ownership
lc	phase of process	tense	going to
	> phase of process: thing	> noun	> prospect
ld	conation	phase	try to
	> conation: thing	> noun	> attempt
le	modality of process	modal	can
	> modality of process: thing	> noun	> possibility; may/must
			> permission/ necessity
lf	circumstance	adv. group/prep. phrase	'how quickly?'
	> circumstance: thing	> noun	> rate [of growth]
	minor process	preposition	with
	> minor process: thing	> noun	> accompaniment
lg	relator	conjunction	so
	> relator: thing	> noun	> cause, proof

Table 4: Shift to 'thing'

The corpus was analysed to determine the number of instances of each of these sub-types according to age and the percentage of instances per number of clauses calculated for each sub-type.

3.1.1. (Ia) quality: thing

In the oral data we find fairly predictable instances of low-level metaphor from an early age:

> S: Mum there's a *DIFFERENCE* between slice and cut. Slice means you're cutting something soft and cut means medium or hard. [age 6]

(N discussing sneakers)
N: They're pretty good but they haven't got much WIDTH. [age 10]

Stefan's use of 'difference' is technically metaphorical given that a viable congruent alternative was possible ('Slice and cut are different'[3]). The choice of 'difference' however is not particularly significant as he appears to be simply picking up on a commonly used expression. Nick's use of 'width', however, is more interesting as this is a more unusual choice (cf. 'they're not very wide').

Examples from the written core data:[4]

> There was still *a lot of POVERTY and BACKWARDNESS* [age 9]
> [*'People were still very poor and backward'*]
>
> From these two encounters, *Slake's CONFIDENCE* grows. [age 13]
> [*'From these two encounters, Slake becomes more confident'*]

There was no use of this type of metaphor until age 9, at which point there was a dramatic increase.

3.1.2. (Ib) process: thing

This, the largest of all the sub-categories, can be further broken down according to type of process:

    (i)   'doing' process: thing
    (ii)   'sensing' process: thing
    (iii) 'saying' process: thing
    (iv) 'relating' process: thing

Each of these sub-types will be treated in turn.

3.1.2.1. Ib (i) 'doing' process:[5] *thing.* In the oral data Stefan, discussing his project on Ancient Egypt at age 12, is quite conscious of the shift from the more congruent 'keep the body intact' and 'keep the corpse from decaying' of the oral mode to the metaphorical 'mummification' and 'preservation' of the written mode:

> S: Mum, is 'preservation' a word?
> M: Why?
> S: Because I need it for my project. I've written 'Mummification was necessary ...' you know, to keep the body intact and keep the corpse from decaying. Can I say '*MUMMIFICATION* was *NECESSARY* for *the PRESERVATION of the corpse*'? (cf. *'They had to mummify the body in order to preserve the corpse'*)

The following examples are from the written core data at a variety of ages:

Today I started earning poket money from fireweed *brik WORK* and *snail and grub WORK*. [age 5]
['Today I started earning pocket money from picking fireweed, working at cleaning the bricks and working at picking snails and grubs off the plants']

After *the COLLAPSE of the Qin dynasty* there were several other dynasties. [age 9]
['After the Qin dynasty collapsed ...']

There hasn't been *many CHANGES* except for the barn, [age 11]
['Things haven't changed much except for the barn']

and are faced with *EXTINCTION* [age 12]
['and are about to die out']

On *his RETURN to the prison* he met Lawrence Kavenagh and George Jones [age 13]
['When he returned to the prison ...']

In the data we find no substantial use of grammatical metaphor of the 'material process: thing' type until the age of 9. There is a handful of instances before age 9, but while these are of interest, they are not statistically significant. At age 5, 'brik WORK' and 'snail and grub WORK' would appear to be genuine attempts at metaphorical creations as Nick would not have heard such phrases being used around the house. Similarly, 'trout CAMPING' at age 6 was not a phrase used by the family, although this could be a simple transfer from the more common 'trout fishing'. At age 7, 'after ten SHOTS he was dead' and 'its CRYING reached the ears of the feared sailors' both seem to have a literary ring which could be attributed to adventure stories being read at the time. After age 9, there is a substantial increase in the use of 'material process: thing' metaphors, though the growth is uneven, with an unexpected spurt at age 11.

3.1.2.2. Ib (ii) mental process: thing. In the oral data, Stefan reflects on his use of the term 'estimate', perhaps aware of the fact that he is using language in a more 'adult' way and wanting to make sure that he has nominalised correctly:

S: How long till we get home?
N: I predict it will take half an hour.
S: Before you said two hours .... I'm not saying *your ESTIMATE* was wrong .... Is there such a thing as an *'ESTIMATION'*? [age 9 & 10]

Several months later another example shows him using 'estimation' in adult company rather than the more congruent 'When do you think dinner will be ready?', possibly in an attempt not to sound too 'pushy':

S: Bruce, what's your ESTIMATION of dinnertime? [age 10]

The following are some typical examples from the written core data:

Marty is an inexperienced camper with *no KNOWLEDGE of camping whatsoever.* [age 10]
['... who doesn't know anything about camping at all.']

After *ANALYSIS* he classified it as Pithecanthropus erectus [age 12]
['After he had analysed it, .. '']

Our CONCERN for Antonio heightens [age 13]
['We become more concerned for Antonio']

Again we find virtually no instances in the written data until age 9, at which point there is a relatively steady pattern of growth, except for another 'blip' at age 11. The fact that there are fewer instances overall of this type of metaphor reflects the fact that mental processes occur much less frequently in our language use than material processes.

3.1.2.3. Ib (iii) verbal process: thing. Examples from the written core data:

Personal definition: *My personal DEFINITION of a lever* is something that can prise up something [age 10]
['The way I define a lever is ... ']

The battle is still continuing with *verbal ABUSE* etc. [age 13]
['... with people abusing each other verbally.']

Because the general use of verbal processes is relatively low and because the motivation to use them metaphorically is probably even lower, it is not unexpected that there would be few instances found in the data. Again few instances were found before age 10, while after this age there is growing evidence of its use.

3.1.2.4. Ib (iv) relational process: thing. Examples from the written core data:

His *APPEARANCE* is very nice with short straight fur. [age 8]
['He looks very nice with short straight hair.']

caused by *his LACK of control over his emotions.* [age 13]
['because he did not have enough control over his emotions.']

Here again the small number of instances make it difficult to generalise in any way, except to note that in the early years there is no evidence of the use of 'relational process: thing' grammatical metaphor, while in the later years there appears to be an increase in its use, particularly at age 13.

In the related category of existential processes, no instances of its metaphorical use were to be found in the data.

3.1.3. (Ic) phase of process (time): thing

In addition to considering the nominalisation of different types of processes, we can look at the nominalisation of various aspects of processes, such as phase (time), phase (reality), modality, and the like.

The following are the only instances of metaphorical phase in the data (and even a couple of these are borderline interpretations):

I had a bit of trouble at *the START off the race.* [age 7]
['I had a bit of trouble when we started racing']

it was near *the END of the game.* [age 8]
['they had nearly finished playing']

Sixteen of the twenty motorcyclists were out in *the BEGINNING of the race* because of a major collision. [age 11]
['... when they began to race ...']

Germination is *the RESTARTING of growth* by the embryo inside a seed.
[age 12] *['Germination is when the embryo inside the seed starts to grow.']*

Garraty meets a few people before *the BEGGINING of the walk*
[age 12]
['Garraty meets a few people before they begin to walk']

At *the very BEGINNING* he collects three warnings [age 12]
['When they first begin [to run], he collects three warnings']

how he had seen *the END of the race* [age 12]
['how he had seen them finishing the race']

Events throughout the book bring their outlooks to a normal standard and
a fresh START to life.) [age 13]

['... and they start to live life afresh']

The instances in the data are so few that any statistical analysis would be invalid.

While there are numerous instances in the data such as 'the end', 'the finish', 'the beginning', in most cases these are generally nominalisations of material processes ('to end', 'to finish', 'to begin') rather than examples of metaphorised phase:

> In *the BEGINNING of the play* Bassanio asks for a loan from Antonio.
> [age 13]
> *['When the play **begins**, Bassanio asks for a loan from Antonio.']*

Nominalisations of phase are distinguished from the above by the fact that they are accompanied by a nominalisation of the process to which the phase refers:

> Garraty meets a few people before *the BEGGINING of the WALK*
> [age 13]
> *['Garraty meets a few people before they **begin to walk**']*

We might conclude that metaphorical phase (time) is one aspect of grammatical metaphor which develops later, perhaps due to the fact that phase is used in the data primarily in narrative contexts where nominalisation is not as prevalent.

Similarly, there are no instances of metaphorical reality phase, even though there is evidence of this being used congruently:

> *[Max has got a cute little face]* wich *seems* to smile all the time. [age 7]

> and they *seemed* to take about fifty photographs . [age 9]

> and they *seem* to be dead according to the viewer. [age 10]

Again, we might assume that, while metaphorical reality phase is possible in certain contexts, it is simply not called for in the sort of texts that Nick was writing.

3.1.4. (Id) conation: thing

Halliday identifies another aspect of processes, conation, as a candidate for metaphorising. In the data we find instances such as the following:

and therefore it would be *a financial SUCCESS* [age 9]
[*'and therefore they would succeed in raising a lot of money'*]

Mr Wood made *a stupendous ATTEMPT* to save his three children
[age 11]
[*'Mr Wood tried really hard to save his three children'*]

and goes on *his QUEST to find back his inheritance* [age 12]
[*'and goes off to try and find back his inheritance'*]

Again we find relatively few examples of metaphorical conation, even though conation in its congruent form is used frequently from an early age. When conation is nominalised, it tends to occur in Process + Range constructions.

3.1.5. (Ie) modality of process: thing

The following are representative examples of metaphorised modality from the written core data:

His main RESPONSIBILITY is to bring things together [age 9]
[*'He has to bring things together'*]

Ned had *the OPTION*[6] *of shooting them* [age 10]
[*'Ned could have shot them'*]

There would be *a NEED to have modern firefighting equipment hidden*
[age 11]
[*'They would have to have modern firefighting equipment hidden'*]

because there is *the POSSIBILITY that somebody will read the books*
[age 12]
[*'because somebody might read the books'*]

But the main climax is when Garraty sits down for *WANT of rest*
[age 13]
[*'... because he has to rest'*]

The analysis of the data reveals a sprinkling of instances in the data, increasing after age 11 with an unexpectedly high proportion at age 12.

3.1.6. (If) minor process: thing (including 'circumstance: thing')

This is one of the less clearcut categories to identify. Halliday gives examples of 'minor process: thing' as well as 'circumstance: thing'. While there may be reason to separate these out at times, they are so close that they will be treated as a single group here.

In the oral data, Stefan (at age 9, following a visit to the dentist where he has been told that his new teeth are too big for his jaw) comes out with "*Amazing RESEMBLANCE to a vampire* – big teeth, little jaw.", instead of the more congruent 'I look like a vampire'.

We also find instances such as the following where Stefan [age 10] is conscious of the need to compact the congruent expression 'how many people die each year', but needs help to come up with 'death rate': "Mum, on my graph of *how many people die each year*, what word could I use?".

In the written data we also find several instances of congruent expressions which in adult written language would probably have been metaphorised:

> Australia has 200 years worth of coal
> but that depends on *how quickly we use it.* [age 9]
> [cf. *'rate of use'*]

> They had special rules in the tribe and the penalties varied
> from *how big crime it was* [age 11]
> (cf. *'the size of the crime'*)

> But we also find several metaphorised instances, e.g.:

> This gave us *an Idea of the DISTANCE it would be* [age 9]
> [*'This gave us an idea of how far it would be'*]

> because a train couldn't climb *such a HEIGHT* in one go. [age 10]
> [*'because a train couldn't climb so high in one go'*]

> but a large ovalic one on the bottom *in RESEMBLANCE to a head.* [age 11]
> [*'but a large ovalic one on the bottom like a head'*]

> The tree hurtled down with *such VELOCITY* that we couldn't escape [age 12]
> [*'The tree hurtled down so fast that we couldn't escape'*]

Following an absence of this kind of metaphor in the early years, we find a somewhat uneven occurrence of instances from age 9 onwards.

3.1.7. (Ih) relator: thing
The following are typical of this type of metaphorisation:

> to set *the PLACE* (London) and *TIME* (1850) [age 9]
> [*'to set where and when we would do it'*]

In serious *CASES* of cowardice, poor fighting, etc. they were drowned in swamps. [age 11]

['If someone was very cowardly, or fought poorly, etc. they were drowned in swamps.']

as petrol was found all over *the crash SIGHT* [age 11]

['as petrol was found all over where he crashed']

Once again we find no use of this kind of metaphor before age 9. From age 9 onwards there is an uneven pattern of usage.

3.1.8. Summary of 'shift to thing'

Table 5 indicates the frequency of use of this type of metaphor across age levels (5 years to 13 years) as a percentage of the total number of clauses written.

Age	5	6	7	8	9	10	11	12	13
Instances in the data	2	7	7	8	67	114	148	182	168
Total number of clauses	73	441	183	285	694	1433	932	1638	966
Percentage	2.73 %	1.58 %	3.82 %	2.8 %	9.65 %	7.9 %	15.87 %	11.11 %	17.39 %

Table 5: Summary of 'Shift to thing'

3.2.   (II) Shift to 'quality'

This type of experiential metaphor is the second largest grouping to be found in the data. As with the 'shift to thing' group of metaphors, this group can be further subdivided into a range of subtypes (see Table 6).

3.2.1.   (IIa) thing: class (of things)

The only instances of this type of metaphor in the data are the following:

Anyone interested in *GOLFBALL finding* should start off with suitable clothing.[age 10]

The only possibility it could have been is *ENGINE failure*. [age 11]

[cf. 'when the engine started to fail' earlier in text]

The fire was prevented from burning further houses on Shoalhaven St by *an unexpected WIND change*. [age 11]

the main changes I have noticed in my time here is that it has changed

from *a CEDAR logging area* to a farming community with dairying and
wheat products. [age 11]

and crashed into *the back of a ROAD maintenance truck* which was parked
on the side of the road. [age 11]

These have not been included in the final tally as they are simply part of a
syndrome accompanying the metaphorisation of another element. Their status as
metaphors therefore is relatively incidental.

#	semantic shift	class shift	example
IIa	thing > thing: class (of things)	noun head > noun premodifier	engine [fails] > engine [failure]
IIb	thing > thing: circumstantial quality	noun head > prep. phrase postmodifier	glass [fractures] > [the fracture] of glass
IIc	thing > thing: possessor (of thing)	noun head > possessive determiner	government [decided] > government's [decision]
IId	process > process: quality	verb > adjective	[poverty] is increasing > increasing [poverty]
IIe	phase of process > phase of process: quality	tense/phase verb (adv) > adjective	begin > initial
IIf	modality/modulation of procecc > modality of process: quality	modal verb/adverb > adjective	will, always > constant; may, must > permissible, necessary
IIg	circumstance > circumstance: quality/class	prep. phrase/adverb > noun premodifier	[acted] brilliantly > brilliant [acting]; [argued] for a long time > lengthy [argument]; [cracks] on the surface > surface [cracks]
IIh	relator > relator: quality	conjunction > adjective	before > previous

Table 6: Shift to 'quality'

3.2.2. (IIb) thing: circumstantial quality[7]

In this category, things which, in the congruent case, had functioned as noun
head have taken on a 'circumstantial' role as Qualifiers as a result of the
metaphorising process. As above, because these are simply the secondary

outcome of a primary metaphorisation, they have not been counted in the tally of instances, but are reported here for interest.

> I had a bit of trouble at *the start OFF THE RACE.* [age 7]
> [*'... when the race started'*]

> After *the collapse OF THE QIN DYNASTY* there were several other dynasties. [age 9]
> [*'After the Qin dynasty collapsed, ...'*]

> Therefore seeing *the change IN TECHNOLOGY* meant to Abigail a change in time. [age 12]
> [*'So when she saw how technology had changed ...'*]

> The other factor for *this increase IN CHURCHES* was that so many different nationalities had come out [age 13]

3.2.3. (IIc) thing: possessor (of thing)

This category is similar to the above two and as such will not be included in the tally. Examples in the data include:

> *HIS appearance* is very nice with short straight fur. [age 8]

> so I'll refresh your memory about the sorts of things that have happened since *OUR arrival in Jamberoo.* [age 11]

> and give me *YOUR oppinion on it.* [age 12]

> On *MACQUARIE'S arrival in England* he was already a thing of the past. [age 13]

3.2.4. (IId) process: quality

There are interesting examples of Nick and Stefan using this type of metaphor from the oral data. At age 8, Stefan shifts from the congruent 'it erupts' to the more metaphorical 'eruptive':

> S: If we're living on top of a volcano and it erupts ....
> M: Are we living on a volcano?
> S: Well, *an ERUPTIVE area* ... Saddleback was a volcano.

This is a significant instance, given that it is from a relatively early age. Its motivation is also of interest. Stefan had recently been involved in a very stimulating school project on rocks in the local area, where the children were encouraged to take on the role of apprentice geologists and to scientifically study the rock formations in the surrounding region. In the course of the project, the children were encouraged to use the technical terminology of the field, and it could be that his use of 'eruptive' is a carry-over from the project. On the other hand, this could be an example of Halliday's 'trailer strategy', where the child ventures into a new area which is beyond his or her current level of ability.[8] This instance highlights the issue of whether the use of grammatical metaphor in children is a matter of 'maturity' at around adolescence, or whether it is a matter of the type language to which they are exposed and the expectations placed upon them to use more 'adult' language.

On the same day, Stefan was watching a documentary on television about Diprotodonts. When the presenter stated that '... these giants are no more', Stefan asked:

S: Why doesn't he say *'EXTINCT'*?

Here again we have a sensitivity to the nature of more technical registers, with a conscious awareness of metaphorical options.

Examples from the written core data include:

and we got BLESTING feet and BLESTING hands [age 6]
['and our feet and hands were blistered']

to turn the MOISTURISED pulp into paper form [age 10]
['to turn the pulp moisturised by the water into paper form']

She was also looking at the freshly DUG fields which showed signs of my toil and labour. [age 11]
['She was also looking at the fields which I had recently dug up ...']

and changed from foul SMELLING dirt tracks to ORGANIZED PAVED towns [age 13]
['and changed from dirt tracks which smelled foul to town which were organised and paved.']

The analysis of the data in this category reveals a trend similar to that found previously – a few instances up till around age 9 followed by a significant increase.

3.2.5. (IIe) aspect or phase of process: quality
The oral data gives an example of Nick (age 11) commenting on a wasp which refuses to fly out of the car "This wasp is *PERSISTENT*!", instead of the more congruent 'keeps on flying around'.

In the written data there are only two instances of 'aspect of process' (conation) realised metaphorically:

Ned is not guilty of the ATTEMPTED murder of Fitzpatrick [age 10]

Charge: ATTEMPTED murder of Constable Fitzpatrick [age 10]

Even these instances are not very significant as they appear to have a somewhat formulaic nature.

3.2.6. *(IIf) modality/modulation of process: quality*
This type of metaphor is very common in the children's oral language from an early age:

(N & S playing with toy raft in bathtub)
N: This is automatic control. It's INVINCIBLE.
S: It's FLOATABLE.
N· It knows where it wants to go. [ages 7 &9]

(S. always loses the secateurs, leaving them in the bushes.)
G: Did you put the secateurs away or leave them where I can see them?
S: At least I know where they are and at least they're SEEABLE. [age 10]

(Watching monster movie).
N: In bat form he's SHOOTABLE. [age 11]
['when he's the form of a bat you can shoot him']

(S enquiring about leprosy)
S: Is it CATCHABLE? I mean ... what's the word? ... contagious? [age 12]

(Looking at man flying model aeroplane.)
N: It's a glider but it's got a CONTROLLABLE rudder – he's able to control it.
     [age 13]

There are few examples in the core written data:

and it is POSSIBLE that not many people will come to see it [age 9]

Vladimir Vostov, the most LIKELY to win the election, said [age 11]

it is most PROBABLE that the chamber should expand or contract [age 12]

The main factor for the CONSTANT criticism is due to Macquarie's mismanagement and his policies. [age 13]

3.2.7. (IIg) circumstance: quality

The written core data contains several instances of this category, exemplified by the following:

> Have *WEEKLY meetings* with the director [age 9]
> *['Have meetings every week with the director']*

> he did *no MANUEL work* [age 11]
> *['he didn't work with his hands']*

> but his sentence was reduced to *LIFE imprisonment* [age 13]
> *['but his sentence was reduced to imprisonment for life']*

3.2.8. (IIh) relator: quality

Only one instance could be found in the data:

> where in *the ENSUING fight* Martin Cash shot Constable Winstanley through the left breast. [age 13]

3.2.9. *Summary of 'shift to quality'*

Age	5	6	7	8	9	10	11	12	13
Instances in the data	0	2	1	1	8	25	43	67	53
Total number of clauses	73	441	183	285	694	1433	932	1638	966
Percentage	0%	.45%	.54%	.35%	1.15%	1.74%	4.61%	4.09%	5.48%

Table 7: Summary of 'shift to quality'

3.3. (III) Shift to 'process'

As with the other types of experiential metaphor, this third major grouping can be further subdivided into a range of subtypes presented in Table 8.

3.3.1. (IIIa) circumstance: process

This category has been discussed previously as a protometaphorical strategy. It is included here as a relatively low level class of metaphor. The following are instances found in the data:

> But Egypt had made the first thing that *RESEMBLED* paper hundreds of years [age 9]
> *['looked like']*

#	semantic shift	class shift	example
IIIa	circumstance > circumstance: process	be/go + preposition > verb	be about > concern; be instead of > replace; comes after > follows
IIIb	relator > relator: circumstance	conjunction > verb	and > complement; then > follow; so > lead to ; by > enable; because > cause; while > overlaps; whereas > contrasts with; like > resembles, etc
IIIc	process type A > process type B	verb A > verb B	On the fifth day they arrived at the summit > The fifth day saw them at the summit

Table 8: Shift to 'process'

Some of the arguments they had *CONCERNED* their lives [age 10]
*[cf. age 9: This project **is about** what I discovered about Chinese history from one of the earliest remains ever found up to the present time.]*

he would have to find something that *would have SUBSTITUTED* for real currency [age 11]
['put instead']

ABSCONDING a second time [age 13]
['running away']

3.3.2. (IIIb) relator: process

Halliday (seminar handout)[9] refers to these as 'clausalised logical-semantic relations' and claims that in the English language there are some one to two thousand verbs which are metaphors for logico-semantic relations.

Examples from the core written data include:

I *MADE* everyone scream. [age 6]

we *GOT* some one to be blindfolded [age 8]

but this expansion *LED TO* too much responsibility [age 9]

This *MEANT* that one train could not cover all the distance from Victoria to Queensland in one go [age 10]

CAUSING expansion and contraction [age 11]

FORCING children to receive their early education at home either from their parents or from a tutor [age 12]

[and this] *CONTRIBUTED* to more expensive buildings being built [age 13]

3.3.3. (IIIc) process type A > process type B

The following are the only examples of this category to be found in the data:

and it's crying *REACHED* the ears of the feared sailors [age 7]

I was paralysed by the sound which had just *HIT* my ears, the unmistakeble voice of Aunt Agatha Augustus and Uncle Urvine Urine.[age 11]

when my eyes *FELL* upon the only photo that I ever owned of my dearest parents. [age 11]

which made us *FALL* upon a large camping pot which had small dints on the side .. [age 11]

What followed could *SEE* the changing of dress attire at school. [age 13]

3.3.4. Summary of 'shift to process'

Age	5	6	7	8	9	10	11	12	13
Instances in the data	0	1	1	2	7	7	17	14	17
Total number of clauses	73	441	183	285	694	1433	932	1638	966
Percentage	0%	.22%	.54%	.70%	1%	.48%	1.82%	.85%	1.75%

Table 9: Summary of 'shift to process'

Age	5	6	7	8	9	10	11	12	13
Instances in the data	2	10	9	11	82	146	208	263	238
Total number of clauses	73	441	183	285	694	1433	932	1638	966
Percentage	2.73%	2.26%	4.91%	3.85%	11.81%	10.18%	22.31%	16.05%	24.63%

Table 10: Summary of all instances of experiential grammatical metaphor

3.4. Summary of all instances of experiential grammatical metaphor in the written core data

Table 10 summarises the preceding tables, consolidating all the findings in the data of various types of experiential grammatical metaphor.

It is obvious from the summary presented in Table 10 that there is an increase in Nick's use of grammatical metaphor between the ages of 5 and 13. The nature and significance of this increase will be discussed in the concluding section of this chapter.

4.   Discussion

From the above evidence we can confirm Halliday's suggestion that grammatical metaphor is a feature which is more characteristic of the language of adolescence than of earlier childhood. That is, that the congruent is ontogenetically prior to the metaphorical.

When we examine the detail, however, some interesting questions are raised. It is certainly not a matter of a dramatic increase at puberty. Rather we observe a relatively steady, though uneven, progression from the earliest texts through to the later. The earlier instances could be explained in terms of Halliday's notion of 'trailer' strategies where the child ventures beyond his or her current ability and anticipates a future developmental step. Many of the examples in these early texts are also of a relatively 'low level' type of metaphor – Process + Range constructions, formulaic expressions, and the like.

At age 9, however, we find an unexpectedly marked increase in the use of grammatical metaphor. This would appear to contradict Halliday's assertion that grammatical metaphor is related to the onset of puberty and entry to secondary education.

The unevenness of the growth could be attributed to the influence of context. The expectations of the teacher in any particular year could be seen as significant. In the primary years, certain teachers displayed 'child-ist' tendencies in terms of what they felt children should and could be writing, while others were quite demanding and challenged the students to write more mature texts. The amount of writing undertaken doesn't appear to have been a significant factor in the development of metaphor. At ages 6, 10 and 12 in particular, Nick wrote copiously with no corresponding increase in the incidence of grammatical metaphor. More important would appear to be the nature of the writing tasks. It is more likely, for example, that we would find instances of metaphor in texts dealing with abstract or technical fields rather than in narratives, recounts, procedures and the like which tended to predominate in certain years. Exposure to written texts containing grammatical metaphor could be another significant variable, and the degree of engagement with such texts. Nick at age 9, for example, undertook an unusually substantial project for a child of this age in writing a multi-chapter historical account of Chinese history. The type of genre, the expectations of his teacher, the number of redraftings, the nature of the source materials, and the effort expended could all have contributed to the unusually high proportion of metaphorical instances at that age.

Of greater significance than the uneven pattern of growth over the years is the uneven development between different types of metaphorical categories. The data analysis demonstrates earlier and greater use of types such as 'quality: thing', 'process: thing', 'process: quality', and 'circumstance: quality'. In other categories there is very little evidence of the development of grammatical metaphor (e.g. 'phase: thing', 'conation: thing', 'phase: quality', 'modality: quality', and 'relator: quality'). And in certain categories there was no evidence at all of metaphorical usage ('circumstance: thing', 'conation: signifying process', and 'relator: process').

In order to explain this phenomenon adequately, it would be necessary to look at the relative congruent frequency of use of each of these categories in the data and the motivation to metaphorise the different categories. It would also be informative to investigate the relative frequency of use of these categories in adult texts and to see whether Nick's rate of use reflected similar tendencies. In addition, a more protracted study of Nick's written language might have shown the development in later adolescence of certain types of grammatical metaphor. With such evidence, it might then be possible to speculate on whether certain types of metaphor develop later and if so, whether they constitute a more 'complex' type of metaphor.

The question of complexity is beyond the scope of this study. In considering whether certain types of metaphor are more complex than others, however, we could refer to Ravelli's (1985, this volume) identification of two major types of complexity. Paradigmatic complexity is recursive in nature, involving the potential to pass through the network more than once to retrieve the congruent. Examples of this in the data would include:

The Cultural revolution was meant to be *a time of MODERNISATION*
[age 9]

where 'a time of modernisation' could be unpacked to 'when things were being modernised' and then taken a step further with 'when things were becoming more modern'. In a similar vein, the following nominal groups could go through at least two stages in their unpacking:

> My OPINION on mountain CLIMBING is that it is very dangerous. [age 10]
> *[> I think that mountain climbing is very dangerous.*
> *> I think that it is very dangerous to climb mountains.]*

> Even though the people are rejoicing at *the THOUGHT of Gorbachev's*
> *RESIGNATION* [age 11]
> [> Even though the people are rejoicing when they think about Gorbachev's resignation.
> *> Even though the people are rejoicing when they think about the fact that*
> *Gorbachev is resigning.]*

Syntagmatic complexity on the other hand refers to those instances where the metaphorisation of one element co-involves the metaphorisation of other elements, resulting in a syndrome effect:

> *The main CRITICISM of him* was *the ever increasing EXPENDITURES* on
> the colony. [age 13]
> *['They mainly criticised him because he kept on spending too much*
> *money on the colony.']*

In the above example, when the process in the congruent version 'they mainly criticised him' ('criticism'), is nominalised, the elements 'him' and 'mainly' must also undergo a metaphorical transformation ('of him' and 'main'). A similar syndrome is found in the second nominal group, where metaphorisation of 'spending money' ('expenditure') necessitates the metaphorisation of 'kept on' ('ever increasing').

And finally, the data analysis has suggested that while grammatical metaphor is characteristic of adult texts in the written mode, it is in the spoken mode that much of the experimentation takes place. The oral data contains numerous instances where the boys are obviously 'having a go' in a context where they are not committing themselves in writing. At times they make explicit reference to their use of 'adult' language and sometimes they use highly metaphorical language when they want to send up pretentious conversation:

> S: Mum would regular consumption of licorice be beneficial to one's health because of its laxative properties? For example in the prevention of bowel cancer ... no, hang on ... I've got the word – bowel disorders ... *[giggles]* oh piss off mum

M: Why did you say that?

S: I was being a snob. [age 14]

At other times they use it when they want to be taken seriously in the context of an adult conversation. At age 10, for example, Stefan senses frustration in his search for metaphorical variants of relational and mental processes as he discusses the nature of clones:

M: What's a clone Stef?

S: What scientists have discovered is that they can take a cell from a body and make an artificial human. And how many cells you take from it, that's how many artificial things you'd get. But they might not have the same intelligence and they might not have the same voice. And they might not have the same um ... *likeness*, I mean *looking* ....

M: Mmm, they might not look the same?

S: Yeah, because they could grow up differenter. More different. I don't know if they have got the same sort of you know, *what they want to do*. Because ....

M: What would you call that? The same ....?

S: The same .... I dunno what you'd call it. Maybe um .... but I don't think they'd all grow up to be um ... murderers ... murderers even if it did come from a ∖ murderer.

M: Why's that?

S: Because they could grow up different with a different *liking*. Different *thing*!

And Nick at age 11 confidently rejects his father's more congruent formulation:

D: Yes. What would you say? A lot of ... *we export a lot of* .....

N: We are also *a big exporter of natural gas*.

The use of oral metaphorical expressions is often accompanied by an 'unpacking', as if conscious of their incursion into adult territory:

N: Um, U.S.A, Canada and Sweden and China are very greedy, and U.K, West Germany, U.S.R, France are less greedy. Japan, Brazil, Iraqi, India are not greedy.

D: Greedy about what, Nick?

N: Um, *the energy consumption* per person. ***How much energy each person uses.***

In addition, the oral mode provides opportunities for adults to model the use of grammatical metaphor and provide a scaffold in a similar way that the caregivers of young children do:

M: Now, I just said 'this silly machine'. And Nick just said 'I know, it's *never reliable*'. Which is true, isn't it!
S: What?
M: This machine. *You can't depend on it.* [age 8]

The oral mode appears to provide an unthreatening context where children can be exposed to adult use of metaphorical constructions and can explore their own use of this type of language.

5. Conclusion

The results of this study have confirmed Halliday's suggestion that grammatical metaphor is a significant dimension of language development in later childhood, distinguishing children's use of language from that of adults. The results indicate that while it is possible to identify instances of grammatical metaphor in young children's language (used usually either in a formulaic way or in the sense of 'trailers' or 'gateways'), it is not until age 9-10 years that we find a dramatic increase in the number of instances. This finding not only lends substance to Halliday's claim that grammatical metaphor becomes a feature of older children's language use at around this age, but also confirms his description of phases of development in terms of 'generalisation > abstraction > metaphor'.

The study went further, however, than simply demonstrating the growth of grammatical metaphor. Because of the degree of delicacy built into the taxonomy, it was able to show how different types of metaphor emerged at different rates – those types which were more frequent, and those which developed earlier or later. It also suggested that certain protometaphorical types might be seen as important precursors of grammatical metaphor 'proper', providing models of the nature and function of metaphor. The more significant development, however, is when the child begins to deploy the resources of grammatical metaphor in a motivated, creative manner, often tentatively and awkwardly but increasingly with a sense of confidence and purpose.

In a more general sense, this study has contributed towards the development of a linguistic theory of learning, examining in an explicit way what is meant by 'expanding a child's meaning potential' in later childhood and adolescence. It has demonstrated the continuities between earlier and later language development in terms of the expansion of the choices available in the linguistic system, but has argued that the nature of that expansion is qualitatively different – not simply more of the same, but a redeployment of grammatical resources to realise semantically complex notions.

Notes

1. In the oral data, N refers to Nick, M refers to Mum, and S refers to Stefan. All written work cited is Nick's.

2. For example many uses of the possessive form, such as *the champion's defeat by the newcomer* (Halliday & Matthiessen 1999: 199); the shift from Attribute to Epithet as in *her eyes are brown* ⇒ *she has brown eyes* (Halliday 1985a: 327; 1990b: 16)

3. This could of course be taken a step further in terms of the number of 'loops through the system' needed to arrive at the congruent – 'Slice and cut differ' – though it is unlikely that this would have represented a plausible alternative for Stefan.

4. Possible congruent alternatives have been suggested in italics.

5. Included in the category of 'doing' processes has been the related category of 'behavimg' processes.

6. Martin sees 'option' as metaphorical, though Halliday would not. (p.c.)

7. In his an earlier version of his taxonomy, Halliday uses the term 'circumstantial quality' to refer to this category. In a later version, he uses the term 'possessor' (followed with a question mark). Neither of these appears to capture the exact nature of this category.

8. When asked (at age 14) to reflect on his use of 'eruptive' at age 8, Stefan felt that it was more a case of 'trying things out' and experimenting, than transferring a possible 'stock phrase' from the geology project.

9. Macquarie University seminar, 1994.

References

Cooper, D.E. (1986) *Metaphor.* Cambridge, Mass.: Basil Blackwell.

Halliday, M.A.K. (1975) *Learning How to Mean: Explorations in the development of language.* London: Edward Arnold.

Halliday, M.A.K. (1985) *An Introduction to Functional Grammar.* London: Edward Arnold.

Halliday, M.A.K. (1986) Language in School. Lecture 4 in a series of lectures at the University of Singapore, University of Singapore Press.

Halliday, M.A.K. (1990) New ways of meaning: A challenge to applied linguistics, paper presented to the Ninth World Congress of Applied Linguistics, Thessaloniki, (Greece).

Halliday, M.A.K. (1991) *The Language of Learning.* (Prepublication draft).

Halliday, M.A.K. & C.M.I.M. Matthiessen (1999) *Construing Experience through Meaning.* London: Cassell.

Matthiessen, C.M.I.M. (1995) *Lexicogrammatical Cartography: English systems.* Tokyo: International Language Sciences Publishers.

Painter, C. (1992) The development of language as a resource for thinking: A linguistic view of learning. Paper presented at the International Systemic Functional Congress, Macquarie University, July 1992.

Ravelli, L. (1985) *Metaphor, Mode and Complexity: An Exploration of Co-varying Patterns.* B.A. (Hons) thesis, Department of Linguistics, University of Sydney.

Part III

Interpersonal metaphor:
Enactment and positioning

Lexical metaphor and interpersonal meaning

Anne-Marie Simon-Vandenbergen
University of Ghent

1. Introduction: Aims of this article

Within systemic functional linguistics a great deal of attention has been given to grammatical metaphor, and relatively little to lexical metaphor. There are various explanations for this focus, the most important ones of which are the following. First, the concept of grammatical metaphor has not been dealt with as such in other linguistic theories and the way in which it is handled in systemic linguistics has contributed much to our understanding of the relationship between agnate lexicogrammatical structures. Second, the finding that grammatical metaphor is so evidently linked to textual complexity and the development of particular discourse styles has stimulated applied research in this area, especially with a view to obtaining a better insight into the nature of scientific language and the problems it presents to lay readers. A third angle from which grammatical metaphor has been studied is that of child language development, and such research has thrown further light on the relationship between congruent and non-congruent language forms. This book reflects the concentration on these aspects within the theory. Where does that leave lexical metaphor?

According to Goatly (1997), lexical metaphor has been "marginalised" within both the generative tradition and the functional Hallidayan tradition because linguists within these traditions "have found metaphor difficult to integrate with their theories" (p.4). While it is true that a great deal of innovative work on lexical metaphor in recent decades has come from the cognitive linguistic approach (Lakoff & Johnson 1980 was the starting point for many studies on metaphor from a cognitive point of view), it seems to me unjustified to refer to problems of integrating lexical metaphor in the Hallidayan framework. It is the aim of this article to show the inaccuracy of such a claim.

First I shall look at the relationship, differences and similarities between grammatical and lexical metaphor. Next I will further explore this relationship on the basis of a small corpus of lexical metaphors, and examine the 'payoff' of lexical metaphor. It will be argued that the interpersonal function is crucial in the make-up and function of lexical metaphors. The results of this study show that, far from being a problem to the theory, lexical metaphors can most harmoniously find a place in it, precisely through the presence of three vital assets of systemic functional theory: its emphasis on the inseparability of lexis and grammar, its concept of grammatical metaphor and its recognition of the simultaneous operation of the three metafunctions at all ranks of the lexico-grammar. As a natural conclusion of the argumentation the term 'lexico-grammatical metaphor', to subsume both 'grammatical' and traditional 'lexical' metaphor, is found to be a more adequate term, as suggested by Halliday (1994: 341–342), who states that "metaphorical variation is lexicogrammatical rather than lexical".

2.   Preliminary observations:
How is lexical metaphor (un)like grammatical metaphor?

Mostly drawing on remarks made by Halliday (1998), parallels and differences between grammatical (GM) and traditional lexical metaphor (LM) are briefly surveyed.

2.1. Parallels between GM and LM

(i) *GM and LM involve a realignment between a pair of strata.* Because of the stratified nature of the linguistic system, whereby meaning is mapped onto abstract lexicogrammatical form, different realisations are possible. This allows for the possibility of so-called 'congruent' and 'non-congruent' mappings. In the case of GM this means, for instance, that a process, congruently realised as a verb, is metaphorically realised as a noun (see Ravelli, this volume, for an elaborate discussion of realignment and stratal tension). In the case of LM, the stratified nature of language allows for the possibility of, for instance, referring to a greedy person as a *pig*. In both cases a remapping of meaning onto form has taken place, thereby creating a new meaning. This meaning creating function is the second parallel.

(ii) *GM and LM are not simply rewording but remeaning.* Halliday points out that GM gives the system "indefinitely large semogenic power" (1998: 227), because new meaning is created through the recoupling of meaning and grammar. The result is the construction of a new way of looking at experience, a different conceptualisation of the world, a different ideology. For instance, in the case of nominalisation, processes come to be conceptualised as static things, a development which has had far-reaching ideological consequences in scientific discourse (e.g. Halliday & Martin 1993; Martin & Veel 1998). Likewise, the power of LM as a means of creating new ideologies has been demonstrated by Lakoff (1992), who showed how metaphor can be used to justify war. More crucially, Lakoff & Johnson (1980), Lakoff (1987) and Johnson (1987) have thrown new light on the way in which our conceptualisation of the world takes place through metaphor.

(iii) *GM and LM show a move towards 'thinginess'*. As Halliday formulates it, we can recognise in the operation of GM a general drift towards "thinginess" (1998: 211). This means that the different types of GM all tend to realise shifts in the direction of the noun. For instance, when a verb such as *vibrate* is turned into *vibration* we get a so-called 'abstract noun', and one discourse type in which this type of metaphor abounds, namely scientific discourse, is known for its high level of abstraction. However, because nouns typically refer to participants in processes, whether objects, animals or persons, the shift is, paradoxically, also towards greater concreteness in the senses of boundedness and stability. For instance, the noun *vibration* takes on the meaning of its class, which is that of Things, and thereby represents a process as if it were something concrete, to be counted, to be given qualities such as *strong*, etc. Similarly, LM typically involves a transfer from a more concrete donor domain into a more abstract domain, so that abstract concepts come to be conceptualised in more concrete terms. Thus *fruit* is a concrete object which has come to represent 'result' in *the fruits of our endeavour*. In this example we see a gradual shift towards 'thinginess', since *result* is already a GM and is in its turn reconceptualised as *fruit*.

(iv) *GM and LM come later in the phylogenetic and ontogenetic development of language*. In the history of the language system, the congruent construal of experience comes before the metaphorical one. This has been demonstrated very convincingly for grammatical metaphor in the evolution of one type of discourse, the language of science (Halliday & Martin 1993; Martin & Veel 1998). Halliday (1998: 223) remarks in this connection that "[o]nce again there is a parallel with metaphor in its traditional, lexical guise". The history of the lexicon is indeed one of constant metaphorical extension and conventionalisation (see for instance Goossens 1995 and Rudzka-Ostyn 1995 for interesting discussions of the historical development of linguistic action metaphors in English).

It has further been amply shown (e.g. Derewianka 1995 and this volume; Painter 1993 and this volume; Torr and Simpson, this volume) that young children gradually come to terms with GM. They first construe experience in congruent terms, in the grammar of everyday life, while nominalisation, for instance, presents problems of interpretation. The extent to which metaphor is indeed characteristic of adult language is also taken up by Holme (this volume), who takes a critical look at the view that young children would not produce metaphors. It seems to be he case that one's viewpoint depends on what one classifies as metaphor (cf. Holme's contribution to this volume), but on the other hand it seems obvious that the more complex metaphors – grammatical as well as lexical – present problems of understanding because of the mental step that needs to be taken to reconstrue and reclassify experience.

(v) *GM and LM move from the instantial to the systemic.* Instantial constructs can be unpacked, which means that they can be reworded in a more congruent form. However, instantiations of the system ultimately reconstrue the system which they manifest, so that the instantial becomes systemic. For instance, the potential of representing relators or processes as nouns has created many technical terms in scientific discourse which cannot be unpacked, because there is no agnate wording in a more congruent form: the semogenic power of GM includes the possibility of creating meanings which ˋcan apparently be expressed only through the metaphor. This also implies that metaphors are no longer recognised as such, that the non-congruent is the most frequent, most 'normal' expression. Similarly, LMs become conventionalised and reshape the system. In their turn they offer the potential for the creation of new metaphors. I shall come back to this point further in this paper.

So far the parallels pointed at seem to warrant at least the use of the term 'metaphor' to cover both the phenomena of what SFL calls grammatical metaphor and what is traditionally recognised as lexical metaphor. The question remains to what extent the phenomena are different enough to be treated as completely separate. Let us examine two apparently obvious differences.

2.2. *Differences between GM and LM*

(i') *GM involves 'same signified, different signifier'; LM involves 'same signifier, different signified'.* This difference is pointed out by Halliday (1998: 191), who gives the following example to illustrate it:

GM: *the brakes failed* (congruent construal):
       brake failure (metaphorical construal)

This means that what is basically the same signified is realised once as a clausal structure and once as a nominal group. In contrast, the traditional way of explaining LM is as follows:

> LM: *spoonfeed* 'feed baby or invalid with small quantities of easily digested
> food on a spoon' (literal): 'provide learner with small quantities of
> carefully chosen instructional materials' (metaphorical) (Halliday 1998:
> 191)

This presentation suggests that LM can indeed be theorised as one signifier (*spoonfeed*) being used once in a literal/congruent sense and once in a metaphorical/non-congruent sense: one signifier, different signified. However, the distinction is only apparent, since one can also look upon LM as a non-congruent realisation of the same signified. Depending on whether one considers the phenomenon from above or from below, a different perspective results (cf. also Halliday 1994: 342). Looked at from 'below' one sees indeed one wording (*spoonfeed*) and two senses; looked at from above, one can see *spoonfeed* as the incongruent counterpart of a congruent realisation:

The pupils were provided with small quantities
of carefully chosen materials (congruent):
The pupils were spoonfed (metaphorical)

In the same vein, GM can also be looked at from below (same signifier, different signified) in the following way: a particular grammatical class (e.g. that of nouns) stands for different types of signified: nouns prototypically, thus congruently stand for concrete Things (persons, animals, objects) and metaphorically for processes. In the same way that certain features of the literal meaning of a lexical item are carried over into the metaphorical use, certain features of the class of nouns are carried over into the nominalisation of processes.

(ii') *GM involves the substitution of one grammatical class by another; LM involves the substitution of one lexical item by another.* This is the most obvious difference, which seems to warrant the use of the two terms. However, there are reasons for seeing both types of phenomena as 'lexicogrammatical' because the shifts involved affect the grammar as well as the lexicon. First, as mentioned, GMs may become part of the lexicon. This is not only the case with technical or scientific terms but also with more general abstract terms which have arisen out of metaphorical instantiations. Consider the following example from Halliday (1998: 193):

GM: Fire intensity has a profound effect on smoke injection.
Unpacked: A fire grows more intense so more smoke is injected.

A lexical item such as *effect* has arisen from the language users' choice to realise a logical relation as a noun. Furthermore, the fact that *injection* (still) has a verbal counterpart and *intensity* has an adjectival one, from which they have been morphologically derived, is a historical coincidence and irrelevant to grammatical metaphor: these words, too, are additions to the lexicon. Similarly, LM involves grammatical changes to a greater or lesser degree (see also Ravelli and Veltman, this volume). Though different grammatical configurations are possible (cf. Goatly 1997: 198ff for an overview), the result is always that the lexical item is used in a lexicogrammatical context which is noncongruent. The following example may illustrate the point:

LM: *This kitchen is a pigsty* (example from Thibault 1997: 584)

While this looks at first sight like a 'pure' LM, in which the noun *pigsty* is used not in its literal sense of 'place where pigs are kept' but in its metaphorical one of 'a place which is dirty and/or messy', the shift also has a grammatical consequence, in that the intensive clause must be interpreted as an attributive one, in which *a pigsty* is then used as an Attribute of *this kitchen*, which makes *pigsty* into a class of Things of which this kitchen is a member. In other words, the quality which is congruently realised as an adjective (*dirty, messy*) is here realised as a noun, which entails a more permanent or more 'inalienable' perspective on the state of affairs concerned. Compare in this respect: *This kitchen is messy* vs *This kitchen is a mess* or *She is beautiful* vs *She is a beauty*. I shall come back to the grammatical implications of lexical metaphors further in this paper.

At this point I would like to conclude that there seem to be sound reasons for considering both GM and LM as types of 'lexicogrammatical' metaphor. This is also what Halliday (1994: 341–342) suggests. However, I decided to continue using the term 'lexical metaphor' in the title of this article in order to specify that the concern will be with expressions which are traditionally subsumed under that term. I shall also use it later in the discussion of my data, which have been gathered from a dictionary.

3.   Data: Metaphorical realisations of verbal Processes

This study is based on a corpus of 300 metaphorical expressions of verbal Processes. They have been collected from the *Longman Dictionary of Contemporary English* and are actually a subsection of the corpus of 1916 entries which were selected from this dictionary for the studies reported on in Goossens et al. (1995). In that book the authors examined the metaphorical expression of linguistic action from the point of view of donor domains and value judgements involved. With regard to donor domains it appeared that reification is one of the major metaphorical patterns, relating abstract conceptions to concrete experiences. Domains which frequently give rise to metaphors of linguistic action range from fairly schematic ones (such as 'object', 'container', 'motion', 'transfer') to more specific and concrete ones such as 'the human body', 'war', 'animal behaviour', 'eating'. Since these domains have been amply illustrated and discussed in Goossens et al. (1995), whose findings were confirmed by Goatly's (1997), I shall not go into this in great detail, though the domains will come back further in the discussion of transitivity. The study of value judgements implied in the metaphors revealed that they are among the most imortant factors facilitating metaphorical transfer (Pauwels & Simon-Vandenbergen 1995; Simon-Vandenbergen 1995).

Goossens et al. (1995) looked at metaphors from a cognitive viewpoint, mainly drawing on the views presented in Lakoff (1987) and Johnson (1987). So does Goatly in his description of the metaphorical lexis for language. Goatly's study is based on items incorporated in *Collins Cobuild English Language Dictionary*. He examines what he calls 'root analogies' structuring the lexicon, and arrives at an overview of the diverse 'vehicles' for language in the lexicon which comes very close to Goossens et al.'s overview of donor domains. In order to explain the functions of metaphors, Goatly adds to his cognitive approach (in particular the Experiential Hypothesis) a functional perspective, in an attempt to remedy the so-called marginalisation of metaphor in Hallidayan functional linguistics. The way in which my own perspective in this paper differs from Goatly's can be summed up as follows: Goatly restricts his functional analysis to the linkage of the external functions of metaphors to the three metafunctions. I shall briefly explain how this relates to the functional analysis I adopt here.

The theses in this paper are the following: first, metalinguistic metaphors have an external ideational, interpersonal and textual function; second, metalinguistic metaphors reflect on the three metafunctions; third, metalinguistic metaphors realise the three metafunctions internally.

First, the external functions of metaphors can be classified under the general headings of experiential, interpersonal and textual. Goatly (1997: 148ff) recognises no less than 13 such functions, including: filling lexical gaps (experiential), expressing ideology (interpersonal), expressing emotional attitude (interpersonal), decoration, disguise and hyperbole (all three interpersonal), enhancing memorability, foregrounding and informativeness (all three textual). Since this aspect has been treated at length in Goatly, it is not the concern of this paper.

The second thesis, that metalinguistic metaphors reflect on the meta-functions, means that the expressions refer to the content of what is said in the primary situation, to language in its function of representation (ideational), to language used as exchange in the primary situation (interpersonal), and to language as it is used for creating relevance and relating to the context (textual). This link with the metafunctions also involves that expressions may refer to register choices to do with field, tenor and mode, to conventions of communicative behaviour, to styles of speaking. For instance, in the utterance *How rude of her to barge into the conversation*, reference is made to the breach of rules of conversational behaviour. Reference to rhetorical functions is illustrated for instance in *They bombarded him with questions*, a metaphorical expession referring to the speech function of demanding information ('asking someone questions'), while *Stop pushing me around* refers to the speech function of demanding services ('giving someone orders').

The third thesis, that metalinguistic metaphors realise the three functions internally, means that they reconceptualise experience, express interpersonal meanings and reorganise the clause as message. The ideational function of metalinguistic metaphors involves the reconceptualisation of verbal Processes in terms of other Processes. For instance, a verbal Process may be conceptualised as a material Process denoting an exchange of objects or physical violence. I shall come back to this angle in the discussion of transitivity shifts.

The textual function as realised internally in metalinguistic metaphors involves the possibility that they create of focussing on various aspects of the total verbal interaction scene. Some elements can be foregrounded to background or disguise others. For instance, in *The words poured out of her* the Verbiage is focused on by being made both Actor and Theme, while the Sayer has been turned into a Circumstance and backgrounded. The following sentences from G. Orwell's novel *1984* also illustrate how this pattern can be built on and exploited for literary purposes:

The stuff that was coming out of him consisted of words, but it was not speech in the true sense: it was a noise uttered in unconsciousness, like the quacking of a duck . (p. 47)

For what was there that they had not screwed out of him under the torture? (p. 220)

In both passages the verbal Process is metaphorised as a material Process (*come, screw*), but the Sayer does not become Actor but a Circumstance expressing the source. The meaning which is conveyed by these metaphors is the passive role and helplessness of the subjects in the totalitarian regime (Simon-Vandenbergen 1993, 1994).

The internal realisation of the interpersonal function means that the metalinguistic metaphors express the secondary speaker's personal attitude to or evaluation of the verbal action in the primary situation. The interpersonal aspects of meaning will be the focus in this article. Before turning to these, however, I shall first take a closer look at the transitivity shifts involved in the metaphorisation processes in my data. Such shifts show that these so-called lexical metaphors are better termed lexicogrammatical, as grammmatical changes necessarily accompany the lexical transfer.

4.   Transitivity in metaphors of verbal Processes

When otherwise congruent verbal Processes are realised metaphorically, they typically take the form of material Processes. This is not surprising, as such a metaphorical transfer involves the representation of a more abstract type of activity in terms of a more concrete one. There are, however, different ways in which the transfer can take place. The following patterns are frequent:

4.1.   Verbal Process as material Process

This means that the verb has both a 'literal' and a metaphorical meaning, and that the latter is that of 'verbal Process'. The participant roles can likewise be interpreted on one level (congruently) as Actor and Goal, and on another level (noncongruently) as Sayer and Target. Compare:

The journalist *attacked* the Prime Minister
congruent: Actor ^ P: material ^ Goal
metaphor: Sayer ^ P: verbal ^ Target

Other examples:

'May I ask a question?' – 'Certainly, *fire away*'.

After some initial *sparring* about who would take the minutes, the meeting started.

Verbs such as *attack, fire, spar* belong in the domain of 'fighting' which serves as the donor for the metaphors. It will be noted that the transfer involves other shifts which point to the degree in which the metaphorical sense has become the 'normal' one. In *fire away* the collocation of *fire* with the adverb *away* has only one meaning, which is that of 'begin to speak'. In other words, the expression has no existence in the system of (present-day) English except in the sense of verbal process. This does not mean, however, that it would not have a metaphorical basis: just as in grammatical metaphor the potential for non-congruent grammatical realisations allows for shifts from the instantial to the systemic, the processes at work in the lexicon allow for the possibility of fully exploiting the potential and in consequence changing the system. The representation of verbal action as physical fighting is frequent in the English language (cf. Vanparys 1995: 31; Goatly 1997: 75) and is thus responsible for the existence of many metaphorical expressions which have become conventionalised and are hence no longer recognised as such. In the third example above, the metaphorical meaning of *sparring*, literally a term from boxing, is 'betrayed' by the presence of the preposition *about* introducing a circumstance of Matter. This shows again that, although the metaphorical origin is beyond doubt, grammar and lexicon together point to the complex nature of shifts into the noncongruent.

4.2. *Verbal Process as Participant or Circumstance in a material Process*

The second important pattern is that in which the verbal Process appears in the metaphorical expression in the guise of a participant in a material Process. Most integrated in the system of English is the type *give an order*, *make a promise*, which have as 'congruent' counterparts the verbs *order* and *promise* respectively. In the metaphorical expressions the verb carries little semantic weight and it is the noun which conveys the meaning of verbal Process. This noun functions as Range of the material process (Halliday 1994: 147). It is a nominalisation, a grammatical metaphor, and such expressions are a good illustration of the interconnectedness of grammatical and lexical metaphor in the same configuration.

Related to the above type are expressions in which the verbal Process noun also functions as Goal, but in which the material Process verb carries more semantic weight. Examples are: *return a compliment, heap praise on someone, deliver a speech, drop a suggestion, ladle out advice.*

The verbal Process may also appear as Circumstance in a material Process, as in the following instances:

> They fell *into conversation.*
> How rude of her to barge *into the conversation.*
> She at once plunged into a description of her latest illness.

In all three instances above the Circumstance expresses 'direction towards a container': just as one may literally fall into a pit, barge into a room or plunge into water, one can metaphorically fall into some sort of verbal (inter)action, which is very frequently conceptualised as a container (Vanparys 1995: 28).

If the verbal Process is conceptualised as a material one, the participants involved in it, i.e. Sayer, Verbiage, Target, Receiver, and the circumstance of Matter inevitably take on different functions within a material Process configuration, such as Actor, Range, Goal or Circumstance (especially Direction and Manner). Here is a non-exhaustive list of possible shifts:

1. Verbiage as Goal:
   I take back *my words*
   The stories being bandied about are completely false
2. Matter as Range or Circumstance:
   His talk covered *the history of medicine from Roman times to the present day.*
   Our conversation ranged *over many subjects.*
3. Target as Goal:
   She was his most persistent enemy, assailing *him* at public meetings.
   He was pilloried in the newspapers.
   Receiver as Goal:
   They bombarded *him* with questions.
   Please fill *me* in on what happened.
4. Target as Circumstance:
   The teacher came down *on me* for talking in class.
   You're always getting *at me.*

If we look at the metaphorical expressions from the point of view of their relation to the congruent counterparts, we can see how complex the shifts are that are involved in these lexicogrammatical metaphors. Let's consider one example:

LM: *They bombarded him with questions.*

Congruent: *They kept asking him aggressive questions* (COBUILD)

They	kept	asking	him	aggressive	questions
Sayer	Phase	P:verbal	Receiver	Verbiage	
				Epithet	Head

Actor	P: material	Goal	Circ: Manner
They	bombarded	him	with questions

It can be seen that much more is involved than the replacement of one lexical item by another one, and that the verb *bombard* here conveys both the meanings of 'aggression' and 'repetition', realised in the more congruent version as Epithet and Phase respectively.

5.   Donor domains of verbal Process metaphors and the link with transitivity shifts

As the analogies which underlie a great deal of metalinguistic metaphors have been extensively dealt with in previous literature (especially Goossens et al. 1995; Goatly 1997), I shall not elaborate on this aspect again. However, it is useful to survey briefly the major metaphorical transfers which take place in order to try and establish links both with the ideational shifts involved (transitivity configurations) and with interpersonal meaning (see further below). The following analogies give rise to many conventionalised metaphorical expressions of verbal actions:

5.1.   Verbal interaction = possession and exchange of object

Underlying this very general donor domain is the reification of language (Vanparys 1995: 12ff.; Goatly 1997: 46ff.). This means that the speaker is represented as the source, origin, or creator of language, the hearer as the receiver, and the verbal interaction as the exchange of an object between speaker and hearer. There are numerous instances of conventional metaphors in which the notion of exchange of object is salient. They include:

> bandy words with, return a compliment, exchange words, give away the answer/information, fling dirt at someone, furnish the right answer, give an order, hand out advice, peddle an idea/information, pass a comment, put one's meaning across, take back one's words, withdraw a remark, etc.

Several subtypes make the exchange less salient but nevertheless also conceptualise the Sayer as bringing the Verbiage into the scene, as making it visible to the Receiver. Here are some examples:

bring up a subject, drag up a subject, keep sth back, raise a subject, rake up a subject, etc.

Also the conceptualisation of a verbal Process as the creation of an object fits into this category of metaphors:

coin a phrase, make a promise, fabricate a story, spin a yarn, weave a story, etc.

Objects may be manipulated in various ways and this gives rise to metaphorical expressions such as:

adorn a story, belabour the point, colour one's account, mince one's words, polish one's speech, wrap up one's meaning, etc.

Expressions which are based on the speaker as being in possession of or 'containing' information and which conceptualise 'speak' or 'cause to speak' also belong here:

drag out, extract, leak information, open out, pour out (one's feelings), spit out, throw out, etc.

5.2. Verbal interaction = location and movement

The representation of verbal Processes in terms of location and movement is again a very general and very productive basic metaphor, realised in numerous expressions. The Sayer is the moving Actor:

stick to (the point), stay with (a subject), dwell on (a subject), come back at so, approach so about sth, come out with, falter, flounder, get at so, go back to, go into, jump from one topic to another, meander, come to the point, return to, stumble, etc.

A subcategory here consists of expressions realising the metaphor 'conversation = a container/a bounded area':

barge into the conversation, break in, fall into conversation, horn in, plunge into a description, etc.

Yet another subtype sees the Verbiage rather than the Sayer as mover:

flood in, flow, get round (of news), pour out of so, etc.

Apart from these two general donor domains of 'possession/exchange' and 'location/movement' there are a few more specific domains which likewise underlie a great many expressions.

5.3. Verbal interaction = physical violence/fighting/destruction

This is a rather concrete and specific donor domain which is brought into play to refer to such speech functions as criticising, reproaching, scolding, arguing. The more general domains of 'exchange' and 'movement' underlie these expressions as well, but the more specific domain has a high level of salience. Here are some examples:

attack, assail, barrage (so with questions), besiege, bombard, chastise, come down on, cross swords with, fence, flay, grill, hit out at, rap so over the knuckles, lace into so, lash, rap so, wade into so, etc.

Typical shifts here involve the representation of the Target or Receiver of the verbal Process as the Goal of an effective material Process or as the Circumstance of a middle material Process. The following examples illustrate such shifts:

I was assailed with rude words. (*LDOCE*)
I lashed the amazed trio with my tongue. (*COBUILD*)
They listened to Jimmy lashing into the extremists. (*COBUILD*)

5.4. Verbal interaction = vocal and non-vocal behaviour

There are two basic subtypes here. One consists of expressions in which verbal (inter)action is represented as the production of sound normally produced by animals or natural elements:

babble, bark, bleat, twitter, crow, cackle, thunder, squawk, yap, etc.

The other subtype consists of expressions in which verbal (inter)action is conceptualised as human or non-human non-verbal behaviour:

applaud, drool, snap, trumpet, etc

There are many other specific domains which have given rise to conventionalised metaphors of verbal Processes (cf. Van Parys 1995 for an overview) but the two given above are very productive ones. The two general domains contain, as shown, various subtypes and hence give rise to expressions with varied meanings, while the domain of physical violence is more specific and will therefore produce expressions with more predictable meanings. The domain of vocal and non-vocal behaviour is, while fairly specific, too, nevertheless more heterogeneous than 'physical violence' and will hence also give rise to expressions with more varied meanings.

6.   Interpersonal meaning in verbal Process metaphors: Evidence from the dictionary

In the previous sections the interconnectedness of lexical and grammatical metaphors in the so-called conventionalised lexical metaphors has been demonstrated. What I shall examine in this section is the 'payoff' of such lexical (read 'lexicogrammatical') metaphors. The ideational function of reconceptualising verbal Processes in terms of other Processes has appeared from the discussion of donor domains. It is the interpersonal function of expressing appraisal that I want to concentrate on here and I want to propose that this may well be at least as crucial a motivating factor in the creation of most lexical metaphors.

Let us start by considering again the type of basic metaphor which represents verbal Processes in terms of a semantically rather 'weak' verb plus a nominalised Process which actually carries the semantic weight. These are metaphors building on the 'possession/exchange' meaning: *make a remark, have a chat, give an order.* Verbal communication as exchange of information is a basic conceptualisation, as can be seen from such metaphorical theoretical metalinguistic terms as *language as exchange*, the *Receiver* and the *Target* roles in a verbal Process configuration. Also basic are expressions building on the 'movement' meaning in which the 'neutral' verbs *come* and *go* are used metaphorically: *go on, come back to sth.* While the latter type will typically be classified as a lexical metaphor, because the verbal Process is represented as a material one, the former is called grammatical metaphor in SFL because a process is noncongruently realised as a noun. However, it is obvious that such expressions also involve the bringing in of lexical items such as *have, make* and *give.* These items, which are also used in the grammatical representation of other types of Processes (*have a bath, give a smile, do a dance*) are 'core' expressions and hence not prominently attitudinal.

However, the interpersonal function of expressing attitude becomes much more salient in expressions building on these basic ones but drawing on less core items. For instance, both *give advice* and *ladle out advice* conceptualise the speech function of 'advising' as an exchange of object. In *give advice* no extra additional meaning is superimposed on that, but in *ladle out advice* another domain is called into the picture, viz. that of the literal meaning, i.e. transferring liquid with a ladle from one receptacle to another. The salient aspect in the literal *ladle out* is the large quantity of food or liquid that is served with a ladle, and in the metaphor this aspect of 'large quantities' is added to the basic analogy of 'giving'. The choice of *ladle out* is thus motivated by the speaker's judgement that a norm of quantity has somehow been transgressed.

Summarising, it appears that the basic conceptual metaphor 'reification and transfer of goods' is realised in such expressions as *give advice* , which have become part of the core system of the language, as well as in less core items such as *ladle out advice*, which include the speaker's value judgement in terms of quantity: the expression conceptualises deviation from a norm. The core item *give* can in that sense be said to be 'neutral', while the more specific items are 'coloured'. The following are all verbs which represent verbal Processes metaphorically as exchange of 'goods' such as advice, information, a speech, secrets, stories:

	deliver		
ladle out			bandy about
dish out		give	peddle
hand out			put about
	leak		

An examination of the metaphorical expressions in my corpus reveals that they can be categorised according to types of interpersonal meanings they most saliently convey. Here follows an attempt at systematisation, based on the types of appraisal meanings built into the expressions. The classification draws on the APPRAISAL system as set out in Martin (1997; 2000) and White (1999; 2000). It must be stressed, however, that metaphorical expressions often fit into several categories because more than one type of evaluation is implied. I shall refer to some examples below. Further, the classification given here captures the most important evaluations that I came across in the corpus but makes no claim to exhaustiveness.

6.1. Judgement: social esteem: capacity

These expressions refer to lack of competence or of fluency:

babble: repeat sth foolishly; talk in a confused way
bumble: speak in a confused way
drool: talk foolishly
falter: speak in a weak and broken manner

6.2. Judgement: social esteem: courtesy

I tentatively introduce the category of 'courtesy' here, as it is not included in Martin's nor in White's classification but is important in the evaluation of verbal behaviour, which is regulated according to certain norms of politeness. Examples expressing disapproval because politeness norms are violated are:

bite someone's head off: speak or answer rudely and angrily
barge into a conversation: rudely interrupt

6.3. Judgement: social sanction: propriety

In these expressions the subject matter is judged to be undesirable in some way, for instance because it should have remained secret or because it harms people:

muckrake: tell unpleasant stories about so
sling mud at so: speak badly of
peddle: spread about, esp.harmful stories about people
rake up sth: talk about sth that should be forgotten
spill: tell secret information

6.4. Judgement: social sanction: veracity

These expressions typically refer to untrue statements, deception:

adorn a story: make more attractive, perhaps with untrue elements
embellish: heighten with fictitious additions
fabricate: invent in order to deceive
lay it on: tell sth in a way that goes beyond the truth

6.5. Appreciation

Several metaphors refer to the speaker's evaluation of the verbal behaviour in terms of the impact it has on the audience (e.g. boring, dull), the quality (e.g. appealing, ugly), the composition (e.g. elegant, disorganised). These are typically the expressions which construe human verbal behaviour in terms of sounds produced by animals, though they can also be other sound-imitative expressions:

babble:	talk in a confused way so that you are difficult to understand
bumble:	speak in a confused way so that you are difficult to understand
cackle:	talk loudly and unpleasantly with henlike sounds
chirp:	speak in a highpitched voice
jabber:	speak rapidly and not clearly
rumble:	talk in a boring way

Types (i) to (v) can express either positive or negative appraisal but it appears from the corpus that in nearly all cases the evaluation is negative, involving criticism. In the following types (vi and vii) verbal behaviour is evaluated in terms of deviation from expected positions on scales of quantity, duration, frequency, speed and loudness. Evaluations of deviation from a norm appear to be negative and in addition are often associated with other negative qualities such as aggression, stupidity, dullness, etc. Types (vi) and (vii) are therefore expressions of graduation, while at the same time often (though not necessarily) involving social esteem, social sanction or appreciation:

6.6. Graduation: Scales of quantity, duration and frequency

These expressions typically evaluate the speaker as speaking too much, too long, or too frequently. In expressions referring to the speech functions of demanding (information or goods and services) the negative judgement is due to the amount of pressure put on the addressee:

badger so:	ask or tell repeatedly
barrage so:	ask a large number of questions very quickly one after another
besiege so:	make so many requests, complaints, that they are unable to deal with them
dish out advice:	give a lot of advice
ladle out advice:	give freely and in large quantities
flood in:	arrive in such large numbers as to be difficult to deal with
hold forth:	speak at great length

6.7. Graduation: Scales of speed and loudness

These expressions focus on the manner of speaking and typically judge it too be too fast or too loud. The donor domain is typically that of noises made by animals (Simon-Vandenbergen 1991)

cackle.	talk loudly and unpleasantly
twitter:	talk rapidly, as from nervous excitement
yap:	talk noisily about unimportant things
snap:	say quickly, usually in an annoyed or angry way

It will be noted that in some of these expressions the system of APPRECIATION is also drawn upon, in that the verbal behaviour is evaluated as boring or unpleasant, and the content as unimportant.

6.8. Graduation: Scale of intensity

In type (viii) the scale is more abstract in the sense that 'force' or 'intensity' is involved. While many of the expressions in this class realise intensity as 'degree of violence' (and hence correlate it with negative propriety judgements), this is not necessarily so. A high degree of intensity is not by itself positive or negative but it combines with other more concrete evaluations, which may be positive but are typically negative:

applaud:	express strong agreement with
assail:	criticise strongly
come down on:	scold severely
cut up:	judge severely
flay:	scold violently
hit out at so:	disagree violently
lash into so:	attack violently
lam into so:	attack violently

A number of metaphors conceptualise inceptive phase. Intensity then typically combines with the evaluation of verbal behaviour as unexpected and/or sudden:

break out:	say suddenly
burst out:	speak suddenly, loudly, with strong feeling
chip in:	enter a conversation suddenly
come out with:	say, especially suddenly or unexpectedly
plunge into:	begin suddenly or hastily

The above types of judgement, appraisal and graduation are found in so many metaphors of verbal Processes that they can be said to be motivating forces in the majority of cases. Two further comments are in order here.

First, it will have been noticed that I have not drawn the system of AFFECT into the picture. Nevertheless, affect is part of the meaning of several metaphors. Cases in point are the expressions for 'criticise, attack, scold', such as *flay, hit out, lash,* which refer to behaviour resulting from negative feelings. The reason why I classified them under GRADUATION is that their most salient feature seems to be the high degree of intensity which they express, made explicit in their congruent counterparts by such adverbs as *violently, severely, strongly.* Another example is *bleat* . Literally denoting the sound made by sheep, the metaphor is defined in *COBUILD* as follows:

> If someone bleats, they speak in a weak,high, complaining voice, usually because they are unhappy or nervous about something, e.g. *They bleat about how miserable they are*

The expression thus clearly refers to the feelings of the speaker (affect) as well as to the manner of speaking (appreciation). However, it seems to me that the negative judgement conveyed in the metaphor is its most salient feature: the action of *bleating* is evaluated as showing lack of stamina and strength, and it is this negative judgement of social esteem that motivates the metaphor. Having said that, however, I want to emphasise that the classification of individual metaphors in one category or another is less important than the finding that very often various evaluations are present in the metaphors, in different layers. Their congruent counterparts often contain more than one explicit appraisal item.

The second point I want to make is that all of the evaluations discussed so far are evaluations of the verbal actions, i.e. as skilful, rude, boring, aggressive, etc. However, these evaluations of actions are at the same time used in contexts which clarify the speaker's evaluation of the proposition as well. The following invented examples illustrate two possible evaluations of the proposition:

(i)   *It is horrible* that she slings mud at people all the time.
(ii) *It is surprising* that he fabricated those stories about his family.

Lemke (1998) proposes seven semantic dimensions for a classification of evaluative attributes of propositions and proposals: Desirability / Inclination, Warrantability / Probability, Normativity / Appropriateness, Usuality / Expectability, Importance / Significance, Comprehensibility / Obviousness, Humorousness / Seriousness. In order to find out the relative frequency of particular evaluations scoping over the LG metaphors at issue, one needs to study them in a large number of texts. My hunch is that the frequent dimensions are Desirability / Inclination (negative pole) and Normativity / Appropriateness (negative pole). This is indeed to be expected, as Lemke found on the basis of his own corpus data that "evaluations of propositions and proposals are not independent in connected text from evaluations of the participants, processes, and circumstances within propositions or proposals" (1998: 43). In the next section I shall take a look at the use of some of these expressions in a corpus in order to shed further light on speakers' evaluations accompanying them.

7.   Interpersonal meaning in metaphors: An illustration from corpus data

The assignment of value judgements to particular expressions in the preceding section has been based on definitions and examples given in dictionaries. However, an examination of the actual use of an expression in context may reveal more about its interpersonal meaning than a dictionary definition. The occurrence of a word in a great many contexts can be studied in large electronic corpora, which provide some insight into how the language community actually uses particular expressions, in what sort of evaluative contexts. Such very large corpora represent the "discourse of a community" and in that sense they can "mimic, though not of course replicate" the language experience of its users (Thompson & Hunston 2000: 15).

I looked more closely at four expressions, i.e. *barge into (a conversation)*, *fabricate (a story)* , *plunge into (a description)* and *dish out (advice)* as they are used in the British National Corpus. The purpose of the exercise was to detect their usual collocations, the types of participants they attract and the interpersonal elements in the clauses in which they tend to occur. These four expressions have been selected more or less at random, except that they represent different types of metaphorical expressions. First, from the experiential point of view, both *barge into* and *plunge into* are based on the basic analogy of 'verbal Process = movement' (Sayer is the Actor who moves), while *fabricate* and *dish out* are realisations of the metaphor 'verbal Process = possession/exchange' (Sayer is the producer, possessor of an object, which he or she may give away). From an interpersonal point of view, they express different attitudes towards the primary communicative event: *barge into* expresses a negative judgement of courtesy, *fabricate* expresses a negative judgement of veracity, *plunge into* conveys high force on the scale of graduation, combined with phase, and *dish out* expresses negative appraisal due to a judgement in terms of quantity (graduation) as well as social sanction (propriety) (cf. Section 5 above). The examination of their actual use should reveal more about the motivating factors involved in the conceptualisation of verbal Processes in terms of these particular material Processes, both experientially and interpersonally.

The verb *barge* is not a frequent one (28 occurrences in the 100 million word British National Corpus), and its use as a metaphor of a verbal Process appears to be even less common (no instance found in the BNC). It is defined in *LDOCE* as follows:

> Barge: 'to move in a heavy ungraceful way, perhaps hitting against things in addition': *He kept barging along/about, until I told him to stop.*
> Barge into: 1. 'to interrupt': How rude of her to barge into the conversation! 2. bump into

COBUILD explicitly mentions that it is 'a fairly informal word, used showing disapproval'. The metaphorical use is defined as follows:

> 'If someone barges in or barges into a conversation, they rudely interrupt what someone else is doing or saying'. E.g. *He just barged into the conversation.*

From the BNC data it appears that the negative value judgement is present in the use of the verb as a material Process, and that it has to do with the disapproval of somebody invading a private space. In most instances that space is a physical one (a room), and this is the congruent use. The following extracts from the BNC data illustrate this use:

> How dare you think you can *barge into* my property!
> He gets a bit fussed and fidgety if I *barge into* his bedroom.
> We can't *barge into* a private garden and start searching their trees.
> That he was going to *barge into* her bedroom and ...
> So you *barge into* my bedroom and wake me up?
> when the masked raiders, armed with a pistol and a knife *barged into* his home
> At that moment James Morris *barged into* the office without knocking.
> He *barged into* her house with the sole purpose of making trouble
> Thank God he hadn't *barged into* the bathroom
> someone who *barges into* a room unannounced ...

The 'evaluators' (cf. Lemke 1998: 41) in the above examples are all indicators of negative Desirability and negative Appropriateness. They appear in various lexicogrammatical forms. In some instances, evaluation is expressed in the grammar, viz. in the MOOD type (*How dare you think ...; That he was going to ..., So you barge into my bedroom ...?*) or in a modal auxiliary (*We can't ...*). In other instances there are explicit lexical signals of negative evaluation, viz. the exclamation *Thank God,* adjectives denoting negative consequences of the action (*fussed* and *fidgety* are states signalling dissatisfaction), and the reference to *making trouble.* In still other instances there are apparently non-evaluative terms which reflect an unspoken, shared value system. The words *without knocking* and *unannounced* are 'ideational tokens' of judgement (cf. Martin 1997: 25), suggesting that a rule of an accepted behavioural code has been broken. Even in these, however, there is still an explicit indication of 'deviation from a norm' in the negative elements *without* and *un-* (cf. Thompson & Hunston 2000: 21 on the evaluative meaning of expressions of negativity). Finally, *masked raiders, armed with a pistol and a knife* evoke negative value judgements purely by their referential content.

A person can by extension be barged into, in which case the meaning aspects of 'rough movement' plus 'invasion of private space' are carried over:

Croft deliberately *barging into* an umpire
I *barged into* Nolan bodily, pushing him off line
Now that she was doing the crawl (painfully) she *barged into* people all the time
I just *barged into* Shirnette

A further extension is found in the following instance, where one's life is conceptualised as a private space:

Until Dane Jacobson had *barged into* her life she'd done pretty well, too, she
    thought darkly.

The further metaphorical extension to 'interrupting a conversation' can thus clearly be seen to have resulted from the experiential pattern of the conceptualisation of verbal Processes as movement and of conversation as a bounded area (cf. Simon-Vandenbergen 1995: 89). What has motivated this particular expression, however, is the interpersonal meaning which is transferred from the material Process use into the verbal Process use. The congruent and metaphorical uses thus share the value judgement.

The case is different with *fabricate.* In *LDOCE* it is defined as:

1. to make or invent in order to deceive: *The story was fabricated and completely untrue. 2.* to make, esp. by putting parts together

The use of *fabricate* as a material Process verb with the meaning of 'manufacture' is amply represented in the BNC data and illustrated in the following instances:

And just as an effective fishing lure may be *fabricated* from cheap, shiny material
The rather elegant frame (...) was designed by Ted and *fabricated* by John Welbourne

Instead of material objects, one may fabricate texts:

The above text is *fabricated* for the purposes of illustration.

What is focused on in the above example is the aspect of 'artificiality', as compared with natural creation; it represents the fabricated object as somehow not real. The step from 'artifical' to 'false' is a small one, and hence the verb acquires a negative meaning in collocation with nouns referring to events (such as *a Cold War, an encounter, a crisis, an interview* , as in the following instances), meaning 'invent in order to deceive':

this forced the American government to *fabricate* a Cold War with the Soviet Union
Bhutto also accused the government of *fabricating* an encounter on May 8-9 with Al Zulfiqar
accused the ANC of *fabricating* an artificial crisis
They have been accused of *fabricating* an interview with Richard, one of the Birmingham Six

A frequent collocation is *fabricate evidence:*

police officers do not *fabricate* evidence against men they know to be innocent
Prosecution witnesses were allegedly tortured or subjected to other pressure to *fabricate* evidence against them
allegations that officers *fabricated* evidence
in his first writings Leavis had *fabricated* evidence as quotations
for offences he certainly never committed, on *fabricated* evidence

In combination with verbal Process nouns (such as *allegation, claim, report, story,* as in the following instances), the main motivating factor is the negative veracity judgement, the 'falsity' aspect:

On Nov. 2 Saudi Arabia denied the allegation, describing it as "totally
fabricated"

On Nov. 24 the Iraqi News Agency (INA) denied as "*fabricated*" a claim
broadcast by the Voice of America

The SLORC continued to accuse the foreign media of carrying "exaggerated and
fabricated" reports about the situation ...

I studied fellow patients, *fabricating* their life stories

fabricating a story to try to avoid criminal proceedings

The most salient meaning aspect of the verb in present-day English seems
to be the artificiality and falseness of the thing which is 'fabricated', so that
fabricate a pack of lies is in a way tautologous, as the falseness of the statement
is expressed both in the verb and in the noun. On the other hand, the metaphor
allows for quantification and qualification more easily (cf. *a pack of*) and
Process and Range reinforce each other semantically.

then he is guilty of *fabricating* a pack of lies

The example of *fabricate* further illustrates that the value judgement may
be the most salient meaning aspect in the metaphorical sense of a verb, while it
is not there in the non-metaphorical sense. What happens is that one feature of
the meaning motivates the metaphorical extension, and in the process acquires
interpersonal meaning. Thus 'artificiality' is the motivating feature for the
metaphorical extensions of *fabricate* and turns into the value judgement of
'falseness'.

The third example is *plunge into (a description)*. The material Process of
plunging into something refers to movement in a sudden and violent or quick
manner. The thing into which someone or something plunges is typically water:

The 42,000-ton rock, which had threatened *to plunge* into the lake when there's
an inviting pool *to plunge* into to cool down

There are several meaning aspects here which can motivate metaphorical
extensions: the prototypical downward movement, the total immersion resulting
from it, the risky aspect of it (not knowing where one will end up), the
suddenness of the movement, or a combination of these. In the following
instances the prototypical, congruent meaning is still present (in the equally
metaphorical *deep waters* and in the literal *a tank of water*), so that these
examples clearly show the nature of the extension:

Will German think-tanks ever go the way of some of their English-speaking
   counterparts and *plunge into* the deep waters of ideology?
She *plunged into* the noise as into a tank of water

The following instances illustrate the use of *plunge into* as a verbal Process
verb:

Before we *plunge into* that debate we ought to recognize that ...
we must not just *plunge into* descriptions of the world of school and football
   ground
they immediately *plunge into* an uncritical and largely irrelevant answer
She was about to *plunge into* her story when Bridget spoke first
Alexandra's brother *plunged into* a series of statistics and examples
Tim *plunged into* the discussion, justifying himself
and once more they *plunged into* conversation to the exclusion of all around them
R.S.K. Barnes and R.N. Hughes's An Introduction to Marine Ecology *plunges*
   right *into* the nature and global distribution of marine organisms
She began, excitedly, *plunging into* her strategy of convincing her grandfather she
   was prospering
sometimes the hysterical story teller and raconteur *plunging into* that great bath of
   imitation
he waved to them an unceremonious halt and *plunged into* his sermon

The motivating factor in the metaphorical extension is the manner
(suddenness), and the effect (being immersed or absorbed). The metaphor
inherently expresses high force (a high degree on the graduation scale), which is
the speaker's appraisal of the way in which the verbal action was carried out. At
the same time there are evaluators in the clauses which explicitly convey the
speaker's evaluation of the proposition, and this evaluation is often negative: the
immediacy of the action (cf. adverbs such as *immediately, excitedly, right*) is
judged as entailing lack of rational planning and perhaps absence of
consideration for one's audience. Consider e.g. the modal auxiliary *we mustn't*,
adjectives such as *uncritical, largely irrelevant, hysterical*, and the prepositional
phrase expressing the effect *to the exclusion of all around them*.

The fourth expression I examined in the BNC corpus is *dish out*. The
literal meaning is that of serving food and no particular value judgement is
attached to it. Some examples from the corpus are:

by the time the Unimix – a high protein gruel – is *dished out* of the cooking
   drums

getting a bit tired of the sameness and predictability of the food which was *dished
out* to us

I'm just giving *dishing out* the the dinner love

The first step in meaning extension seems to have been that *dish out*
acquires the sense of 'distribute', not only food but other concrete things as well.

you children helped in *dishing out* plates of curry and rice every day

who would be *dishing out* leaflets advertising the shops

In this sense the expression acquires the sense of 'giving freely, generous-
ly, a lot of', which easily becomes a negative value judgement: the liberal
distribution of things is appraised as a breach of propriety:

one of the little pleasures of life in Downing Street is the opportunity it affords *to
dish out* baubles of one kind or another

the people who *dish out* honours are not really my people

where pensionable music executives *dish out* prizes to superannuated superstars

the system of *dishing out* automatic awards to civil servants, diplomats and
councillors

Edward should not have abused his divine right and curried favour by *dishing out*
peerages

the majority of higher honours are *dished out* to people who have done nothing
more than their job

The negative appraisal may also come from the fact that the free and
generous distribution of something is forced upon the receiver, and that the thing
distributed is in fact unwanted. A frequent collocation is with words such as
punishment, penalty, rough justice, sentence. This meaning extension of 'giving
a lot of something unasked for' has created the metaphorical expressions for
verbal Processes. The BNC yielded the following instances:

has been more than happy to *dish out* expensive advice to clients

although I still tend to *dish out* unsolicited advice

never afraid to dish speak its mind and *dish out* criticism

Mr Schmidt has appointed himself Germany's agony-aunt and scold, *dishing out*
advice to politicians left and right.

don't think, though, that I'm *dishing out* blame

This was very much the kind of stuff that Quigley was used to *dishing out.*

I am not saying that a bream leader *dishes out* orders to his underlings in the same
way that an army commander does.

The author of Poor Robin's Almanac of 1729 *dished out* all sorts of advice to
readers.

yet another string of personal insults, all *dished out* in that patronising way that
got her blood heated to boiling-point.

and *dished out* more than her fair share of barefaced cheek

I am ashamed of all the slagging off I *dished out* to Jony boy

In sum, the contexts of the metaphorical expressions confirm that the
appraisal element is very strong and prominent in their semantic make-up. They
corroborate the thesis which I advanced on the basis of the dictionary data, viz.
that the motivating force behind the creation of lexicogrammatical metaphors is
primarily interpersonal. This means that the speaker's attitude towards or
judgement of (some aspect of) the primary speech event is a crucial factor in the
process of the experiential representation of verbal behaviour as some other type
of behaviour.

8. Conclusions

The findings discussed in this paper allow us to draw a number of conclusions.

(i) *The dichotomy between GM and LM is artificial.* It appears that the
dichotomy GM versus LM is an artificial one. The former involves the
realisation of meaning by means of a noncongruent grammatical category, the
latter by means of a noncongruent lexical item. However, changes of one type
necessarily entail changes of another type, so that in real text, i.e. on the level of
the clause, it makes more sense to talk about lexicogrammatical metaphor. In
isolation it is useful to refer to say nominalisation of *analyse* into *analysis* as
grammatical metaphor, and to refer to *fruit* as a lexical metaphor for the
congruent *result*. In practice, i.e. when these forms are used in larger
configurations, they will cause all sorts of other shifts to take place. The link
between GM and LM is also clearly seen from the existence of such
conventionalised patterns as *give an order* or *make a comment*, which can be
seen as GM because the verbal Process is expressed as a noun, while the verb
itself has little or no semantic weight. However, looking at such expressions
from another angle one can see that they are based on a basic metaphor in
English which reifies language as a Thing and reconceptualises the verbal
Processs as possession and exchange of objects. While this is not at all salient in

such conventionalised patterns, the salience increases when the verbs are replaced by less core words such as *hand out, dish out, ladle out* (for 'give') or *fabricate* (for 'make'), which would more readily be accepted as lexical metaphors in the traditional sense.

(ii) *Metaphors provide the basis for further metaphorisation.* Basic analogies in the lexicon generate metaphorical expressions, which may in their turn give rise to new expressions. For instance, the basic analogy of verbal (inter)action as movement leads to such expressions as *go into details.* While *go* is 'neutral', other verbs such as *plunge* carry stronger value judgements. Some of the 'derived' metaphors may in their turn become part of the system, i.e. of the lexicon as recorded in the dictionary. However, conventionalised noncongruent expressions can be revived in particular contexts, which points to their real identity as metaphors. This happens in literary texts (cf. Simon-Vandenbergen 1993 and 1994 on metaphors in G. Orwell's novel *1984*), but also in other text types. In the following example from the BNC both *plunge* and *deep end* are used metaphorically, but their co occurrence in the same clause enhances their shared 'literal' domain of 'water':

> Without *plunging into* the moral and intellectual *'deep end'* of the arguments
> about retribution, I suspect there is a relationship (...)
> (E. Powell, *Reflections of a statesman.* BNC text A69).

The question whether so-called 'dead' metaphors are appropriately termed 'metaphors' at all has therefore no simple answer. Ravelli (this volume) takes a balanced position. My own view is that, while it is true that no speaker of present-day English will, for instance, interpret *take a look* as a metaphorical version of *look* (and *take* as having the same meaning as in the congruent *take a biscuit*), there are lexicogrammatical arguments for treating such expressions as metaphors. One argument is that a Process is presented as the Range of another Process, with all the consequences this entails for quantification and modification (e.g. *take another look, take a good and proper look*). A second argument is that the metaphorical value can be enhanced by the context (as in the *plunge into* example from the BNC above). Thirdly, new metaphors typically build on 'stale' ones, which is a further indication that the metaphorical construal is present in the system as an option. For instance, *take a look* is built on as a metaphor in the expression *steal a glance*, which adds further meaning dimensions (especially the manner component 'surreptitiously'). The examples of verbal Process metaphors given in this paper illustrate the same point.

(iii) *Appraisal is a strong motivating factor for the creation of lexico-grammatical metaphors.* The examination of a subsection of the lexicon of verbal Process metaphors has revealed that they typically express negative evaluations of the primary communicative event. These evaluations can be judgements of various types and/or assessments that some norm has been transgressed. Such evaluations seem to create the need for metaphorical transfers. The value judgements are either carried over from the donor domains or are newly created in the metaphorical expressions. In the latter case a particular aspect of the congruent meaning of the expression is focused on, is as it were blown up, and becomes the salient feature in the metaphorical expression. This feature contains an evaluation of the verbal Process.

Because evaluation is inherent in metaphors, they collectively reflect the ideology of the language community. In other words, value judgements as they are implied in the creation as well as in the use of lexicogrammatical metaphors in actual texts, signal the ways in which society approves and disapproves of types of behaviour. This makes conventionalised metaphors interesting, precisely because they have become part of the lexicon and thus part of the system which reflects the cultural norms in construing reality.

(iv) *Compression of information is a payoff in lexicogramatical meta-phors.* A consequence of appraisal being built into the metaphors is that compression of information is also a payoff of lexicogrammatical metaphor of the type discussed, i.e. of what is traditionally called LM. Compare:

Metaphor: They barraged him with questions.
            (Longman Dictionary of Contemporary English)
Unpacked: They asked him a large number of questions very quickly one after
            another.

The metaphorical *barrage* here expresses at the same time the verbal Process itself as well as the circumstances of Manner and Frequency: the fact that the action of asking is carried out quickly and repeated several times. In addition, the metaphor conveys that the effect is aggression committed against the Receiver. *COBUILD* gives the following definition of *barrage* in its metaphorical sense:

1. A barrage of questions, complaints, criticisms, etc is a great number of them when people suddenly raise them in an angry or aggressive way.

The negative appraisal is implicit in the metaphor and needs to be spelt out in the conguent expression. GM has the same effect of compression:

Metaphor: Pollution leads to diseases
Unpacked: Because the air is polluted people get ill

This points to another parallel between GM and LM: both are at the same time a move towards the concrete ('thinginess') and towards the abstract (loss of explicitness). Veltman (this volume) argues that the congruent form is the 'functionally most transparent' one. In the case of the LG metaphors studied in this paper the congruent 'equivalents' certainly spell out the meanings more explicitly and these metaphors provide therefore good grounds for supporting Veltman's thesis.

(v) *Lexicogrammatical metaphor finds a natural place in the SF model.* The analysis in this paper suggests that many metaphorical expessions of the type discussed, i.e. what are traditionally referred to as lexical metaphors, can be related to basic conceptualisations of verbal Processes in terms of possession and location. These basic meanings entail further analogies such as exchange and movement. They give rise to basic metaphors in the language, involving the verbs *have, give, take, go, come*. These verbs are used for the metaphorical representation of various other types of processes as well (e.g. *take a look, give a smile, have a chat*), and involve grammatical as well as lexical reconceptualisations. The basic patterns are then built on to give rise to more salient lexical transfers: the more specific the donor domain (e.g. fighting, eating), the more prominent the lexical reconceptualisation. This fundamental integration of lexical and grammatical conceptualisations and reconceptualisations finds a natural place within the SFL model. In addition, the factors motivating the transfers are explained from the simultaneous operation of ideational, interpersonal and textual functions. The concept of the metafunctions manifested at the levels of the group, clause and text, is a powerful explanatory device when one tries to account for the creation and functioning of lexicogrammatical metaphors.

References

Collins Cobuild English Language Dictionary (1987) London: Collins.
Derewianka, B. (1995) *Language Development in the Transition from Childhood to Adolescence: The role of grammatical metaphor.* PhD thesis. Macquarie University.

Goatly, A. (1997) *The Language of Metaphors*. London: Routledge.

Goossens, L. (1995) From three respectable horses' mouths: Metonymy and conventionalization in a diachronically differentiated data base. In: Goossens et al. (1995). 175–204.

Goossens, L., P. Pauwels, B. Rudzka-Ostyn, A.-M. Simon-Vandenbergen & J. Vanparys (1995) *By Word of Mouth: Metaphor, metonymy and linguistic action in a cognitive perspective*. Amsterdam: Benjamins.

Halliday, M.A.K. (1994) *An Introduction to Functional Grammar*. 2nd edition. London: Arnold.

Halliday, M.A.K. (1998) Things and relations: Regrammaticising experience as technical knowledge. In: J.R. Martin & R. Veel (eds.) (1998). 185–235.

Halliday, M.A.K. & J.R. Martin (1993) *Writing Science: Literacy and discursive power*. London: Falmer.

Hunston, S. & G. Thompson (eds.) (2000) *Evaluation in Text: Authorial stance and the construction of discourse*. Oxford: Oxford UP.

Johnson, M. (1987) *The Body in the Mind*. Chicago: Chicago UP.

Lakoff, G. & M. Johnson (1980) *Metaphors We Live By*. Chicago: Chicago UP.

Lakoff, G. (1987) *Women, Fire and Dangerous Things*. Chicago: Chicago UP.

Lakoff, G. & M. Turner (1989) *More than Cool Reason: A field guide to poetic metaphor*. Chicago: Chicago UP.

Lakoff, G. (1992) Metaphor and war: The metaphor system used to justify war in the Gulf. In: M. Pütz (ed.) *Thirty Years of Linguistic Evolution*. Amsterdam: Benjamins. 463–481.

Lemke, J.L. (1998) Resources for attitudinal meaning: Evaluative orientations in text semantics. *Functions of Language* 5.1: 33–56.

Longman Dictionary of Contemporary English (1978, 1987) Harlow: Longman.

Martin, J.R. (1997) Analysing genre: Functional parameters. In: F. Christie & J.R. Martin (eds.) *Genre and Institutions: Social processes in the workplace and school*. London: Cassell. 3–39.

Martin, J.R. (2000) Beyond exchange: APPRAISAL systems in English. In: S. Hunston & G. Thompson (eds.) (2000). 142–175.

Martin, J.R. & R. Veel (eds.) 1998 *Reading Science: Critical and functional perspectives on discourses of science*. London: Routledge.

Orwell, G. (1949) *Nineteen Eighty-Four*. Harmondsworth: Penguin.

Painter, C. (1993) *Learning through Language: A case study in the development of language as a resource for learning from 2.6 to 5 years*. PhD thesis, University of Sydney.

Pauwels, P. & A.-M. Simon-Vandenbergen (1995) Body parts in linguistic action: Underlying schemata and value judgements. In: Goossens et al. (1995). 35–69.

Rudzka-Ostyn, B. (1995) Metaphor, schema, invariance. The case of verbs of answering. In: Goossens et al. (1995). 205–243.

Simon-Vandenbergen, A.-M. (1991) Who think too little and who talk too much (Dryden). A study of metaphors. In: M. Demoor (ed.) *De kracht van het woord*. (Studia Germanica Gandensia, 24). Ghent: University of Ghent. 131–147.

Simon-Vandenbergen, A.-M. (1993) Speech, music and dehumanisation in George Orwell's *Nineteen Eighty-Four*: A linguistic study of metaphors. *Language and Literature* 2.3: 157–182.

Simon-Vandenbergen, A.-M. (1994) Metaphorical verbal clauses in George Orwell's *Nineteen Eighty-Four.* In: K. Carlon, K. Davidse & B. Rudzka-Ostyn (eds.) *Perspectives on English.* Leuven: Peeters. 395–407.

Simon-Vandenbergen, A.-M. (1995) Assessing linguistic behaviour: A study of value judgements. In: Goossens et al. (1995). 71–124.

Thibault, P.J. (1999) Communicating and interpreting relevance through discourse negotiation: An alternative to relevance theory – A reply to Franken. *Journal of Pragmatics* 31: 557–594.

Thompson, G. & S. Hunston (2000) Evaluation: An Introduction. In: S. Hunston & G. Thompson (eds.) (2000). 1–27.

Van Parys, J. (1995) A survey of metalinguistic metaphors. In: Goossens et al. (1995). 1–34.

White, P. (1999) Appraisal theory and the rhetorical properties of news reporting. Workshop given at the University of Ghent, March 1999.

White, P. (2000) Dialogue and inter-subjectivity: Reinterpreting the semantics of modality and hedging. In: M. Coulthard, I. Cotterill & F. Rock (eds.) *Working with Dialogue.* Tübingen: Niemeyer. 67–80.

The elided participant
Presenting an uncommonsense view of the researcher's role

Geoff Thompson
University of Liverpool

1.   Introduction

The main focus of my discussion in this paper will be an examination of what happens to the researcher who is a real-world participant in certain processes when those processes are talked about in the text. Broadly speaking, the processes fall into three overlapping groups (see Thompson & Ye 1991, for this idealised view of research as construed in the transitivity of reporting verbs): material processes expressing research actions – performing an experiment, collecting data, etc.; mental processes expressing the act of observing and interpreting research findings; and verbal processes expressing the act of discussing these and other findings. The groups are inherently overlapping, in that collecting data involves observation, and interpreting data is frequently done through discussing them; but the basic model has practical heuristic value. I should point out that I am using the term 'researcher' to include the writer(s), and/or other researchers, and/or the readers (since, in the texts that I am investigating, the readers are construed as peers who are, at least potentially, involved in similar research and are competent to participate in and evaluate the writer's argumentation).

2. Resources for eliding

2.1. An example

I would like to start the analysis of resources for eliding participants with a simple example from an article on economics (in the *Guardian* newspaper of 27th June 1992), in order to establish the kinds of phenomena that will be focused on:

(1)   The north emerges from every statistical comparison that can be made as significantly poorer than the south.

The researcher is elided from this sentence in (at least) three ways. The first resource that the writer draws on for this purpose is nominalisation. One of the consequences of construing a process as a 'thing' is that mention of the participants involved in the process becomes structurally optional. Here the nominal group 'every statistical comparison' can be 'paraclaused' (i.e. paraphrased as a clause) as 'every time *someone* compares the statistics': the 'comparer' has been elided from the nominalisation. The second resource is passivisation: the Agent by whom the comparison 'can be made' is elided. With the passive, it is easy to probe for the elided participant ('Who by?'); and even with the nominalisation the participant can be recovered without too much difficulty (particularly by expressing the process congruently as a verbal group – 'Who compares the statistics?'). In other words there are traces in the text of the participant, as inherent argument of the verb.

In the case of the third resource, on the other hand, recovery is less straightforward: the participant is more thoroughly elided. The reconfiguration of meanings brought about by the nominalisation allows the interpretation of the results of the comparison to be represented as 'emerging' from the comparison. Of course, an interpretation like this depends on there being an interpreter – a more congruent wording would be: 'every time someone compares the statistics *they understand that* the north is significantly poorer'. However, to recover the participant who interprets means recasting the wording more radically than with the nominalisation or passive. It involves reconstructing, at least partially, a plausible version of a physical and mental event (people looking at statistical data and drawing conclusions) which is referred to in the clause. The arguments of the verb 'emerge' do not map at all onto the participants in this event, and it is only by referring 'outwards' to that event that the analyst can see which potential participants have been elided.

This example suggests that, to explore eliding fully, it is useful to distinguish between what may be termed C-participants (where 'C' stands for 'clause') and W-participants (where 'W' stands for 'world'). C-participants are those entities which either are explicitly represented in the wording as involved in the process, or can be recovered as arguments of the verb. In the latter case, recovery may be necessary because they are not explicitly mentioned (as can occur with the Agent of a passive clause). It may also be necessary if the process is nominalised: here the participants may not be mentioned, or they may appear as various kinds of modifiers of the nominalisation. In such cases, paraclausing can bring the participants to the surface and show their relationship to the process. W-participants, on the other hand, are those entities which can be plausibly assumed to participate in the physical or mental event or state represented in the clause, whether or not the entities are also C-participants. The extent of the match between these two kinds of participants can vary in many ways, but there are three major possibilities:

a.   the W-participant and C-participant correspond more or less congruently: e.g. 'someone compares the statistics'

b.   the W-participant corresponds to a recoverable C-participant: e.g. 'every statistical comparison [by someone]'

c.   the W-participant has no corresponding C-participant: e.g. 'the north emerges as poorer' ['someone understands that the north is poorer']

It is the last two categories which are relevant to a discussion of the eliding of participants.

Before leaving the discussion of 'emerges', it is worth relating this to the alternation identified by Halliday (1994: 114) in mental processes. He pointed out that these can be construed as generated in the sensing mind or as stimulated by external phenomena:

(2)   I understood the situation of the north
      = mental cognition process construed as Senser apprehending (and thereby construing/creating) Phenomenon

(3)   The situation of the north struck me
      = mental cognition process construed as (pre-existing) Phenomenon affecting Senser – note the common mental-as-material blend in the choice of process

The wording in the example can be seen as taking this a step further towards representing the Phenomenon as the dynamic entity in the process:

(4)   The situation of the north emerged
       · = mental cognition process construed as material action of
       (pre-existing) Phenomenon

This type of dynamic representation of what is congruently a mental process in a sensing mind will be further explored in the discussion in 3.1 below of verbs such as 'demonstrate'.

2.2. Nominalisation

I have so far assumed without discussion that nominalisation allows participant eliding. However, it is, of course, possible with nominalisations to mention the participants as modifiers of various kinds – e.g. '*student* self-assessment', 'government *of the people by the people*'. In a small-scale study of nominalisations in a range of randomly-chosen university textbooks and academic papers,[1] the distribution shown in Figure 1 was found (the study covered only nominalisations functioning as Head of a nominal group – the total number was 489).

1	no participants mentioned	37%
2	'done-to' mentioned	26%
3	'doer' mentioned	22%
4	Carrier mentioned	14%
5	both 'doer' and 'done-to' mentioned	1%

Figure 1: Participants in nominalisations

Here are representative examples for each category, with paraclauses to show the congruent participant roles and with elided participant slots marked by 'X' and 'Y':

(1)   the illumination   [X illuminates Y]
      an acceleration equal to g   [X accelerates at the speed of g]
      quantitative analysis   [X analyses Y quantitatively]

(2)   prolonged exposure of the body to   [X exposes the body to less extreme
      less extreme heat   heat for a long time]
      addition and subtraction of vectors   [X adds and subtracts vectors]
      increased electron absorption and X-   [X absorbs electrons and generates
      ray generation   X-rays more]

(3)   the constant acceleration of a freely   [a freely falling body accelerates
falling body   constantly]
the body's cooperation   [the body cooperates]
increase in accelerating voltage   [accelerating voltage increases]

(4)   the coherence of an electron source   [an electron source is coherent]
the presence of a suitable potential   [a suitable potential is present]
the instability in the sources   [the sources are unstable]

(5)   ion bombardment of the filament by   [gas ions bombard the filament with
gas ions   ions]

These findings actually suggest that in academic writing it is the norm for C-participants in nominalised processes to be mentioned in some way: 63% of the instances have at least one participant mentioned. For reasons which will be made clear below, I am particularly interested in cases where what may be called the 'natural Subject' of the more congruent clausal wording is expressed.[2] Since categories 3, 4 and 5 all share this feature, they can be counted together in terms of looking at which participants are mentioned: they comprise 37% of the total. This makes it appear that nominalisations are as likely to occur with natural Subject expressed as they are to occur with no participants expressed. Even if, in order to concentrate on the relative frequency of mention of natural Subject in contrast to other options, we add categories 1 and 2 together, this still means that well over one-third of instances have natural Subject mentioned.

However, the natural Subject may be a range of different types of W-participants: as the examples above show, they are mainly the phenomena being studied (a freely falling body, gas ions, etc.). The processes are equally varied, but are mainly material and relational, referring to the actions and qualities of those phenomena. On the other hand, the picture alters dramatically when the focus is restricted to nominalisations that refer to processes in which the researcher is a W-participant. (The following figures are based on the same texts as above, but more extracts were examined in order to accumulate a comparable overall total: 447.) I found no cases in which the researcher, if mentioned, was anything but natural Subject, so I have simply divided the relevant nominalisations into 2 categories – see Figure 2.[3]

1	researcher not mentioned	91%
2	researcher mentioned	9%

Figure 2: Researcher as participant in nominalisations

Examples of each category are:

(1)   simultaneous collection of the   [X collects the whole range of X-rays
       whole range of X-rays   simultaneously]
       parameter measurements   [X measures parameters]
       a sophisticated understanding of the   [X understands the nature of voice in a
       nature of voice   sophisticated way]
       a metaphorical interpretation of the   [X interprets the process meta-
       process   phorically]
       most discussions of these issues   [usually, when X discusses these issues]
(2)   *his* analysis   [he analyses Y]
       our scrutiny   [we scrutinised Y]
       our preliminary speculations   [we begin speculating about Y]
       our discussion   [we discuss Y]

Thus with regard to the particular case of the researcher, participant elision is very much the unmarked option in nominalisation in academic text (though other participants in those processes – e.g. the 'natural Objects' – may well be mentioned).

2.3. Passivisation

As noted above, the example with which we began also draws on the other familiar resource for participant eliding in academic text, passivisation. In a survey of 438 finite passives in the same texts, the great majority were agentless, but there is again an interesting difference when the findings are divided into those with the researcher as understood or expressed Agent, and those with other Agent – see Figure 3.

	Agent: researcher	Agent: other
no Agent mentioned	56%	31%
Agent mentioned	1%	12%
Total	57%	43%

Figure 3: Presence of Agents in passive clauses

The researcher is the Agent in slightly more than half the occurrences. However, whereas over one quarter of the cases with 'other' Agents have the Agent mentioned, when the Agent is the researcher participant elision is overwhelmingly the unmarked option. Even the few cases in the agentive/ researcher category that do occur are often marginal: for example, in one the researcher mentioned is not the researcher who wrote the paper: 'The story was recorded by Eiríksson'. (It is worth mentioning that 'other: no Agent mentioned' includes one instance of the researcher as Subject of a passive form: 'the investigator can be forced to attend ...' – though this could equally be categorised as objective modulation rather than a true passive. It is also worth mentioning that 2% of cases included in 'researcher: no Agent mentioned' are where the elided Agent refers specifically to the reader – e.g. 'It will be observed ...'.)

Representative examples of each category are:

agentless/researcher	the brightness of a scanning image *can be scaled*
	different kinds of grammaticalization *have to be distinguished*
	when the issue of context *is raised*, it *is* typically *argued* ...
agentive/researcher:	a term that *will be used by most papers* in this volume[4]
agentless/other:	X-rays *will be generated*
	at the moment the utterance *is produced*
agentive/other:	his adversary's villainous tongue *is eaten out by a shrimp*
	the vacancy *can be filled by an electron*

Thus, the traditional picture of nominalisation and passivisation as two important resources for 'depersonalisation' of academic text – where I am interpreting 'depersonalisation' as meaning participant elision – is correct as long as it is made clear that it is one particular type of participant that is routinely elided (cf. Iedema 1997, on similar strategies in administrative directives; and Coffin 1997, on eliding the historian in school history textbooks). But that is not the whole story. There are a number of other resources which have not received as much attention but which also make a substantial contribution to avoiding the need to mention the researcher in the text.

3.   Eliding in text

3.1.   Eliding the Senser in methods and findings

The eliding of the W-Senser – the researcher as observer in a perception process and interpreter in a cognition process – is in fact a wider phenomenon (small 'p'!). In order to illustrate this point, it will be useful to examine a stretch of text that is representative of one kind of academic writing, an extract from a medical case study reported in the *Journal of Trauma* (Deluca et al. 1996). This extract focuses on the events which are later to be interpreted by the writers of the paper (i.e. it is oriented very much towards the research action/observation end).

(5)   On admission [*to hospital*], no fetal heart tones were detected by Doppler examination and no fetal movement was seen with ultrasound evaluation,

indicating fetal death. The patient underwent an emergency laparotomy with splenectomy, and repair of the diaphragmatic injury. A moderate sized, nonexpanding pelvic hematoma was noted. The bladder rupture was treated by urethral catheterization and bladder decompression. There was no evidence of uterine injury. The consultant obstetrician chose not to perform a cesarean section at the time of surgery because the patient had already sustained significant blood loss and had developed a coagulopathy. Postoperatively, the patient was hemodynamically stable without clinical signs of placental abruption or disseminated intravascular coagulation, and a decision was made to electively induce a vaginal delivery at a later time.

On the first postoperative day, the patient developed sudden onset of oliguria with progression to anuria over a 3-hour period. Her vital signs were stable , and a physical examination was unremarkable. She demonstrated no signs of symptoms to suggest the onset of labour. A repeat cystogram showed the urethral catheter within the bladder without obstruction or contrast extravasation.

There is only one sentence here ('The consultant obstetrician ...') in which the research participants – in the broad sense used here – come to the surface. How are they elided the rest of the time? There are clearly a number of nominalisations and passives which play a major role in this. In the following version I have italicised words and inserted *[by R]* wherever the researcher has been elided by either of these two resources (note that 'by' is used in the text on two occasions to encode Circumstance: Means rather than Agent; and two cases which are not unambiguously nominalisations have been marked as queries).

(5')   On admission, no fetal heart tones were *detected [by R]* by Doppler
          examination [by R] and no fetal movement was *seen [by R]* with
          ultrasound *evaluation [by R]*, indicating fetal death. The patient
          underwent an emergency laparotomy with splenectomy, and *repair [by R]*
          of the diaphragmatic injury. A moderate sized, nonexpanding pelvic
          hematoma was *noted [by R]*. The bladder rupture was *treated [by R]* by
          urethral *catheterization [by R]* and bladder *decompression [by R]*. There
          was no evidence of uterine injury. The consultant obstetrician chose not to
          perform a cesarean *section [?by R]* at the time of *surgery [?by R]* because
          the patient had already sustained significant blood loss and had developed
          a coagulopathy. Postoperatively, the patient was hemodynamically stable
          without clinical signs of placental abruption or disseminated intravascular
          coagulation, and a *decision [by R]* was *made [by R]* to electively induce a

vaginal *delivery [by R]* at a later time.

On the first postoperative day, the patient developed sudden onset of oliguria with progression to anuria over a 3-hour period. Her vital signs were stable , and a physical *examination [by R]* was unremarkable. She demonstrated no signs or symptoms to suggest the onset of labour. A repeat cystogram showed the urethral catheter within the bladder without obstruction or contrast extravasation.

However, there are several sentences in which a further set of resources for the elision of Senser is drawn on. These are processes which imply the existence of a real-world observer; they are bolded and marked **[to R]**.

(5")   On admission, no fetal heart tones were *detected [by R]* by Doppler *examination [by R]* and no fetal movement was *seen [by R]* with ultrasound *evaluation [by R]*, **indicating [to R]** fetal death.

She **demonstrated [to R]** no signs or symptoms to **suggest [to R]** the onset of labour.

A repeat cystogram **showed [to R]** the urethral catheter within the bladder without obstruction or contrast extravasation.

These processes, and a small set of others like them (*show, demonstrate, suggest, indicate, reveal, imply, signify, prove, display, manifest*, etc.), frequently cause problems in doing a transitivity analysis since they can refer to a complex type of process that is not adequately captured by any one of the major categories. The simplest solution seems at first sight to be to label them as verbal processes, taking a very broad view of these as including any process which involves the 'symbolic exchange of meaning' (Halliday 1994: 140). In the instances above, there is no projection, so the labelling would be Sayer and Verbiage – e.g. 'She [Sayer] demonstrated [Process: verbal] no signs or symptoms ... [Verbiage]'. However, Halliday (1994: 142) argues that cases like these are best seen as identifying relational clauses (Token^Value). With instances like the first in the extract:

(6)   no fetal movement was seen with ultrasound evaluation, <u>indicating</u> fetal death

this is certainly more convincing than the verbal process analysis, since there is a clear relationship of identity: 'no fetal movement' = 'fetal death'. However, the line between relational and verbal readings is somewhat indeterminate. For instance, in the final sentence of the extract:

(7)   A repeat cystogram <u>showed</u> the urethral catheter within the bladder
        without obstruction or contrast extravasation.

it is harder to see a relation of identity between the cystogram and the absence of
obstruction that it showed. The difference here seems to arise from the fact that
in the first 'no fetal movement' is an observation, which can be equated with an
interpretation since both are phenomena of the same kind (mental constructs);
whereas in the second 'the cystogram' is the means of observation (the
messenger rather than the message), and the 'no obstruction' is the observation.
In this latter, there are close similarities to examples such as 'my watch says six
o'clock', and the arguments in favour of a verbal process reading seem very
strong – 'a repeat cystogram [Sayer] showed [Process: verbal] the urethral
catheter ... [Verbiage]'.

One possible reason why these processes are on the borderline between
verbal and relational (symbolising) is that they appear to construe the exchange
of meaning from both ends, as it were: not only as something conveyed by the
Sayer but simultaneously as something grasped by the Receiver – meaning
extracted/constructed from phenomena rather than passed on. Relational
processes are different from other process types in that 'relating' is something
done not by the participants but by the speaker (in transitivity terms, s/he might
be called the Relator – except that s/he cannot normally appear in the clause
except as Circumstance: Angle: '<u>for me</u>, this book was the clear winner'). In a
clause such as 'the patient was hemodynamically stable', the process 'was' is a
record of the speaker's attribution of the quality of stability to the patient. Thus
relational clauses have an inherent link with 'extracting meaning from
phenomena'. Note, however, that a relational clause expresses a relation – i.e.
the product of the relating. The *demonstrate* type of process, on the other hand,
might almost be seen as 'relating' rather than 'relational' – it expresses the
process of constructing the relation on the basis of evidence. For example, 'no
fetal movement indicat[ed] fetal death' construes the process of moving from an
observation (of lack of movement) to a conclusion as to what this represents
(fetal death). At the same time the Relator/Receiver is typically not mentioned in
such clauses: the meaning is construed as immanent in, or embodied by, the
phenomenon. (It is worth noting that in all cases there is the structural possibility
of making the Relator/Receiver explicit – 'indicated fetal death *to us*'; but in my
data this does not occur even once.)

What both suggested analyses, as identifying and as verbal processes, miss
is precisely what makes these processes so useful for, and frequent in, academic
text: the fact that they simultaneously indicate that a process of interpretation by

the researcher of the relation is going on (thus validating the Token-Value relation being represented by giving the grounds for the relation), and yet construe the interpretation as self-generated by the phenomenon and not as dependent on any particular Relator. The Relator role is implied but left open – anyone could fill it and would arrive at the same interpretation. The Relator's real-world role is dual: perceiving the evidence (the Token) and interpreting the significance (the Value). These are, of course, roles that in other construals of the real-world events are attributed to the Senser in mental processes, which is why I have talked about the processes as eliding the Senser. Admittedly, all this does not actually help with the question of what transitivity label to give the processes which are not clearly verbal. Both perspectives on the process – as identifying and as reflecting the cognitive process involved in establishing the identification – seem equally important. For what it is worth, I therefore find it useful to label them as identifying/mental blends.

To look at the issue from a different perspective, it is significant that it seems natural to use 'by R' to tag the nominalisations and passives, and 'to R' for this group, even though both may involve the researcher as Senser. It corresponds in certain respects to the distinction mentioned above between Senser as 'doer-to-Phenomenon' and Phenomenon as 'doer-to-Senser'. This suggests that this semantic distinction is applicable beyond the basic structure of clauses with a mental process, and underlies other structural options – a view which, of course, fits in with general systemic functional theory (see especially the discussion of proportionalities in Martin 1992). The 'to R' tag also fits in with the idea of the observer merely receiving the interpretation from the phenomenon.

3.1.1. Indexing the W-participant

Before leaving this extract, it is worth noting a number of other wordings where the real-world participation of the researcher might be said to be pointed to, or 'indexed', rather than elided: that is, wordings which refer to physical actions and states that inherently involve the researcher but where there is no straightforward way of paraclausing them to reinstate the researcher as C-participant. These include both the 'by R' type, where nouns such as 'laparotomy' are not strictly speaking nominalisations but refer to actions by the researchers, and the 'to R' type, where nouns such as 'evidence' and adjectives such as 'unremarkable' may or may not be related to mental processes ('evidence' is not, but 'unremarkable' is) but nevertheless imply a W-participant as Senser. The justification for including these is that they contribute to the overall sense of the text as imbued by the unstated presence of the researcher:

they resonate with the other eliding choices (see Thompson 1998, on the concept of resonance in text). These have been added below, using the same conventions as above, to give a fairly full picture of the extent of researcher elision in the extract.

(5''')   On admission, no fetal heart tones were *detected [by R]* by Doppler *examination [by R]* and no fetal movement was *seen [by R]* with ultrasound *evaluation [by R]*, **indicating [to R]** fetal death. The patient underwent an emergency *laparotomy [by R]* with *splenectomy [by R]*, and *repair [by R]* of the diaphragmatic injury. A moderate sized, nonexpanding pelvic hematoma was *noted [by R]*. The bladder rupture was *treated [by R]* by urethral *catheterization [by R]* and bladder *decompression [by R]*. There was no **evidence [to R]** of uterine injury. The consultant obstetrician chose not to perform a cesarean section *[?by R]* at the time of surgery *[?by R]* because the patient had already sustained **significant [?to R]** blood loss and had developed a coagulopathy. Postoperatively, the patient was hemodynamically stable without clinical **signs [to R]** of placental abruption or disseminated intravascular coagulation, and a *decision [by R]* was *made [by R]* to electively induce a vaginal *delivery [by R]* at a later time.

On the first postoperative day, the patient developed sudden onset of oliguria with progression to anuria over a 3-hour period. Her vital **signs [to R]** were stable , and a physical *examination [by R]* was **unremarkable [to R]**. She **demonstrated [to R]** no **signs [to R]** or **symptoms [?to R]** to **suggest [to R]** the onset of labour. A repeat *cystogram [?by R]* **showed [to R]** the urethral catheter within the bladder without obstruction or contrast extravasation.

3.2.   *Eliding the Senser in discussion and conclusions*

As mentioned above, this extract focuses on the data collection stage of research (the fact that the events were presumably originally seen by all concerned as treating a patient who unfortunately died is not relevant: in the text they are reconstrued as evidence in a research project). I want now to carry out the same kind of analysis with an extract that focuses on interpretation and discussion, from a paper by Louise Ravelli, 'A dynamic perspective: implications for metafunctional interaction and an understanding of Theme' (1995, slightly abridged). To save space I will immediately highlight the resources described in the preceding analysis using the conventions already introduced.

(8)   In contrast [to the synoptic perspective], spoken language, which presents
         text as active and on-going, encourages a *view [by R]* which is less
         totalising, and more process-like. To account for this aspect of language, a
         dynamic perspective is *needed [by R]*. Yet it is too easy to make a false
         equation [by R] between written language and a synoptic perspective on
         the one hand, and spoken language and a dynamic perspective on the
         other. .... It is therefore inappropriate to equate one mode with only one
         perspective: all language is both product and process. Given that
         linguistics models have largely arisen in conjunction with the *study [by R]*
         of written language, the relatively recent *focus [by R]* on spoken language
         has **revealed [to R]** the inability of available models to account for the
         process nature of language. However, both modes can – and should – *be
         accounted for [by R]* from both perspectives. This **suggests [to R]** that a
         perspective on language should be independent from any 'intrinsic'
         qualities of the data. A dynamic perspective, then, is a way of modelling
         or explaining language as, or as if it were, unfolding.
                 Within the systemic functional approach the dynamic perspective
         has tended to be most vigorously *pursued [by R]* in relation to certain
         linguistic phenomena. These phenomena include the *study [by R]* of
         generic structure ... As these phenomena can be *seen [by R]* to unfold in
         time, and to be dependent on the nature of the current environment, they
         could be *said [by R]* to be 'inherently' dynamic. Certainly a full *account
         [by R]* of them demands that they be *considered [by R]* as processes, and
         doing so **reveals [to R]** inadequacies and weaknesses in synoptically
         oriented models. However, the *suggestion [by R]* that some types of
         linguistic phenomena are 'dynamic', and that by *inference [by R]* others
         are not, is an *equation [by R]* as false as the *equation [by R]* of a dynamic
         perspective with a specific mode of discourse. A dynamic perspective
         should not be *reserved [by R]* just for certain types of data, but should be
         applied [by R] broadly to language as a whole.

This indicates that the same resources play an important part in both data
reporting and discussion sections. However, it is clear that the analysis above by
no means covers all the cases where the researcher is elided: there are some
resources which are perhaps more typically found in discussion sections. An
important group of omissions are the non-finite verbal groups, which appear in
the following sentences – the groups are underlined, and [R] is inserted where
the Subject is elided. I also include two extra 'to R' instances – 'too easy' and
'inappropriate' – which will be discussed below.

(8) a. [R] To account for this aspect of language, a dynamic perspective is
          needed [by R].
     b. Yet it is **too easy [to R]** [R] to make a false equation [by R] between
          written language and a synoptic perspective on the one hand, and spoken
          language and a dynamic perspective on the other.
     c. It is therefore **inappropriate [to R]** [R] to equate one mode with only one
          perspective: all language is both product and process.
     d. A dynamic perspective, then, is a way of [R] modelling or [R] explaining
          language as, or as if it were, unfolding.
     e. Certainly a full account [by R] of them demands that they be considered
          [by R] as processes, and [R] doing so **reveals [to R]** inadequacies and
          weaknesses in synoptically oriented models.

Non-finite verbal groups, by definition, have no Finite; and they also have
no Subject, though the 'doer' can of course be expressed elsewhere in the clause
complex. Indeed, a crude rule-of-thumb that language teachers often invoke is
that a non-finite verb typically 'takes' its Subject from a finite verb nearby in the
clause complex. One thing that is noticeable about the instances in the extract is
that the 'doer' is completely elided from the complex in each case. Three of
these cases ('modelling', 'explaining', doing') are gerunds: they are therefore on
the edge of nominalisation and do not depend on finite verbs elsewhere in the
complex. One ('to account for') occurs with an agentless passive verb in the
clause on which it depends: the use of the non-finite form harmonises with the
use of the agentless passive, precisely because they both elide the researcher.

   The other two cases ('to make', 'to equate') are of particular interest. The
embedded clauses in which they appear are extraposed extraposition Subjects of
evaluative clauses. When such structures involve modality (e.g. 'it is
possible/necessary to ...'), they are described as explicit objective modality and
recognized as interpersonal grammatical metaphor (Halliday 1994: 355).
Although Halliday does not explicitly extend the discussion to attitudinal
expressions, it can be argued that, just as with modality, the expression of
personal stance is being treated as if it were an attribute of the proposition – the
similarity is underlined by the fact that 'it is inappropriate to' could be viewed as
objective modulation. What is being disguised in each case, of course, is the
outcome of an assessment by the researcher. If the researcher's role in this
assessment is made explicit, the result is a projecting clause with a mental
process in which the researcher is Senser ('I think/believe/feel/etc. that...'). Thus
it is again the researcher in their role as W Senser that is being elided. I have
therefore included these two evaluations, though somewhat awkwardly, as
falling into the 'to R' category.

The usefulness of these anticipatory 'it' structures in expressing writer stance in a depersonalised way is already well established; but I am interested in the fact that the embedded clause is a non-finite 'to'-infinitive clause rather than a finite 'that'-clause. Both these types of embedded clause can occur in the structure (though usually with different types of evaluation in the matrix clause – see Thetela 1997). Compare, for example:

> (8) c.'It is inappropriate to equate one mode with only one perspective
>   f. It seems reasonable that learners should be helped to progress in the direction of some variety of standard competence.

In one sense, the selection of an objective evaluative clause and of the type of embedded clause can be seen as two separate choices. However, the Subject in 'that'-clauses in this pattern is normally some participant other than the researcher (as in the second example above, where the Subject is 'learners'). When the researcher is the 'doer' of the process in the embedded clause, the normal option is the non-finite one (it is the researcher who 'equates' in the first example), which avoids the need to mention the doer. Thus, a good case can be made for viewing the choice as a single one, led by the writer's desire to elide themself from the message. The 'it ... to ...' structure kills two participant birds with one stone: it elides the researcher as evaluator in the text and as doer in the physical event.

This suggests that wordings in academic text may at times be selected in order to accommodate a non-finite form so that it is not necessary to have an expressed Subject. This is, of course, one of the reasons that has been claimed for choosing nominalisations. Non-finites and nominalisations can therefore be viewed as competing for the same ecological niche in this respect.

3.2.1. Metonymy

There is in fact yet another resource for not mentioning the W-participant that needs to be mentioned, one which appears to draw on the familiar category of metonymy. The word 'perspective' could be seen as implying a Senser, but it does not fit easily into the two main categories established so far: it perhaps suggests a separate category – 'of R'. This could also be applied, though less obviously, to 'models' and in fact to any terms which refer to the products of the researcher as thinker or writer when they are used as metonyms for the researcher.[5] These can again be seen as indexing the researcher, in the sense in which I have used it above. Cases are included in the version below marked by bold italic, together with the other elidings identified above.

(8")   In contrast, spoken language, which presents text as active and on-going, encourages a *view [by R]* which is less totalising, and more process-like. [R] To account for this aspect of language, a dynamic ***perspective [of R]*** is *needed [by R]*. Yet it is too easy [R] to make a false *equation [by R]* between written language and a synoptic perspective on the one hand, and spoken language and a dynamic perspective on the other. .... It is therefore inappropriate [R] to equate one mode with only one perspective: all language is both product and process. Given that linguistics ***models [of R]*** have largely arisen in conjunction with the *study [by R]* of written language, the relatively recent *focus [by R]* on spoken language has **revealed [to R]** the inability of available ***models [of R]*** to account for the process nature of language. However, both modes can – and should – *be accounted for [by R]* from both ***perspectives [of R]***. This **suggests [to R]** that a ***perspective [of R]*** on language should be independent from any 'intrinsic' qualities of the data. A dynamic ***perspective [of R]***, then, is a way of [R] modelling or [R] explaining language as, or as if it were, unfolding.

Within the systemic functional approach the dynamic ***perspective [of R]*** has tended to be most vigorously *pursued [by R]* in relation to certain linguistic phenomena. These phenomena include the *study [by R]* of generic structure ... As these phenomena can be *seen [by R]* to unfold in time, and to be dependent on the nature of the current environment, they could be *said [by R]* to be 'inherently' dynamic. Certainly a full *account [by R]* of them demands that they be *considered [by R]* as processes, and [R] doing so **reveals [to R]** inadequacies and weaknesses in synoptically oriented ***models [of R]***. However, the *suggestion [by R]* that some types of linguistic phenomena are 'dynamic', and that by *inference [by R]* others are not, is an *equation [by R]* as false as the *equation [by R]* of a dynamic ***perspective [of R]*** with a specific mode of discourse. A dynamic ***perspective [of R]*** should not be *reserved [by R]* just for certain types of data, but should be *applied [by R]* broadly to language as a whole.

3.3.   Summary of environments for eliding participants

To summarise, I have discussed the following range of lexicogrammatical environments in which the researcher as participant may be elided:

'by R' (Agent): nominalisations; passives; 'action' nouns
'to R' (Senser): identifying/ mental processes; explicit objective assessment;
                 'mental' nouns and adjectives
'of R' (Carrier): metonymy
'R' (Subject) :   non-finites

At this stage the reader may have the impression that the study has turned into a manic 'hunt-the-participant' chase which has been stretched beyond the necessary limits. However, it should be emphasised that what the 'full' analyses above are doing is showing the places where the participation of the researcher in the physical or mental activity is discernible in some way but is not explicitly encoded in the wording. In other words, at each of these places, it would have been possible in principle to mention the researcher. It is not being claimed that in a more congruent wording the researcher might be mentioned in every one of these slots – obviously that would not be feasible. However, the analyses do give some idea of just how absent the researcher is; and they also indicate the interweaving configurations of mutually supportive lexicogrammatical choices which contribute to that absence.

At the same time, there is a further crucial feature of all these resources, which has been touched on in relation to the identifying/mental blends discussed above. All the wordings trail diffuse clouds of researcher behind them; and what I have been doing in the analyses, I would claim, is to trace the sources of the vapour trail. Academic text is largely depersonalised, but it is also intended to come across as deeply imbued with the sense of an observing, interpreting mind. Indexing the researcher, leaving a trace of their presence even while eliding them from the explicit wording of the text, is a highly distinctive characteristic of this register. If I tell an anecdote about a funny event that I witnessed, I do not typically preface every statement with 'I saw ...' or 'I heard ...' even though I was the W-Senser: in casual conversation there is not the conventional expectation that I will project a sense of everything being filtered through my interpreting mind. In academic writing, on the other hand, a sense of the filtering mind is essential; and the resources described above are designed to achieve the delicate balancing act of eliding the researcher and simultaneously infusing the text with their presence.

4.   Issues remaining

The discussion so far raises a number of issues, of which three seem to me to be particularly interesting (though I cannot as yet see any way of resolving the last two).

I have so far presented the reasons for eliding the researcher as relatively unproblematic – essentially as a question of conforming to conventions. However, the possible motivations in any particular case are likely to be much more complex.[6] In the first extract, the events described are clearly highly charged in emotional terms. The writers' main purpose is to present data to be interpreted rather than to tell an unhappy story of someone who died; but the sensitive nature of those data must presumably affect to a certain extent the way the writers present them and provide a further reason for construing them impersonally (potentially at least, omissions on the part of the medical staff could be seen as having contributed to the death). In relation to the second extract, Ravelli (personal communication) has pointed out that talking about 'the researcher' as an undifferentiated entity obscures important distinctions, especially in texts putting forward views that could be controversial – as hers does. In particular, there is the question of alignment: whether 'the researcher' represents the author and like-minded scholars, or researchers against whose views s/he is arguing. The reasons for not mentioning the researcher in these two cases are presumably different. Similarly, although I have found it convenient to include the reader under the umbrella term of 'the researcher', the reasons for not mentioning the reader are likely to be different again (for some discussion of this, see Thompson, 2001). There is clearly room for more delicate description of the phenomenon of participant eliding, especially in terms of the factors that encourage it, within the framework set out here.

The second issue takes us into areas where I tread more warily. I argued earlier that what might be seen as separate choices are probably best viewed as different manifestations of the same choice. That can clearly be applied to complete texts (indeed, the whole register): the decision to present the uncommonsense view of the researcher's role that we associate with academic writing can be seen as opening up, or weighting the probabilities heavily in favour of, the syndromes of choices outlined above. (Of course, it is somewhat misleading to talk about it as a 'decision': for most academic writers on most occasions it is a more-or-less automatic acceptance of working within the conventional probabilities, with just occasional Prufrockian hesitations – 'Do I dare to eat a peach? Do I dare to mention me?').

However, such 'signing up' to a particular register (which we might call the writer's 'registration'?) brings doubts about the picture that has been implied so far of the process of producing and understanding the wordings. In very simple terms, I have been writing as if the writer experiences the 'real-world' events and deliberately recasts them in uncommonsense terms in the text, selecting certain aspects to highlight and others (especially their own role) to background. In understanding the text, the reader then reconstitutes as far as possible the physical events, reinstating the researcher as a W-participant. See Figure 4.

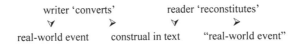

Figure 4: The simple view of uncommonsense construal

However, it seems at least as likely that the process is shortened by familiarity, and that both writers and readers understand the uncommonsense construal without calling directly on experience of, or general familiarity with, the physical events. See Figure 5.

Figure 5: Shortened uncommonsense construal

My own guess (and it is only that) is that both processes must occur, to differing degrees according to external factors. It seems unlikely that a researcher who has carried out an experiment can blank out that experience completely: the process of 'converting' may play more of a role here than in, for example, the presentation of abstract argumentation. (Evidence from comparing spoken presentations with published versions of the same paper indicates that the 'conversion' is typically much less pervasive in the former. For example, presenters talking about their own research frequently intersperse short narratives of the physical sequence of events – see S. Thompson 1997.) However, it seems plausible that the second process dominates most of the time – though, as argued above, the wordings are still designed to evoke traces of the researcher's presence. The case for shortened construal but with traces remaining of what has been excluded in the construal is perhaps strongest with nominalisation. It is generally accepted that the meaning of grammatical metaphor involves recognition at some level that there are two strands: that something which could potentially be worded as a clause has not been (this is especially clear when the clausal wording precedes the nominalised one in the text, and the nominalisation re-enters that meaning as a participant in another clause). As has often been pointed out, it is difficult to know at what stage in the analysis to stop the conversion to more congruent wording; and this corresponds to difficulty in knowing how far writers and readers do the same kind of conversion. But the assumption in including more congruent wordings in analyses is that they somehow correspond to at least part of what the reader understands. The same argument would seem valid (though perhaps to differing degrees) for all the types of participant eliding listed above.

This leads on to the third issue. To what extent – if at all – are all these resources kinds of grammatical metaphor? From one angle, they could be seen as metaphorical, since they construe the events referred to in ways which are not congruent with the physical events: one of the central W-participants in those events remains indexed but unmentioned. Most discussions of grammatical metaphor (and also traditional lexical metaphor) rely to a greater or lesser extent on a perceived lack of congruence between what is felt to be the 'real' state of affairs being talked about and the wording chosen to represent it: the more congruent wording is one which is intuitively more 'faithful' to the world (though see Ravelli 1988, for a different perspective). However, the criterion of participant eliding by itself may not be enough to label the resources as metaphorical, since all clauses involve a selection from the range of possible features that might be mentioned – as Winter (1982) points out, we cannot ever say everything, and the clause is a means of constructing coherent messages without saying everything.

From another angle, there appears to be a fundamental difference between nominalisation – representing something (a process) for which a 'natural' linguistic category has evolved (verbs) in terms of a different category (nouns) – and, say, identifying/mental processes like 'demonstrate' – which use the natural category but simply omit to mention one of the elements of the real-world event. On the other hand, it could be argued that the issue is simply one of delicacy: a verb like *show*, for example, presumably evolved originally to refer to a material process, and its use in identifying processes is an expansion of its semiotic potential which is essentially of the same kind as the semiotic expansion represented by nominalisation, though at a greater degree of delicacy. Similarly, non-finite forms represent an expansion of wording potential from the most natural forms which have all the clausal trappings (Subject, finiteness, etc.) explicitly represented.

At this stage, I do not know whether the resources should all be counted as grammatical metaphor (though on the whole I am inclined to believe that they should). The answer depends on exactly what our definition of grammatical metaphor is. Although the concept is intuitively clear and heuristically valuable, and the central types are easily identifiable, there are still indeterminacies. Perhaps it is simply a concept that, like so much else in linguistics, we have to accept as being fuzzy, with prototypical instances at the core and less clear-cut cases around the periphery; but this still means that there is work to do in describing the periphery and in identifying the characteristics which may contribute to, even if they do not determine, the status of a linguistic feature as grammatical metaphor. The present paper is designed to be a participant in that process.

Notes

1. The sample consisted of extracts chosen at fairly regular but random intervals from 9 university textbooks in biology, physics, chemistry, medicine, business and linguistics, and from 12 journal articles in linguistics, materials science and medicine. Since the figures and examples are intended to be merely illustrative, I did not attempt to establish systematic categories of sources to ensure proper coverage of relevant text types.

2. I do not know of any good term which covers Actor/Senser/Carrier/Sayer/Behaver – the transitivity participants which can be seen as typically mapping onto the choice of Subject in an unmarked way: I am therefore using the admittedly unsatisfactory term of 'natural Subject'.

3. It should be borne in mind that I have only considered the nominal group itself in assigning instances to the categories. In a small number of category 1 cases there is explicit mention of the researcher elsewhere in the clause, most clearly in instances where the nominalisation is Range in a process with the researcher as Actor, Senser or Sayer:

    we reached the conclusion that the virus is a set of parasitic genes encased in a protein coat

4. On the use of 'papers' to stand in for the researchers, see section 3.2.1 on metonymy.

5. It might be worth considering the possibility that nominalisations with the researcher (as 'doer') elided can also be seen as a kind of metonymy: the action stands in for the person performing the action. (However, as yet I am not quite sure what would be gained by seeing them in this way.)

6. I am grateful to Louise Ravelli for raising the issues discussed in this paragraph.

References

Christie, F. & Martin, J.R. (eds.) (1997) *Genre and Institutions: Social processes in the workplace and school.* London: Cassell.

Coffin, C. (1997) Constructing and giving value to the past: An investigation into secondary school history. In: F. Christie & J.R. Martin (eds.) (1997). 196–230.

Deluca, M., Peerless, J.R., Matthews, L.A. & Malangoni, M.A. (1996) Acute obstructive uropathy in a gravid Patient with pelvic injuries: Case report". *The Journal of Trauma* 41.3: 556–7.

Halliday, M.A.K. (1994) *An Introduction to Functional Grammar.* 2nd edition. London: Arnold.

Halliday, M.A.K. & J.R. Martin (1993) *Writing Science: Literacy and discursive power.* London: Falmer.

Iedema, R. (1997) The language of administration: Organizing human activity in formal institutions. In: F. Christie & J.R. Martin (eds.) (1997). 73–100.

Martin, J.R. (1992) *English Text: System and structure.* Philadelphia: Benjamins.

Ravelli, L. (1988) Grammatical metaphor: An initial analysis. In: E.H. Steiner & R. Veltman (eds.) *Pragmatics, Discourse and Text: Some systemically-inspired approaches*. London: Pinter. 133–47.

Ravelli, L. (1995) A dynamic perspective: Implications for metafunctional interaction and an understanding of Theme. In: R. Hasan & P. Fries (eds.) *On Subject and Theme*. 187–234. Amsterdam: Benjamins.

Thetela, P. (1997) Entities and parameters in academic research articles. *English for Specific Purposes* 16.2: 101–118.

Thompson, G. (1998) Resonance in text. In: A. Sánchez-Macarro & R. Carter (eds.) *Linguistic Choice across Genres: Variation in spoken and written English*. Amsterdam: Benjamins. 29–46.

Thompson, G. (2001) Interaction in academic writing: Learning to argue with the reader. *Applied Linguistics* 22.1: 58–78.

Thompson, G. & Y.Y. Ye. (1991) Evaluation in the reporting verbs used in academic papers. *Applied Linguistics* 12.4: 365–82.

Thompson, S. (1997) *Presenting Research: A study of interaction in academic monologue*. Unpublished PhD thesis, University of Liverpool.

Winter, E. (1982) *Towards a Contextual Grammar of English: The clause and its place in the definition of sentence*. London: Allen & Unwin.

Imperative readings of grammatical metaphor
A study of congruency in the imperative

Inger Lassen
Aalborg University

1.   Introduction

Grammatical metaphor (GM) is a notion that was introduced into Systemic Functional Theory by Halliday in the 80s. Since then the theory has been developed by a number of Systemicists, including primarily Halliday (e.g. 1987, 1989, 1994, 1995a, 1995b, 1998a, 1998b), Ravelli, (1985, 1988), Halliday and Matthiessen (1999), Halliday and Martin (1993) and Martin (1992). Providing examples of the two GM categories, metaphors of transitivity and metaphors of mood, Halliday (1994: 40–367) characterises both categories as incongruent realisations of meaning that might in other situations be rendered through less metaphorical variants. The designation Halliday uses for language that makes sparing use of metaphorical configurations is 'congruent'. (For a more detailed explanation of the notion of GM, see Section 2).

A question that may present an obstacle to a deeper understanding of the nature of GM is how 'congruent' and 'incongruent' should be interpreted. The problem seems to be particularly pronounced for metaphors of mood, an observation originally made by Halliday (1994: 365), who points to the "very considerable semantic load" carried by mood variants. He states that "these categories lend themselves to a rich variety of metaphorical devices; and it is by no means easy to decide what are metaphorical and what are congruent forms". Now, Halliday's concern is directed at various modalized and modulated mood resources functioning as warnings, advice, commands, etc., while one of the key resources within the mood system, viz. the imperative, is not discussed in any detail as regards congruency. At one point Halliday (1994: 356) refers to the imperative as the congruent 'default' option for proposals, but otherwise it is not being made very clear which role the imperative plays in congruency.

The primary purpose of this article is therefore to address congruency with the imperative as a case in point. My research question is whether the imperative is – by nature – always congruent, or whether there might be instances when this grammatical form carries metaphorical meaning. To pursue the task I have set for myself, I shall devote some space to identifying similarities and differences between lexical metaphor, grammatical metaphor, indirect speech acts and literal utterances, since I believe an overview of these areas will facilitate comprehension. My point of departure will be Halliday's definitions of lexical and grammatical metaphor (1994: 342; 1999: 7). However, in addition to Systemic Theory I shall resort to Indirect Speech Act Theory as described by Searle (1979), with the purpose of examining what part context plays in determining congruency.

2. Defining grammatical metaphor

Halliday has defined GM as "variation in the expression of a given meaning" (1994: 342), a definition that he juxtaposes with a pun in which he defines lexical metaphor as "variation in the meaning of a given expression" (ibid.: 342). A perhaps more explanatory definition is offered in Halliday & Matthiessen (1999: 7) where GM is referred to as "a phenomenon whereby a set of agnate (related) forms is present in the language having different mappings between the semantic and the grammatical categories". GM is perhaps best understood as a metaphor of lexical metaphor, which – for lack of a commonly accepted definition – may be defined on an ad hoc basis as

> any semantically equivalent identification or any association of one thing with another by replacing a word or phrase from the semantic field it naturally belongs to with a word or phrase from another in the context less usual semantic field.

Against this background GM is to be understood as any association of the category meaning of one semantic category with another by replacing the original semantic category with a different semantic category in the lexico-grammar (Lassen 1997: 68 based on personal communication with Halliday 1997). It is important to note that semantic category is to be understood here as a metalinguistic notion involving the semantics of the grammar. One of the key mechanisms of GM is that of *semantic junction* as explained by Halliday and

Matthiessen (1999: 260, 243) and Halliday (1998b). A semantic junction arises if for example an element displays a combination of the feature of the element (the congruent meaning of the grammatical class 'noun') and a process (the congruent meaning of the grammatical class 'verb'). (For a thorough description of elements and figures, see Halliday and Matthiessen 1999: 59–65). The principles of lexical metaphor and grammatical metaphor are illustrated in Figures 1, 2 and 3.

The features of a fruit 'orange' coincide with the features of the nature phenomenon 'sun'

Semantics	The 'sun'	is an	'orange'	(two meanings)

semantic junction

Lexico-grammar	The sun	is an	orange	(grammatical choices)
				(one realization option)

Figure 1. Lexical metaphor

Two readings are required to make sense of the statement 'the sun is an orange'. If read literally, the statement does not make sense, and it is therefore given an additional metaphorical reading.

In GM the features of a process may coincide with the features of an entity (verb and noun). This is the case in ideational metaphors of transitivity as shown in Figure 2 below:

Installation of cylinder (GM)
How to install the cylinder (more congruent version)

Semantic category	Process (action, event)	Entity (person, thing)
	'install'	

semantic junction

Grammatical class	verb	noun (grammatical choices)
	install	installation (two realization options)

Figure 2: Grammatical metaphor (ideational metaphor of transitivity):
Remapping[1] of a process 'to install' into a nominal form 'installation'

In addition to the notion of *semantic junction*, the notion of *typicality* or *markedness* seems to be crucial to the understanding of GM. According to Halliday (1994: 343), knowing a language is knowing its typical ways of expression. In this sense he looks upon typical patterns of wording as 'congruent' forms, a point that is also raised by Ravelli (1988: 135), who – like Halliday – equates typical with unmarked. Eggins seems to support Halliday and Ravelli in their stances on typicality and congruency in that she equates typicality with congruency (1994: 63). Along the same lines, Martin (1997: 26) talks about "unmarked correlations between meanings and wordings" and continues that "we may expect statements to be realized congruently as declaratives, questions as interrogatives and commands as imperatives". The same sort of reasoning may be applied to the ideational level where, in Martin's words, "participants are congruently realized as nouns, processes as verbs, properties as adjectives and logical relations as conjunctions" (ibid.: 26–27). If this realization pattern is not followed, tension in the form of a *semantic junction* arises, and it is in this 'denaturalized' state of affairs that GM thrives. These formulations might suggest that the notions of congruency and incongruency are seen as a dichotomy. However, researchers have recently begun to question this point of view. Thus, using semo-history as their theoretical platform, Halliday and Matthiessen (1999: 17–18; 235) propose that rather than maintaining a simple dichotomy of literal and metaphorical, it would be more appropriate to look at grammatical metaphor as a continuum with a 'least metaphorical' pole and a 'most metaphorical' pole. In my discussion of the metaphorical potential of the imperative later in this article I shall adopt this point of view.

3.   Types of grammatical metaphor

An overview of GM types is offered in Halliday (1994: Ch 10) where GM is subdivided into ideational metaphors and interpersonal metaphors. In ideational metaphors a metaphorical shift takes place between two or more of the following classes: relator, circumstance, process, quality and thing. The principle of mapping a process onto a thing was shown in Figure 2 above. According to Halliday and Matthiessen (1999: 264) the general drift of ideational metaphor is from the abstract towards the concrete, i.e. from process towards thing, and the simultaneous shifts that take place at the level of rank between e.g. clause complex, clause and group/phrase forming syndromes of GM further support this impression.

The second type of GM introduced by Halliday, viz. interpersonal metaphor is usually subdivided into metaphors of modality and metaphors of mood. As observed by Martin, who quotes Halliday (1992: 412), one of the primary purposes of interpersonal metaphors is that of 'modal responsibility' as illustrated in the subjective explicit clause 'I think it's going to rain' which in a less metaphorical clause might be rendered as 'It's probably going to rain' (objective implicit clause). The second type of interpersonal metaphor is the metaphor of mood. An example of this type is e.g. 'I'll shoot the pianist' (Halliday 1994: 363), which may be reported as 'he threatened to shoot the pianist'. In this clause the wording selects for mood in that it realizes the illocutionary act of offer.

Now, two GM categories have been introduced on the basis of the ideational and interpersonal metafunctions. However, since there is a third metafunction, the textual function, one may wonder why only Martin (1992: 416–417) uses this category in his classification. According to Martin (ibid.: 416), certain discourse elements organize text rather than field. These include certain anaphoric, cataphoric and exophoric references as well as a number of conjunctive relations, all of which are text-organizing pro-forms such as: *that's* ridiculous, *that point* is just silly, *for example, let me begin by, another example.* There is not necessarily a contradiction between the stance Martin has taken and that of other systemicists even if the categories of textual metaphor offered by Martin seem to have gone unnoticed by the majority of other GM theorists. The latter have primarily focused on ideational and interpersonal metaphors. In mainstream GM theory (see e.g. Halliday & Matthiessen 1999: 238–241) it is the general view that metaphoric shifts have textual implications. This is the situation if for instance sequences are realized as clauses and processes as nouns, as is the case in ideational metaphor. The same thing can be said for propositions realised as proposals in interpersonal metaphor. An example would be 'defective rolls can be returned for free replacement', which is a proposition. If we wrote instead 'return any defective roll for free replacement', the proposition would now assume the form of a proposal. It is clear from the example that the shift has textual implications in that 'defective rolls', which is Theme in the proposition becomes Rheme in the proposal. For the present purpose, I shall therefore refrain from a discussion of the feasibility of establishing a third GM category for textual metaphor and instead focus attention on the imperative, which I believe is a borderline case of GM within the area of interpersonal metaphors of mood. A discussion of GM as textual metaphor is offered in Lassen (to appear).

That the imperative seems to belong to a fuzzy area when attempts are made to categorise it as congruent or incongruent becomes clear if one looks at a number of claims made by systemic theorists. Following Halliday's point of view that the imperative is the most direct and typical way of expressing a command – and hence congruent –, Eggins (1994: 67) indirectly comes to the same conclusion, demonstrating that the variable of tenor impacts on how we use the mood structure of a clause. In an informal context of situation we would use the imperative for getting an action carried out by somebody else, as in 'Give me a hand here'. But if we try to get our boss to do something, we would construct a clause like 'I wondered if you'd mind giving me a hand with...'. According to Eggins the imperative is the typical choice for commanding family and friends, while statements and questions are preferred in formal situations. Eggins refers to clauses using structures other than imperatives to express commands as grammatical metaphor. Martin (1997: 26) cites Halliday for the view that the relationship between lexicogrammar and discourse semantics is 'natural'. On this basis Martin concludes that meanings and wordings will correlate, and that we may therefore expect statements to be realised as declaratives, questions as interrogatives and commands as imperatives. However, as we all know, this does not always happen, and declarative clauses are sometimes used instead of imperative clauses to express a command, as shown in the above example by Eggins. This way one mood is 'acting as another' in Martin's terminology. Following Halliday, Martin (1997: 28) observes that such 'denaturalized' use of speech acts is what gives rise to the formation of interpersonal GM in that the two speech acts must be read on two levels because it is the interaction of the two levels that creates the meaning. In the examples offered above, the imperative would seem to be the most direct way of expressing a command. However, since the imperative may be used for indirect speech acts other than commanding, like e.g. advice, warning, inviting, etc., it is not entirely clear why the imperative should always be characterised as congruent. In the clause 'use recommended pastes only' it seems that the imperative is not the most direct way of expressing a piece of advice because, as noted by Martin, the unmarked way of expressing statements is through declaratives. Therefore, I am going to argue that the imperative holds a vast meaning potential that may require a number of readings on different levels – incongruent as well as congruent – and it is to this aspect that I shall now turn.

4.   The imperative

The imperative has been studied in a variety of theories including speech act theory (e.g. Searle 1979, Lyons 1977), grammar and linguistics (e.g. Holdcroft 1978; Davies 1986), politeness theory (Brown & Levinson 1987), relevance theory (Sperber & Wilson 1986) and Systemic Functional Linguistics (e.g. Halliday 1994; Martin 1992, 1997; Eggins 1994). But, while there seems to be general consensus that the imperative is the most direct way of rendering for instance an instruction, very few articles on the topic focus on the imperative as a carrier of various indirect speech acts such as implicit warnings, promises, offers, advice, etc., and the metaphorical potential this multi-purpose grammatical form seems to entail. And while Searle (1979: 115) suggests criteria for distinguishing between indirect speech acts and lexical metaphor, no one seems to have defined the differences and similarities between indirect speech acts and grammatical metaphor. As a result there is a need for clarifying the metaphorical potential of the imperative and to try to provide a more varied picture of the possible uses that may be imposed on this grammatical form. This aim may be achieved by discussing metaphorical variation in some of the indirect speech act realizations that the imperative may accommodate. As a first point I am going to demonstrate that the imperative is not always congruent. To motivate this point – and on the basis of data from an experimental study – I shall discuss to what extent context influences the meaning that can be inferred from different uses of the imperative in LSP texts. As a second point, and building on Searle's categorization of literal meaning, metaphorical meaning and indirect speech acts, I wish to suggest that as carrier of metaphorical tension,[2] the imperative shares a number of features with lexical metaphor, on the one hand, and GM, on the other, but that in other respects it is also different from those two categories. I am therefore going to introduce a cline of metaphoricity for the imperative. For these purposes I shall provide a brief overview of some of the most relevant aspects of indirect speech act theory and how this theory relates to the approach advocated in Systemic Functional linguistics. In the process I shall include certain elements of Grice's principles of co-operative conversation (1975). But before approaching this task, I intend to look at the relations between the imperative, lexical metaphor, grammatical metaphor, indirect speech acts and literal meaning in order to gain more knowledge about possible similarities and differences.

4.1. *Categorization of the imperative*

In a chapter on metaphor, Searle (1979: 112–116) provides a graphical overview of different kinds of meaning relations represented through lexical metaphor, indirect speech acts and literal utterances (see Figure 3).

As observed by Searle, the 'speaker's utterance meaning' and the 'sentence meaning' come apart in metaphor as well as in indirect speech acts (see Figure 3 below), but in spite of this apparent similarity there is a major difference between them. In indirect speech acts the speaker means what he says but he also means something in addition to that. If he says (1) *can you pass the salt,* he asks at the same time about your ability to pass the salt and your willingness to do so. In this sense 'meanings are amplified', to use Searle's terminology. In lexical metaphor the speaker says something but means something else. If s/he says (2) *no man is an island,* the most probable interpretation would be that s/he does not intend to convey the idea that the phenomenon has been studied, and it has been found that none of the islands in the world is a human being. Rather the speaker intends to say that every person's actions have consequences. We may say then, as suggested by Halliday (1994: 342), that lexical metaphor has two meanings, but one expression – a gloss it shares with the imperative as carrier of different indirect speech acts. If the imperative is used simultaneously to instruct, warn and recommend as in the utterance (3) *use recommended pastes only,* there are three meanings combined in one expression. There is an element of inducing action, an element of trying to persuade the user to buy exactly the pastes recommended by the seller and an element of implicitly warning the user against possible failure by taking the chance of using non-recommended and – as a result – perhaps harmful pastes.

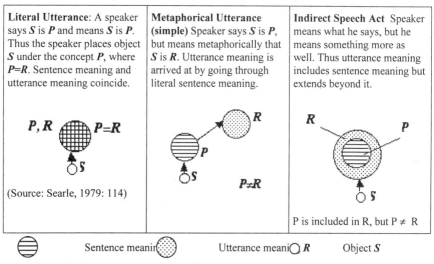

Literal Utterance: A speaker says S is P and means S is P. Thus the speaker places object S under the concept P, where $P=R$. Sentence meaning and utterance meaning coincide.	**Metaphorical Utterance (simple)** Speaker says S is P, but means metaphorically that S is R. Utterance meaning is arrived at by going through literal sentence meaning.	**Indirect Speech Act** Speaker means what he says, but he means something more as well. Thus utterance meaning includes sentence meaning but extends beyond it.
P, R $P=R$ S (Source: Searle, 1979: 114)	R P S $P{\neq}R$	R P S P is included in R, but P $\neq$ R

Sentence meaning   Utterance meaning R Object S

Figure 3: A graphic comparison of sentence meaning and utterance meaning

However, even if indirect speech acts, lexical metaphor and grammatical metaphor seem to have a number of common traits, something that makes it difficult to obtain a clear understanding of the relations between lexical metaphor and indirect speech acts, on the one hand, and indirect speech acts and grammatical metaphor, on the other, is the fact that the imperative is not the only way in which instructions, warnings and recommendations may be rendered. An instruction could also be rendered as a statement such as (4) *it is time you went to bed,* or as a question in (5) *would you like to calm down now* or even as a hint

(6) *bedtime*. These examples potentially share the same meaning, but there are a number of expression forms available to them. Interestingly, similar variation of expression is found in GM, which in Halliday's words may be seen as "variation in the expression of meanings" (1994: 341). It might be assumed then that GM and indirect speech acts such as instructions, warnings, recommendations, etc. are shaped in the same mould since in GM one meaning and two or more expression options combine to amplify meaning, and similar forces seem to be at work in the realization options used for various indirect speech acts. Along the same line of thought, there seem to be certain similarities between lexical metaphor and the imperative as carrier of different illocutionary acts in that in lexical metaphor there are two potential meanings to be derived, but only one expression; this interpretation may be closely associated with the way in which the imperative performs, combining two or more meanings in one expression. Figure 4 is a graphic presentation of Searle's interpretation of literal utterances, metaphorical utterances and indirect speech acts in which I have extended Searle's interpretations with alternative interpretations of the relations between sentence meaning and speaker's utterance meaning in indirect speech acts as well as in GM.[3]

Now, what possible inferences may be drawn about the imperative on this basis? It seems that the imperative may be viewed from two perspectives. The first perspective includes its function in the grammar as carrier of a number of illocutionary acts. And the second perspective focuses on its function as one of the options available for expressing each of these illocutionary acts. The question that invariably arises at this point is whether the imperative can be shown to be congruent in all of these expression options. My intuitive answer is that the imperative is congruent in some functions, but metaphorical in others. It is well-known that the imperative is the conventional way of issuing military commands and other orders backed by some authority, and in such uses it is therefore seen as congruent in that there is an accurate fit of function and form. Other directives that are closely related to the issuing of orders are instructions, and these may therefore be assumed to come close to orders in terms of congruency. However, as we shall see later, the imperative has a much wider metaphorical potential when it is used for indirect speech acts such as offers or promises.

A further question that has puzzled indirect speech act theorists is how it is possible for the listener to interpret an utterance if what Searle refers to as 'sentence meaning' differs from its illocutionary force. To be able to talk about these different types of meaning, Searle introduces the notions of 'primary illocutionary force' and 'secondary illocutionary force', of which the former is to

Literal Utterance: A speaker says *S* is *P* and means *S* is *P*. Thus the speaker places object *S* under the concept *P*, where *P=R*. Sentence meaning and utterance meaning coincide.	Metaphorical Utterance (simple) Speaker says *S* is *P*, but means metaphorically that *S* is *R*. Utterance meaning is arrived at by going through literal sentence meaning.	Indirect Speech Act Speaker means what he says, but he means something more as well. Thus utterance meaning includes sentence meaning but extends beyond it.
P, R $P=R$ S (Source: Searle, 1979: 114)	R P S $P{\neq}R$	R P S P is included in R, but P ≠ R
Indirect Speech Act I (**The imperative as carrier of three speech acts**): Speaker says *S* is *P* but means that *S* is *P* as well as R_1 and R_2. (See sentence 3).	**Indirect Speech Act II** (**The imperative as one of several realization options**): Speaker realizes *S* as P_4, but listener interprets *R* as an amplification of meaning based on a combination of P_1, P_2, P_3 and P_4. (See sentence 3).	**Grammatical metaphor** Speaker realizes *S* as P_1, but listener interprets R as an amplification of meaning based on a combination of P_1 and P_2.
R_1 R_2 P S **Three meanings – one expression** (like lexical metaphor)	P_1 P_2 P_3 P_4 R S **One meaning – two or more realizations** (like grammatical metaphor)	R P_1 P_2 S One meaning – two realizations
	P_1: Statement P_2: Question P_3: Offer P_4: Command	P_1: Process realized as actor P_2: Process realized as process

⊜ Sentence meaning, *P*   ⊙ Utterance meaning *R*   ○ Object *S*

Figure 4: A graphic comparison of sentence meaning and utterance meaning

be understood as the speaker's utterance meaning and the latter as the sentence meaning (ibid.: 33). Thus a sentence such as (7) *Can you reach the salt?* might evoke different types of response. One of these could be (8a) *'Yes, I can'* (doing nothing). This would be a response reacting to the secondary illocutionary force, which is a question about a person's ability to reach the salt. As an alternative reply we might have (8b) *Yes, I can. Here it is*, – a response to the primary illocutionary force of the utterance, which we would normally interpret as a request for the listener's assistance in moving the salt into the speaker's reach. In example (7) we might say that if the illocutionary force of the sentence is that of a request, sentence meaning and speaker's utterance meaning is not the same, and there is, in Searle's terms, "an ulterior illocutionary point beyond the illocutionary point contained in the meaning of the sentence" (ibid.: 47), which in the example would be the illocutionary points relating to the directives of asking information and requesting assistance respectively.

In Systemic Functional linguistics (e.g. Halliday 1994), illocutionary points are dealt with as categories of exchanging goods, services and information. Halliday's fundamental speech role notion of 'inviting', which embraces 'inviting to give' and 'inviting to receive', seems to correspond to the illocutionary points explained in Searle (1979), and further elaborated in Sperber & Wilson (1986, 1995) and in Downing & Locke (1992) as desirability on the part of the speaker or listener, respectively.

In Halliday (1994: 69; 1994: 365) the fundamental congruent speech act patterns work as follows: 'giving acts' (inviting to receive) are expressed through offers and statements, while 'demanding acts' (inviting to give) are expressed through commands and questions. Inferring from the examples provided by Halliday (ibid.: 69), the speech acts of offer and statement are used to express desirability on the part of the listener/reader, while questions and commands are used to express desirability on the part of the speaker/writer, corresponding to the notion of illocutionary point in mainstream speech act theory. The four speech functions then subsume a vast range of illocutionary forces such as e.g. advice, warnings, promises, invitations, requests, orders, injunctions, instructions, etc.

Halliday's distinction between 'inviting to give' and 'inviting to receive' is crucial to understanding how speech acts are defined in Systemic Theory compared to mainstream speech act theory since in Systemic Theory there seems to be a sharp division between the activities the two speech functions can achieve. If invited to give, the listener/reader is invited to do something that may benefit the speaker/writer whereas if there is an invitation to receive, the speech act will benefit the listener/reader.

As mentioned, Searle's categorisation is different in that he does not make the distinction between giving or demanding acts, but instead subsumes these two categories under the category of 'directives' – a category whose main characteristic is that it includes 'attempts to get a listener/reader to do something', no matter whether the speaker/writer invites or insists. However, as noted by Searle (1979: 14) his category of 'Commissives', which subsumes 'promises' is in fact closely related to the category of 'Directives' because the two categories have "the same direction of fit". Now a confusing point is that the notion of 'command' has different meanings to Halliday and Searle. Halliday uses 'command' as a speech function at the same level as Searle's 'Directive'. Searle also uses the notion of 'command', but as a sub-category of illocutionary forces within the category of Directives.

In what follows, I shall be using the notion of 'offer' for illocutionary acts that subsume the illocutionary point of *inviting to do something that benefits the listener/reader* and 'command' for illocutionary acts that subsume the illocutionary point of *inviting to do something that benefits the speaker/writer*. I shall then be using 'directive' as an umbrella term for offers and commands, since the basic illocution of a directive is – in Halliday's terminology – to 'invite' the addressee to do something. Searle (1979: 46) has suggested that to begin to understand the nature of the interplay between primary and secondary illocutionary points, we need a model based, not only on speech act theory but also on the shared background information of the speaker and the listener, the listener's ability to infer meaning and, not least, on conversational rules and conventions. The model Searle (ibid.: 32) suggests for explaining the indirectness of indirect speech acts is partly based on Grice's idea of the Co-operative Principle as described in his famous article "Logic and Conversation" (1975: 45). According to the Co-operative Principle, each discourse participant is expected to contribute to the conversation when it occurs while offering the exact amount of information required and observing the general drift of the exchange in which the interlocutors participate. He then distinguishes four main categories which he refers to as "the maxims of Quantity, Quality, Relation and Manner".[4] By analysing an example of indirection, Searle illustrates how he perceives the process of Student X deriving primary illocution from literal illocution

> Student X: Let's go to the movies tonight
> Student Y: I have to study for an exam

I shall not go into the details of Searle's analysis, but only mention that it proceeds through a number of steps drawing on inferencing, principles of conversational co-operation, factual background information and speech act theory. On this basis Student X is able to conclude that Student Y's primary illocutionary point probably is to reject the proposal.

As noted by Searle (ibid.: 35) the analysis is probably 'underdescribed' in spite of its 10 steps, and moreover it must be said to be probabilistic, since we do not know for certain whether this is what Student X would infer from the exchange. However, the example serves as an illustration of how primary illocutionary points may depart from secondary illocutionary points, thereby causing tension between two illocutionary forces. As suggested earlier the tension thus created may be observed in the imperative when this form is used for indirect speech acts. The research question I am therefore going to ask is: how do readers/listeners manage to differentiate between primary illocutionary points and secondary illocutionary points in the imperative? To explore this question, I set up an experiment designed to test whether non-specialist readers were able to identify more than one illocutionary point in a clause. The experiment, which I am going to describe more closely below, was based on clauses that had been isolated from their context, a design that was made to elicit as much information about meaning potentials in the imperative as possible. I attempted to achieve this goal by asking respondents to provide as many replies as possible to the stimuli they were exposed to, which meant that they would have to invent different contexts in which the clauses would make sense. I made the assumptions that (1) for some of the clauses, it would be possible to imagine different contexts in which different replies would make sense, and (2) for some of the clauses it would be possible to imagine only one context and consequently provide only one sensible reply. Examples falling under the first category would then be incongruent, while examples under the second category would be congruent. To argue this point, I am going to suggest that context is of paramount importance in the inference process and that specialist readers, who are deprived of a context when exposed to a verb in the imperative will make up for the contextual loss by inventing a context of their own, while non-specialist readers will tend to respond to the imperative on the understanding that the relationship between lexico-grammar and discourse semantics is 'natural', as suggested by Halliday (in Martin 1997: 26). This would mean that, unable to think of a relevant context, non-specialists would probably interpret the imperative as having only one illocutionary point, viz. that of a command. However, before I begin providing answers to the question asked above, it will be necessary to devote some space to the concept of context with the purpose of explaining the extent of losses we are likely to incur by not having access to this dimension.

4.3. Context

Context is dealt with in Systemic Functional theory as a layer that interacts with language in a stratified metaredundancy system. As a higher stratum in a hierarchy of strata, context is realized through 'preselections' in the lower language strata of semantics, lexico-grammar and phonology/ graphology. Context is thus seen as "a more comprehensive environment" than the language strata (Halliday & Matthiessen 1999: 375).

But what information is it that context may provide? What potential clues might knowledge of contextual dimensions offer in a text dominated by directives such as is the case in instruction manuals? And how do we make up for the lack of a context? To answer some of these questions, we need to study some of the situational features involving context. Susana Murcia-Bielsa (2000: 118–146) has studied variation in the expression of directive force in instruction manuals, which she argues is determined by a number of situational features. Basing her argument on the situational dimensions of field, tenor and mode, Murcia-Bielsa discusses context in terms of task-relevance, authority relations and production circumstances. In her study, she found that the imperative seems to be the syntactic form that typically realizes directives in instruction manuals (79.3% of the directives studied), and that it is mainly used to express necessity. Using politeness theory (as discussed in Brown & Levinson 1987), she claims that the imperative seems to be acceptable in the context of written instruction manuals, if the action can be seen as beneficial to the instructee, as also observed by Downing & Locke (1992: 198). On the tenor dimension, Murcia-Bielsa suggests that the frequent use of the imperative may be explained by the nature of power relations between the writer and the reader/user. When using the imperative, the writer does not impose authority on the reader/user. Instead, in the context of an instruction manual, the imperative will indicate necessity, leaving the reader/user no option if the product is to be used without problems (2000: 127). As for the dimension of field, Murcia-Bielsa suggests that due to their priority of urging a reader/user to act according to a directive, instruction manuals tend to avoid indirectness by using imperatives instead of using 'embroidered' directives that would distract the reader/user's attention (ibid.: 142). Now this may work if the interpreter has contextual literacy. If, in other words, the interpreter has access to the context of culture as well as to the context of situation involving the dimensions of genre, field, tenor and mode, s/he is likely to interpret the imperative in accordance with writer intentions.

There are two situations in which an interpreter may not have access to a context. Either s/he is not a specialist within a given field and is therefore contextually illiterate, or we have an arranged situation where one or several of the contextual dimensions are not readily accessible. This is the case when we analyse isolated sentences. If an imperative clause such as (10) *stay clear of rotating components* appears in isolation, we have no idea of the extent of the risk we might run by not following the directive because we have limited information about its field and context. Besides, since we do not know which genre the clause belongs to, we would not be able to say whether the directive is beneficial to the writer or to the addressee and we have difficulty in interpreting its illocutionary force(s). Therefore, our interpretation is limited to the information that can be derived from semantics and to the background information we may or may not have as readers of various LSP texts where clauses such as (10) would normally be found.

When discussing contextual dimensions we must distinguish between the immediate textual context of an utterance and the situational and cultural contexts, since the former category may be the only interpretation clue a reader has access to. In (11) *to determine the plunger load setting, press the plunger load set,* although it is not quite clear who will benefit from the action of 'pressing', there is no doubt that the writer urges the reader/user to engage in an action. However, the immediate textual context constituted by the purpose clause of 'to determine the plunger load setting', suggests that the 'pressing' should not be done right away. Rather, the plunger load set should only be pressed, if it is considered desirable to determine the plunger load setting. Thus a temporal dimension is suggested in that three stages may be identified in the clause. At stage 1 the decision concerning the desirability of plunger load setting is taken. Then at stage 2 the pressing is done, and at stage 3 the plunger load setting is determined. That it is possible to interpret clause (11) along these lines is partly a result of the syntactic pattern, which largely pivots on the semantic features carried by the lexis and grammar of the verbs.

4.4.   Towards a typology of processes based on semantic features

I would therefore assume that if for one reason or another a reader were denied access to the cultural and situational contexts of a text, it would be necessary to study the semantic features of verbs to obtain a deeper understanding of their contribution to the total meaning potential. Such a situation may be realistic if a translator is to translate a complicated technical text without being familiar with a given genre or the technology described in this genre as is sometimes the case when freelance translators are given translation tasks by agencies. It may be argued that all written text suffers from some degree of context deprivation as – by necessity – the production side is something we can only speculate about.

This is an important difference between written and spoken text, which may help justify the procedure I have followed in the experiment I am going to describe.

A discussion of the semantic features of verbs will conveniently take its point of departure in what Halliday refers to as processes. As demonstrated by Halliday and Matthiessen (1999: 466–467) processes have two functions. They are organizers of participants in figures, and they are organizers of time. In Halliday and Matthiessen's terminology therefore, they may be seen as having two profiles: a transitivity profile and a temporal profile. Focusing in particular on Vendler's treatment of temporal typology of processes (1967), Halliday and Matthiessen (1999: 469–506) explore and discuss process typologies suggested by other researchers without exhausting the field of investigation. On the basis of their explorations and taking a critical stance towards typologization that does not account for the interplay of the transitivity profile and the temporal profile of processes, Halliday and Matthiessen conclude that no process typology can be universal.

For the purpose of exploring the use of the imperative in proposals and following Halliday and Matthiessen (1999), I shall therefore use a typology in which Vendler's event taxonomy as described in Halliday and Matthiessen (1999: 474) intersects with the typology of figures proposed within Systemic Functional theory (ibid.: 151), viz. those of doing, sensing, saying and being/having. The typology is shown below as Table 1:

	doing	Sensing	saying	being and having
Activities	run, walk, swim, push/pull sth, ponder	ponder	speak, talk, chat	be [naughty/difficult]
accomplishments	paint a picture, make a chair, grow up		tell a story, ask a question	become, grow, go
Achievements	reach a peak, win a race, die, start	recognize, realize, spot	convince, remind	turn, fall
States	[habits, e.g.: he smokes]	desire, want, like, dislike, love, hate, know, believe, think that	say, ask, tell	have, possess, dominate, rule

Table 1: Typology combining Vendler's temporal profile
intersected with SFL process types
(Source: Halliday & Matthiessen 1999: 475)

In Halliday and Matthiessen's interpretation, Vendler's contribution is a typology based on a temporal profile, which includes activities, accomplishments, achievements and states (ibid.: 470). Activities are of a generic nature, while accomplishments embrace the completion of specific tasks over a span of time. Achievements are described as short transitions to an end state, and states are expressed through processes that involve no change. The advantage of combining Vendler's temporal profile with the process typology suggested by systemic theorists is that such combination allows us to consider – in addition to elements of time – also semantic features inherent in the transitivity system. In the following I am going to apply the process typology explained above to imperatives found in various professional genres such as sales brochures and instruction manuals. The purpose of this is to argue the point suggested earlier that the imperative holds a rich metaphorical potential. To explore this assumption, I shall be using data from an experiment described below.

5.   Describing the experiment

Aiming at producing as varied a picture of the imperative as possible, I selected 25 examples from a variety of professional texts (instruction manuals and brochures). The examples are listed in Table 2 below. I entered these examples into a reply sheet in random order and presented the sheet to native speakers of English who were at the same time non-specialists in the fields of technology as well as technical writing. The reason for choosing native speakers was that I wanted to eliminate possible comprehension problems caused by foreign language incompetence. By addressing non-specialists, I intended to come close to the real-life situation of readers struggling with texts whose contents they have to read for some mandatory purpose without being able to do so on an informed basis. In other words if students or translators are asked to translate a complicated technical text, they may often be unaware of the social and discursive practices determining the syntax and lexis of the text, because they only have the reading context as guidance, being deprived of the situational and cultural contexts in which the text was produced. Specialists would be able to imagine the contexts in which such texts are produced, but this does not apply to non-specialists.

Another reason for addressing non-specialists was that a primary purpose of the experiment was to explore whether the imperative may be viewed as congruent in all situations. I assumed that while specialists would be able to interpret the intended meaning of the imperatives presented to them without having to resort to more than one reading level, non-specialists would be wondering how to make sense of it all and consequently apply a number of readings. This way I hoped to be able to obtain more information about the metaphorical potential of the imperative, assuming that imperative clauses, which were unambiguous in the sense that they would trigger one – and only one – reaction, because they were not interpreted as having a secondary illocutionary force, might be defined as congruent.

To achieve this goal, I asked the respondents to imagine that each of the imperative clauses represented input in a dialogue between a writer and a reader, and that this input might trigger various responses. The respondents were asked to provide – if possible – two types of replies for each imperative clause: one co-operative, the other one non-co-operative. To facilitate comprehension, I had provided the following typical example of a non-co-operative exchange: 'Can you reach the wine?' 'Yes' – (doing nothing).

In this situation the most direct (and natural) way of expressing the command intended by the utterance would be by way of an imperative like: 'Pass me the wine, please'. The co-operative reply would be: Yes, sure (passing the wine), and the only non-co-operative reply possible would be a flat refusal.

To further exemplify the task that the respondents were asked to do, I had provided illustrative responses in both response categories for the following sample clause:

Save and receive voice messages into a 'mailbox'.

Examples of co-operative replies where the illocutionary direction has been understood as intended:

(a)   Is that possible?
(b)   Really!
(c)   I see!
(d)   No thanks, not interested

Example of a non-co-operative reply where the illocutionary direction has been misunderstood: *Yes, I'll do so!* (Understanding the imperative as a command). The example shows that a non-co-operative reply does not have to be negative and, similarly, a co-operative reply does not have to be positive. Against this background it will be appear that I used the term non-co-operative as synonym for miscommunication, whether deliberate or unintended.

As already indicated above, the purpose of the experiment was to acquire more information about the meaning potential present in imperative utterances.

Deprived of a context, the respondents would have to rely on a semantic interpretation of the clauses presented to them, and – to a certain extent – on background knowledge gained from possibly having read similar LSP texts without being specialists in the area.

I assumed that respondents without any background knowledge at all would not be able to differentiate primary illocutionary points from secondary illocutionary points since they would have to rely on a semantic interpretation only. The consequence of this is that they would most likely interpret all the imperatives as commands because of the natural relationship assumed to exist between the two (Martin 1997: 27). For certain imperatives this strategy would generate meaningless responses, since in some of the imperative clauses used in the experiment, speaker's utterance meaning was not the same as sentence meaning, – a point that I intended to explore by asking the respondents to provide both co-operative and non-co-operative replies.

6.   Results and discussion

When analysing the results I found that the co-operative principle had been flouted in two distinct ways. In the first type of flouting, respondents replied to sentence meaning rather than to speaker's utterance meaning. In other words the response took account of form rather than of function like in (13) *Hold it in your hand. Feel its weight. Take a closer look at its features,* to which one respondent replied by saying *Yes, I'll do that.* Surprisingly, this reply is non-co-operative since the speaker's utterance meaning is misinterpreted, the respondent interpreting the example to be a command, while it was intended as an implicit promise of customer satisfaction. A response of this sort might trigger a reaction like 'this was not what I meant'. The second type of flouting found in some of the replies involved a response that replied to an interpretation of the speaker's undisclosed intention. In other words, in replying, the respondent unpacked an illocutionary point that was not actually meant to be made explicit. Unlike the example above such flouting might cause the first speaker to comment 'this was what I meant, but you were not supposed to make it explicit'. An example of the flouting explained appears in one of the responses to (14) *use recommended pastes only,* which triggered a response like *Why – it's a sales ploy.* The respondent reveals the seller's strategy of pretending to give advice, while there probably is an illocutionary point beyond the apparent service-mindedness of the utterance.

	doing
activities	1) and receive messages (offer)
accomplishments	2) Repair leaks in the engine immediately (Recommendation);
	5) ....read this manual carefully (Recommendation);
	7) Do not weld hydraulic piping (Warning/advice);
	12) Add a fibreglass cab, and the Cushman dealer .... (Promise);
	13) Go where you want to go ... (Promise);
	14) Never start the tractor with ... (Warning);
	17) Remove the dipstick (Instruction);
	18) To determine the plunger load setting, press the plunger load set (Instruction);
	19) If necessary, insert an iron bar under the twines on the end of the bale (Recommendation);
	22) Return any defective roll with its label for free replacement (Offer);
	24) Avoid skin contact with all fuels, oils, acids, solvents, etc. (Warning).
achievements	9) Flip up the passenger seat and you ... (Promise)
states	16) For best results, rake with some dew moisture on the hay crop (Recommendation);
	17) Permit the crop to dry (Recommendation);
	23) Use recommended pastes only (Recommendation/advice).
	sensing
activities	
accomplishments	3) feel its weight – take a closer look at its features (Offer).
achievements	8) Understand that your safety is measured by .... (Warning);
	10) know the positions of all controls before .... (Warning).
states	6) Do not hesitate to ... (Offer/non-state);
	10) Know the positions of all controls before you ... (Warning);
	21) Believe it or not, pistons can go seriously out of true (Threat/Warning).
	saying
activities	
accomplishments	4) Ask your Cushman Dealer for a demonstration (Offer).
achievements	
states	25) When ordering service parts, always quote the model and serial number (Request).
	being and having
activities	3) Hold it in your hand (Offer).
accomplishments	11) Stay clear of rotating components (Warning);
	15) become acquainted with .... the relative legislation in your country (Recommendation).
achievements	
states	15) Respect the relative legislation applicable in your country (Recommendation).

Table 2: Examples used in the experiment
(Numbers in the table refer to the way the examples were numbered in the experiment.)

Interestingly, in some of the examples the respondents had extreme difficulties in suggesting non-co-operative replies that went against the primary illocutionary point of the imperative. I take it that these imperatives are congruent in that there is co-incidence of form and function. An example of a congruent imperative is offered in (15) *Never start the tractor with the PTO engaged*, which is a warning based on prohibition. In the example the imperative is used to prevent action and the circumstance of time 'never' makes the prohibition definitive and something it is impossible to argue against. There seems to be no illocutionary point beyond that.

Now, as suggested earlier, verb processes play a crucial part in determining the illocutionary force of the message. And since some of the imperatives that the respondents were asked to interpret seemed to create difficulties, I shall now take a closer look at the processes involved. I shall use Vendler's temporal profile in intersection with SFL process types as a framework for categorizing the processes that occurred in the experiment. The purpose of doing this is to see whether the imperatives to which the respondents seemed to have difficulty in finding a non-co-operative reply might share common features in terms of process types.

Of the 25 imperative clauses shown in Table 2, the majority (11 of 25) belong to the category of doing/accomplishment, while the categories of saying and being/having in different combinations are nearly empty. It may therefore be assumed that processes in the imperative mood belonging to the doing/ accomplishment category are frequently found in instruction manuals. This probably has something to do with the nature of the imperative, in that an important semantic feature of this syntactical form is that it induces action. It is interesting to note that the illocutionary points in the category of doing/ accomplishment include a wide range of directives such as recommendation, warning, prohibition, instruction, promise and offer. It should be added though that there is only one example of an offer in the category even if the total sample has 6 examples of offers. However, these fall in different other categories and do not seem to prefer any single category, while instructions are only found in the category of doing/accomplishment. It is of course not possible to say whether this observation would still hold if the experiment were extended to include a larger sample of imperative clauses. Interestingly, however, of the 25 examples the doing/accomplishment category seems to be by far the preferred category for the texts studied.

Now, if we look at the respondents' attempts at producing non-co-operative replies it would appear that they found this task particularly difficult for the category of doing/accomplishment processes since non-co-operative replies were only possible in 3 of the 11 examples in this category. Of the 3 examples (clauses 12, 13 and 22) for which non-co-operative responses could be produced, 2 replies (12 and 13) were promises and 1 reply (22) an offer. On a narrow basis, it may be assumed, therefore, that the process category of doing/accomplishment has limited scope for metaphoricity, but is instead a category in which the imperative is primarily congruent. I have to emphasize once again, though, that the examples were studied out of context. This means that it was in fact possible to misinterpret examples 2, 17, 18 and 19 on temporal grounds. In example (18) *To determine the plunger load setting, press the plunger load set*, a respondent misinterpreted the temporal perspective due to the absence of an immediate situational context, thereby neglecting the asynchronic element of the message. As a result the respondent could pretend that s/he was being asked to act immediately upon reading the clause. One of the non-co-operative responses produced against this background was *I can't press it* as if the respondent was trying to press the plunger load set while participating in the experiment.

There is of course a fair amount of guessing involved when trying to imagine how a reader would make sense of an utterance, or in other words which interpretation strategies would be the most probable choice in a given situation. In my treatment of indirect speech acts I introduced Searle's approach to analysing how a reader/listener might infer meaning from verbal or written interaction. I suggested that a point of weakness in Searle's approach is that it does not include context to any significant degree. However, for that very same reason, it might be useful for analysing individual clauses in the experiment described. Using Searle's model, I shall therefore analyse one of the imperatives occurring in my experiment, viz. a warning, which I have selected from the category of sensing/achievements. And to shed further light on the distinction between co-operative replies and non-co-operative replies, I shall analyse the example from each of these two perspectives.

6.1. *Analysis of non-co-operative response to a warning*

An imaginary exchange between the writer of a manual representing a manufacturer (A) and a respondent representing a potential customer (B) may be interpreted as follows:

Example 8:
Understand that your safety and the safety of other persons is measured by how you service and operate this machine.

Step 1: A warning consisting of a projecting clause in the imperative (*understand*) and a projected proposition *(... that your safety and the safety of other persons is measured by how you service and operate this machine)* has been made by A, and B responds by saying: *I do not understand* (Facts about the exchange).

Step 2: B may be assumed to be co-operating in the conversation, thus making an effort to produce a reply that makes sense (The Co-operative Principle).

Step 3: If B follows the co-operative principle, A's utterance will most likely trigger responses that confirm B's willingness to observe the warning such as a promise (I'll take care to operate it safely) or a counter-statement (I agree) (Theory of Speech Acts).

Step 4: However, the response does not include any of these options, but is instead a response to the initial projecting clause: *I do not understand* (Inference from steps 1-3).

Step 5: Therefore the response is either not relevant, or the warning to which B replied carries two illocutionary points one of which is embedded in the sentence meaning, while the other point is the speaker's utterance meaning (Theory of Speech Acts).

Step 6: Now, the use of the mental process '*understand*' may be assumed to be rather unusual in a projecting clause in the imperative form, since, as we have seen, the imperative tends to favour processes of doing (Semantics).

Step 7: Apparently B has disregarded the semantic potential of the imperative form of '*understand*' , failing to unpack the interpersonal metaphor held by the projecting clause. In an unpacked version, the imperative '*understand*' might be interpreted as having vocative force as in '*I am telling you ...*' (a vocative declarative statement). In an alternative interpretation unpacking would reveal advisory force as in '*you should know that ....*' (an advisory declarative statement). This would be clear if a tag-test were used as follows: *Understand that your safety and the safety of others is measured by how you service and operate this machine, isn't it.* In this case the tag question relates to the projected proposition and not to the projecting part of the clause. We would not say '*understand that your safety and the safety of others is measured by how you service and operate this machine, won't you*' (Grammatical metaphor theory, Halliday).

Step 8: In a real communicative situation, A would probably realize that B has misinterpreted the message, and the reaction might be: I did not ask you to understand something; I intended to warn you against possible hazards. Therefore the co-operative principle has been flouted.

6.2. Analysis of co-operative response to the same example

Example 8:
Understand that your safety and the safety of other persons is measured by how
you service and operate this machine.

Step 1: A warning consisting of a projecting clause in the imperative
(*understand*) and a projected proposition *(... that your safety and the safety of
other persons is measured by how you service and operate this machine)* has
been made by A, and B responds by saying: *I will take care to operate it safely*
(Facts about the exchange).

Step 2: B may be assumed to be co-operating in the conversation, thus
making an effort to produce a relevant reply (The co-operative principle).

Step 3: If B follows the co-operative principle, A's utterance will most
likely trigger responses that confirm B's willingness to observe the warning such
as a promise (I'll take care to operate it safely) or a counter-statement (I agree)
(Theory of Speech Acts).

Step 4: B's response 'I'll take care to operate it safely' is a promise
responding to A's proposition, viz '... your safety and the safety of other
persons is measured by how you service and operate this machine'. Thus B, by
implication, accepts the proposition as a warning and promises to act on it, if
necessary. Therefore B has not interpreted the initial projecting clause
'understand' as part of the propositional content, but instead unpacked the
meaning of the interpersonal metaphor (Inference from steps 1-3).

Step 5: The exchange is successful because B has responded to the
primary illocutionary force, which is a warning (Inference from step 4).

That it is possible to supply at least two different replies shows that the
clause may be seen in more than one contextual situation. Therefore, to interpret
the meaning of the speech act embedded in the clause, more than one reading is
needed, and the clause may therefore be seen as incongruent. It is possible to
read the clause as a literal utterance, in which the imperative 'understand' is
interpreted as a command – hence the pun 'I do not understand'. But seeing that
this interpretation does not make sense, a second reading becomes necessary,
thus bringing out a new layer of meaning. Similar analyses would be possible for
all of the incongruent examples in the experiment. However, the congruent
examples would necessitate only one reading.

7.   Towards a cline of metaphoricity

Against this background, I would suggest that rather than look upon the imperative as inherently congruent, it may be more rewarding to place it on a cline of metaphoricity, with lexical metaphor at one end of a scale and grammatical metaphor at the other.

My justification for suggesting this method of categorisation is Halliday and Matthiessen's (1999: 87–88) description of the relationship between the 'grammatical zone' and the 'lexical zone' as one of delicacy. Focussing on the 'ideation base', which must be said to carry the heaviest semantic load of meaning, Halliday proposes a move in delicacy from grammar as the 'most general' to 'lexis' as the 'most delicate'. Starting from the grammatical end of the scale, we have processes and participants which can be sub-categorised into still more delicate degrees until we reach the smallest units of meaning represented by lexical items. Along a sliding scale of delicacy, the lexical items invariably carry the heaviest load of semantic meaning. This observation is important to the argument that lexical metaphors may be seen as more metaphorical than grammatical metaphors because of their potential for amplifying meaning. All things being equal, the more semantic features are involved in a metaphorical process, the stronger their impact on meaning.

Table 3 below serves as illustration of this point. It shows lexical metaphor at one end and literal utterances at the other with grammatical metaphor closer to the literal end and indirect speech acts closer to the lexical end of the scale. It should be noted that metonymy and synecdoche are listed both as lexical metaphor and as grammatical metaphor. This is because these two types of lexical metaphor are a result of grammatical metaphor, and it is therefore impossible to imagine one of these tropes without the other. An example is 'The White House issued a statement', which is an example of metonymy. The congruent version of the sentence would be 'they issued a statement in the White House'. In the metaphorical version there is semantic deviation between the Actor 'The White House' and the process 'issued' because normally houses do not issue statements. This creates metaphorical tension in lexis. However, it is at the same time possible to identify a GM in the sentence since congruent circumstance 'in The White House' dresses up as incongruent Actor 'The White House' in the metaphorical sentence, and it is this shift that gives rise to the creation of a lexical metaphor. The table further serves as illustration of what was a preliminary conclusion to the experiment described above, viz. that it is possible to perceive different kinds of indirect speech acts as having different metaphorical values. In the experiment, it turned out that it was generally more difficult for the respondents to provide non-co-operative replies to imperatives used for instructions and warnings than to imperatives used for offers and promises, which might indicate that imperatives used for offers and promises entail primary as well as secondary illocutionary forces. It should be noted that the spread of illocutionary acts shown in Table 3 is not an attempt to categorize the illocutionary acts carried by the imperative as either lexical or grammatical metaphor. Rather it should be read along a cline of metaphoricity.

Lexical metaphor	Indirect speech acts realized as	Grammatical metaphor	Literal utterances
Simile Metaphor Catachresis Metonymy Synecdoche	┌ Statement ├ Question ├ Offer └ Command	Metonymy Synecdoche	

A spread of illocutionary acts carried by the imperative:

(the imperative as carrier of two or several indirect speech acts)

Lexical end   Metaphorical end

       Offers

      Promises

          Requests

                            Instructions

                            Warnings

                    Recommendations

                  Advice

                                Military commands

                                   Injunctions

                                 Prohibitions

Lexical end ◄————————————————————► Metaphorical end

Augmenting metaphoricity   Declining metaphoricity

Table 3: Cline of metaphoricity based on lexical metaphor,
indirect speech acts and grammatical metaphor

Based on a rather limited sample, this overview is neither exhaustive nor in any way representative of the real-world situation of metaphoricity involving indirect speech acts, lexical and grammatical metaphor. However, it offers an approach to perceiving the relationship between the imperative and the many functions this grammatical form has. The map would possibly change if the experiment were enlarged to cover a wider sample of imperatives. On the other hand there seems to be a certain logic in thinking that metaphoricity declines as the conflation of form and function intensifies.

Displaying the imperative on a cline with a lexical end and a grammatical end raises the question as to whether the metaphorical potential held by the imperative is of a lexical rather than of a grammatical nature. I believe there is no straightforward answer to this due to the many functions open to the form studied. However, I believe it is safe to say that from an experiential point of view, the imperative only approaches the concept of grammatical metaphor if a semantic junction between different functional categories can be identified. In other words, for the imperative to be seen as ideational GM, it has to represent one of at least two realization options such as e.g. *'pay by visa'* (metaphorical) instead of the unpacked declarative statement of *'we allow you to pay by visa'* (congruent) in which the imperative mood has been replaced by an infinitive clause. Similarly for an imperative to be seen as interpersonal GM, certain requirements have to be fulfilled. In the example *'believe it nor not, pistons can go seriously out of true'* , there is an interpersonal metaphor in the initial clause *'believe it or not...'*. An unpacked version might read *'Whether you believe it or you do not believe it, pistons ....'* where the imperative clause has been substituted by a concessive clause. However, it seems that metaphoricity in imperatives is often a result of the interplay of illocutionary forces, in which case it is closely connected with the way in which GM works without using exactly the same resources. The difference seems to be that no junction of semantic categories in the grammar can be identified when illocutionary forces interact, and the metaphorical potential of the imperative as simultaneous carrier of different illocutionary forces may therefore best be explained by resorting to a level of discourse semantics that has not so far received much attention within SF theory.

8.   Summary and conclusions

This article has aimed at demonstrating that the imperative is not by definition congruent or metaphorical, but that it is instead a sentence type that may be used both for metaphorical and congruent purposes. To bring home this idea, I have studied the imperative out of context and found that its metaphorical range is best illustrated on a cline of metaphoricity. In the process I have related the imperative in its different functions to the concepts of lexical metaphor, grammatical metaphor and indirect speech acts respectively and found that all of these constructs share a number of features while there are also significant differences to be identified, as illustrated in Figure 4. The imperative is like lexical metaphor in that one expression option may carry a number of meanings. But it is also like grammatical metaphor in that it is one of several realization options. As a third point my data seem to suggest that a reader has to rely more on semantics and background knowledge. if contextual information is not available either because s/he is contextually illiterate and therefore unable to recognize the genre in which an utterance appears, or because s/he has to react to written text, which is usually removed from its proper context. Both of these situations may give rise to communication breakdown because of the increased risk of confusing speaker's utterance meaning and sentence meaning.

What seems to be a crucial point in determining the metaphorical potential in imperatives is the junction of illocutionary forces and the meaning amplification resulting from such junction. Unlike ideational GM, whose primary characteristic feature is a junction of semantic categories in the lexico-grammar, the metaphorical potential in the imperative is characterized by a junction of illocutionary forces. Now illocutionary forces do not usually manifest themselves explicitly in the semantic system, and as a result the lexico-grammar is involved only implicitly, through mental maps so to speak. It is therefore difficult to decide whether the interplay of illocutionary forces in the imperative can be classified as GM. My suggestion would be that only when the imperative can be identified as either ideational metaphor or interpersonal metaphor of mood can it be classified as GM proper. In other situations a more appropriate designation might be 'illocutionary metaphor'.

Acknowledgements

I am grateful to professor Torben Vestergaard, Aalborg University, for valuable comments on earlier drafts of this article.

Notes

1. The term 'remapping' is used in Halliday (1998b).
2. By metaphorical tension I allude to tension caused by semantic junctions as illustrated in Figure 2. However, I suggest that the potential tension of certain uses of the imperative may be caused by semantic junctions between illocutionary forces. Such tension arises when one mood is acting as another, as suggested by Martin (1997: 27).
3. Speaker and listener are used synonymously with writer and reader in this article.
4. The maxim of Quantity requires the quantity of information provided to be adequate. Under the maxim of Quality the participant is required to make his or her contribution 'true'. The maxim of Relation deals with the 'relevance' requirement and according to the maxim of manner, the participant should be brief and orderly, and avoid ambiguity and obscurity of expression (1975: 46).

References

Austin (1962) *How to Do Things with Words.* Oxford: Oxford UP.

Brown, P. & Levinson, S. (1978/1987) *Politeness. Some universals in languge usage.* (Studies in Interactional Sociolinguistics, 4.) Cambridge: Cambridge UP.

Davies, E. (1986*) The English Imperative.* London: Croom Helm.

Downing, A. & Locke, P. (1992) *A University Course in English Grammar.* London: Prentice Hall.

Eggins, S. (1994) *An Introduction to Systemic Functional Linguistics.* London: Pinter.

Grice, H.P. (1975) Logic and conversation. In: P. Cole, P. & J.L. Morgan (eds.) *Syntax and Semantics. Vol. 3: Speech Acts.* New York: Academic Press. 41–58.

Halliday, M.A.K. (1987) Spoken and written modes of meaning. In: R. Horowitz & S. Samuels (eds.) *Comprehending Oral and Written language.* London: Academic Press. 55–82.

Halliday, M.A.K. (1989) *Spoken and Written Language.* Oxford: Oxford UP.

Halliday; M.A.K. (1985/1994) *An Introduction to Functional Grammar.* London: Edward Arnold.

Halliday, M.A.K. & J.R. Martin (1993) *Writing Science: Literacy and discursive power.* London: The Falmer Press.

Halliday, M.A.K. (1995a) *Scientific English.* Paper given at University of Trieste,. Facoltà de Economia, Sala Conferenze, October 1995.

Halliday, M.A.K. (1995b) Language and the reshaping of human experience. National and Kapodistrian University of Athens. *Honorary Lectures* (1994–1997). Athens: The University of Athens Publications. 1247–1276.

Halliday, M.A.K. (1998a) Linguistics as metaphor. In: Anne-Marie Simon-Vandenbergen, Kristin Davidse & Dirk Noël (eds.) *Reconnecting Language: Morphology and syntax in functional perspectives.* Amsterdam: Benjamins. 3–27.

Halliday, M.A.K. (1998b) Things and relations: Regrammaticizing experience as technical knowledge. In: J.R. Martin & R. Veel (eds.) *Reading Science: Critical and functional perspectives on discourses of science.* London: Routledge. 185–235.

Halliday, M.A.K. & C. Matthiessen (1999) *Construing Experience through Meaning. A language-based approach to cognition.* London: Cassell.

Holdcroft, D. (1978) *Words and Deeds.* Oxford: Clarendon Press.

Lassen, I. (1997) On the cohabitation of grammatical metaphor and conventional figures of speech. In: I. Lassen (ed.) *Interactional Perspectives on LSP (Language and Cultural Contact* 22). Aalborg: Aalborg UP. 67–83.

Lassen, I. (to appear). *Accessibility and Acceptability in Technical Manuals: A survey of style with the emphasis on grammatical metaphor.* Unpublished Ph.D thesis. The Faculty of Humanities, Aalborg University.

Lyons, J. (1977) *Semantics. Vol. 2.* London: Cambridge UP.

Martin, J.R. (1992) *English Text: System and structure.* Amsterdam: Benjamins.

Martin, J.R. (1997) Analysing genre: Functional parameters. In: F. Christie & J.R. Martin (eds.) *Genre and Institutions: Social processes in the workplace and school.* London & Washington: Cassell. 3–37.

Murcia-Bielsa, S. (2000) The choice of directive expressions in English and Spanish instructions: A semantic network. In: E. Ventola (ed.) *Discourse and Community: Doing Functional Linguistics* (= *Language in Performance,* 21). Tübingen: Gunter Narr Verlag. 117–146.

Ravelli, L.J. (1985) *Metaphor, Mode and Complexity: An exploration of co-varying patterns.* Honours Thesis. Department of Linguistics, University of Sydney.

Ravelli, L.J. (1988) Grammatical metaphor: An initial analysis. In: E. Steiner & R. Veltman (eds.) *Pragmatics, Discourse and Text: Some systemically-inspired approaches.* London: Pinter Publishers. 133–147.

Searle, John R. (1979) *Expression and Meaning: Studies in the Theory of Speech Acts.* Cambridge: Cambridge UP.

Searle, John R. (1983) *Intentionality: An essay in the Philosophy of Mind.* Cambridge: Cambridge Univesity Press.

Sperber, D & D. Wilson (1986/1995) *Relevance. Communication and Cognition.* London: Blackwell.

Vendler, Z. (1967) *Linguistics in philosophy.* Ithaca: Cornell UP.

Part IV

'Metaphor' in grammar and in other modes of meaning

Phonological metaphor

Robert Veltman
University of Kent, Canterbury

> *The voice of the surf now and then was a positive pleasure,*
> *like the speech of a brother, it was something natural, that had*
> *its reason, that had a meaning.*
>
> (Joseph Conrad *Heart of Darkness* 1902)

1.   Engagement with phonological metaphor

Joseph Conrad's powerful description of the way his hero, Marlowe, senses the sound of the surf familiarises us with *phonological* metaphor in two ways. First, it offers an insight into what the process of meaning, or *semogenesis* (Halliday 1992: 27), both in its logogenetic (textual) and phylogenetic (historical) manifestations, is: meaning has *natural* origins, which can be related *rationally* to the symbols which convey it, a relation Saussure portrayed as being 'motivated' or 'partially motivated'. Secondly, the sound of the surf as it reached the shore is *metaphorically* heard as a human, brotherly 'voice'; but the perceived sound is itself a *congruent* realisation of the actual sound of surf. The point about sound as metaphor is that motivation of the congruent side of the relation is, at its most natural, one of identity and *transparency* – transparency, as we shall see, is presented here as a fundamental characteristic of a type of relationship between meaning and form. This relationship has come to be known as *congruency*, an appropriate term drawn from Euclidean geometry, which has both an expressive aspect – identity and proximity of physical form – and a deeper, structural aspect, derived from computation of size of angles and application of various axiomata.

Sound in language relates to other strata via two principles: arbitrariness and duality of patterning. Both these principles are negations of the principle of 'naturalness', which in respect of arbitrariness is manifested as iconicity, the 'looks- or sounds-like' relation. Iconicity itself is a cline (although arbitrariness is not), governed by mechanisms of perceptual tolerance (Holówka 1981). Transparency of resemblance between phenomenon and symbolic realisation exists at one end of the iconic cline. Therefore, with respect to sound in language, as well as to grammar and vocabulary, forms of natural transparency govern congruency.

In summary, Conrad's surf metaphor teaches that, while the actual sound of the surf was 'congruent' with its perception, the 'meaning' it had, or symbolic value it had for Marlowe was metaphorical. I suspect that semogenesis is fundamentally metaphorical and, in relation to sound in language, this is most accessibly reflected in its prosodic manifestation.

2.   A framework for phonological metaphor

Consider the following texts, for which the context provides a semantically equivalent re-wording of an utterance or part of it:

(1)   Innovatory jargon: University final degree appeal board in November 1999 interrogates an appellant's tutor about his view of her academic career:
Tutor: I have always been impressed by students who perform relatively better in their final year than in their previous two years at university.
Board member: Oh you mean their *exit velocity?*

(2)   Quiz question: What term is used for <u>fractures occurring in young children, in which the softness of the bones allows them to bend in response to stress, rather than break</u>? Answer: *greenstick* (Christmas quiz in The Observer Magazine 26th December 1999)

In the light of these textually occurrent metaphors, I want to propose that wherever a meaning is realised in some linguistic expression, the opportunities for metaphor are created. Let us call this set of opportunities 'metaphorical potential'. Halliday and Martin (1993: 128) neatly describe this process in relation to semantics and grammar as follows: "A semantic feature that is typically realised by one grammatical means comes instead to be realised by another". This entails that:

A single meaning may be realised by two or more forms, of which one is 'congruent' with the meaning. Although metaphorical congruency is loosely interpretable as an equivalent of literalness, it is different from literalness in that it specifically designates a relation concerned with the realisation of *meanings* and not of forms, for which the term 'literal' is conventionally appropriate. Later, I shall try to refine the device of 'congruency', as it might apply in a functional grammar in the light of the principle of *functional transparency*. The construal of metaphor as being grounded in meaning rather than form is in keeping with Halliday's and Ravelli's pioneering reconstruction of the relation (Halliday 1985/94 and 1998, Ravelli 1988) and is illustrated by the metaphors themselves in (1) and (2) above and their textualised glosses. Turning to (1) above, the meaning underlying both the tutor's description of the student's career (see underlined portion) and the panel member's terminological re-phrasal (*exit velocity*) of this description is realised *congruently* by the tutor and *metaphorically* by the panel member. Here, the discussion will focus analogously on the realisation of semantic features by phonological, rather than lexico-grammatical features.

To the extent that vocalised sound processes may play a 'sense-determinative' and not merely 'sense-discriminative' role in the higher linguistic levels of meaning and wording (lexico-grammar) (Jakobson 1978, Jakobson & Waugh 1979) i.e. they may 'have meaning' or 'have lexical or grammatical function', these vocal processes may function metaphorically, as 'greenstick' in text (2) above demonstrates. The vocal processes concerned, following Firth (1948 passim), are known as *prosodies*, which include features of intonation systems, as well as features normally associated with the construction of *phonematic* units, such as nasalisation, length, sonority, etc. Therefore, prosodies are here defined as phonological features and units which function at other meaning-related levels, such a lexis, grammar and meaning itself. In (2) above, the prosodic (and orthographical) realisation '*greenstick* (fracture) is metaphorical, while *green* '*stick* (two words, with stress on the second) is clearly a congruent realisation of a different meaning.

The 'naturalness' of interstratal relations has normally been taken as that inhering between meaning and wording. However, the existence of barriers between phonological and non-phonological levels of language, such as arbitrariness and duality of patterning, as well as that between the lexis and the grammar, has tended to preclude or at least complicate any natural explanations of language. This limitation is reinforced by what appears to be a paradox: how can sounds mean things other than sounds themselves and a limited range of phenomena which can be pictorially represented by sound? Sound, characteristically iconic only in a limited fashion, is responsible for the *linear* nature of linguistic signals (visually captured, bodily linguistic signs are less linear), *which bears away from representable reality*, thus stretching the iconic principle to breaking-point. This principle remains in human, natural languages in a 'natural' guise (Halliday 1985/94: xvii-xviii), which is neither iconic nor completely arbitrary, in which not only lexical items, such as *city*, 'have, or determine meanings', but also grammatical devices and constructs, such as *subject* (Kress 1976: 16). The significance of this linearisation of meaning-making processes is that 'representation' as such is no longer the sole semantic relation to be resolved in a semiotic system; the linearised, sound-realised linguistic system is abstract enough to incorporate what we now recognise as interpersonal or textual types of meaning, those meanings that are *intrinsic* to the communication process itself, and to the communication of which prosodies, in particular, lend themselves.

Intonation systems and features have been known for a long time to be *motivated* by context, semantics and grammar. Some of these phenomena of English intonation will form the main part of the tentative claim that prosodies are not only dynamic, functionally motivated and determine meanings, in the Jakobsonian sense, but that they, as meaning-bearing entities, can also participate in *metaphorical* processes. Moreover, phonematic features have been found to participate in such processes. Thus, for instance, Gell (1995), in his study of phonological iconicity in the language of the Umeda people (New Guinea), notes an opposition between front/alveolar consonants (/d/) in words glossed as conveying cultural 'centrality' and back/velar consonants (/g/) in words glossed as conveying cultural 'peripherality': *edi* (man), *edie* (middle) vs. *agwa* (woman), *agea* (arm, branch), Thus, /d/ in *edi* and *edie*, and /g/ in *agwa* and *agea* can be considered in the light of this reading to be metaphorical 'extensions' of a broad gloss, which lacks particular congruent realisation. Veltman (1998) offers further examples of this natural, sense determining relation between sound and the other levels of language.

The sense-determining functions of prosodic features are described, and their metaphorical potential hinted at, by Jakobson and Waugh (1979: Ch. 4), who detail and discuss the terminology that has evolved in the last 150 years to describe and classify sounds in the work of scholars such as Gabalentz (1840-1893), Grammont (1866-1946) and, more recently, Sapir (1949) and Chastaing (1964). Laver (1994: 392), speaking of the dimensions auditory space offers for sensory discrimination, notes that "many of them, such as 'bright'/'dark', 'rough'/'smooth', or 'clear'/'dull', are able to be identified by means of metaphorical labels derived from other sensory modalities". Thus, despite the strictures of the duality of patterning principle, sound features not only have/determine meanings, but these meanings appear to be in a significant measure metaphorical, and their congruent source is extra-linguistic. These characteristics ('bright/dark' etc.) provide frameworks within which metaphorical relationships may thrive and emerge, between fundamental, congruent meaning realisations and metaphorical ones. This can be provisionally stated in the following way:

For a phonetic feature Pm to realise a meaning M metaphorically, there must also exist, a phonetic feature Pc, which realises M congruently. This is analogous with the network of relations outlined in the discussion of Conrad's *Heart of Darkness* metaphor, where an abstract sound form, the ocean surf is congruently and transparently realised in acoustic perception, on the one hand, and realised in the words of a metaphor 'voice', 'like a brother', etc., on the other. Thus, the phonological characteristics of '*greenstick* (as opposed to green '*stick*) in the context of 'fracture' has a congruent equivalent in the explanatory wording. Furthermore, there exist in principle metaphorical equivalents at the level of sound, between, a neutral intonation and a marked intonational contour. This effect is reflected in Cruttenden's (1986: 80–87) distinction between 'broad' and 'narrow' focus; Halliday's notions of unmarked and marked intonation patterning, where the latter is reflected in systems of 'key', and 'wide' and 'narrow' tones (Halliday 1970, 1979); Brazil's (1985) constructs of 'mid' in contrast with 'high' and low' keys; and Couper-Kuhlen's (1986: 158–187) studies of the relation between intonation and illocution (ibid.: 158–172) and attitude (ibid.: 173–187).

3. Phonological metaphor and the problem of channel

At first sight, the very notion of 'phonological metaphor' sounds glib, a result of simple analogising with grammatical metaphor. However, within linguistics and particularly SFG, such 'analogical heuristics' has proved quite fruitful. Halliday has offered three such powerful analogies, diagrammatised below (Figure 1):

IF,	THEN,
lexical tone languages	? grammatical tone languages (1967);
lexis has meaning	? grammar has meaning (1973);
lexical metaphor	? grammatical metaphor (1985/94)
and here,	
lexical and grammatical metaphor	? phonological metaphor

Figure 1: Productive analogical processes in the development of SFG

Less obvious analogising may have taken place in the treatment of the metafunctional component, when Halliday developed *interpersonal* grammatical metaphor, along the lines of his more central *ideational* grammatical metaphor, intrinsically concerned with accounting for *nominalisation* processes. Martin (1992: 417–418) continues this pattern, in setting up the domain of *textual* metaphor. The value of such analogising is that, if it succeeds, it helps revise conventional thinking, as, for instance, in structural linguistics earlier in the last century in the application of methods, honed in phonology, to syntax. Even if this procedure is not successful or only partially successful, analogising assists further understanding of the constituent parts of the phenomenon: phonology and metaphor.

It may be possible, for instance, to argue that sound cannot function metaphorically in language, for intrinsic reasons, unlike lexical or grammatical contrasts, such as 'city' vs. 'town' or nominalisation vs. clausal equivalent; that is, the physical channel alone cannot be identified with metaphor. If, however, metaphor can be Interpersonal or Textual in function, as well as Ideational, then phonological metaphor cannot be objected to on functional grounds, for Interpersonal and Textual meanings are precisely those realised by prosodies and intonation systems, in particular (Halliday 1979, Brazil et al. 1980), those "on-the-spot features of language, the things that tie it to the particular moment and context of speaking" (Halliday 1985/89: 32). Indeed, even grammatical functions of intonation, equating with logical scope, and identifiable with the Ideational metafunction of language, may have metaphorical potential as exemplified in (3) and (4) below:

(3)   // 1 he doesn't gamble / 1 because he's poor//
      ('he is poor and that is why he does not gamble')

(4)   //4 he ↑doesn't gamble because he's poor//
      ('he is poor but that is not why he gambles')

Later discussion will suggest that the marked prosody of (4) is metaphorical, while (3), with its unmarked intonation is a congruent realisation of a different meaning. After all, the notion of 'scope' has strong iconic resonance, and (4) has a marked negative scope, which is matched and conveyed by a marked intonation pattern, warning almost 'please understand this message in a special way'.

One may argue additionally that any sound or sequence of sounds that has meaning or extra-phonological function, is automatically a morpheme, and therefore the notion of 'phonological metaphor' is redundant. After all, many languages have morphemes which consist of single phonemes, which can even be content-rich lexical items (Japanese {/e/} meaning 'picture' and {/i/}

meaning 'stomach', for instance) and, as morphemes, may participate in metaphorical processes. However, in terms of the duality of patterning principle, /e/ is a sound unit at the level of phonology, and {e} is a morphological unit at the level of wording. Moreover, since sounds qua prosodies are features and are not bound by the duality of patterning principle, as phonemes are, they may 'have' or 'determine' meaning, and have the potential to participate in metaphorical processes. The sound of the Japanese, content-rich word 'e', /e/ is not, in respect of the argument proposed here, a prosody, since as a phonematic unit or functional complex of phonetic features (mid-high, front, unrounded), it cannot be said to have a meaning; indeed, it is *features* that contribute to meaning, not the phonemic complex which they cluster into.

Sounds which can determine meaning are phonetic and acoustic *features*, such as voice; these harbour a contrast such as + or − voice, a contrast which in turn can serve as a vehicle for meaning determination. Moreover, the contrast is at least partially *systematic* in a language, such as the alternation of voice in the final fricative consonant in some English verb-noun pairings, such as /hauz/ vs. /haus/ and /liv/ vs /laif/, etc. In intonation systems, sense determinative oppositions are conveyed by contrasts in the tonic segment pitch movement patterns, prominence assignment and information distribution and segmentation. Hence, returning to the original objection to phonological metaphor on intrinsic grounds, can these sense-determinative contrasts serve metaphor, as well as simply 'have meaning'? These issues are raised in work within semiotics, some of which is relatively recent, which argue for an 'integrationist' approach to the status of channel identified forms, such as writing and other graphic modes, speech and music, and signing (Armstrong et al 1995, Gell 1995, Harris 1995, Forceville 1996, Kress & Van Leeuwen 1996, Van Leeuwen 1999). According to this approach, phenomena are gathered in and correlated, hitherto considered to belong to 'separate levels' or to be disparate and 'arbitrarily related'. The answer of these scholars to the question just asked points up the metaphorical potential of channel-defined devices, like sound, but does not go far enough, as further discussion below will show.

It is not a coincidence that the linearised character of spoken languages, introduced in Section 2, is dynamic in the axis of time and that prosodies of different kinds are intrinsically dynamic as sounds – they are variations along the possible parameters that vocal sound can take, short-lived departures, if you like, from the linear base. Just think of the rough diacritics, exemplified in ancient Greek writing and called 'prosodies' in that tradition, which attempt to represent some of these voice potentials, and the ways in which phonologists, since Joshua Steele in the 18th century, represent intonation melodies, as *pictured* or *picturable* movements (Allen 1981, Sumera 1981). The fact that it is possible to iconicise prosodies graphically or at least in terms of some texture seems to be the basis for the metaphorical potential of vocalised sound. Textures and pictures can thus be said to 'have sounds', as artists such as Edvard Münch believed, and sounds are picturable or physically comparable with textures. We can access meaning as sound through pictorial, visual or textural resonances, as fundamental acoustic vocabulary suggests: 'bright', dark', 'sharp', 'blunt', 'rough', 'smooth' etc. According to Allen (1981: 122), sounds in Ancient Greek could be "bent around" as the Greek term, 'perispomene', which calques as 'circumflex', suggests,. The rising or fall-rise tones ('referring', Tone 4) point backwards; while falling tones and congeners (Tone 1, 'proclaiming) point forwards. Tench (1992) speaks about varying 'status' of information in different tone groups endowed by tone selection. When we speak, we *shape* or mould each utterance in a variety of meaningful, communicative ways.

The visual medium, both linguistic and artistic, offers important parallels. Gombrich (1972: 378) tells us in discussion of a relief from the tomb of Ti (IVth dynasty): "We do not know how the Egyptians viewed the separation of the calf from its mother, but it is obvious that I have sentimentalised the scene in calling it a little tragedy". What this suggests is the commonplace that representations are open to different interpretations, some of them culturally bound, with the proviso that it is likely that at least some of these interpretations will be linked in meaning, through metaphorical processes, as the just cited example tells us. Metaphors inhere in all linguistic symbol systems: in scripts, the image of a sparrow determined the sense of the accompanying graph as 'baleful' in Ancient Egyptian; in Chinese a character showing two hands clasping a stalk of millet, determines meanings such as 'poor', 'humble', 'sincere', 'glean', 'hamster', 'spoonbill', 'winnow', all metaphorically related (Cooper 1978). Sign languages of the deaf "can ascend to any height of metaphor or trope" (Sacks 1989: 123), but because signs are, in origin anyway, iconic, this does not mean that they are more capable of metaphor than non-iconic, arbitrariness-defined spoken languages. However, iconicity, although dependent on channel, as a meaning relation can lend itself to metaphor, in two ways: firstly, in terms of individual lexemic signs in British Sign Language 'tomorrow' is represented by a single raised finger being projected *forward,* while 'ago', 'yesterday' are conveyed by the *backwards, over-the-shoulder* projection of the hand. In these examples, the metaphorical link between movement and time is exploited. Secondly, metaphorical utterances are conveyed by utilising the multiplicity of devices at the service of the signer; thus, in the 1986 feature film about deaf education, 'Children of a Lesser God', the simultaneous display of eyes, brow, tongue, hands, fingers and body posture is used by Sarah, the deaf assistant in the school, to metaphorise on the image of a begging dog in order to mean the equivalent of the ironic 'I can't wait' (to have a class with Jim, the teacher). However, there is a clear difference between this last example, which is a 'living' metaphor, though possibly conventional, in the American deaf community, and the others drawn from logographic scripts and sign language lexicons, which are not merely conventionalised, but are only metaphorical in origin. Moreover, in reading and writing and in signing, such symbols are processed at speed and are not sensed etymologically. These units are no longer motivated by their origins, iconic or otherwise, but form part of a functional whole, where their alleged, individual iconicity no longer matters, but what does matter are their relations with the other units in the syntagm or cluster (Halliday 1985/89: Ch. 2).

It is interesting that in the recent 'integrationist' exploration of image and other semiotic systems, defined above, little obvious effort was made to investigate fully the metaphorical potential of the phenomena discovered. This is surprising given the fundamental, not peripheral role of metaphor in semo-genesis, as characterised in Langacker 1976, for instance. As far as sound in language is concerned, Van Leeuwen's recent work (1999) is quite radical; it points up this potential, but advances only tentatively into the 'promised land' of metaphor of sound. Speaking of intonation patterns, Van Leeuwen observes that "Melodies are not just 'prosodic'. They are not just some colour for verbally expressed meanings. They can also stand on their own" (ibid.: 103). Melodies express "the dynamic and interactive character of sound" (ibid.: 97). In treating tempo, Van Leeuwen draws attention to the 'disjunctive' force of staccato phrasing and the 'connective' sensation of legato phrasing, assigning meanings to disjunctive phrasing, such as 'lively', 'energetic', 'bold', 'aggressive' and to connective phrasing, meanings such as, 'smooth', 'sensual' and 'relaxed'. *Disjunctive* and *connective* articulation provide frameworks for metaphorical interpolation. However, neither Van Leeuwen nor Gell, whose work among the Umeda of New Guinea was discussed earlier, either go far enough or fully understand what is entailed by the relation between sound and 'higher' linguistic strata, seeming to conflate the suspension of arbitrariness (the relation between sound and meaning in language) and of duality of patterning (the relation between sound and systematic lexical and grammatical paradigms). So, Van Leeuwen (1999: 149), enthused by Schafer (1986), contrasts the constituent sounds of the English words *womb* and *crypt*. The former is glossed as phonologically 'describing' an unconstrained (/w/), deep, enclosed (/u/), enclosing, calm interior (/m/); the latter as conveying 'a cramped space (/i/), thoroughly guarded by obstructions and constrictions (/kr/ and /pt/)'

(Phonological interpolations mine – author). However, these items are not contrasted systematically in English, and the analyses could even be said to be contradictory: crypts are, after all, calm interiors, deep and quite enclosed and sometimes quite vast! These attempts by Van Leeuwen and Gell at demonstrating phonological metaphor are very valuable in that they provide data in a data-impoverished area, but they defeat any purpose they may have had by re-emphasising the perception of peripherality of these phenomena. Gell tries to resolve this problem by arguing that, for cultural and environmental reasons, English is not an acoustically sensitive language, as Umeda is alleged to be. This view merely explains the scarcity of collected data rather than the peripheral status of such data in descriptions of the world's languages.

While confusion or fusion of the principles of arbitrariness and duality of patterning occurs in some of the literature, others such as Bühler (1933), argue passionately for onomatopoeia and sound symbolism of various types in language to be taken seriously by linguists; he writes of the speaker's "thirst for concrete reality" to explain the need to "penetrate directly the intimacy of universal life" (ibid.: 101) and the emergence of sound symbolism in language. However, he observes the solidity and impenetrability of duality of patterning, seeing it as the boundary separating sound symbolism from the rest of language.

I hope that I have shown above that the channel of expression may, independently of more abstract units (e.g 'silent' words), engage in metaphorical relations; at the same time I hope to have demonstrated the power and limitations of the principles of arbitrariness and duality of patterning. It is the *limitations* of duality of patterning, in particular, in language, argued for in Veltman (1998), which in theory would support and permit the occurrence of phonological metaphor, since unlike the ad hoc working of the principle of arbitrariness, duality of patterning is concerned with system.

4.   Metaphor in SFG and phonological metaphor

In arguing for phonological metaphor, I am going to extend some of the fundamental precepts (e.g. in Halliday 1985/94 and Ravelli 1988), which have inspired and driven the theory of what I am henceforth going to call 'lexico-grammatical metaphor' (LGM). These are:

a.   LGM is a device which explains the relationship between certain agnate forms in a language.

b.   Grammatically identifiable constituents, such as nominalisations, thematic or propositional variants, etc. could be seen as metaphorical and as alternants of *congruent* realisations (see (5) below):

> (5)   ... and another late night beckoned' (metaphor – spoken by BBC commentator on Donald Dewar – then a Westminster M.P. – reported as having to attend subsequent late night parliamentary sessions M.P.). (metaphor)
> <... and he was to stay up late again> (agnate, congruent form).

c.   Lexical metaphors invariably entail some grammatical contrast with their congruent equivalents. If (5) can be unscrambled congruently as <he was to stay up late again>, then we note that content rich 'another late night' replaces anaphoric 'he' as theme, subject and actor (while retaining its cohesiveness with the prior context – 'another' for 'he'). Most tellingly, 'beckoned', clearly a lexical, metaphorical realisation of a verbal process is semantically equivalent to the *grammatical* form 'was to', as a marker of future-in-past tense.

d.   Metaphor need not be exclusively aesthetic, literary, inventive or sensational – it is and more often is mundane, occurring in every type of text or utterance.

e.   To obtain this perspective, we, I repeat, do not ask whether a particular word or expression can be used metaphorically (as well as literally), but whether a particular use or meaning is expressed metaphorically or not. Indeed, it is nonsense to ask whether (5) above ('... and another late night beckoned') can mean anything else in the context. Can it possibly have a literal but simply contextually odd meaning? What we should ask rather: in what other ways, more congruent with the intended meaning, can the meaning itself be expressed?

f.   Metaphors can be *unpacked* to reveal their congruently realisable counterparts. Every meaning has at least one congruent realisation. How can then the notion of congruency be formulated in SFG terms? My answer to this is that the congruent realisation of a meaning is the one that is most *functionally transparent* or *motivated*. It must somehow 'look like' or more probably correspond directly with the elements of meaning, as the underlined elements in (1) and (2) above show.

g.   LGMs also tend to be more concise, indeed 'packed', less explicit versions of their counterparts, e.g. nominalisations versus explicit clausal equivalents, while congruent forms are by definition 'transparent' in relation to their meanings.

While a. to e. above would be broadly accepted in contemporary Systemic-Functional thinking, elements of f. and g. extend or modify founding statements of grammatical metaphor. f. imposes an additional condition of 'functional transparency' on congruency. Furthermore, g. poses a special problem for LGM theory as it stands, since the version provided by Halliday (1985/94) of interpersonal grammatical metaphor, the metafunctional aspect of metaphor most at play in phonological metaphor, is at variance with LGM theory. If phonological metaphor is a plausible process in language, then the motivations for interpersonal metaphor need to be revised.

To justify phonological metaphor at least some of the defining characteristics of LGM, outlined above ought to be able to apply to it:

a'.   There would have to exist two or more agnate prosodic patterns realising the same meaning;

b'.   One of the prosodic agnate patterns would have to be congruently related to the meaning concerned and the other metaphorically;

c'.   is irrelevant;

d'.   The metaphors concerned would not be limited to poetry and other literarily privileged domains; in fact the corpus is drawn from light radio and television broadcasts;

e'.   Although some work (e.g. O'Connor and Arnold 1973) shows how one particular prosodic configuration may fulfil a variety of sometimes unrelated functions, the task of charting the converse relation: how one meaning can be realised in different prosodic patterns, needs further attention. Some data e.g. my 'Magic Rectangle' texts, provide a variety of similarly functioning responses. What these varying responses have in common may be attributable to what Couper-Kuhlen (1986) calls 'the one-to-one hypothesis' deriving from work by Liberman and Sag (1974), according to which particular illocutionary meanings inhere in individual prosodies, and are delicately differentiated through particular contexts. A methodological problem remains, however: the corpus tends to supply the metaphors – the investigator *invents* the congruent forms with which the metaphorical forms can be paired in agnation (hence, the value of (1) and (2));[1]

f'.   It is not entirely clear how prosodic patterns, if metaphorical, can be 'unpacked' to reveal a functionally motivated counterpart, congruent with the meaning concerned. Some suggestions are made below, prompted by more traditional insights into metaphor, such as the demand for 'novelty' and 'precision' and the presence or absence of 'attitude' (Tench 1996);

g'.   As indicated above, the treatment of interpersonal metaphor, pioneered by Halliday (1985/94), is at variance with his description of ideational metaphor, in that the latter requires of the metaphorical form to be 'packed', implicitly concise and inexplicit (e.g nominalisations need not display accompanying argument nominals), and the congruent form in its 'unpacking' to be explicit and transparent. Interpersonal *congruent* forms are said to be typically realised by the systems of modality and mood in English, yet these are far more concise and inexplicit than their alleged metaphorical counterparts.

(6)   <It may rain during Wimbledon> (Congruent), versus;

(7)   'I think that it is going to rain during Wimbledon' (Metaphorical).

Phonological metaphor, if it is to be valid, requires a reworking of interpersonal metaphor.

5.   Metaphor and phonological metaphor as exploratory precision tools

It is not the aim here to make a general statement about metaphor. This is done elsewhere in abundance. However, if phonological metaphor is to be treated seriously, it must meet some of the conditions which determine not only the nature of grammatical metaphors, but also of metaphors in general.

Metaphorically interpreted relations lie outside the narrow range of the denotative extension of an expression, but not so far as to be treated as just another homonymous pairing, e.g. *bark* (of a dog) and *bark* (of a tree) or 'scales' (in weighing, as a type of hide, or as used in music, mathematics and statistics). They may be said to lie within the polysemous range of an expression (as suggested by *exit velocity* in text (1) above), but only loosely. The *mouth* of a river may be metaphorically related to the *mouth* on a face, but only in its origins; a metaphor has to have some synchronic character – it has to be invented or result from the act of 'metaphorising', rather than 'using a metaphor'. (Tyler

1978: 320). Tyler says of these acts: "We do not consciously construct old metaphors on every occasion of use" (ibid.: 319). Consensus seems to support strongly a view that *metaphor flees habituation and explores new experience.* Thus, Knight (1998: 82): "Metaphor counters a process of decay intrinsic to conventionalisation"; and Montgomery et al. (1992: 133): "New metaphors are constantly being developed whenever a new area of experience or thought needs new descriptive terms". This approach chimes with the role of metaphor in giving rise to new registers in different languages, often in so-called 'developing' languages (Halliday 1978, Joseph 1987, Godman & Veltman 1990). What is important in these definitions of metaphor is not only the notion of exploration but also the strongly implied ideas of search for precision and mutliplication of options. I.A. Richards, having insightfully recognised the role of metaphor in non-literary scientific language, describes metaphor as 'a semi-surreptitious method by which a *greater variety of elements* can be wrought into the fabric of experience' (my italics) (Richards 1924/48: 240).

What science and literature have in common as discourse genres is that they explore novel experiences and that metaphor as a heuristic device in these genres is stylistically foregrounded, playing an iconic role in these purposes. They also typically 'integrate' non-linguistic visualisations with the linguistic: diagrams, formulae, pictures and illustrations (Harris 1995, Kress & Van Leeuwen 1996). What about spoken language, then, in particular its most natural form, conversation? Typically, spoken conversation promotes, reinforces and maintains the relationships of solidarity among participants (Goffman 1959, Brown 1982). Much of the interaction, therefore, will rely on given/old reference schemes, which draw conversational parties together: 'you knows' and 'referring' Tone 4s (Fall-Rise), as well as integrating other modalities of channel, such as paralinguistic activity. Conversation too, again prosodically, facilitates evaluation and adjudication of propositions and proposals (Brazil 1985), allowing for options of disagreement, rebuttal and refusal.

Metaphor is highly typical of conversation and, more narrowly, of its *register*, in the sense that it is not 'incidental' to the activity. Drew and Holt (1998) discovered that in their data, 'figurative' speech, which is clearly metaphorical, has important conversational discourse roles: it summarises preceding talk; it marks the sequence of management of topic transition; and, in the course of this process, the next turn is constructed as the next topic. The type of figurative expressions concerned here are old metaphors like *take it with a pinch of salt* and *had a good innings*, which fall short of metaphorising, a clear marker of new metaphor use, exploration of experience, the search for precision and the construction of variety. However, in certain types of conversation, there is a need to signal that what one is saying *is* a new experience for the speaker and possibly for the hearer. This occurs typically in responses to questions, challenges and perceived criticism and insult. I will argue that it is intonation and other prosodic devices which fulfil this role of signalling precision and novelty. In that sense sound can be said to be metaphorical. Tench summarises this verbal behaviour, which takes on a metaphorical guise at the level of phonology, in terms of *attitude*. The physical resources required correspond with what Halliday calls 'key' (Halliday 1970, 1979). Tench sees attitude as an independent variable that is managed by prosody, contrasting with *neutral* verbal behaviour (Tench 1996: 107–137 and 136 for summary). Tench tellingly suggests that until recently it was believed that intonation was centrally concerned with 'attitude', but like Brown (1977/1991) considers attitude marked since there are many genres of spoken discourse, like news-reading, which are allegedly unmarked for attitude. He concludes therefore that "the expression of attitude is an optional element ... the ideational, interactional and textual components are obligatory, the attitudinal component is optional" (1996: 108). This account of the role of attitude runs parallel with the semantic increment provided by metaphor and by marked, attitudinal intonational choices e.g. Halliday's 'key' system (Halliday 1970,1979, Van Leeuwen 1999: Ch. 6), marked by wide or narrow pitch range.

Tannen (1989: 29), following Bakhtin, suggests that the involvement strategies of conversationalists "contribute to the meta-message, the level on which a speaker's relationship to the subject of talk and to the other participants in the talk are negotiated." The way this talk about talk is conducted is, metaphorically, through intonation, combining as it does both textual and interpersonal strategies, as do Brazil's Key/Termination and Tone systems, respectively. Prosodic activity is metaphorical, precisely because a) it explores the ever-changing novelties of the talk experience, and b) because attitudes are expressed which are relatively 'ineffable' and therefore, where words and propositions fail, prosodies come to the rescue.

Lemke (1998), also building on Bakhtin's thought, exploits the latter's notion of 'heteroglossia', of different communally identifying discourse voices, realised as 'discourse formations', which are either ideational (ideological) or evaluative. Lemke says that "we often encounter phenomena of language that reveal new semantic resources at text level. This is particularly true for the semantics of evaluation, because of its tendency toward 'prosodic' realizations, i.e. realizations that tend to be distributed through the clause and across clause and sentence boundaries" (ibid.: 47). Evaluative semantics is constructed on two functional bases: evaluative metaphor and textual propagation of evaluations. In relation to evaluative metaphor, usuality, realised in the text as 'too often', is a metaphorical signal for 'un-desirability'. Textual propagation, on the other hand, draws on Hasan's (1989) key notions of a text's *structure* and its *texture*.

Prosodies, especially intonation, have a vital role to play in texture, since they associate, through their pervasive and durative character, elements which would otherwise be isolated, thus making patent their covert semantic relations. Brazil's notion of *localised knowledge* enables, for instance, *new* and *red* or *going to town* and *shopping* to be semantically equivalent, relationships which a conventional linguistic dictionary would ignore (Brazil et al. 1980). These local, private, rare and untaught understandings are managed and articulated by intonation patterns, which explore the field of knowledge concerned, as it relates to the hearer, at the same time as the relationships of the speaker with the hearer are being explored.

Drew and Holt, Tannen, Lemke, Hasan, Halliday and Brazil, in summary, have constructed frameworks within which it is sensible to locate metaphor of a sounded, phonological kind. These frameworks extend Tench's notion of 'attitude' to highly metaphorically related functions of 'novelty' and 'precision'.

Couper-Kuhlen (1986: 165), advancing this approach by drawing on work by Searle (1975) and Glenn (1977), notes that "intonation distinguishes illocutionary force only when there are no explicit performatives". Where felicity conditions underlying illocutionary acts are modified in the performance of indirect, non-literal speech acts, these shifts in conditions are signalled by marked intonation choices. This is illuminating but has a problem. Alistair Cook on BBC World Service on 26th March 1998, discussing American identity, said the following:

AC:

//winston chur		ber/↑he		
		mem	was half am	can//
	chill/re			eri

Here, Alistair Cook exploits tonality, pitch range and height extensively in this relatively brief utterance, an act of reminding, but which is made overt by the clearly performative item *remember*. However, although this item has a performative function, its lexico-grammatical form is a command to carry out a mental process, surely a metaphorical phenomenon.[2] What is metaphorical about this utterance is not simply the wording but also the intonation. Cook could have said simply with a falling, non-undulating contour:

(8)　　Winston Churchill was half-American.

The marked, metaphorical intonation offers an alternative world for the meaning to visit. Simple proposition-like declarative utterances, like (6) and explicit performatives of the 'I hereby request you to ...' kind, are living evidence of semantic-formal transparency and congruency, in which intonation in the shape of falling tones participates.

6.   Two 'Magic Rectangle' texts

The 'Magic Rectangle' texts or rather 'textlets', because they are no more than one brief turn in length, were recorded some years ago from a BBC television programme, 'The Magic Rectangle', in a search for suitable EFL teaching material. An unexpected section in the programme provides very much what is a functional linguist's dream: a reasonable number of subjects (prominent TV performers) responding to the same question ('What is it like to be a television personality?'), which though simple enough, provokes complex emotional reactions, which are broadly similar across the range of respondents. Fundamentally, as the intervening producer's gloss heard in the middle of the extract explains, these television performers all like the idea of being a TV personality (TVP), but are obliged to be self-effacing and pretend offence or embarrassment at the term, TVP, when it is overtly applied to them. The problem of expressing their feelings is solved in a variety of ways, all displaying 'attitude', realised throughout by marked prosodic choices, defying conventional *propositional elaboration*.

As a group, the respondents select from 3 moves:

MOVE I: REJECT TVP AS A NAME
MOVE II: JUSTIFY REJECTION
MOVE III: OFFER ALTERNATIVE NAMES OR CHARACTERISATIONS

The intonation, unlike the wording, subject as wording is to pragmatic restrictions of a Gricean kind, is complete – it tells all. You can have pragmatically implied but unworded *information*, but at the level of *intonation* nothing is omitted as far as the role of intonation is concerned. Intonation articulates in a precise way matter which no propositionally elaborated equivalent in neutral prosodic guise could, at least in the sense of economy of effort. In other words, the recorded utterance is agnate with a set of hypothetical, non-recorded, but propositionally complex utterances with their own *unmarked* intonation patterning. Two examples, from the 'Magic Rectangle' texts are analysed in detail below, spoken by Angela Rippon, a high-profile TV presenter of the 1970s and 1980s and David Frost, who has figured prominently in television broadcasting in Britain and in America since the early 1960s. For both contributions, I have marked the tone group division, and melody direction, and shall informally describe the processes.

AR:

The first tone group contains a stepping head, followed by a high rising tonic – 'emphatic' 'strong' and 'intense', according to Tench's summary (1996: 136). The wide falling head also displays authority. It certainly expresses paralinguistically annoyance and through its High Key (Brazil 1985), a strong sense of adjudication of the questioner's assumption. The next move is to spell out 'this feeling' attributed to her. This element too has a descending head, but at low key it mimics the ideas behind the name TVP; thus, it is not her voice, but the low key makes it textually equivalent to its antecedent, 'this feeling', which it attempts to elaborate paratactically in three stages. Note that AR uses the marked form of the English indefinite article /ei/ before 'personality' – a phonological variant, which impersonates the way children recite or read aloud. This is a good example of *metaphorical switching* (Fishman and Giles 1978), exploiting a conventionally recognised phonetic conversion of lax to tense articulation of the vowel. So far AR has scolded the questioner (tone group 1), belittled him (tone group 2) and in tone groups 3 and 4 AR raises her own profile: low heads (involvement) are followed suddenly by low to high rises. This combines the maximum impact of the expressive and vocative functions (This is who I am! And not what you think I am!). Three significant rises to high peaks and the prevalence of stepping heads combines the sense of deeply felt injury with authoritativeness, examples of attitude marking and marked attitude. The meta-message of prosodic aspect of the utterance is virtually ineffable. However, a 'propositional', congruent equivalent is given in the course of the following section.

David Frost solves the problem of affront in a different way from Angela Rippon, but nonetheless uses prosodic resources to conserve effort and to make his point plain, in ways which Smith and Wilson (1979: Ch. 6) and Sperber and Wilson (1986) adumbrated in ascribing a role for intonation in the relevance model. He responds to the question 'What is it like to be a television personality?' by focusing on an alternative name (Move III), which phonologically and morphologically chimes with the word 'personality', namely 'person', and relatively gently rejecting the name TVP (Move I) by saying that the alternative name 'would be better'. He does not go to the lengths that Angela Rippon does to justify rejection (Move II). In the six Magic Rectangle texts Moves II and III seem to be mutually exclusive.

DF:

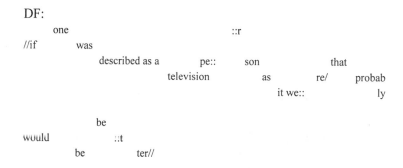

David Frost utilises a stately downwards stepping head to leave room for the rise-fall on his focus *person*. By docking the tail of the word *personality*, presented to him in the question, he is implicitly rejecting the presupposition with which the phrase TVP is charged and thus making the question pragmatically void and invalid. At the same time, he shows that he despises the 'industrial' connotations of *personality*, by substituting it with its back-formation, *person*, the connotations of which are 'individual' and 'human'. The acute turn at the peak of the rise-fall tone on *person* may express annoyance, but here, it is directed towards another discourse goal associated with dominance, that of 'reminding' his audience – of the ills of the industry in question (Brazil et al. 1980), reflected emblematically in the term, *personality*. The rise of the melody to High Key on what would amount to the conflation of onset and nuclear syllable of the Tone Unit expresses adjudication, contradiction and self proclamation: 'you are wrong and I am right', a combination of devices reoccurring in the second tone unit, where gentle rejection via comparison occurs. *As it were*, low pitched with fall-rise shape suggests 'I know and you do also that I am being impudent in rejecting your language as well as your ideas, but I know you understand'. His tone as well as his wording is tentative: *If one was described, probably*. This explication of David Frost's response includes an outline of the prosodic contribution to the message conveyed, which goes far beyond the words uttered but allows the speaker to construct and convey his point. This point could in theory and with much convolution and effort be conveyed explicitly, transparently and congruently in propositions, which would amount to a commentary rather than a sponsored utterance. The prosodic devices used in the relaying of attitude are metaphorical, and as sound, phonologically metaphorical.

7.   Interpersonal grammatical metaphor and phonological metaphor

From an a priori point of view there should be a great deal of connection between interpersonal metaphor and phonological metaphor, since the latter's function, relying as it does on prosodic feature realisation, would be typically interpersonal. However, characteristics so far tentatively outlined of phonological metaphor, suggest that it is at variance with the accepted version of interpersonal metaphor, but not, ironically, with the formulation, as it stands, of ideational metaphor.

Ideally, an attitudinally marked metaphorical prosody will have as its congruent equivalent a more strung-out, propositionally marked explicit version exhibiting unmarked, neutral intonation choices. A rough example relating to AR's utterance would be: // I hereby object to the assumption in your heavily loaded question that I am a television personality / I am justified in objecting to it / because it suggests I feel that I am famous and / that I am a television personality when I go out into the world / which is quite wrong / because I tell you that I am not a television personality / but an ordinary person whose name is Angela Rippon / and who works on television //.

In this hypothesised 'congruent' version, all propositions which may be pragmatically concealed but which spell out AR's attitude and feelings, are made available. Because they are spelt out, there is no requirement for the hypothesised speaker to draw on the full range of her prosodic resources.

In Halliday's view of interpersonal grammatical metaphor, it is the propositional equivalent of the more concise and packed exploitation of the systems of modality and mood that is considered metaphorical, the converse of the formulation of ideational grammatical metaphor. Langacker (1974) proposes that the function of modal verbs in English is to highlight the 'objective content' of the main clause, otherwise this would be submerged in a subordinate clause. It is my contention that in so doing modal verbs are behaving metaphorically. The fact that a modal verb can disguise itself as being the predicate of the main subject and the fact that it can superficially appear to be within the scope of negation suggests that as a class modal verbs in English are highly 'surreptitious', as Richards suggests above, in infiltrating the clause. The main verb is 'tricked into believing' that it can participate in the mood system, which of course only the modal can. Indeed, grammatical metaphor is an ideal, semantically-motivated way of explaining such structural phenomena as 'Raising'. Moreover, historically and comparatively, modals are main verbs, as their congeners still are in other European languages, which have in English become 'grammaticalised', itself a metaphorical process, a change of role (Langacker 1976, Hopper & Traugott 1993, Givón 1979). Mood choices in English are metaphorical too, since they substitute for semantically and syntactically explicit, stylistically prolonged, propositional performative verbs. The choices in mood are managed in terms of theme, itself partially iconic and metaphorical: the finite precedes the subject in interrogatives, for example, as it is the bearer of polarity, hence of the truth value of the proposition, and will therefore be a fitting starting point of the message.

However, Halliday and others make the assumption that, what is a 'normal' realisation of a meaning e.g. *may* for non-commitment or uncertainty (versus *I think*) is therefore a congruent one. Arguments in the preceding paragraphs suggest that this is not the case. The false assumption corresponds with conventional time-worn arrangements of grammars. Fictions about language are important; they are part of the data and cause the objective reality to modify. Kress and Van Leeuwen (1996: 7) say of the socially conditioned, transient nature of metaphor : "which metaphors carry the day and pass into the semiotic system as 'natural', neutral classifications, is [...] governed by social relations". A grammar of a language is a set of current beliefs about it and primacy or typicalness of function or realisation can be nothing more than types of belief.

8.   Concluding remarks

Prosodies are concise and non-propositional, but can be vaguely translated into propositions, provided that the accompanying prosodic pattern is unmarked and neutral. In specific contexts, for instance, where the speaker is challenged interpersonally or intellectually, prosodies will perform the task of functional precision, of summarising the moment to moment changes in the truth values being negotiated and the relationships between participants. They borrow heavily from each other, which adds up to an especially rich source of meanings, given that prosodic systems and choices are non-discrete. It is in these senses that prosodies not only are sense-determinative – Freese and Maynard (1998) give an account of clearly differentiated prosodic representation of good and bad news delivery and Van Leeuwen (1992) an explanation of spoken rhythm in terms of different social, speech defined contexts – but they are also metaphorical.

This study attempts to extend yet further the range of metaphor within the language system to the level of sound in language or phonology. Of course, the scope of the 'system' is one of the most hotly debated issues within linguistics, with entrenched minimalist and maximising positions. However, as the recognised linguistic system has expanded throughout the last century under increasingly rigorous critique, it is justifiable to look forward to freshly systematised domains, previously uncharted, rather than look backward to narrow, perhaps more disciplined, but comfortable interpretations of 'system' in language.

Phonological metaphor has therefore much to commend it, provided that the account of interpersonal grammatical metaphor is revised, so that the rich metaphorical content of the 'normal' realisations of mood and modality in English is acknowledged and their propositional counterparts seen to be what they are, explicit, wordy but functionally transparent congruents. In parallel, prosodies perform the metaphorical tasks of exploration of interpersonal and textual needs, in particular, and in so doing 'hit the right spot', in a concise and precise manner, which a good metaphor always does.

Notes

1. I am grateful to a referee for pointing out further contexts in which both congruent and metaphorical realisations are common e.g. child-parent discourse.

2. Similarly, a horoscope tells us metaphorically 'Expect life to be busy'.

References

Allen, W.S. (1981) The Greek contribution to the history of phonetics. In: Asher & Henderson (eds.) (1981). 115–122.

Armstrong, D.F., W.C. Stokoe & S.E. Wilcox (1995) *Gesture and the Nature of Language.* Cambridge: Cambridge UP.

Asher, R.E. & J.A. Henderson (1981) *Towards a History of Phonetics.* Edinburgh: Edinburgh UP.

Brazil, D. (1985) *The Communicative Value of Intonation in English.* (Discourse Analysis Monograph, 5.) Birmingham: English Language Research.

Brazil, D., M. Coulthard & C. Johns (1980) *Discourse Intonation and Language Teaching.* London: Longman.

Brown, G. (1977/91) *Listening to Spoken English.* 2nd edition. London: Longman.

Brown, G. (1982) The spoken language. In: R. Carter (ed.) *Linguistics and the Teacher.* London: Routledge & Kegan Paul. 75–87.

Bühler, K. (1933) L'onomatopée et la fonction représentative du language. *Journal de Psycholoie Normale et Pathologique* 30: 101–119.

Chastaing, M. (1964) L'opposition des consonnes sourdes aux consonnes sonores et muettes: a-t-elle une valeur symbolique? *Vie et Langage* 147: 367–370.

Cooper, A. (1978) *The Creation of the Chinese Script.* London: The Chinese Society.

Couper-Kuhlen, E. (1986) *An Introduction to English Prosody.* London: Edward Arnold.

Cruttenden, A. (1986) *Intonation.* Cambridge: Cambridge UP.

Drew, P. & E. Holt (1998) Figures of Speech: Figurative expressions and the management of topic transition in conversation. *Language in Society* 27: 495–522.

Fishman, J. & H. Giles (1978) Language and society. In: H. Tajfel & C. Fraser (eds.) *Introducing Social Psychology.* Harmondsworth: Penguin. 380–400.

Firth, J.R. (1957) [1948] Sounds and prosodies. In: J.R. Firth, *Papers in Linguistics 1934-1951.* London: Oxford UP. 121–138.

Forceville, C. (1996) *Pictorial Metaphor in Advertising.* London: Routledge.

Freese, J. & D.W. Maynard (1998) Prosodic features of bad news and good news in conversation. *Language in Society* 27: 195–219.

Gell, A. (1995) The language of the forest: Landscape and phonological iconism in Umeda. In: E. Hirsch & M. O'Hanlon (eds.) *The Anthropology of Landscape: Perspectives on place and space.* Oxford: Clarendon. 232–254.

Giegerich, H. (1992) *English Phonology.* Cambridge: Cambridge UP.

Givón, T. (1979) *On Understanding Grammar.* New York: Academic Press.

Glenn, M. (1977) *Pragmatic Functions of Intonation.* Ph.D. Thesis, Michigan, University of Ann Arbor.

Godman, A. & R. Veltman (1990) Language development and the translation of scientific texts. *Babel* 36.4: 193–212.

Goffman, E. (1959) *The Presentation of Self in Everyday Life.* New York: Anchor Books.

Gombrich, E.H. (1972) Action and expression in Western art. In: R.A. Hinde (ed.) *Non-Verbal Communication.* Cambridge: Cambridge UP. 373–392.

Halliday, M.A.K. (1970) *A Course in Spoken English: Intonation.* London: Oxford UP.

Halliday, M.A.K. (1978) *Language as Social Semiotic: The social interpretation of language and meaning.* London: Edward Arnold.

Halliday, M.A.K. (1979) Modes of meaning and modes of expression: Types of grammatical structure and their determination by different semantic functions. In: D.J. Allerton, E.Carney & D.Holdcroft (eds.) *Function and Context in Linguistic Analysis: Essays offered to William Haas.* Cambridge: Cambridge UP. 57–79.

Halliday, M.A.K. (1985/89) *Spoken and Written Language.* Oxford: Oxford UP.

Halliday, M.A.K. (1985/94) *An Introduction to Functional Grammar.* London: Arnold.

Halliday, M.A.K. (1992) Learning how to mean. In: M. Davies & L. Ravelli (eds.) *Advances in Systemic Linguistics: Recent theory and practice.* London: Pinter. 20–36.

Halliday, M.A.K. (1998) On the grammar of pain. *Functions of Language* 5.1: 1–32.

Halliday, M.A.K. & J.R. Martin (1993) *Writing Science: Literacy and discursive power.* London: Falmer.

Harris, R. (1995) *Signs of Writing.* London: Routledge.

Hasan, R. (1989) The structure of a text. In: Halliday & Hasan (eds.) *Language, Context and Text.* London: Oxford UP. 52–69.

Holówka, T. (1981) On conventionality of signs. *Semiotica* 33.1: 79–86.

Hopper, P.J. & E.C. Traugott (1993) *Grammaticalization.* Cambridge: Cambridge UP.

Jakobson, R. (1978) *Sound and Meaning.* Hassocks: Harvester Press.

Jakobson, R. & L. Waugh (1979) *The Sound Shape of Language.* Brighton: Harvester Press.

Joseph, E. (1987) *Eloquence and Power.* London: Pinter.

Knight, C. (1998) Ritual/speech coevolution: A solution to the problem of deception. In: J.R. Hurford, M. Studdert-Kennedy & C. Knight (eds.) *Approaches to the evolution of language: Social and cognitive bases.* Cambridge: Cambridge UP. 68–91.

Kress, G. (ed.) (1976) *Halliday: System and function in language (selected papers).* London: Oxford UP.

Kress, G. & T. van Leeuwen (1996) *Reading Images: The grammar of visual design.* London: Routledge.

Langacker, R.W. (1974) Movement rules in functional perspective. *Language* 50.4: 630–664.

Langacker, R.W. (1976) Semantic representations and the linguistic relativity hypothesis. *Foundations of Language* 14: 307–357.

Laver, J. (1994) *Principles of Phonetics.* Cambridge: Cambridge UP.

Lemke, J. (1998) Resources for attitudinal meaning: Evaluative orientations in text semantics. *Functions of Language* 5.1: 57–84.

Liberman, M. & I. Sag (1974) Prosodic form and discourse function. *Papers from the 10th Regional Meeting, Chicago Linguistics Society*: 416–427.

Martin, J.R. (1992) *English Text: System and structure.* Amsterdam: Benjamins.

Montgomery, M., A. Durant, N. Fabb, T. Furniss & S. Mills (1992) *Ways of Reading: Advanced reading skills for students of English literature.* London: Routledge.

O'Connor, J.D. & G.F. Arnold (1973) *Intonation of Colloquial English.* 2nd edition. London: Longman.

Ravelli, L. (1988) Grammatical metaphor: An initial analysis. In: E. Steiner & R. Veltman (eds.) *Pragmatics, Discourse and Text: Some systemically-inspired approaches.* London: Pinter. 133–147.

Richards, I.A. (1924/48) *Principles of Literary Criticism.* 2nd edition. London: Routledge & Kegan Paul.

Sacks, O. (1989) *Seeing Voices.* London: Picador.

Sapir, E. (1949) *Selected Writings.* Edited by D. Mandelbaum. Berkeley: Berkeley UP.

Schafer, R.M. (1986) *The Thinking Ear.* Toronto: Arcana Editions.

Searle, J.R. (1975) Indirect speech acts. In: P. Cole & J.L. Morgan (eds.) *Speech Acts, Syntax and Semantics.* New York: Academic Press. 59–82.

Smith, N. & D. Wilson (1979) *Modern Linguistics: The results of Chomsky's revolution.* Harmondsworth: Penguin.

Sperber, D. & D. Wilson (1986) *Relevance: Communication and cognition.* Oxford: Blackwell.

Sumera, M. (1981) The keen prosodic ear: A comparison of the notations of rhythm of Joshua Steele, William Thomson and Morris Croll. In: R.E. Asher & J.A. Henderson (eds.) (1981). 100–112.

Tannen, D. (1989) *Talking Voices.* Cambridge: Cambridge UP.

Tench, P. (1992) Some remarks on Halliday's description of British English intonation. *Network* 1/: 1–16.

Tench, P. (1996) *The Intonation Systems of English.* London: Cassell.

Tyler, S.A. (1978) *The Said and the Unsaid.* New York: Academic Press.

Van Leeuwen, T. (1992) Rhythm and social context: Accent and juncture in the speech of professional radio announcers. In: P. Tench (ed.) *Studies in Systemic Phonology.* London: Pinter 231–262.

Van Leeuwen, T. (1999) *Speech, Music, Sound.* Basingstoke: Macmillan.

Veltman, R. (1998) The silence of the words: Duality of patterning as a natural relation, not a barrier. *Functions of Language* 5.1: 57–84.

Intersemiosis in mathematics and science
Grammatical metaphor and semiotic metaphor

Kay O'Halloran
National University of Singapore

1. Introduction

Investigation of the functions of language in mathematics and scientific discourse becomes more complex when these discourses are viewed as multi-semiotic construals which also involve the use of mathematical symbolism and visual display. In this paper I discuss the impact of the use of these semiotic resources on the development of grammatical metaphor in scientific language. Following this, I extend the concept of grammatical metaphor to 'semiotic' metaphor to partially account for the expansions of meaning which occur inter-semiotically in mathematics and science.

The systemic functional approach of this investigation is based on the social semiotic theory of Michael Halliday (1978; 1994). As investigations in this tradition (for example, Halliday & Martin 1993; and Martin & Veel 1998) have tended to concentrate on analysing scientific language as a separate resource rather than one that interacts with other semiotic resources to create meaning, in this paper I discuss the impact of the use of mathematical symbolism and visual display on the evolution of scientific language, in particular the development of grammatical metaphor. Although, as Lemke (1993) claims, language has always been co-deployed with other semiotic resources and thus has co-evolved in relation to these other resources, the nature of this co-evolution has not really been theorised. Following this, I discuss semantic expansions which occur through intersemiosis, the interaction between the semiotic resources of language, mathematical symbolism and visual display in mathematical and scientific discourse.

The approach I have adopted is situated at the micro-level of analysis, the grammatical, to investigate how semiotic resources interact and impact on each other to create semantic construals which are only possible through the integrated use of these resources. The reason for investigating the micro-level is explained by Halliday (1998: 189): "The semiotic energy of the system comes from the grammar". Nonetheless, because the discussion is restricted to this level of analysis, what follows is somewhat incomplete because the macro-level of the historical is not fully developed. With this restriction in mind, I discuss the phylogenesis of scientific language at the level of the grammatical; that is, the historical development of scientific language which has occurred through its co-deployment with mathematical symbolism and visual display. This is followed by a discussion of inter-semiotic processes which occur in the logogenetic unfolding of the mathematical and scientific texts.

2.   Multimodal discourse

Lemke's (1993; 1998; 2000; forthcoming) early interest in the multimodal nature of scientific discourse together with theoretical advances in the theory and analysis of semiotic modalities other than language in seminal works such as Michael O'Toole's (1994) *The Language of Displayed Art* and Gunther Kress and Theo van Leeuwen's (1996) *Reading Images: The Grammar of Visual Design* have created intense interest in the theory and analysis of multisemiotic texts (for example, Baldry, 2000a; Martin & Iedema, in press; Ravelli, 2000; Thibault, 2000). As Kress (in press) claims, however, interest in multimodality, the simultaneous use of a number of semiotic modes, is not new (for example, in psychology, education, film theory, semiotics and drama), but now this issue is being placed at the centre of theoretical attention rather than at the periphery. Kress also echoes previous claims that a diachronic approach to the co-deployment of different semiotic resources can be instructive in learning about any one semiotic resource (Baldry 2000b, Lemke 1993; O'Halloran 1999a; 1999b; 2000; Thibault 1997).

The nature of contemporary scientific and mathematical language is therefore perhaps best understood historically in relation to its use with mathematical symbolism and visual display. Adopting this strategy, in this paper I recontextualise the development of grammatical metaphor in order to suggest reasons for the 'regrammaticising of experience' found in the language of science (Halliday & Martin 1993; Martin & Veel 1998). From this vantage point, I discuss semiotic metaphor (O'Halloran 1996; 1999a; 2000) which accounts for semantic reconstruals through the interaction between semiotic resources.

While ideational meaning is the focus in this discussion, this is not to downplay the significance of interpersonal and textual meaning in mathematics and science both across and within the different semiotic modalities. Rather, the significance of interpersonal meaning and the sophisticated nature of the textual organisation of mathematics have been demonstrated (O'Halloran 1996). Unfortunately, there is no place in this paper to explore these dimensions of meaning-making in mathematics.

3.   The language of science: The stable experience

The regrammaticising of experience which takes place in scientific language has been described in detail from the systemic perspective (Halliday 1993a; 1993b; 1998; Martin 1993a; 1993b). In what follows, I provide a brief overview of Halliday's (1998) most recent and comprehensive account before discussing the impact of mathematical symbolism and visual display on the development of scientific language.

Halliday (1998) is primarily concerned with the use of grammatical metaphor and relational processes to repackage experiential content, which he terms "the favourite grammatical pattern ('syndrome' of grammatical features) in modern scientific English" (Halliday 1998: 193).

In this pattern, (1) a (semantic) sequence of two figures (grammatically a clause complex) is construed as a single clause, typically a relational clause of the intensive or circumstantial type (cf. Halliday (1985/1994), Chapter 5); (2) each figure (clause) is construed as a nominal group, and (3) the logical-semantic (conjunctive) relation between them is construed as a verbal group (Halliday 1998: 193).

Halliday (1998: 202) gives the following example in contemporary science writing to demonstrate this metaphorical repackaging of experience:

> If electrons weren't absolutely indistinguishable, two hydrogen atoms would form a much more weakly bound molecule than they actually do. The absolute indistinguishability of the electrons in the two atoms gives rise to an 'extra' attractive force between them. (David Layzer, Cosmogenesis, 1990: 61)

The sequence realised as a clause complex, *If electrons weren't absolutely indistinguishable, [then] two hydrogen atoms would form a much more weakly bound molecule than they actually do*, is replaced by a single clause which contains a causative relational process, The absolute indistinguishability of the electrons in the two atoms gives rise to an 'extra' attractive force between them. In addition, the clause *If electrons weren't absolutely indistinguishable* is replaced by nominal group, the absolute indistinguishability of the electrons in the two atoms.

Halliday (1998) lists the 'pay-offs' of these grammatical strategies in scientific discourse as an increased potential for categorisation and taxonomic organisation together with an increased potential for effective reasoning and logical progression. In the latter case, the repackaging of a clause into a nominal group has a discursive textual function in carrying forth the momentum of the reasoned argument. Thus for Halliday the two motifs in the logogenesis of scientific language are 'technicalising' and 'rationalising'.

Halliday (1998: 209–210) categorises the different types of grammatical metaphor and thus demonstrates that the general semantic shift in scientific language is towards concrete entities. Halliday (1998: 211) captures this shift in the following form:

relator → circumstance → process → quality → entity

Halliday (1993a; 1998) cites several examples from Newton's (1704) *Opticks* to demonstrate that the features which characterise the grammar of modern scientific writing in English had begun to emerge in this work. One such example is the following:

> If the Humours of the Eye by old Age decay, so as by shrinking to make the Cornea and Coat of the Cystalline Humour grow flatter than before, the Light will not be refracted enough, and for want of a sufficient Refraction will not converge to the bottom of the Eye but to some place beyond it, and by consequence paint in the bottom of the Eye a confused Picture, and according to the Indistinctness of this Picture, the Object will appear confused. This is the reason of the decay of sight in old Men, and shews why their Sight is mended by Spectacles. For those Convex glasses supply the defect of plumpness in the Eye ... (Halliday 1998: 201–202).

Halliday (1998) argues that although reason is carried forth congruently by conjunctions such as *if*, *so as*, and *and*, the grammatical resource of nominalisation (where a process, for example, becomes an entity) is also employed to carry forth the argument. Halliday (1998: 202) cites the following examples:

make ... grow flatter than before :	supply the defect of Plumpness
will not be refracted enough :	for want of sufficient Refraction
paint ... a confused picture :	according to the Indistinctness of this Picture

The question arises as to how and why Newton and others started to construe this new world view of stability and order in the seventeenth century when linguistic construals of sensory experience had previously tended to register change, flux and process. In other words, what provided the impetus for the shift from congruent dynamic linguistic constructions of the material world to metaphorical accounts of cause-and-effect such as those found in the new language of science? Here I am concerned with the semiotic tools which were at the centre of the creation of this new world view, namely mathematical symbolism and visual display. In what follows, I investigate the evolution of scientific language with its grammatical strategies for construing technical causality relations in terms of its interaction with mathematical symbolism and visual display. The interplay between the three semiotic resources must be a critical factor determining the evolution of the functions, semantics and grammar of each resource. To investigate these claims, in other words to unearth the role of mathematical symbolism and visual display in the evolution of scientific language, I examine Newton's (1967) early writing in mathematics. From this analysis we may be able to appreciate the semantic contribution of the symbolism and visual display in order to re-examine Newton's (1931) use of scientific language. The aim of this exercise is to understand the nature of the relationship between linguistic and mathematical construals, for in Newton (1931) we not only find "the birth of scientific English" (Halliday 1993a: 57), but we also have the foundations of modern mathematics.

4.   Mathematical symbolism: The dynamic experience

In this section I examine the linguistic and symbolic text in one of Newton's (1967: 248–251) early mathematical research papers which was published in 1664. This paper appears in *Volume 1, The Mathematical Papers of Isaac Newton,*[1] where Newton is concerned with investigating the slope of curves. We may appreciate the integrated nature of his work across mathematics and science as these mathematical writings in *Volume 1* gave rise to calculus as well as geometrical optics (Rickey 1994).

To find ye Quantity of crookednesse in lines
December 1664

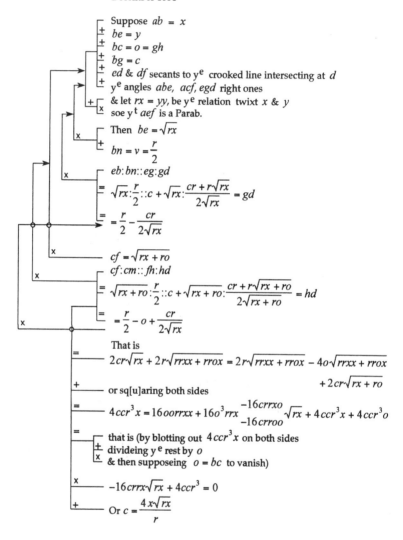

Figure 1: The logico-semantic relations in Newton (1967: 248–250)

Along with problems of area and volume, calculus is concerned with the
of change of quantities which may be interpreted as the slope of a curve, or
Jewton's 1664 terminology, *ye Quantity of Crookednesse in lines*. In the first

section of this paper Newton (1967: 248–250) seeks to establish that *ye Quantity of Crookednesse* in a parabola at point *e* is the same as *ye Quantity of Crookednesse* in a circle with radius *de*. In the first part of the symbolic text transcribed in Figure 1, Newton is concerned with finding an expression for *c*. The original text also contains a diagram which is not reproduced here due to space constraints.

From Figure 1, we may see that while the text is primarily symbolic, the linguistic selections function to contextualise the mathematical derivation of the solution to the problem. In what follows, I discuss the ideational meaning of this extract in terms of the linguistic selections for logical meaning and the symbolic selections for experiential meaning. From this analysis, we may gain an appreciation of the contribution of mathematical symbolism in the construction of scientific reality, and therefore the role of the language in this multisemiotic construal.

4.1. Logical meaning in Newton's mathematics paper

The analysis for the logico-semantic relations (Halliday 1994: Chapter 7) is displayed in Figure 1. From this analysis we see that:

(i)   The logico-semantic relations of expansion (elaboration, extension and enhancement) and taxis span the entire extract.

(ii)   These relations are extremely complex in their constituent structure.

(iii)   The semantic sequences are construed congruently through explicit and implicit conjunctions and conjunctive adjuncts.

(iv)   There are relatively few cases of grammatical metaphor, the exceptions being *ye crookednesse in lines* and *ye relation*.

The linguistic choices for logical meaning (some of which are now symbolised in contemporary mathematics discourse) appear to have several functions. Firstly, they establish the links between the symbolic participants and the diagram; for example, *Suppose $ab = x$*, [and] $be = y$, [and] $bc = o = gh$. [and] $bg = c$. [and] *ed & df secants to ye crooked line intersecting at d* refer to points, line segments and curves which are displayed visually in the diagram. Establishing these relations is significant because the visual representation provides an overview of the relationships between these participants, and these relations provide the basic conditions from which the symbolic solution to the problem is derived as we shall later see. Secondly, the linguistic choices for logical meaning (for example, *&, soe, then, that is,* and *or*) realise the sequence of steps in the symbolic solution to the problem. Lastly, linguistic selections provide a gloss for the sequence of steps; for example, *by blotting out* $4ccr^3x$ *on both sides, divideing ye rest by* o, *and then supposeing* $o = bc$ *to vanish.*

It thus appears that Newton's mathematical text contrasts with the nature of his writing in *Opticks*. Instead of making use of grammatical metaphor to discursively construct a reasoned argument, logical meaning is construed congruently through (explicit and implicit) structural conjunctions and conjunctive adjuncts in Newton's mathematics text. This is not to say, however, that logical reasoning is not buried in mathematical discourse. On the contrary, reasoning is buried in the symbolism through the use of pre-existing mathematical results, axioms and theorems (O'Halloran 1996; 2000). In Section 4.2, however, I attempt to demonstrate that the primary lexicogrammatical strategy for packaging the experiential aspect of this buried reasoning is radically different from that found in grammatical metaphor in language.

Significantly, the complexity of mathematics discourse appears to be similar to that found in spoken discourse; it is dynamic and intricate (Halliday 1985). This may be compared to the static and dense complexity of written discourse. As Halliday (1985: 87) explains "The complexity of the written language is its density of substance ... By contrast, the complexity of spoken language is its intricacy of movement".

It appears that while scientific writing evolved to become static and dense to construe a stable world of entities which are causally related, this analysis of logical meaning in Newton's mathematical writings together with the analysis of contemporary mathematical discourse (O'Halloran 1996; 2000) indicates that mathematics continues to construe the world dynamically as a flux of sequences, a world of processes and happenings reminiscent of spoken language.

> The natural consequence of the spoken language's preference for presenting things as processes is that it has to be able to represent not just one process after another in isolation but whole configurations of processes related to each other in a number of different ways. This is what the clause complex is about. (Halliday 1985: 86)

In what follows I attempt to demonstrate that the potential of language to configure processes and participants in spoken discourse pales in comparison to the potential of mathematical symbolism. This is a critical point for it means that dynamical construal of reality is not confined to the logical relations in the clause complex in mathematics, but extends to the grammatical systems for encoding experiential meaning in mathematical symbolism.

4.2. Experiential meaning in Newton's mathematics paper

Before investigating the experiential meaning of the mathematical symbolism in Newton's (1967) paper, we may note that this text shares many similarities with contemporary mathematics discourse. Although Newton's (1967) paper is relatively unsophisticated in terms of textual organisation and contains dated notation (for example, indices or powers are not used consistently) and outmoded mathematical terms (such as *ye crookednesse in lines*), the paper nonetheless represents the origins of contemporary mathematics, which is no surprise given that Newton is considered along with Leibniz to be the founder of modern calculus. In addition, Newton uses much of Descartes' notation which Rickey (1994) explains has been adopted in contemporary mathematics.[2]

My argument concerning the grammar of mathematical symbolism is simple. Basically the grammar of the symbolism differs from the grammar of scientific language in that it operates to preserve, firstly, the (semantic) sequences realised through the clause complexing as we have seen above, and secondly, the (semantic) configurations, the figures of process and participant structures in the clause. At the rank of clause, unlike the language of science where experiential meaning is packed through downranking the clause into extended nominal group structures, nuclear configurations of process/participant remain intact in mathematical symbolic statements. Rather than exploiting the expanded potential of the experiential structure of the nominal group, a different strategy is used in mathematical symbolism, and that strategy is clausal rankshift. This grammatical strategy is deliberate for it allows the process/participant structures to be reorganised and thus regrouped, and this provides the basis for the derivation of the solution to mathematical problems. This is a critical point, for it appears that mathematical symbolism is the semiotic in which the semantics of flux and change are maintained.

This claim concerning the nature of the grammatical strategies for encoding experiential meaning in mathematical symbolism is best illustrated by analysing mathematical symbolic statements in Newton's (1967) paper on curvature. To situate this analysis, the ranks and the units of analysis in the systemic model for language (Halliday 1994; Martin 1992) are compared to those proposed for mathematical symbolism (O'Halloran 1996) in Table 1. The metafunctionally organised systems for the mathematics and language are not displayed here, though it is assumed that mathematical symbolism is metafunctional (and thus realises experiential, logical, interpersonal and textual meaning), and tri-stratal (the semantics are realised through the lexicogrammar which is realised through typography).

Stratum	LANGUAGE Unit of Analysis	MATHEMATICAL SYMBOLISM Unit of Analysis
SEMANTICS	TEXT	TEXT
LEXICO- GRAMMAR	CLAUSE COMPLEX (Sentence)	CLAUSE COMPLEX (Sequence)
	CLAUSE // // (Clause)	STATEMENTS // // (Clause)
	WORD GROUP/PHRASE (nominal groups)	EXPRESSIONS [[ ]] (Rankshifted Clauses)
	WORD (Word)	COMPONENTS (Atoms)
TYPOGRAPHY		

Table 1: The systemic model: Language and mathematical symbolism

From the framework in Table 1, we may see that the units of analysis for language and mathematical symbolism are similar at the ranks of text, clause complex and clause. This is not surprising because mathematical symbolism evolved from language (Lemke 1998; forthcoming; O'Halloran 1996). Contemporary symbolic discourse evolved from the prose form of verbal rhetorical algebra and syncopated algebra which contained abbreviations for recurring participants and operations (Joseph 1991).

However, at the lower ranks of word group/phrase, the proposed unit of analysis for mathematical symbolism is the 'expression' which contains the rankshifted process/participant structures. This is best explained by examining Newton's (1967: 248) equation for the parabola:

$$rx = yy$$

This is a statement with the ranking process "is equal to" realised through "=". However, the left hand side, rx, is equivalent to $r \times x$ and the right hand side, yy, is equivalent to $y \times y$. These expressions are therefore composed of rankshifted configurations of process/participants structures in the form of multiplication between r and x, and y and y. I have extended Halliday's (1994: Chapter 5) categories of process types in the system of TRANSITIVITY to include Operative processes in mathematics (O'Halloran 1996; 1999b; 2000). These Operative processes include arithmetical processes and more abstract processes in mathematics. Thus using [[ ]] to indicate configurations of symbolic participants and mathematical Operative processes we have:

$$rx = yy \text{ is equivalent to } [[rx]] = [[yy]]$$

Similarly, if we consider:

$$\sqrt{rx} = y$$

This may be re-represented as:

$$\sqrt{r \times x} = y$$

$$\text{or } (r \times x)^{\frac{1}{2}} = y,$$

$$\text{or } [[(([r \times x]])^{\frac{1}{2}}]] = y$$

Although linguistically 'the square root of rx' is a nominal group, I am conceptualising $\sqrt{rx}$ as an Operative process because there is an operation or a process to be carried out on rx, illustrated by $\sqrt{xx} = (xx)^2 = x$. I return to the problem of the linguistic version of the 'square root' in Section 6 in connection with semiotic metaphor.

Now let's consider Newton's (1967: 249) result for gd:

$$eb:bn::eg:gd$$

$$\sqrt{rx}:\frac{r}{2}::c + \sqrt{rx}:\frac{cr + r\sqrt{rx}}{2\sqrt{rx}} = gd$$

Through substituting the values for eb, bn and eg and rearranging configurations of the process/participant structures, Newton obtains the following equation:

$$gd = \frac{cr + r\sqrt{rx}}{2\sqrt{rx}}$$

If we re-examine Newton's result by showing the sequence of steps through which the above equation is derived, we gain an idea of the level of reconconstrual of process/participant structures that takes place:

$$\frac{eb}{bn} = \frac{eg}{gd}$$

$$\frac{\sqrt{rx}}{\dfrac{r}{2}} = \frac{c + \sqrt{rx}}{gd}$$

$$gd \times \sqrt{rx} = (c + \sqrt{rx}) \times \frac{r}{2}$$

$$gd = \frac{r(c + \sqrt{rx})}{2\sqrt{rx}}$$

$$gd = \frac{cr + r\sqrt{rx}}{2\sqrt{rx}}$$

These reconfigurations are possible because the grammar of mathematical symbolism operates to retain participant/process configurations where, in this case, the participants are c, r, x and 2 and the Operative processes are multiplication, division, addition and the square root. The depth of rankshift for each expression is indicated below:

$$\frac{eb}{bn} = \frac{eg}{gd}$$

$$[[\frac{[[\sqrt{[[rx]]}]]}{[[\frac{r}{2}]]}]] = [[\frac{[[c + [[\sqrt{[[rx]]}]]]]}{[[gd]]}]]$$

$$[[gd \times [[\sqrt{[[rx]]}]]]] = [[[[(c + [[\sqrt{[[rx]]}]])]] \times [[\frac{r}{2}]]]]$$

$$gd = [[\frac{[[r[[(c + [[\sqrt{[[rx]]}]])]]]]}{[[2[[\sqrt{[[rx]]}]]]]}]]$$

$$gd = [[\frac{[[cr + [[r[[\sqrt{[[rx]]}]]]]]]}{[[2[[\sqrt{[[rx]]}]]]]}]]$$

Mathematical symbolism appears to maintain configurations of participants and processes through the grammatical strategy of clausal rankshift, the potential of which exceeds that found within language. This potential for such a degree of clausal rankshift is possible through specific grammatical systems in mathematical symbolism which permit unambiguous encoding of deeply embedded configurations. Such systems include spatial graphology, (for example, the use of indices for multiplication as demonstrated by r^3 for $r \times r \times r$), spatial positioning and use of horizontal line segments for division, the rule of order of operations (expressions are evaluated in a specific order; brackets, powers, multiplication/division and addition/subtraction), variation in the rule of order through use of brackets, implicit realisation of the process of multiplication (for example, rx means $r \times x$) and the conventional use of symbolism for variables and constants. In this way, the continual reconstrual of the relations between participants is possible. This potential for dynamic reconstrual means that while appearing to be abstract and divorced from reality, paradoxically mathematical symbolism is the semiotic which most closely reconstrues, albeit metaphorically, our sensory perception of material reality in that it records flux, change and process.

With mathematics fulfilling the role of describing and recording flux in terms of continuity, change and covariation (Lemke 1998; forthcoming) through the grammatical strategies described above, language evolved to provide causal explanations for these patterns. The language we see in the 'regrammaticising of experience' in science may therefore be a result of the development of the semiotic resource mathematical symbolism with its inter-semiotic relation with graphical representation. Language shifted semantically to the concrete in terms of entities and explanation of cause-effect because the dynamic construal of the description of the patterns of relations was achieved symbolically. The functionality of the two semiotic codes diverged, and this is reflected in the development of their grammatical resources for construing experience.

I discuss the nature of experiential meaning in mathematical symbolism in answer to the possible objection that mathematics is a tool for logical reasoning alone in Section 5. In the preceding discussion I have assumed the existence of processes and participants (and thus experiential meaning) in the symbolism without providing a strong basis for this formulation. In addition, in Section 5 the significance of intersemiosis, or the interactions between language, symbolism and visual display, for semantic expansions in multisemiotic texts is explained. This provides the context for the discussion of semantic expansions which occur through the process of semiotic metaphor in Section 6.

5.   Experiential meaning in mathematical symbolism

With seemingly lexically empty pronouns and idealised processes in, for example, Newton's equation $rx = yy$, in its abstractness one could claim that mathematical symbolism is devoid of content or experiential meaning, and that the dominant function of this semiotic is logical reasoning. However, in what follows I explore the possibility that an important component of the ideational meaning of mathematics is experiential as well as logical. This will involve re-examining mathematical symbolism through its relationship to the visual semiotic.

The question of the 'reality' of mathematics has been the subject of much philosophical enquiry from antiquity to the present (for example, Azzouni 1994; Boyd 1991; Davis 1986; Grabiner 1986; Janich 1989; Kitcher 1983; Kline 1985). This includes today a backlash against feminist and postmodern critiques of mathematics and science which posit mathematics as a social and cultural construction which is politically motivated (Koertge 1998). There is no place here for a discussion of such philosophical enquiries, but instead I examine two historical texts in order to explore the experiential meaning of mathematical symbolism. Here it appears that, paradoxically, the symbolism is the semiotic which is closest to our pre-semiotic experience of the material world in terms of the semantics of flux and change, but one that is not recognisable as such because it captures this experience in terms of reductive formalised relationships between entities. However, the significance of the relationship between the visual image and the mathematical symbolism becomes apparent.

According to Saussure (1966), language is used to circumscribe and delimit pre-semiotic perceptual and sensory motor experience to create order and value. As Thibault (1997: 183) explains: "This reality is not simply given; rather it emerges in and through the value-producing resources which the users of a language deploy to construe it, act on it and intervene". Following Thibault (1997: 183) and others (for example, Kress & van Leeuwen 1996; O'Toole 1994) these formulations of language may be extended to other forms of semiosis including visual images. Pictures and drawings are not simply replications of our sensory experience, rather they impose order on that experience.

If we examine Figure 2, Niccola Tartaglia's investigation of the path of cannon shot published in the Nova Scientia [The New Science] in 1537, we may see participants engaged in the action of firing a cannon, presumably aimed at the house on the other side of the river. We may also see that a line-arc-line model is used to trace the path of the projectile as it travels through the air, for at this time the question of the range of the cannons was important for purposes of war and defence. Thus Tartaglia's visual representation construes salient visual categories which are culturally specific, that is, the concern is the prediction of the path of the cannon shot.

Figure 2: Tartaglia's drawing: The cannon (Swetz 1994: 465)

If we now look at one of Descartes' (1954: 15) mathematical drawings in Figure 3, we see an uncanny resemblance in that the concern with arcs and lines is still apparent, but the background scene which contextualises those arcs and lines is missing. In addition, mathematical symbolic and linguistic text appear alongside the visual representation. Linguistic and symbolic text may have also been present in Tartaglia's original manuscript, but these are not reproduced as part of the historical document (Swetz 1994: 465). This absence and apparent relative insignificance of mathematical symbolism in Tartaglia's work accords with Kline's (1972) report that before Descartes, algebra was in a stage of 'disarray', which we may gloss as meaning that it had not fully developed as a semiotic resource. Descartes is concerned with lines and arcs of circles, but these are now represented inter-semiotically with mathematical symbolism and language.

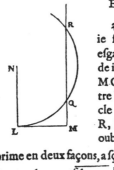

Enfin fi i'ay

$z \infty a z - bb:$

ie fais N L efgale à ½ a, & L M efgale à b cóme denât, puis, au lieu de ioindre les poins M N , ie tire M Q̂ R parallele a L N. & du centre N par L ayant defcrit vn cercle qui la couppe aux poins Q & R, la ligne cherchée z eft M Q; oubiê M R, car en ce cas elle s'exprime en deux façons, a fçauoir $z \infty \frac{1}{2} a + \sqrt{\frac{1}{4}aa - bb}$, & $z \infty \frac{1}{2} a - \sqrt{\frac{1}{4}aa - bb}$.

Et fi le cercle, qui ayant fon centre au point N , paffe par le point L, ne couppe ny ne touche la ligne droite M Q R, il n'y a aucune racine en l'Equation, de façon qu'on peut affurer que la conftruction du problefme propofé eft impoffible.

Au

Figure 3: Descartes' *Geometrie* (Descartes 1954: 15)

The experiential content of Tartaglia's image is explicit, and order is imposed visually on the observable sensory world. The circles, arcs and line segments have experiential meaning as the path of the projectile in relation to the ground, vertical height and time. When these circles and arcs appear in mathematical texts such as Descartes' *Geometrie*, however, they enter a different form of relationship in construing experience. In Descartes' text, the visual image enters into a direct inter-semiotic relationship with mathematical symbolism rather than our sensory experience of the world. No longer is the dialectic with sensory perception, the activity now becomes one of semiotic mediation between mathematical symbolism and visual display. The experiential meaning of the symbolism extends to the lines and circles which become describable through this semiotic; the curve becomes a function of the relationship, for example, between the participants x and y. In other words, the curve is construed experientially through configurations of participants and processes in the mathematical symbolism.

This move away from our sensory experience of the material world to sensory experience of the inter-semiotic mediation between mathematical symbolism and visual display is significant. While the visual image remains our most obvious link to the sensory material world (even in the case of mathematical graphs and diagrams), with the symbolism we are mediating with the visual semiotic rather than directly with the material world. The experiential meaning of mathematical symbolism is one removed from our experience of the world to our experience of the visual semiotic, at least initially. We may of course say, *let x be the width of the river, or let x be the time elapsed after firing the cannon*, in which case the symbolism is contextualised through our material experience of the world. From here, the x is nonetheless represented visually on the diagram. Once the description has been achieved visually and symbolically and the problem modeled and solved symbolically, the mathematical results may then be used to intervene on the material world. Newton's $rx = yy$ thus means experientially in relation to the mathematics diagram, and in relation to the grammar of the mathematical symbolism.

Meaning-makers appropriate and adapt the resources and conventions of the system in order to construct meanings which are relevant to specific contexts. We may extend this argument to include the development and refinement of semiotic resources. The impetus for the development of mathematical symbolism as a semiotic resource may lie in its relationship to visual representation because the first fully developed descriptions of continuity, change and patterns of covariation in mathematics (Lemke 1998; forthcoming) are perhaps demonstrated in the work of Descartes, the mathematician who developed the inter-semiotic relationship between the symbolic and the visual. As Boyer (1994) explains:

> [...] there appears to be no conception before their time [Descartes and Fermat] [...] – the fact that in general an arbitrary *given equation* involving *two unknown quantities* can be regarded as determining *per se*, with respect to a coordinate system, a plane curve. This latter recognition, together with its fabrication into a formalised algorithmic procedure, constituted the decisive contribution of Fermat and Descartes. (Boyer 1994: 462)

Lemke (forthcoming) describes language as primarily describing typo-graphical or categorical difference and mathematics as describing topological or degree of difference, though he points out that the topological descriptions of continuity in mathematics are achieved using 'quasi-linguistic' or algebraic selections which evolved from language. How is this possible? Perhaps through the work of Descartes where the inter-semiotic link between the symbolism and the visual display was fully established; the curve became describable as a function between variables. That is, the symbolism developed as a resource which construes experience as change and flux, the semantics of which also reside implicitly in the visual representation. As this change and flux, however, is recorded symbolically as variation between a discrete number of variables, the semiotic construal must inevitably be reductive in nature.

How and why Descartes started to use a co-ordinate system to describe curves is suggested by the drawing displayed in Figure 4, which depicts the materiality of his first investigations into the relationship between equation and curve. This picture shows the material experience of drawing a curve using a ruler and string which is braced against a horizontal line.

Figure 4: Descartes' *Geometrie*: Drawing a curve (Descartes 1954: 122)

Descartes describes the mechanism of "describing these ovals":

There are many other ways of describing these same ovals. For example, the first one, AV (provided we assume FA and AG equal) might be traced as follows: Divide the line FG at L so that FL : LG =A5 : A6, that is, the ratio corresponding to the index of refraction. Then bisecting AL at K, turn a ruler FE about the point F, pressing with the finger at C the cord EC, which, being attached at E to the end of the ruler, passes from C to K and then back to C and from C to G, where its other end is fastened. Thus the entire length of the chord is composed of GA+AL +FE=AF, and the point C will describe the first oval in a way similar to that in which the ellipse and hyperbola are described in *La Dioptrique*. (Descartes 1954: 123–124)

Descartes, however, developed a method to replace these material actions where the curve becomes a matter of the deviation from the horizontal and vertical. He discovered that the symbolic semiotic could describe this curve through the notion of co-ordinate axes. The symbolic representation replaced the act of using mechanical devices to describe the curve.

Mathematical symbolism therefore means experientially in relation to the visual representation and in relation to its own grammar, and this is an important aspect of the semantics of mathematics. If we return again to Newton's mathematical equation for the parabola, the x in $rx = yy$ means in different ways: extending Saussure's theory of language (Saussure 1966; Thibault 1997), the x means through its value in the grammar of mathematical symbolism, both in terms of its paradigmatic difference with other symbols r and y, and the syntagmatic relations it enters into in the equation $rx = yy$. That is, x means through the grammar of mathematical symbolism, both in terms of the system and in terms of the relationships it enters in any instantiation. In addition, the x means inter-semiotically through the grammar of visual representation. In other words, x means what it means with respect to the grammar of mathematical symbolism and the grammar of visual representation.

The x therefore means intra-semiotically and inter-semiotically. If we return to Tartaglia's drawing, the reason for the use of x rather than *the distance across the river* is not only linked to the generalisable result sought by mathematicians in their descriptions of continuous relations, but also with strategies of unambiguous condensation through which the grammar of the symbolism functions. The x is easily manipulated to reconfigure the relationships it possesses with other mathematical participants. This reconfiguration is essential for the derivation of the solution to mathematics problems.

Although I have referred rather generally to inter-semiotic processes in this discussion of the experiential meaning of mathematical symbolism, I now consider specifically one such process which allows semantic expansions to occur in mathematics. The x means what it means, not only as a choice in the grammar of mathematical symbolism but also as a choice in the grammar of visual display. However, there is added mechanism for further semantic expansions apart from the exploitation of the meaning potential of the different semiotic resources, and here I am interested in one micro-inter-semiotic process which occurs when a functional element such as x is reconstrued in a second semiotic resource. That is, I am concerned with semiotic metaphor which occurs with movements between semiotic codes.

6.   Semiotic metaphor in mathematics and science

The scientific process, along with many other forms of human activity, involves repeated semiotic reconstruals of experience. In the case of science and mathematics, sensory perceptions and experience of the material world are construed linguistically, these sensory perceptions and/or linguistic construals may be represented visually, the relations between participants in these sensory/ linguistic/ visual representations may be described symbolically and there may be a linguistic reconstrual in the form of description and/or causal explanation. This is not to say that the construals are uni-directional, that is from one resource to another in a pre-determined pattern, rather the process is dialectical in that there is a dialogue or movement back and forth between the different forms of semiosis. Generally, however, we may conceptualise an underlying sequence in regard to the use of a primary semiotic at different stages in the solution to a mathematics problem. For example, Stewart (1999: 59–60) summarises the problem solving steps in mathematics:

> Understand the problem. The first step is to read the problem and make sure you understand it clearly [*linguistic*] [...] for many problems it is useful to draw a diagram and identify the given and required quantities on the diagram [*visual*] . Usually it is necessary to introduce suitable notation [*symbolic*] [...] Think of a plan [a method of solution] [...] Carry out the plan [*symbolic*] [...] Look back [*linguistic, visual, symbolic*].

We may see in this formulation the process of repeated semiotic mediations. That is, initially order is created from the flux of sensory experience of the material world using linguistic and visual resources. From this point, rather than engaging with the pre-semiotic sensory world, as previously discussed, one perceptually engages with the visual semiotic form, the diagram. That is, the focus shifts from the world out there, to the salient features of the visual representation imposed on that world. And this world created by the visual image is selective and culture specific. It is not a distillation of material reality, but rather like a superimposed structure which functions to situate constituents in a particular relationship with each other through some sort of happening. We may now speak of a second stage, an inter-semiotic stage where one engages materially and perceptually with a semiotic construct rather than the world out there, and as such this world is now further filtered and circumscribed. I return to this point in the final section of this paper.

It becomes apparent that not only are the intra-semiotic processes and the exploitation of the meaning potential of each semiotic significant, but also the repeated inter-semiotic processes through which the scientific world is constructed become critical. I now turn to the micro-processes in the inter-semiotic action in order to trace the shifts in meaning in functional elements which occur with transitions between codes, and here I discuss the notion of semiotic metaphor.

In a manner similar to grammatical metaphor, semiotic metaphor may involve a shift in the function and the grammatical class of an element, or the introduction of new functional elements. However, this process does not take place intra-semiotically as for grammatical metaphor in language, rather it takes place inter-semiotically when a functional element is reconstrued using another semiotic code. With such a reconstrual, we see a semantic shift in the function of that element. In addition, the shift to a new semiotic resource may allow the introduction of completely new functional elements. For illustrative purposes, I give several examples of semiotic metaphor which occur in the writings of Descartes and contemporary mathematical discourse.

In the following extract, Descartes (1998: 86) is concerned with the problem of the colours in a rainbow:

> ... it was easy for me to judge that it [the colour red] came merely from the way in which rays of light act against those drops and from there tend towards our eyes. Then, knowing that these drops are round, as we have demonstrated above, and seeing their size does not affect the appearance of the arc, I decided to make a very large [drop] so as to be able to examine it better. For this purpose, I filled a perfectly round and transparent large flask with water, and I discovered that, for example, when the Sun came from that part of the sky marked AFZ [fig 26], my eye being at point E, when I placed this globe at the spot BCD, its part D appeared to me completely red and incomparably more brilliant than the rest. (Descartes 1998: 86)

In this translation[3] Descartes' linguistic construal of his sensory experience of the world is dynamic and congruent in the sense that conjunctive relations construe sequence and, with the exception of *the appearance of the arc,* there is an absence of grammatical metaphor.

The drawing accompanying Descartes' linguistic account is reproduced in Figure 5. Here the participants include a man (with a sword!) standing on the ground, a rainbow which is indicated by two parabolas, and a circle which represents a large drop of water. There is a sequence of episodes portrayed; the rays of light from the sun enter the drop of water and these rays are refracted towards the man who is looking up at the rainbow.

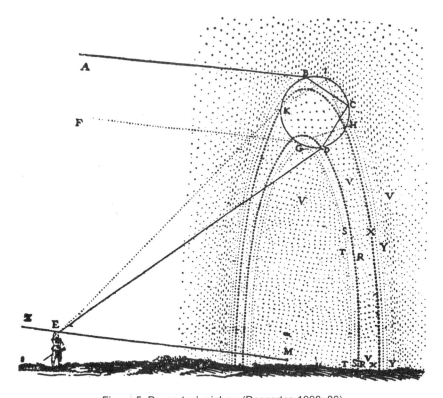

Figure 5: Descartes' rainbow (Descartes 1998: 86)

Semiotic metaphor occurs in Descartes' writing in the shift between the linguistic construal and the visual representation. As the linguistic text is constructed around the visual representation as evident from reference to the drawing, for example, *that part of the sky marked AFZ*, and *point E*, the relationship is dialectical. However, we may examine the semantic shifts which occur with the re-representation of functional elements in each semiotic. These semantic shifts primarily involve reconstruing processes in language as participants in the visual representation. For example, in *when the Sun came from that part of the sky marked AFZ* we may see that the process of the sun *coming* from a particular location in the sky results in the introduction of new participants, the parallel line segments which are accordingly named AB, FG and ZM. Here the visual construal allows the introduction of participants from the process of the sun *coming*.

Further to this, the process of *acting* [on the drops] in *the way in which rays of light act against those drops and from there tend towards our eyes*, is reconstrued as participants in visual representation in that they become a series of line segments BC and CD. The process of *tend* also becomes an entity, the line segment DE. There has been a shift here from linguistic clausal configurations of participant/process and process to visual entities in the form of line segments in the drawing.[4] Similarly, in *these drops are round* the linguistic attribute or quality *round* shifts semantically to an entity, the circle in the drawing. These shifts to visual entities in the drawing are critical inter-semiotic processes because they allow the introduction of a completely new entity, the angle, which later becomes an important participant in Descartes' linguistic account of the problem (see Descartes 1998: 87).

If we return to Tartaglia's picture, we may imagine similar cases of semiotic metaphor occurring. We may reconstrue linguistically the scene which is portrayed, for example: *A man fires a cannon. The cannon shot travels cross the river so that it hits the house.* The congruent linguistic process *travel* shifts to a participant in the drawing, the line segments and the arcs of the circles. In the visual representation, semiotic metaphor occurs in that new participants, the lines and arcs are introduced. This once again is a critical stage because, as we may see later in the work of Descartes and Newton, the new entity, the triangle is introduced visually. From that point the relationship between the sides and the angles can be described symbolically in order to obtain a mathematical solution to the problem, as demonstrated below in the discussion of contemporary solution to the problem of the rainbow formulated by Stewart (1999).

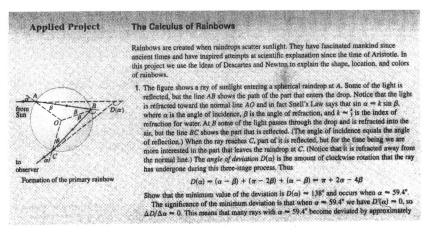

Figure 6: The rainbow problem today (Stewart 1999: 232)

The significance of the introduction of the new participants in the visual semiotic is apparent in Stewart's (1999: 232) construal of the calculus of the rainbow, reproduced in Figure 6. Before examining the examples of semiotic metaphor in this text, we may note that in this contemporary version of Descartes' rainbow problem, the context is introduced linguistically in a congruent manner. The only grammatical metaphors are *scientific explanation* and *location*. However, in part (1), after congruently contextualising the diagram, we have the following (Stewart 1999: 232):

Notice that the light is refracted toward the normal line AO and in fact Snell's Law says that $\sin \alpha = k \sin \beta$, where α is the angle of incidence, and β is the angle of refraction, and $k \approx \dfrac{4}{3}$ is the index of refraction for water.

The proliferation of grammatical metaphor here is evident: *the angle of incidence, the angle of refraction* and *the index of refraction for water*. In the remainder of the problem there is *the angle of deviation, the amount of clockwise rotation*, and *the minimum value of deviation* (Stewart 1999: 232). From Descartes' congruent linguistic rendition, here we have a highly metaphorical account of the refraction of light in contemporary mathematics textbooks. A close examination of the diagram and symbolic description in this text also reveals the occurrence of semiotic metaphor.

The shift between the linguistic, the visual and the symbolic in Stewart (1999) involves two cases of semiotic metaphor, both in the form of the introduction of new participants. That is, the new participant, the triangle, is introduced visually, and the new participant, $\sin \alpha$, is introduced symbolically. The introduction of the line segments noted in Descartes' drawing also appears in Stewart (1999), the difference being that a new entity, the triangle, is also present visually in this contemporary text. This new visual entity, the triangle, is decomposed as a relation between its side and angles to introduce $\sin \alpha$ symbolically. This could only be possible if the triangle were first introduced and then perceived as a whole, which occurs in the visual representation. The introduction of the triangle is therefore a significant step because the derivation of the solution to the problem uses the following mathematical result which depends on the relations between the angles and sides in the triangle:

$$\sin \alpha = k \sin \beta \text{ and}$$

$$D(\alpha) = (\alpha - \beta) + (\pi - 2\alpha) + (\alpha - \beta) = \pi + 2\alpha - 4\beta$$

This result is used to *Show that the minimum value of deviation is* $D(\alpha) \approx 138^{o}$ *and occurs when* $\alpha \approx 59.4^{o}$ (Stewart 1999: 232). While Descartes was aware that there was a critical angle size, unlike Stewart (1999), he did not have the semiotic tools (that is, the mathematical symbolism) to establish the result.

It appears that the visual representation tends to introduce entities through the process of semiotic metaphor. This may involve a shift from clause and process to entity, or it may involve the introduction of new entities as we have seen above. In addition to the dynamic construal of reality afforded by mathematical symbolism, the visual representation perhaps also contributes to the use of grammatical metaphor in language. In other words, after the introduction of the visual image, we see a shift to the use of grammatical metaphor in language when Descartes (1954: 123–124) speaks of *the refraction* and *the reflection* of the light rays.

Finally, let us consider semantic shifts which occur through linguistic and symbolic constructions, for example, the linguistic construal of the symbolic x^5. This case is slightly different to those cited above because the concern is not with semantic expansions or extensions that occur with movements between semiotic codes, but rather unintentional and non-functional semantic shifts that occur, for example, in the oral discourse in the mathematics classroom.

In the grammar of mathematical symbolism for experiential meaning, x^5 encodes the following complex process/participant configuration:

$$x^5 = x \times x \times x \times x \times x$$

However, linguistically, we may say "x to the power of 5" which is a nominal group which construes an entity. This is an example of semiotic metaphor where the linguistic construal involves a semantic shift from a complex process/participant configuration involving the participant x and multiple processes of multiplication in the symbolism to an entity, a nominal group in language. The linguistic rendition can only be unpacked if the grammar of mathematical symbolism is invoked.

A similar phenomenon occurs when $\sqrt{rx}$ is linguistically construed as "the square root of rx". Once again there has been a shift from a process/participant configuration in the symbolism to a nominal group in language. The unpacking of the linguistic rendition can only be achieved through the grammar of mathematical symbolism.

This form of semiotic metaphor commonly occurs with the verbalisation of mathematical symbolism in oral classroom discourse (O'Halloran 1996; 1999b;

2000). The phenomenon of semiotic metaphor may therefore have significant implications for mathematics education where students and teachers may not be aware of the semantic shifts which occur with linguistic construals of the mathematics, especially in the case where language functions as metadiscourse for the mathematical symbolism. This points to the need for an awareness of the different grammatical systems in each semiotic, and the shifts in meaning which occur with movements between semiotic codes. Perhaps neglect of these issues accounts for some learning difficulties in mathematics which could be remedied with further research into the multimodal nature of mathematical and scientific discourse.

Notes

1. There are eight volumes in the series edited by D. T. Whiteside spanning Newton's writing in the years 1664-1722.
2. For a history of the use of mathematical notation, see Cajori (1952, 1974).
3. Series editor K. Ameriks and D. Clarke note: "Wherever possible, texts are produced in complete and unabridged form, and translations are specially commissioned for the series".
4. If these line segments had been represented with arrows (which may be understood to be construing a dynamic process) the 'process' aspect is nonetheless lost in the later visual representation of the triangle.

References

Azzouni, J. (1994) *Metaphysical Myths, Mathematical Practice: The ontology and epistemology of the exact sciences*. New York: Press Syndicate of the University of Cambridge.

Baldry, A.P. (ed.) (2000a) *Multimodality and Multimediality in the Distance Learning Age* Campobasso, Italy: Palladino Editore.

Baldry, A.P. (2000b) English in a visual society: Comparative and historical dimensions in multimodality and multimediality. In: A.P. Baldry (ed.) *Multimodality and Multimediality in the Distance Learning Age*. Campobasso, Italy: Palladino Editore. 41–89

Boyd, R. (1991) On the current state of scientific realism. In: R. Boyd, P. Gasper, & J.D. Trout (eds.) *The Philosophy of Science*. Cambridge, MA: MIT Press. 195–222.

Boyer, C.B. (1994) Analytic geometry: The discovery of Fermat and Descartes. In: F.J. Swetz (ed.) *From Five Fingers to Infinity*. Chicago: Open Court. 458–464.

Cajori, F.A. (1952) *A History of Mathematical Notations. Volume II*. 3rd edition. ILL: Open Court Publishing Company.

Cajori, F.A. (1974) *A History of Mathematical Notations: Volume I*. 2nd edition. ILL: Open Court Publishing Company.

Davis, P.J. (1986) Fidelity in mathematical discourse: Is one and one really two? In T. Tymoczko (ed.) *New Directions in the Philosophy of Mathematics.* Boston: Birkhauser. 163–175.

Descartes, R. (1954) *The Geometry of Rene Descartes* (David Eugene Smith and Marcia L. Latham, Trans.). (1637 1st ed.). New York: Dover.

Descartes, R. (1998) *The World and Other Writings.* Ed. and transl. by S. Gaukroger. Cambridge: Cambridge UP.

Grabiner, J.V. (1986) Is mathematical truth time-dependent? In: T. Tymoczko (ed.) *New Directions in the Philosophy of Mathematics.* Boston: Birkhauser [reprinted from *American Mathematical Monthly* 81.4 (April 1974): 354–365]. 201–213.

Halliday, M.A.K. (1978) *Language as Social Semiotic: The social interpretation of language and meaning.* London: Arnold.

Halliday, M.A.K. (1985) *Spoken and Written Language.* Geelong, Victoria: Deakin UP [Republished by Oxford UP 1989].

Halliday, M.A.K. (1993a) On the language of physical science. In: M.A.K. Halliday & J.R. Martin (eds.) *Writing Science: Literacy and discursive power.* London: Falmer. 54–68.

Halliday, M.A.K.. (1993b) Some grammatical problems in scientific English. In: M.A.K. Halliday & J.R. Martin (eds.) *Writing science: Literacy and discursive power.* London: Falmer. 69–85.

Halliday, M.A.K. (1994). *An Introduction to Functional Grammar.* (1985 1st ed.). London: Arnold.

Halliday, M.A.K. (1998) Things and relations: Regrammaticising experience as technical knowledge. In: J.R. Martin & R. Veel (eds.) *Reading Science: Critical and functional perspectives on discourses of science.* London: Routledge. 185–235.

Halliday, M.A.K. & J.R. Martin (1993) *Writing Science: Literacy and discursive power.* London: Falmer.

Janich, P. (1989) Determination by reality or construction of reality? In: R.E. Butts & J.R. Brown (eds.) *Constructivism and Science: Essays in recent German philosophy.* Dordrecht: Kluwer. 257–269.

Joseph, G.G. (1991) *The Crest of the Peacock: Non-European Roots of Mathematics.* London: I.B. Tauris Company.

Kitcher, P. (1983) *The Nature of Mathematical Reality.* New York: Oxford UP.

Kline, M. (1972) *Mathematical Thought from Ancient to Modern Times.* New York: Oxford UP.

Kline, M. (1985) *Mathematics and the Search for Knowledge.* New York: Oxford UP.

Koertge, N. (ed.). (1998) *A House Built on Sand.* NY: Oxford UP.

Kress, G. (in press) Multimodality: Perspectives on a change in the landscape of communication. In: J.R. Martin & R. Iedema (eds.) *Multimodal Communication: Social semiotic perspectives on meaning making.* Amsterdam: Benjamins.

Kress, G., & van Leeuwen, T. (1996) *Reading Images: The grammar of visual design.* London: Routledge.

Layzer, David (1990) *Cosmogenesis. The growth of order in the universe.* Oxford: Oxford UP.

Lemke, J.L. (1993) Discourse, dynamics, and social change. In: M.A.K. Halliday (ed.) *Language as Cultural Dynamic*. (Special Issue of Cultural Dynamics.) 243–75.

Lemke, J.L. (1998) Multiplying meaning: Visual and verbal semiotics in scientific text. In: J.R. Martin & R. Veel (eds.) *Reading Science: Critical and functional perspectives on discourses of science*. London: Routledge. 87–113.

Lemke, J.L. (2000) Multimedia demands of the scientific curriculum. *Linguistics and Education* 10.3. (Special Edition: Language and Other Semiotic Systems in Education.)

Lemke, J.L. (forthcoming). Mathematics in the middle: Measure, picture, gesture, sign, and word. In: M. Anderson, V. Cifarelli, A. Saenz-Ludlow & A. Vile (eds.) *Semiotic Perspectives on Mathematics Education*.

Martin, J.R. (1992) *English Text: System and structure*. Amsterdam: Benjamins.

Martin, J.R. (1993a) Life as a noun: Arresting the universe in science and humanities. In: M.A.K. Halliday & J.R. Martin (eds.) *Writing Science: Literacy and discursive power*. London: Falmer. 221–267.

Martin, J.R. (1993b) Technicality and abstraction: Language for the creation of specialised texts. In: M.A.K. Halliday & J.R. Martin (eds.) *Writing Science: Literacy and discursive power*. London: Falmer. 203–220.

Martin, J.R., & Iedema, R. (in press) *Multimodal Communication: Social semiotic perspectives on meaning making*. Amsterdam: Benjamins.

Martin, J.R., & Veel, R. (ed.) (1998) *Reading Science: Critical and functional perspectives on discourses of science*. London: Routledge.

Newton, I. (1931) *Opticks* (Reprinted from 4th edition). London: Bell & Sons.

Newton, I. (1967) Normals, curvature and tangents. Section 2: Detailed research into curvature, December 1664. In: D.T. Whiteside (ed.) *The Mathematical Papers of Isaac Newton*. Cambridge: Cambridge UP. 248–271.

O'Halloran, K.L. (1996) *The Discourses of Secondary School Mathematics*. PhD Thesis, Murdoch University, Western Australia.

O'Halloran, K.L. (1999a) Interdependence, interaction and metaphor in multisemiotic texts. *Social Semiotics* 9.3: 317–354.

O'Halloran, K.L. (1999b) Towards a systemic functional analysis of multisemiotic mathematics texts. *Semiotica* 124.1/2: 1–29.

O'Halloran, K.L. (2000) Classroom discourse in mathematics: A multisemiotic analysis. *Linguistics and Education* 10.3 (Special edition: Language and Other Semiotic Systems in Education): 359–388.

O'Toole, M. (1994) *The Language of Displayed Art*. London: Leicester UP.

Ravelli, L.J. (2000) Beyond shopping: Constructing the Sydney olympics in three dimensional text. *Text* 20.4: 489–515.

Rickey, V.F. (1994) Isaac Newton: Man, myth, and mathematics. In: F.J. Swetz (ed.) *From Five Fingers to Infinity: A Journey through the History of Mathematics*. Chicago: Open Court. 483–507.

Saussure, F. (1966) *Course in General Linguistics*. London: McGraw-Hill.

Stewart, J. (1999) *Calculus*. 4th edition. Pacific Grove CA: Brooks/Cole Publishing Company.

Swetz, F.J. (ed.) (1994) *From Five Fingers to Infinity: A Journey through the History of Mathematics*. Chicago: Open Court.

Thibault, P. (1997) *Re-reading Saussure: The dynamics of signs in social life*. London: Routledge.

Thibault, P. (2000) The multimodal transcription of a television advertisement: Theory and practice. In: A.P. Baldry (ed.) *Multimodality and Multimediality in the Distance Learning Age*. Campobasso, Italy: Palladino Editore. 311–385.

Part V

Metaphor in metalinguistic perspectives

The conduit metaphor
and the analysis of meaning
Peircean semiotics, cognitive grammar and systemic
functional grammar[1]

Patrick Goethals
Hogeschool Gent

1. Introduction

In a well-known paper, Reddy (1979) draws attention to the fact that ordinary language expressions about communication reflect a metaphorical way of understanding speech. This metaphor, commonly known as the CONDUIT METAPHOR, presents communication as a (mental) process of transaction where the message is conceived of as an object that is transferred from one mind to another.

(1) Try to get your thoughts across better.
(2) None of Mary's feelings came through to me with any clarity
(3) You still haven't given me any idea of what you mean.
     (examples from Reddy 1979: 286)

In this paper I will try to evaluate the consequences of this metaphorical way of understanding communication. More specifically, I will discuss some of the main theoretical principles of three semiotically oriented frameworks, namely Peircean Semiotics, Cognitive Grammar (CG) and Systemic Functional Grammar (SFG). My purpose is not primarily to investigate what these frameworks say explicitly about the CONDUIT METAPHOR but how they handle one of its main risks, namely the risk of imposing a restrictive view on linguistic signification. Let me first clarify this point.

Firstly, the CONDUIT METAPHOR on communication suggests that a fundamental distinction is to be made between the transferred message and the action of transferring itself. Secondly (and this is the critical point), it might suggest that linguistic meaning or linguistic signification is restricted to building up a message that is transferred in a context of communication which itself does not depend on linguistic meaning. In Figure 1 we represent the most radical and restrictive way of thinking about linguistic meaning.

Figure 1: Meaning and the conduit metaphor

Although this view seems to be implicit in some research within formal semantics, at least since Speech Act Philosophy (Austin 1962) there is fairly general agreement about the need to integrate in a theory of linguistic meaning not only the message-component but also the component of performativity. That is, there is a clear awareness that the meaning of an utterance is not restricted to establishing a representational content, but also specifies characteristics of the speech event. So, for example, in (4) the explicit performative formula *I promise* does not describe an event of promising but indicates that the speaker is actually making a promise; in (5) the function of identifying a speech act of asking is realized by word order and prosody.[2]

(4)   I promise you I will do it.
(5)   Do you agree with me?

The question I want to raise in what follows is how different theoretical paradigms deal with this interactive or performative aspect of meaning. Do they recognize it? Do they establish a clear distinction between performative and representational meaning? And if they do so, which linguistic phenomena do they put in each component? We will see that the three paradigms (Peircean Semiotics, Cognitive Grammar and Systemic Functional Grammar) give different answers. Therefore, the metalinguistic terminology they provide offers different ways of clarifying the metaphorical and intuitive way of talking about communication and linguistic meaning.

First I will introduce some concepts of Peircean Semiotics. This is a framework which is, in my opinion, especially well equipped to both integrate and differentiate representational and performative meaning in an overall semiotic approach. Next, I will compare this particular semiotic analysis with the analysis offered by Cognitive Grammar and by Systemic Functional Grammar. By doing so I hope to enrich the understanding of these linguistic paradigms.

1.1. Peircean Semiotics: Some basic notions

Peirce's philosophical and semiotic thinking is dominated by trichotomic structures. According to Peirce (and in contrast with Saussure, who proposed a binary definition), a sign is a triadic relationship between three poles: the *representamen*, the *object* and the *interpretant*. The *representamen* is equivalent to the *signifier* of Saussure, i.e. the formal side of the sign. The *object* is "what the sign stands for" (*Collected Papers* Vol. 2, §228 -*CP* 2.228), and the *interpretant* is a mediating device that functions as a translator. Although the latter notion will not be our main concern, we quote Peirce:

> Every comparison requires, besides the related thing, the ground, and the correlate, also a mediating representation which represents the relate to be a representation of the same correlate which this mediating representation itself represents. Such a mediating representation may be termed an *interpretant*, because it fulfils the office of an interpreter, who says that a foreigner says the same thing which he himself says. (*CP* 1.553)

Thus, a sign is a complex event that involves a formally identifiable signifier (*representamen*) which produces a mental effect in the mind of the interpreter (*object*) by virtue of a mediating device that ensures that what the interpreter has in his or her mind is indeed what the sign stands for.[3]

Peirce's taxonomy of types of signs is characterized by a trichotomic structure. It distinguishes different subcategories on the basis of the nature of the representamen, the object and the interpretant. The three poles of the sign can belong to the dimension of firstness, secondness or thirdness. As we can read in the following quotation from Deledalle (1987), the first dimension is that of quality; the second dimension that of the individual, of the here and now ("l'haeccéité") and the third dimension is the dimension of abstraction, of mediation, of our thinking.

> [Le phénomène] entre dans l'une ou l'autre des trois catégories de la [...] phénoménologie: la priméité qui est la catégorie de la qualité et du sentiment, la secondéité qui est la catégorie de l'individuel, de l'haeccéité [...], la tiercéité qui est la catégorie de la médiation, de la pensée. (Deledalle 1987: 66)

A particular sign is classified by defining the nature (or the *mode of apprehension*, Pharies 1985: 30) of, respectively, the representamen, the object and the interpretant. In what follows I will restrict myself to the representamen and the object.

When we apprehend the representamen as a quality (in other words, as belonging to the first dimension), the sign is defined as a Qualisign ("A *Qualisign* is a Quality which is a Sign", *CP* 2.244). The sign is a Sinsign when the representamen is apprehended as second, i.e. as a concrete individual ("A *Sinsign* (where the syllable *sin* is taken as meaning 'being only once', as in *single, simple*, Latin *semel*, etc.) is an actual existent thing or event which is a sign", *CP* 2.245). And the sign is finally qualified as Legisign when we apprehend it as a concrete realization (a *token*, or an *instance* in Peirce's terminology) of a type that signifies due to a convention ("A *Legisign* is a law that is a Sign", *CP* 2.246). Some examples will clarify these definitions.

We can think for example of a city map, which can function as a Qualisign, a Sinsign or a Legisign. It functions as a Legisign when we interpret signifiers like the lines, squares or crosses representing respectively the streets, houses and churches, because these are conventional signs, which will probably be explained in a key. It functions as a Qualisign when we interpret the relative structuring and the relative length of the lines because these are qualities of the map. And it is a Sinsign when the signifier is the actual presence of the signifier. So, for example, I interpret the presence of a map on the table as a sign for the fact that somebody is preparing a trip: what signifies is not a quality of the map, nor a convention (except in the case we agreed upon using this sign to communicate that we are preparing a trip), but the fact that it is there. Another clear example of a Sinsign is a column of smoke that shows us that there is a fire. What signifies is not the smoke as an instance of a conventional sign but the actual existence of the smoke. It is the fact that there is smoke that functions as a sign for the fire.

The most prototypical instances of Legisigns are of course linguistic signs which together form a common and conventional code:

> Every legisign signifies through an instance of its application, which may be termed a *Replica* of it. Thus, the word 'the' will usually occur from fifteen to twenty-five times on a page. It is in all these occurrences one and the same word, the same legisign. Each single instance of it is a Replica. (*CP* 2.246)

Secondly, the sign is defined by the nature of the object.[4] When the object is apprehended as something of the first dimension (when the interpreter sees it as a quality) it is called an Icon. This means that an Icon orients us towards a quality without implying the real existence (or the *secondness*) of the signified: "The value of an icon consists in exhibiting the features of a state of things regarded as if it were purely imaginary". (*CP* 4.448)

In the example of the city map, the relative structuring and length of the streets exhibit a quality of the city, and would therefore be defined as an Iconic Qualisign.

A sign is an Index when it orients us mentally towards something we treat as really existent in the here and now. With an Index, we see the object as existing/being of the second order: "[An index is] an appropriate sign for calling attention to the existence of the object" (Fitzgerald 1966: 61).

And, finally, it is a Symbol when the object is of the third order. This means that the interpreter treats the object, not as really existing or present in the here and now, but as an Idea:

> Any ordinary word as 'give', 'bird', 'marriage', is an example of a symbol. It is applicable to whatever may be found to realize the idea connected with the word: it does not, in itself, identify those things. It does not show us a bird, nor enact before our eyes a giving in marriage, but supposes that we are able to imagine those things, and have associated the word with them. (*CP* 2.298)

To illustrate the difference between Indices and Symbols, which are the categories we are mainly interested in, we can think of the difference between a column of smoke and the word *fire*. Both signs have the same object, namely 'fire'. The difference between them is that the object of the (Sinsign) column of smoke is apprehended as really existing (the smoke shows us that there is a fire), whereas it is apprehended as a third-order entity (an idea) when the word *fire* is used in a sentence like *a column of smoke is an indexical sign for fire*.

In Figure 2 I sum up the taxonomy outlined so far.

	First	Second	Third
Representamen	Qualisign	Sinsign	Legisign
Object	Icon	Index	Symbol

Figure 2: Peirce's Semiotic Typology

It is important to note that, in contrast with its sense in post-Saussurean linguistics, the term *symbolic sign* is not synonymous with *conventional sign*. When a sign is part of a conventional code it is defined as Legisign, and a Legisign can be Iconic, Indexical or Symbolic.[5] As such, conventional signs can identify a quality (think of the iconicity of linguistic expressions), can orient us mentally towards a really existing entity or can evoke an idea. In the examples discussed so far we presented Indexical Sinsigns (column of smoke) and Symbolic Legisigns (the word *fire*). The category of signs I will mainly focus on in what follows will nevertheless be the category of conventional indices, or Indexical Legisigns. As non-linguistic examples we can think, for example, of alarm calls in animal communication: the alarm call is a conventional sign (it frequently forms part of a larger code of different alarm and other signals), but it is Indexical: it does not evoke the idea of a possible enemy, but it signals its presence in the here and now.

1.2.   Indexical and Symbolic Legisigns, and the analysis of performativity

In my opinion, Peirce's semiotic taxonomy is an appropriate metalinguistic instrument to describe the two dimensions of linguistic signification involved in the elaboration of the message and the modelling of the speech situation.

These linguistic signs are to be considered Legisigns, since their representamens (such as lexical items, word order, prosody, illocutionary particles, etc.) are all part of a linguistic code and do not signify *per se* but (at least partly) due to a convention. However, this group of linguistic conventional signs is not homogeneous: there are both Indexical and Symbolic Legisigns (in this place I will not consider Iconic Legisigns).

Signs that build up the propositional content of the utterance are Symbolic signs: they construe a proposition that can be evaluated as a true or false idea. Although the propositional content can refer to the speech event or an actual existing entity, it does not belong to the second but to the third order.

By contrast, signs that identify the illocutionary force or the performative value of the utterance are Indexical signs: they indicate that there is a speech act actually taking place. It would not be correct to say that they *refer* to a speech act taking place in the here and now: they *create* it, they *shape* the speech situation instead of referring to it. As a matter of fact, we can see in the above-mentioned quote that (long before Austin) Peirce refers to the absence of a performative value to define the symbolic signs (particularly, when he says they don't "enact before our eyes a giving in marriage").

To come back to our starting-point, namely the question if and how different paradigms integrate the performative component in a theory of linguistic signification, we can see that the metalinguistic terminology offered by Peircean semiotics (1) does not restrict meaning to the message-component: both the propositional content and the performative value can be described as dimensions of linguistic meaning; (2) does not treat linguistic meaning as a homogeneous phenomenon but instead as fundamentally heterogeneous; and (3) motivates the distinction between signs that operate on the content-level and those that operate on the performative level by the ontological status of the object: the former make the interpreter treat the object as a third-order, abstract entity, while the latter make him treat it as a second-order entity or event. Figure 3 summarizes the Peircean perspective

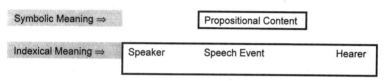

Figure 3: Symbolic and Indexical Meaning

2   Cognitive Grammar and Peircian Semiotics

2.1.   Cognitive Grammar (CG)

Most studies in CG have focused on the way language construes or reflects our conceptualizations (Langacker 1987, 1991, amongst many others). Its particular focus could make us believe that CG excludes the interactional part of communication and pays attention exclusively to the message-component (and so would fall into the trap of the CONDUIT METAPHOR; Figure 1). Interestingly, Langacker (1997) explicitly addresses this question. In his view, CG does not neglect context (or interaction) and to prove this, he argues explicitly against the bias of the CONDUIT METAPHOR. In this section, I will compare Langacker's way of avoiding the bias of the CONDUIT METAPHOR with the framework of Peircean semiotics.

I will approach the question indirectly, looking first of all at Langacker's argument against the claim that a focus on cognition would lead to solipsism and relativism. Solipsism refers to the fact that real communication is impossible if our conceptualizations are individual, not shared by other human minds. According to Langacker, CG avoids both solipsism and relativism because of its emphasis on the idea that our conceptions are shaped by experience (1997: 233). Since the ground of experience is a common ground, we have shared conceptions and so we avoid a solipsist or relativist account:

> Individuals [...] function in a real world [...] which shapes and constrains experience and cognitive development. Thus, since abstract conceptions and imagined worlds are ultimately grounded in real-world bodily

experience, the products of all minds and even the most diverse cultures are to a certain extent commensurable and mutually accessible. [...] Individual minds are thus commensurate because creatures with a common biological endowment develop through interaction with roughly comparable environments. (1997: 233; emphasis added)

The central point of Langacker's argument is indeed that CG excludes solipsism and relativism because it emphasizes the presence of the ground in our abstract conceptions. In other words, our conceptions or ideas are not relativist because they are grounded in and motivated by a common world of experience.

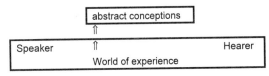

Figure 4: Langacker's argument against solipsism and relativism

In a very similar way, Langacker (1997) refutes the criticism that the analysis of linguistic meaning in CG neglects the component of performativity. In his view, CG does not neglect performativity or interaction in its theory of meaning. On the contrary, the speech situation, or the context, is understood to be part of the meaning of the utterance.

The general idea is that the context (the speech situation) has "the potential to be evoked as part of an expression's semantic value":

A speaker's entire apprehension of the context (including its discourse and interactional dimensions) constitutes the basis for the linguistic meanings, *with any facet of the context having the potential to be evoked as part of an expression's actual semantic value.* (Langacker 1997: 236; emphasis added)

This "potential to be evoked as part of an expression's semantic value" is called "grounding" (see also Davidse 1997, 1998). When the ground or the context is part of the explicitated content (in Langacker's terms, is "put onstage" or is "designated", 1985: 114, 119), by means of, for instance, the personal pronouns *I* or *you*, or deictic expressions like *now* or *here* in *The best place is right here*, it is called "objective grounding". When the ground is left "offstage", and functions as an implicit reference point, the grounding is "subjective" (1997: 243). This is the case when the utterance includes for example a past or present tense or deictic expressions whose reference is to be determined in relation to the speech event.

By introducing the principle of grounding, CG provides a metalinguistic tool to integrate the context of interaction in the analysis of meaning. In fact, it stipulates that in order to account for the meaning of an utterance, it is always necessary to identify the reference point, which coincides with the moment and place of interaction.[6] Figure 5 represents the idea of grounding by the upwards oriented arrows:

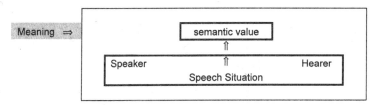

Figure 5: Langacker's view on involving the speech situation in meaning (=grounding)

In what follows I will try to determine whether the idea of grounding can give a full account of the interactive component of meaning. Let's see how this analysis applies to the different "facets of the context", identified by Langacker as "the speech event, its participants, and their immediate circumstances" (Langacker 1997: 243).

The most prominent elements in the context of speech are the speaker and the hearer: they are part of the speech situation and so they are treated as "facets of the context" that are included in the linguistic meaning.

> Conceptualizations [...] do not occur independently of their conceptual-izers. It is thus a basic tenet of the conceptualist semantics adopted in cognitive grammar that meanings comprise **both the subject and the object of conception**, not just the latter. (1997: 242)

Langacker further argues that, by including the subject of conception in the meaning of the utterance, CG avoids the bias of the CONDUIT METAPHOR.

> [The speaker and the addressee] are **actively engaged** as the subjects of conception in the context of the speech event. They are not at all to be regarded as detached observers who passively watch a film projected on a screen, or as uninvolved workers who merely load prepackaged meanings into words and sentences, ship them out, and unload them at the other end (Reddy 1979) (Langacker 1997: 244).

Secondly, there are the spatio-temporal circumstances. Here we can find one of the clearest examples of a subjective construal of the ground, namely primary time reference. A primary time reference (for example, the lexical item *tomorrow* or a morphological device like a past tense marker) does not put onstage the 'now', but leaves it offstage: this temporal reference has to be calculated in function of the speech situation (the ground). As such, the context is always present (although not overtly) in the meaning of the utterance.

Finally, Langacker discusses the illocutionary force of the utterance. We notice that he says little about illocution or performativity, but when he describes it, he uses the same terms as in his description of other grounding devices (i.e. tense and deixis) (1985: 132–123; 1997: 246). As he puts it, the illocutionary force of the utterance is part of the speech situation, conceived of as an interactive 'viewing arrangement' oriented towards the objectively construed message:

> The intended illocutionary force of an utterance is generally presupposed as part of the interactive 'viewing arrangement', the common ground from which, and in relation to which, they [the speaker and the hearer] apprehend an objectively construed situation. (Langacker 1997: 246)

Like the other facets of the ground, the illocutionary force, or the process of speaking, can be construed objectively, by means of explicit performatives (6-7), or subjectively, as in (8-9):

(6)   I ask you why he would ever do such a thing?
      (example from Langacker 1985: 131)

(7)   I order you to pack your bags and leave town immediately.
      (example from Langacker 1985: 131)

(8)   You will leave town immediately. (example from Langacker 1985: 132)

(9)   Will you leave town immediately? (example from Langacker 1985: 132)

It appears that the CG model presented in Langacker (1997) includes performativity in its theory of meaning, combining two ideas: (1) performativity (or the illocutionary force) is part of the speech situation; and (2) the speech situation as such has the potential to be evoked as part of the utterance's semantic value, either as part of the objectively construed message, or as part of the subjectively construed and implicit vantage point. Langacker's comments on (8-9) clearly illustrates the parallel drawn between the different grounding elements:

The speech event [...] specifies a communicative context (abstract domain) in which the designated process (i.e. the hearer leaving town) is situated, and in this respect it is comparable to the offstage points of reference that we have posited for other sorts of examples [e.g. primary tense reference, PG]. (Langacker 1985: 133)

2.2.   Peircean Semiotics and Cognitive Grammar: A comparison

In what sense do the two proposals presented so far, namely Peircean Semiotics and CG, differ in the way they integrate performativity in a theory of meaning? And if they differ, which of these proposals is to be preferred? I will try to argue that Peircean Semiotics and CG do differ in some essential respects[7] and, secondly, that Peircean Semiotics is a metalinguistic model that is more adequate for describing the peculiarity of performativity and the linguistic signs that identify it.

When we compare figures 3 and 5 we see two major differences: (1) in the Peircean semiotic analysis there are no upwards oriented arrows that represent the grounding phenomenon; and (2) Peircean Semiotics puts a clear emphasis on the fact that linguistic signification is heterogeneous, while CG suggests it is homogeneous. These two differences are not independent of each other: in some sense, the presence of the grounding principle provides a way of integrating the speech event in the meaning of the utterance and therefore seems to make superfluous a major inquiry in the semiotic nature of the signs that identify the speech event.

I do not wish to deny the importance of the grounding principle in other semantic issues, but I want to argue that this description is not the most adequate way to describe performativity and the way performative signs function. My central question is: should we understand the grounding involved in performativity (i.e. in the identification of the illocutionary force) as similar to the grounding involved in tense markers or deictic elements?

It is clear that illocutionary force indicators, deictic elements and primary tense references all establish a link with the context and the speech event. But is it the same type of link?

From the semiotic perspective, there is an important difference:[7] tense, unlike illocutionary force, is part of the truth-functional content of the clause. Therefore, when we work with the Peircean terminology, tense is part of the symbolic meaning of the clause and temporal markers will be included in the class of symbolic signs.

Primary tense markers are of course a special kind of symbolic meaning, because they are variables whose concrete reference is calculated in function of the speech situation. But this variability does not prevent their signified from being part of the symbolic content of the clause. Primary tense markers need the ground in order to determine fully their symbolic meaning. Therefore, I would propose to call them *ground-dependent* parts of the symbolic meaning.

Illocutionary force, on the other hand, is not part of the content that can be evaluated for its truthfulness. In our terminology, it is not part of the symbolic content of the utterance. Illocutionary force indicators also relate the utterance to the ground, but this relation is to be distinguished from what tense references do. Illocutionary force indicators shape the speech event, they modify the ground. They are not *ground-dependent parts of the symbolic meaning*, because they do not bring the ground into the symbolic meaning of the clause. Therefore, they are best described as *ground-modifying* indices.

Take, for example, the utterance *Did you read this book yesterday?* According to Langacker, we find three subjective grounding devices in this utterance: the past tense in *did*, the deictic *this* and the word order and prosody, which identify the speech act (the deictic *you* is an example of objective grounding). What I want to emphasize is that these three elements involve the ground in very different ways. *This* and the past tense presuppose the ground in order to become fully interpretable, but they do not modify it: they don't change the spatio-temporal circumstances. In contrast, the illocutionary force marker creates something that was not there before, namely the speech act that establishes a specific interactive relation between the speaker and the hearer. In this sense, it does not presuppose the ground but really modifies it.

From the semiotic perspective, the difference between these types of grounding is in fact more fundamental than what they have in common. From this perspective, primary tense markers have more in common with common nouns than with performative signs.

I summarize the comparison between my analysis of performativity inspired by Peirce and Langacker's analysis:

1.   both proposals clearly avoid the bias of the CONDUIT METAPHOR in that they both integrate performativity into their analysis of meaning;

2.   the difference between Peircean Semiotics and CG is that the former provides a specific semiotic category in order to account for the performative signs, while CG does not provide a supplementary category for performativity, but extends the grounding principle;

3.   as a result, in the semiotic analysis, tense and illocutionary force belong to different semiotic dimensions (and so I would emphasize the differences between them), while Cognitive Grammar treats them in a very similar way, emphasizing the similarities between them.

One possible explanation for the difference between Langacker's analysis and the Peircean one might be the less interactive nature of Cognitive Grammar. Although Langacker does show a number of ways to integrate some aspects of interaction in the cognitive framework, we can still maintain that interaction is indeed not the main concern of Cognitive Grammar.

As we saw, Langacker argued against the CONDUIT METAPHOR by saying that the participants "are not at all to be regarded as detached observers who passively watch a film projected on a screen" (1997: 244). And, indeed, in his alternative, the participants are not detached observers, because, as the subjects of conceptualization, they are part of the viewing arrangement, which is part of the meaning of the utterance. And they are not passive, because the viewing arrangement is construed interactively, through the utterance. That is, the viewing arrangement is not fixed once and for all: the grammar of a language allows the speaker to construe the "same" scene from different vantage points.

However, this is a rather narrow view on interaction. First of all, it focuses almost exclusively on our activities of conceptualization. And secondly, it is based on a very indirect form of interaction. Interaction is presented as a form of coordination between the speaker and the hearer to ensure they take the same vantage point.[8] To put it figuratively: the participants do not seem to look each other in the eyes but instead keep their eyes fixed in the same direction. I think this is a too peaceful view of interaction.

The alternative, semiotic analysis emphasizes far more the dynamic, creative nature of the linguistic signs. Or, more exactly, it distinguishes between two creative functions of linguistic signs: (1) evoking a propositional content (and the whole range of imagery it consists of), which may presuppose or may be dependent upon the speech event, and (2) shaping this speech event through the indexical identification of its interactive coordinates.

So far, the hypothesis that this less interactive nature of the paradigm could explain why Langacker did not provide a separate category for performative signs, can be maintained. To test it further, however, I will confront the Peircean analysis with Systemic Functional Grammar (SFG), whose interest in interaction is obvious.

3.   Systemic Functional Grammar

A quick look at the basic assumptions of SFG makes clear that this paradigm is more interactively oriented than Cognitive Grammar and emphasizes explicitly the fact that language is not to be treated as a cognitive system, internal to the human mind, but as a semiotic system, and more specifically as a *social* semiotic system. Above all, by explicitly distinguishing three different metafunctions (ideational, interpersonal and textual) and by providing a specific place in its overall theory for all these three components, SFG clearly proves that interaction, or the coordination of the participants, is one of its main descriptive concerns.

In this sense, I expected that the analysis of performativity within SFG would be more similar to what I proposed than to the Cognitive analysis. However, this expectation proved to be partially incorrect. Although there are very important differences between SFG and CG, there are also fundamental similarities regarding the analysis of performativity.

The most striking difference between SFG and Cognitive Grammar is that SFG uses a far more active description of interaction. Instead of the 'viewing' terminology of Langacker (1997), we find paraphrases like "the verbal sparring between speaker and hearer" (Davidse 1997: 427) or "setting something up so that it can be caught, returned, smashed, lobbed back, etc." (Halliday 1994: 76). In the terminology used to describe the interpersonal component there is a clear emphasis on the fact that the speaker and the listener confront each other and really "look each other in the eyes", to repeat the image used before.

But there is also an important similarity between the two frameworks. More specifically, like Cognitive Grammar, SFG emphasizes the similarities between performativity (speech function) and e.g. tense or person deixis: we see the same tendency to group these phenomena under a common denominator, be it "grounding" in more cognitive terms or "mood" or "interpersonal grammar" in systemic terms.

I will first give a few bibliographical references in order to exemplify this tendency. Afterwards I shall try to find out what it is that motivates the grouping of these phenomena in both frameworks. The aim is to discover the nature of the difference between a Peircean semiotic analysis and CG/SFG. My initial hypothesis, which explained the difference in terms of the less interactive nature of CG, is clearly wrong, since SFG is an interactively oriented framework. Proceeding in this way, we may perhaps uncover some underlying semiotic principles of CG and SFG.

Halliday's chapter "Clause as exchange" (1994: 68–105) includes references to speech function, modality and tense. We quote Halliday's discussion of the Finite element:

> [The Finite element] brings the proposition down to earth, so that it is something that can be argued about. A good way to make something arguable is to give it a point of reference in the here and now; and this is

what the Finite does. It relates the proposition to its context in the speech event.
    This can be done in one of two ways. One is by reference to the time of speaking; the other is by reference to the judgement of the speaker. An example of the first is *was* in *an old man was crossing the road*; of the second, *can't* in *can't be true*. In grammatical terms, the first is PRIMARY TENSE [time relative to 'now'], the second is MODALITY. (1994: 75)

We can see that the main idea is very similar to the one we found in the analysis of Langacker (1997), namely that the utterance contains devices that establish a link between a decontextualized, abstract content and the speech event, and thus plug the utterance into the concrete context of interaction. The same analysis is found in Davidse (1998), who refers both to Tense/Modality/Person Deixis (ibid.: 160) and to Speech Function (ibid.: 163) as ground-relating functions. It is also found in McGregor (1997) who describes both tense and the scoping operator 'declarative' as grounding devices.

As I argued above (Section 2.2), we have to distinguish between two types of grounding or ways of relating the utterance to the interactive context. The first involves deictic elements or primary tense reference, the second illocutionary force indicators. The first elements are actualizing elements that specify the reference of the utterance by defining it relatively to a zero point. This zero point coincides by default with the moment of interaction between the speaker and the hearer. It can be argued that these elements form a preparatory condition for the interpersonal functioning of the clauses. Due to their presence, the proposition is "something that can be argued about – something that can be affirmed or denied, and also doubted, contradicted, insisted on, accepted with reservation, qualified, tempered, regretted, and so on" (Halliday 1994: 70; see also Davidse 1997: 427). On the other hand, the illocutionary force indicators are (in my view at least) not to be considered as preparatory conditions but as signs that shape the actual interaction. What they modify is perhaps not so much the clause as the actual interaction itself: they create a new social, interactive or "juridical" (Ducrot 1984) relationship between the two participants.

The comparison between the Peircean semiotic analysis and SFG leads to a quite similar conclusion as the comparison with CG:

1. none of these three paradigms neglects the interactive component of meaning;

2. only the analysis inspired by Peircean Semiotics establishes a specific subcategory in which the illocutionary force indicators can be classified; the other two paradigms tend to include illocutionary force indicators, primary tense markers and deictic signs in one overall category.

This means that the taking together of *tense* and *performativity* (in CG and SFG) cannot be explained by lack of interest in interaction. In what follows I will advance an alternative explanation. I shall argue that the difference can possibly be explained by what we consider to be the fundamental questions to be asked about meaning. I will finally maintain that Peircean semiotics suggests other questions about meaning than the paradigms SFG and CG, which are, as far as I can see, more inspired by Saussurean semiotics.

4.   Questions about meaning

In order to distinguish the different types of questions that can be asked about meaning, let us agree we treat the signified of a sign (its "meaning") as a mental representation of an encoded entity A. Although this is a simplification, it reflects the essential feature of a sign, which consists in orienting the mind of the interpreter towards something else than the signifier. This basic idea is represented in Figure 6:

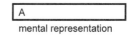

mental representation

Figure 6: Meaning = mental representation of an encoded entity A

A theory about meaning, or indeed any semiotically oriented linguistic framework, can ask different questions about this basic representation. I will basically differentiate between three questions: (1) about the nature of the mental representation, (2) about the represented entity and (3) about the explicitness of the encoding. My claim will be that Peircean Semiotics, more than the other frameworks, leads to focus on the first question.

In fact, what are we doing when we distinguish between indexical and symbolic signs? In my view, this question does not concern the represented entity, nor the type of encoding but instead the ontological nature of the mental representation. More precisely, the distinction between indexical and symbolic signs is based on the fact that we can apprehend the signified object in different ways: we can apprehend it as something of the second order (as something that really exists in the here and now) or as a concept, an idea.

This means that our mental representation of the object of an indexical sign is understood to be fundamentally similar to the experience of perceiving something, while the mental representation in the case of a symbolic sign (or of a cluster of symbolic signs) consists really in representing an idea.

When we perceive something, we build what may be called a non-autonomous mental representation, whereas when we represent an idea, we construe an autonomous mental representation. An idea is an autonomous mental representation because, in order to be an idea, it does not imply that my mental representation corresponds to something in the here and now. Ideas are true if there is something in reality that corresponds to them and that they are false when there isn't. What I want to emphasize is that, independently of their being true or false, they are in both cases ideas. This is not the case with perceptions.

Perceptions are non-autonomous mental representations because, in order to be a perception, they require that what I see is out there in the here and now: "When we see something, we see it as something out there, not just as some painting hanging on the wall of our inner mental gallery." (Harder 1999: 12).

When I think I perceive an oasis with palm trees and cool water and somebody points out that there is no oasis and no palm trees either, I then realize I didn't perceive anything. I did not perceive something false: instead, it was false that I did perceive something. This means that the actual existence of the signified is constitutive of the type of mental experience.

The distinction between indexical and symbolic signs in Peircean Semiotics allows us to understand the peculiarity of the illocutionary force markers in terms of the type of mental experience we have when we interpret them. With indexical signs, the signified is apprehended in a non-autonomous mental representation, or a perception; with symbolic signs it is apprehended in an autonomous mental representation. In Figure 7 the full versus dotted line represents the different nature of the mental representation:

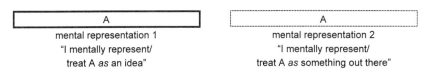

Figure 7: Question 1: what is the nature of the mental representation?

This question is suggested clearly in Peircean semiotics, whereas in Saussurean semiotics it is not, or not to the same extent. From a Saussurean perspective, the signified is said to be conceptual in order to distinguish it radically from its reference, without distinguishing further between types of 'conceptuality'.

A Saussurean approach will focus on the other two questions, i.e.: what is it that is encoded? and how explicitly is it encoded? Figure 8 represents the question *what* is encoded. Figure 9 represents the question *how explicitly* it is encoded.

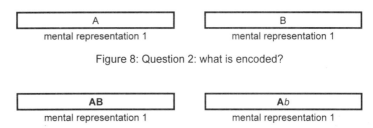

Figure 8: Question 2: what is encoded?

Figure 9: Question 3: how explicitly is it encoded?

As far as I can see, CG and SFG give an important place to the question represented in Figure 8, namely what is encoded, what the signified is about. The reason for taking together illocutionary force indicators, deictic elements and primary tense references seems to be that all those signs encode in one way or another the speech event, one of its participants or the spatio-temporal setting. Their signified concerns the speaker and the hearer: they are all speaker-encoding devices, they all have "to do with the speaker's intrusion in language" (Taverniers 1998). Possibly, it is because of this focus on what the signs encode, that SFG and CG do not make the same distinctions as Peircean Semiotics does.

When SFG and especially CG complement this question about the what of the encoding with a question concerning the how of the encoding, this is primarily understood in terms of explicitness vs. implicitness (see Figure 9). It is in this sense that we understand the distinction made between the objective and the subjective construal of the ground. This distinction is the result of asking consecutively (1) what is encoded and (2) how explicitly this aspect of the meaning of the utterance is encoded. The answer to the first question is that the meaning of an utterance is not to be understood independently from the conceptualizer, and that the conceptualizer is part of its meaning. The answer to the second question, then, is that the conceptualizer can be put onstage, as part of the explicitly encoded content, or can be left offstage, and function as an implicit reference point.

But these two questions will not lead to distinguish between what for example tense does and what the illocutionary force markers do. Both devices encode the ground. And both allow an objective and a subjective grounding. In my view, only a framework that distinguishes between types of signs on the basis of the nature of the mental representation they give rise to will consistently oppose both types of devices.

5. Conclusion

We started this review of Peircean Semiotics, Cognitive Grammar and Systemic Functional Grammar in order to examine whether these paradigms offer metalinguistic tools to avoid the bias of the CONDUIT METAPHOR that dominates our common way of talking about speech. This bias consists in the tendency to focus exclusively on meaning as involved in the message component and to neglect the performative or interactive component. In our opinion, none of these three paradigms could be accused of a lack of interest in this interactive grounding of linguistic meaning, although the terminology used in Cognitive Grammar reflects a rather passive or at least peaceful way of understanding interaction. More interesting is the finding that Peircean Semiotics, and more particularly the distinction between symbolic and indexical signs, leads to opposing tense and illocutionary force markers. In contrast, both SFG and CG treat these in quite similar terms, namely as phenomena involved in the mood component or in the grounding of the utterance. I argued that there are in fact two types of grounding, namely ground-dependency and ground-modification. I reserved the term "indexical sign" to refer to the signs involved in the second type of grounding (for example illocutionary force indicators). The difference between the analysis in terms of symbolic and indexical signs on the one hand and the cognitive or systemic analysis on the other, can ultimately be explained by the types of questions that are asked about meaning. While Peircean Semiotics suggests opposing types of meaning on the basis of the type of mental experience the sign gives rise to, SFG and CG seem to focus on the questions about what is encoded and how explicitly it is encoded.

Notes

1. I wish to thank Nicole Delbecque, Kristin Davidse, Jean-Christophe Verstraete and Liesbet Heyvaert for their helpful suggestions while I was preparing this paper. I am especially grateful to Jean-Christophe Verstraete for the stylistic revision. Of course, all shortcomings are entirely my own.

2. Since the purpose of this paper is to examine the underlying (and quite abstract) principles, I will not discuss in detail which linguistic signs have to be included in the list of speech-act identifying signs. In Goethals (2000) I maintained that also explanatory causal conjunctions have to be included in this class.

3. For more details on the semiotics of Peirce, see, amongst others, Pharies (1985), Deledalle (1987), Petrilli (1999) and Goethals (2000).

4. I must admit that this aspect of the semiotic taxonomy of Peirce is highly complex and possibly controversial. The reason is that Peirce elaborated two slightly different ways of understanding the taxonomy of the object pole of the sign. The first proposal is based on the

ontological nature of the object (first, second or third), while the second focuses on the nature of the relation between the representamen and the object. From this second perspective, Peirce will distinguish between signs that signify through resemblance, contiguity or convention. For reasons I exposed in detail in Goethals (2000: 68–75) I opt consistently for the first way of understanding the taxonomy. See also Burks (1949) and Petrilli (1999) for more details on the underlying contradictions in Peirce's semiotic writings.

5. The reverse is not true: to have an object of the n-th order, the representamen has to be at least also of the n-th order. This means that all symbolic signs are *legisigns*, that indexical signs are *legisigns* or *sinsigns* and that iconic signs are *qualisigns*, *sinsigns* or *legisigns*.

6. Only common nouns, out of context, like *bed*, *water*, *tree* etc. can be said to evoke a meaning without any type of grounding: from the moment that a marker of (in)definiteness is applied to a noun, or a tense/mood marker to a verbal form, the expressions is grounded.

7. On this point I depart from the main analysis of Peirce who considers for example deictic pronouns as (sub-)indexical signs. In my view, they are better classified as (a special kind of) symbolic signs.

8. In this respect, it is worth noting that Langacker (1985) refers to the cooperative nature of communicative activity in order to justify the theoretical position that "the speaker and the addressee regard themselves as a collective SELF capable of arriving at a shared conceptualization as the semantic value of a linguistic expression" (1985: 123–124).

References

Austin, J.L. (1962) *How to do Things with Words*. Oxford : Oxford UP.

Davidse, K. (1997) The subject-object versus the agent-patient asymmetry". *Leuvense Bijdragen* 86: 413–431.

Davidse, K. (1998) The dative as participant role versus the indirect object: On the need to distinguish two layers of organization. In: W. Van Langendonck & W. Van Belle (eds.) *The Dative. Volume 2: Theoretical and Contrastive Studies*. Amsterdam: Benjamins. 143–184.

Deledalle, G. (1979) *Théorie et pratique du signe*. Paris: Payot.

Deledalle, G. (1987) *Charles S. Peirce, phénoménologue et sémioticien*. Amsterdam: Benjamins.

Ducrot, O. (1984) *Le dire et le dit*. Paris: Minuit.

Fitzgerald, J.J. (1966) *Peirce's Theory of Signs as Foundation for Pragmatism*. The Hague: Mouton.

Goethals, P. (2000) *Las conjunciones causales explicativas en español. Un estudio semiótico-lingüístico*. Unpublished PhD-Thesis. Katholieke Universiteit Leuven.

Halliday, M.A.K. (1994) *An Introduction to Functional Grammar*. 2nd edition London: Arnold.

Harder, P. (1995) *Functional Semantics. A Theory of Meaning, Structure and Tense in English*. Berlin: Mouton de Gruyter.

Harder, P. (1999) *Course Notes LOT Winterschool*. Amsterdam, January 1999.

Langacker, R. (1985) Observations and speculations on subjectivity. In: Haiman (ed.) *Iconicity in Syntax*. Amsterdam: Benjamins. 109–150.

Langacker, R. (1987) *Foundations of Cognitive Grammar. Vol. I: Theoretical Prerequisites.* Stanford: Stanford UP.

Langacker, R. (1991) *Foundations of Cognitive Grammar. Vol. II: Descriptive Application.* Stanford: Stanford UP.

Langacker, R. (1997) The contextual basis of cognitive semantics. In: Nuyts & Pedersen (eds.) *Language and Conceptualization.* Cambridge: Cambridge UP. 229–252.

McGregor, William B. (1997) *Semiotic Grammar.* Oxford: Clarendon.

Peirce, Charles S. (1931-58) *Collected Papers of Charles Sanders Peirce.* Edited by Charles Hartshorne, Paul Weiss & Arthur W. Burks. Cambridge: Harvard UP.

Petrilli, S. (1999) About and beyond Peirce. *Semiotica* 124.3/4: 299–376.

Pharies, D.A. (1985) *Charles S. Peirce and the Linguistic Sign.* Amsterdam: Benjamins.

Reddy, M.J. (1979) The conduit metaphor: A case of frame conflict in our language about language. In: A. Ortony (ed.) *Metaphor and Thought.* Cambridge: Cambridge UP. 284–324.

Taverniers, M. (1998) Towards a topology of interpersonal meanings. Paper presented on the 10th Euro-International Systemic Functional Workshop. University of Liverpool, 22-25 July 1998.

Thibault, P.J. (1997) *Re-reading Saussure: The dynamics of signs in social life.* London: Routledge.

Verstraete, J-Ch. (1998) A semiotic model for the description of levels in conjunction: external, internal-modal and internal-speech functional. *Functions of Language* 5.2: 179–211.

Grammatical metaphor as a cognitive construct

Randal Holme
University of Durham

1. Introduction

A key feature in the cognitive interpretation of metaphor (e.g. Lakoff & Johnson 1980, 1999) is that metaphors as a linguistic (or even a visual) phenomenon can be grouped according to the conceptual metaphors that they realise. Language exposes or expresses a deeper process of neural mapping between different experiential domains. Some such mappings are common to growing infants because they are a product of universal experience while others may be peculiar to certain cultures (Grady 1997, Lakoff & Johnson 1999). For example, 'up' and 'balance' would map as a sense of achievement built out of the experience of walking upright and an awareness of all the advantages of the upright position. Therefore 'up' will broadly express positive emotions (Lakoff & Johnson 1980) and 'balance' may constitute the desired state through which uprightness is achieved. Arguably, therefore, a notion of equality may be conceptualised out of the achievement of 'balance' by the body in the physical world (Johnson 1987). By the same token, we engage in logical argument through the schemata that are structured out of our physical experience. Logic is often expressed in the language of spatial relations (Lakoff & Johnson 1999) as in 'one thing *leads to* another'. Logic is therefore conceptualised through metaphor.

Abstract thought is thus conceptualised through schemata that derive from basic physical experiences (e.g. Lakoff 1993). Sensations such as 'balance' 'up/down' or 'blockage' (Johnson 1987) derive from our embodied experience of the world. These schemata group different concepts within metaphors derived from the same experience. Thus two different (though not unrelated) abstract notions such as 'increase' and 'happiness' will be expressed by forming metaphors out of the same schema. Accordingly, we can say that we often conceptualise happiness or increase through the up/down dimension. This use of an image schema to express a particular idea gives us the term conceptual metaphor. In this manner we say that expressions such as 'the market is going up' or 'prices are rising' will derive from a conceptualisation expressing increase through the 'up/down' dimension. This means that such expressions both evolve from the conceptual metaphor 'up is more/down is less' (Lakoff & Johnson 1980). A conceptual metaphor thus groups metaphors according to its schema. Equally, the schema of a physical 'blockage' (Johnson 1987) can be found in the language used to discuss difficulties as in 'overcome the obstacle,' 'get round the problem,' 'get over a difficulty', yielding the conceptual metaphor, 'impediments are physical obstacles'.

The systemic functional linguistic (SFL) view of metaphor involves the identification and description of metaphor according to how it characterises the departure of text from what is deemed to be a congruent use of language. A congruent use of language retains the 'natural' relationship (Halliday 1985) between the lexico-grammar as it is formed to represent specific categories of meaning. Basic to this hypothesis is the contention that a language is structured around the expression of such categories. Thus, most straightforwardly, verbs and nouns are distinct because actions and things are distinct. A problem for this account emerges when nouns not verbs represent processes, as in a nominalisation such as has occurred in 1:

(1)   Walking made me tired

This particular anomaly is accounted for with an idea of metaphor based not as traditionally upon the disjunction of lexical meanings but upon one between a grammatical category and its normal function.

Superficially there is little common ground between the cognitive and SFL approaches since they emerge from the very different goals of each line of enquiry. The social nature of SFL language description means that the representation of experience must then be seen as occurring with different degrees of social construction as these social effects are formulated through register and genre. The SFL interest in metaphor is therefore largely in a lexico-grammatical phenomenon that serves a social function which differs from the one it was originally evolved to fulfil. There is thus a parallel interest, not simply in the structure itself, but in how it fulfils the needs of a given context as this operates through genre and register (e.g. Halliday & Martin 1993, Martin 1997).

By contrast, the cognitive interest is in discovering how the mind conceptualises meaning. The objective is not to describe language but to analyse it in order to find the conceptualisations from which it has emerged. There is an interest both in how language is a product of the schemata that are universal to cognition and in how these schemata may be fashioned by the peculiarities of a given culture or society.

The difference between the SFL and cognitive approaches is therefore fundamental. Yet, we should not forget that each approach is towards the same phenomenon, language and language can exist simultaneously both as a social and a cognitive construct. If physics can attribute a dual nature to light then perhaps linguists can do this to language. My first question, therefore, is to ask whether we cannot see the systemic and cognitive accounts of metaphor as complementary in some sense.

My second question is more specific. Both the cognitive and the SFL views account for how meaning arises from factors external to language. In the cognitive account, language attests to the schematic structure of cognition. Additionally, such structures are held to be imposed upon the world by the nature of mind rather than derived from it. For example, the colour of an object will be perceived as fairly constant despite variations in the quality of light because that colour is in part a function of mind (Thompson 1995). In the SFL account, the search is less for structures of mind and more for those that arise from the interpenetration of language and social context. One could therefore ask if the cognitive account provides a missing piece of the SFL puzzle, namely how the more general properties of cognition can affect the emergence of socially constructed meaning. This question could arise from the nature of a grammatical metaphor.

My argument, therefore, will first allow that a grammatical metaphor is an anomaly in the lexico-grammar. As is traditional, I will treat the anomaly as identifiable according to the SFL precept that a given grammatical category should express a given category of meaning. My second question will ask if we can see such an anomaly as a product of the type of schemata that the cognitive analysis has found in other types of metaphor.

A third point arises from a weakness in the cognitive perspective. There has already been some work on the use of conceptual metaphor in text construction (Albritton 1992) or, more particularly, as its arises from a dual interest in thematic linkages in such ideas as frames (e.g. Tannen 1993). However, there is less sense of how a given conceptual metaphor will come to take a given textual form.

Some types of conceptual metaphor are postulated as sitting nearer to the surface of their textual realisation than others. Lakoff and Johnson (1999: 201–202) identify a hierarchy of conceptual metaphors as producing a particular textual realisation. For example, entailment hierarchies exploit the relational structure of each domain of a metaphor. Thus, if 'actions are self-propelled motions', we can infer that 'aids to action are aids to movement' because an effect upon the source domain, 'motions', will affect the target, 'actions'. A hierarchy implies different levels of reduction in how we analyse a metaphor. Thus 'aids to actions are aids to movement' will operate as the conceptualisation of fewer textual realisations than the more general 'actions are self-propelled motions' which encompasses much of our notion of action. A hierarchy also implies that some conceptual metaphors operate at a different level of generality from others. One can, for example, suggest a final point of reduction and generalisation in seeing reification as being at the core of all abstract language (e.g. Langacker 1990 and 1991).

The metaphor of a hierarchy should perhaps be inverted so that we can talk less of the descent of metaphor towards text and more of its emergence onto a textual surface. A question that then arises concerns the precise role of context as a feature that configures this emergence. Context could be envisaged as restricting lexico-grammatical choice as one comes nearer to the textual surface. For example, let us consider sentences (2–5) below:

(2)   She needed more time. But time would not wait.

(3)   Time had crept up on her and made off with everything she valued in herself.

(4)   The time was getting closer.

(5)   The future stretched ahead of him.

The most general schematic prerequisite for the expression of time in examples (2), (3), (4) and (5) would be that time is perceived as having physical existence. Our conceptual metaphor is therefore reification. Second, in (2), (3) and (4), time is perceived as something that is itself in motion. Our conceptual metaphor is no longer 'time is a thing' but 'time is a moving thing'. Yet this does not fully account for (5) where time is the course down which others move (e.g. Lakoff & Johnson 1980, 1999; Alverson 1995). Therefore, 'time is a moving phenomenon' accounts for fewer examples than a simple metaphor of reification. Now, what is in motion can be animate or inanimate, self-propelled or moved by some force extraneous to it. In (2) and (3), above, because 'time' creeps or waits, we conceptualise it as human or animate in its movement. Therefore, we have 'time is a human'.

As with anything, the more general the conceptualisation the greater the number of instances it can account for. My interest is not in this observation however. The more difficult question is why we will build a text out of one conceptual choice and not another. In order to formulate such a question, we will probably need a method for analysing how context can effect a given set of conceptual and, finally, textual entailments.

Yet the introduction of degrees or levels of specificity in textual choice and context must also raise the issue of what is occurring at these levels. In other words, we are engaging in a shift away from an attempt to represent the processes of cognition towards a focus on the machinations of context and the language with which cognition is inter-related. The description of context closing down textual choice suggests that context requires analysis, perhaps not as itself but as the mediational 'projection' of the 'metafunctions' (Martin 1997) in which its effect is formulated in language. In sum, it might now be appropriate to invoke an SFL framework, utilising genre and register, to plot the emergence of conceptual metaphor as text metaphor.

Therefore, I can summarise the questions I will pose in this paper as follows:

1. Is there any sense in which we can see cognitive and SFL approaches to metaphor as complementary rather than merely conflicting? More specifically, will a contrast of these approaches do anything to illuminate the nature of what is being examined, metaphor in language itself?

2. Is an image-schematic account of grammatical metaphor possible and what would it tell us about the nature of this type of metaphor?

3. Can we use the SFL concepts of genre and register to show how context may affect the preference of one conceptual metaphor over another?

In this paper I will take the above questions in order. I will first contrast the SFL and the cognitive approaches to metaphor and show areas in which they may be complementary. I will suggest that the two modes of analysis can be perceived as complementary if we treat SFL's notion of grammatical metaphor as a form of language, which like all abstract specifications of meaning relations may work by exploiting image schemas grounded in our embodied existence. Controversially, I will suggest that in order to make this argument, we must finally treat the SFL notion of a congruent wording as a metalinguistic device to detect and render metaphorical meaning and not as a direct and natural use of language, since metaphor is itself direct and natural.

My approach to the second question will be a consequence of the arguments advanced about congruent language. I will take the example of grammatical metaphors that express cause-and-effect. I will argue that cause-and-effect structures do not depart from congruency in the sense of breaching a natural relationship between language and meaning. Rather, they are created from conceptual metaphors of reification, rooted in our sense of ourselves as embodied creatures that deal with a world of objects and their physical impact upon us.

Having shown how some forms of grammatical metaphor can be given an image-schematic origin, I will look at a textual example in order to see how we might plot it as having taken its particular form as a consequence of the effect of genre and register.

2.   The systemic and cognitive approaches contrasted

2.1.   The systemic account

First, we should remind ourselves about the nature of the SFL interest in metaphor. This interest is largely in the identification and description of metaphor as ideational or interpersonal in text. Metaphors arise when the language is not congruent. A congruent reading encodes events in a way that is 'straightforward' (Halliday 1985). 'Straightforward' in this sense might almost mean 'natural' in that there seems, for example, to be a natural boundary between 'actions' and 'things'. 'Actions' can only be represented as an effect upon an object. 'Objects' are indubitably there. 'Actions' and 'objects' therefore have a different status that is encoded in language as verbs and nouns. Therefore, a grammatically congruent use of language implies that verbs represent actions and nouns represent objects. However, there are occasions when context as formulated within register or genre may require something different.

I will take as an example, a genre that is used to construct an 'appraisal' of reported business events in order to show their likely future course. Such genres are not dissimilar to those of 'periodic appraisal' in history (Coffin 1997 and Martin 1997) in that they construct and appraise their narrative. However, they are likely to be more clearly motivated by the function of prediction than simple interpretation.

An appraisal will sequence events in order to support a given conclusion. Argument will move text away from a representative function in respect of the world in order to favour its own purpose. For example, events may be selected and organised not according to their chronology but according to need for an argument to sustain a conclusion. In this sense, a genre that makes an appraisal or argues a case attempts to control the nature of its representations of the world even as it makes them. Thus an appraisal or argument genre may pressure its lexico-grammar towards a greater distance from the physical events in which its construction is phylogenetically and ontogenetically grounded.

I illustrate this point with (6), below:

(6)   Forcing it to provide a wholesale version of its broadband product might accelerate meaningful competition (Sunday Times Business News, September 3, 2000).

A process, 'to force' does not achieve a congruent representation as a verb but is expressed by a noun. Since nouns typically represent things, the process receives the grammatical treatment of a thing. Things can precipitate events, as can be illustrated in Langacker's (1994) example of the effect of one billiard ball upon another. Actions are only manifest as an effect upon an object. In the world, therefore, actions do not precipitate events except through the medium of things. This is a difficult point to grasp for those well-inducted into cause-and-effect arguments, which invariably represent actions as able to impact directly on events. The meaning here, of one process causing the acceleration of another, is therefore achieved by separating the 'process' from its typical expression as a verb. Further, in order to precipitate the events described in (6) we would require human agency, yet the extract only represents actions, as if these can impel each other, without physical phenomena to mark their existence. The actions are locked into a relationship of cause-and-effect and the distracting phenomena through which they manifest themselves are allowed to fall away. The actions are thus foregrounded by the metaphor as a sequence that reduces the larger, confusing world of people and objects to an argument that can be understood.

A genre that appraises events may thus use grammatical metaphor to ensure its isolation from the less principled organisation of the events in the world that it has chosen to recount. However, because metaphor posits a use of language that is not congruent, it does not entirely disguise the mechanisms with which it achieves this. Metaphors make themselves known to us as windows in the text. They are windows that afford a view upon the mechanisms of text construction. The view afforded is upon an interaction between the lexico-grammar, as determined by plausible physical events, and the genre/register that will configure this interaction as text. Metaphor can thus be said to open text with its tension between what Martin (1997: 237) identifies as the literal reading that is the prerequisite for our understanding of the metaphorical meaning, and the metaphor to which the contextual displacement of that reading will give rise.

This can be further exemplified with a grammatical metaphor, summarised as 'adjunct to complement metaphor' (Downing & Locke 1992):

(7)   'Dawn found me at the end of my shift'

'Dawn' in this sentence constitutes the circumstances of an occurrence, 'the end' of a 'shift'. In a congruent construction, 'dawn' would be an adjunct as in 'his shift ended at dawn'. The verb 'found' would normally require a 'Senser' to occupy the subject position. Prototypically, the Senser should be animate. Yet 'dawn', the circumstances that background 'the end' to a 'shift', is not, typically, a Senser. A time or event, 'dawn', assumes a function, of which, in the world, it would be incapable.

A narrative genre is likely to foreground its own act of narration, simply because narration is its purpose. Such a genre is likely to treat narration or the unfolding of events, as more important than who is narrating them. The events will therefore be foregrounded and the author may be hidden behind them. A congruent Senser would be the author, a person who sees and feels. Here, circumstances are the Senser, even though they are normally expressed by an adjunct. This departure from congruency is required by a generic purpose, that of hiding the narrator behind the narration. Narratives are temporal sequences. Grammatical metaphor allows a narrative genre to foreground itself by making time into the hero of its particular construction. This is essentially a reader management choice (Thompson & Thetela 1995) which gives the metaphor an interpersonal function. The author chooses not to be an individual whose address can be believed or disbelieved. Instead, the author foregrounds a narrative as if it has itself received the impression of events, signalling to the reader that the recounted events are 'true' because they are unmediated by authorial perception.

In the above discussion, I have elaborated the points made in the introduction about the kind of construction that grammatical metaphor is. I have further situated grammatical metaphor inside the larger SFL concern with the social construction of language through genre and register. I will next briefly extend my opening summary of the cognitive position on metaphor in order to show how this contrasts with the one just summarised.

2.2.   The cognitive approach to metaphor

The cognitive focus on metaphor is upon the linguistic manifestation of a process that is key to the conceptualisation of abstract meaning as it emerges in lexis and grammar. In the cognitive view, metaphors are thus revealing of a process that is sub-linguistic. A key point in this analysis is that much abstract thought is conceptualised through our experience of our bodies as they are engaged in a physical interaction with the world.

This case is partly sustained by studying abstract language for how it carries within it the traces of its genesis from a set of concrete meanings. Most importantly, our idea of abstract language should also include grammar as in the expression of location through prepositions and case, or in the specification of time through tense. For example, prepositions can be traced back to earlier conceptualisations rooted in non-abstract phenomena (e.g. Heine 1997). A clear example of this can be found in the English association between body parts and expressions of direction, for example, ahead, behind, back, forwards (forehead) etc.

Thus, the cognitive approach employs a diachronic analysis in order to tease out the image-schemas that steer grammaticalisation in language. 'Propositional schemas', which represent processes and events (Heine 1993), are found by examining the stages through which some lexical meanings have become grammatical over-time. For example, the schema of possession (Heine 1993: 47) motivated the grammaticalisation of 'have' in the creation of the present perfect, perhaps through the notion of an accomplished action as being in some sense possessed by the agent accomplishing it.

2.3. Difficulties with the SFL view of metaphor from a cognitive perspective

From a cognitive perspective there are two difficulties with the systemic position as it has been outlined. First among these is the location of the metaphor itself or its scope. Second is the status of congruent language as a 'natural' or 'direct' mode of expression and the consequent association of metaphor with generically constructed meaning and the idea of artifice that this involves. I will now examine each of these problems in turn.

2.3.1. The problem of scope: Where a metaphorical meaning begins and ends

I will deal first with what Goatly (1998) calls the scope of the metaphor. 'Scope' refers to the items in a given clause or sentence that are affected by a switch from a literal to a metaphorical meaning. In example 1, above (*walking made me tired*), a normal subject function has been displaced. But there is no certainty that the metaphor is actually located in the displaced function of the subject, or for that matter, in the lexico-grammar at all. I could argue that, in example (7), the verb, 'find', has simply been lexically extended in order to allow the transitive expression of what in the world is the coincidence of two events. Thus, we would not suppose that 'the dawn' has gone off to look for the end to an event. We might rather think that 'find' in example (7) above, might be an economical way to refer to 'broke and cast its light on' to give (8) below as the congruent reading:

(8)   Dawn broke and cast its light on them at the end of their shift

Of course moving the location of the metaphor does not normalise the structural peculiarity in which the grammatical metaphor resides. One may be saying that the grammatical metaphor is required because the meaning of 'find' is not congruent. Thus a metaphorical extension of the term 'find' requires that the adjunct function as a Senser in this case. However, we would then have to say that the grammatical incongruency is a product of the lexical metaphor and not the metaphor of the grammar. A grammatical metaphor identifies a disjunction between language in a text and direct or natural language (Halliday 1985). To state that this disjunction occurs at the behest of incongruent lexis is to suggest that the notion of grammatical metaphor is reduced to the symptom of a lexical departure from congruency.

2.3.2. The problematic nature of a congruent meaning
Most forms of linguistic analysis assume that language has a stable core of sign-meaning relationships, but establishing where these relationships start to destabilise and become figurative has proved difficult. This problem of how to define literality has bedevilled the formal syntactic analysis of metaphor (e.g Davidson 1978), Searle 1978, 1993; Sadock 1993). Deciding what is and what is not a congruent wording may prove equally problematic.

Congruency supposes a language that represents the world according to categories that are fundamental to our perception. For example, it is fundamental that we categorise 'things' as distinct from 'actions' and represent this distinction in the different linguistic categories, nouns and verbs. However, as soon as we move beyond such basic distinctions the idea of a congruent meaning becomes more problematic.

I will now consider this problem of a congruent wording. I will first show why it is difficult to know whether something is literal or metaphorical and how it is even possible for language to be both at the same time. I will argue that these difficulties prevail even when there are formal tests for grammatical metaphor. I will show how the problem is exacerbated by two insights from the domain of cognitive linguistics. The first insight is that language's continuous state of evolution is partly driven by our metaphor-forming capability. Metaphors create new meanings that become socially accepted or standard. The issue of what is literal or not is a matter of social agreement at any one time as to the acceptability of an extended meaning (Elgin 1983). This quite common insight should affect our view of congruency.

2.3.3. Congruent language and the problem of literality

The difficulty of defining congruent language is illustrated by example (9), below, where a wording is both congruent and metaphorical at the same time. The literary genre to which (9) belongs has the ability to make a statement metaphorical without denying its literal truth.

(9)   The frog jumped
       into the pond

As David Cooper (1986) indicates, the metaphorical nature of this statement resides only in the fact that it is a poem of a particular kind. The Japanese poet, Basho, probably witnessed the event he recounts and the language is congruent to it, therefore. However, the interest of this statement lies in our sense that it has a meaning to which the language is not congruent. In other words, we sense that 'pond' does not only mean 'pond, a small stretch of water', but is used to evoke something else, the concealed depth of the unconscious mind, perhaps. The wording is arguably congruent to its meaning and not congruent at the same time. If it is not congruent, it is because we are reading in a poetic genre. Yet, there is nothing in the genre's lexico-grammatical realisation which makes the lack of congruency plain.

Although example (9) may show the problem of trying to distinguish metaphorical and congruent language according to formal linguistic criteria, we should remember that the SFL concept of grammatical metaphor does provide an analytical framework that can identify a figurative form. For example, the interpersonal metaphor, 'I think it's going to rain', can be discovered through a 'tag test,' where the tag, 'isn't it', highlights 'rain' as salient, thus showing 'think' to be a metaphor of modality (Halliday 1985).

However, even this quite limited attempt to formalise the criteria for what is metaphorical is not unproblematic. Though the 'tag test' may elucidate the referent of 'think' as Modal rather than Process, it says less about why such a reference should be construed as metaphorical in late twentieth century English. One could argue that we should accept that 'think' now has the function of Modality and that this meaning has become congruent. Such a difficulty becomes prominent when we consider the wider role of metaphor in language change.

2.3.4. How congruency is a function of the acceptability of a given form at one time

Ullman (1962) expressed the role played by metaphor in language change with the now well-known example of 'muscle'. 'Musculus', the Latin word for little mouse came to mean muscle because of its shape and movement under the skin. The role of metaphor in grammaticalisation has also been a subject of study (e.g. Hopper & Traugott 1993) and figures prominently in the cognitive analysis of grammar (e.g. Heine 1997). The basic argument is that some meanings are constantly being extended towards abstract markers of meaning relations then incorporated as grammatical inflections. In the Hallidayan example, 'think' may be undergoing this type of process and we have no real way of knowing how far it is advanced.

When charting grammaticalisation, Thompson and Mulac (1991: 315) show how the suppression of a subordinator such as 'that' in example (10) below, would mean that 'think' no longer functions as a main verb. 'Think' is therefore moved towards the expression of modality that one finds in (11). The next stage in the process can already be seen in English where modality is expressed through the tag form that is found in (12). The tag is in fact adverbial and this evolution of what was once a main verb towards an adverb marks a step towards grammaticalisation. For all we know, this step may be a preliminary to what has occurred in other languages where the tag 'I think' starts to become a suffix of what is now the main verb, 'rain', thus developing a declension of the verb to express modality, as in a subjunctive.

(10) I think that it's going to rain

(11) I think it's going to rain

(12) It's going to rain I think

The point, finally, is that the association between a given configuration of the lexico-grammar and a given function at one time is always in process of change and development and the associations that are thought to be metaphorical may actually have started to stabilise and become congruent. Such an analysis leads to the view that it is not very profitable to ask what is metaphorical or literal language since this will depend upon the historical vantage point that one chooses to adopt. We should therefore shift metaphor outside language and state that it does not lie in the grammatical disjunction that it may temporarily create. 'Thought' is a metaphor of modality because 'thinking' presupposes a shift from the objective circumstances of the world into the subjectivity of mind. 'Thought events' are therefore 'uncertain events'. 'Think' in Halliday's example, is perhaps in process of becoming a modal and even of replicating the historical development of other modals before it. The difficulty is that we do not know the point at which 'think' has become congruent to the expression of doubt as well as to that of an intellectual process.

Two points can be made here in favour of the SFL position, however. The first concerns how Thompson (1996), for example, acknowledges the haziness of the metaphorical-congruent distinction by expressing it as a continuum. The second point is perhaps more significant and concerns how the SFL interest in congruent language may be placed more in an ontogenetic than a phylogenetic frame of analysis. I will now take each point in turn.

Thompson (1996) sees a metaphorical and a congruent wording as representing the opposite poles of a continuum upon which are spread the murkier and less distinguishable instantiations of social meaning in language. Thus different constructions will be congruent to different degrees. This would account for how a historical process is at work within language and is constantly shifting it off its agreed set of congruent representations. Whether the metaphorical has become congruent again will remain a matter for conjecture and relates to quite how far along the congruent-metaphorical continuum one places a given wording. The problem now is that we are basically back where we started, which is without any definitive sense of when an expression is congruent or not.

2.3.5. Is child language prototypically congruent?
A further difficulty concerns the analysis of congruency within an ontogenetic frame. Congruency is not simply a historical concept characterising some mythical pre-language which could do little more than name objects and represent their impact upon each other. The referential frame of congruency is also to the ontogenesis of language within the individual. Metaphor, therefore, indicates a development away from the mere representation of the physical world as it impacts upon the existence of the infant. The question now is no longer whether a metaphor is actually congruent according to normal, modern usage. The issue is one of whether metaphor can correctly be associated with an adult or mature form of language use (Halliday 1985; Halliday & Martin 1993).

This interest in ontogenesis puts forward the problem of how and when children use metaphor if it is a form of language that is generally associated with greater maturity. The association of metaphor with mature language use would have found support from Asch and Nerlove (1960) and Cometa and Eson (1978) who held that children passed through a 'literal stage' (Gibbs 1994). Winner

(1988), though motivated by her interest in exploring child metaphor, also argued that very young children do not produce original metaphor in the sense of trying to represent meanings for which the lexicon has no equivalent. But this non-use of metaphor may be simply because the child's world does not contain meanings for which there is no standard lexical representation. Both adults and children do the same thing when confronted by meanings for which they do not have lexis. They metaphorically extend one of the categories that they already know. Thus, if a child uses metaphor to make a term represent something it does not normally represent, they cannot be considered non-users of metaphor simply because they are reinventing the linguistic wheel and working to fill gaps in their lexis when they do not need to. If metaphor is to be implicated at all in category extension or catachresis then it must emerge less as a linguistic fact and more as the cognitive process that underlies the child's attempt to represent meanings that are new to it.

Consider examples (13) and (14) below, from a child of four:

(13)   It's a sun moon

(14)   Stop strangling me (to an adult holding them tight by the wrist)
        (the author's data, 1995)

The child perceives the fullness of the moon and conceptualises it through the sun because he/she does not possess adjectives of shape or brightness to do otherwise. The sun is an object that exists in the cognitive 'Frame' of the moon. Arguably the relationship is contiguous. The frame might pertain to light-emitting objects in the sky. The moon's frame provides a source domain, the sun. The sun's circular shape and brightness are made salient by their being mapped onto the target domain of the 'moon' because the moon is now bright and circular.

Sentence (14) is a direct and spontaneous use of language and it clearly reveals how metaphor as a cognitive process can respond to its user's semiotic need. It pits a language's response to an individual's cognitive need against its wider social semiosis. Even as a child grounds language in physical phenomena, they are playing fast and loose with the categories that they thus create. The extension, through metaphor, of one category towards another, supposes a degree of abstraction. The transfer of the action of clenching a hand around the neck to the similar action of the hand around the wrist can only occur after the extraction of the idea of holding tight from the specific physical meaning in which it is first grounded. Actions or things cannot become other actions or things, unless they assert their status as mental constructs and separate themselves from the physical identity in which they were first grounded. From the outset, metaphor as a cognitive process disturbs the status of language as anchored to one set of physical or 'felt' events by extending it to others.

When discussing grammatical metaphor, therefore, we should be aware that it is doubtful if a congruent use of language can be associated with a picture of childhood language as anchored in a straightforward representation of objects and events. Metaphor is not characteristic of mature language use but is part of the process whereby the child extends language that has been given meaning by one context towards another for which he/she does not possess an agreed means of expression. The process of abstraction that underlies grammatical metaphor also exists in the linguistic creativity of children. It would therefore be foolhardy to relate congruent language too strongly to the perceived existence of a child in a world of things, actions and the here and now.

The above conclusion about congruency and child language does not deny that grammatical metaphor may be difficult for less mature language users, or for those not fully inducted into the genres that will employ it. Yet, the difficulty presented by grammatical metaphor may lie less in the fact of a wording that is not congruent and more in the underlying conceptualisation and its distance from the plain effects of physical events that the metaphor has come to express. Such a contention would point us towards a cognitive view of grammatical metaphor. According to such a view, grammatical metaphor would be more a linguistic representation of the process through which we can conceptualise an abstract idea such as a cause-and-effect relationship. I will next examine this idea through a case of nominalisation in a cause-and-effect structure. My conclusion will be the paradoxical one that if a congruent wording is grounded in the direct relationship of language to physical events then, from a cognitive perspective, the wording should be seen as expressing the fundamental embodied experience through which abstract thought is conceptualised.

2.3.6. Congruent language as the representation of the physical experience in which abstract thought is conceptualised

In the SFL view, a social effect, or, acting through this, a generic purpose, draws language away from the physical representations in which its structure originates. In the cognitive view, thought creates meaning out of embodied experience. Each of these views poses difficulties for the other. According to a cognitive approach, example (15), below, is made possible by the fact that we are reading abstract processes as physical ones. Decisions operate as if they were objects or agents acting upon other objects. In short, cause-and-effect relations derive from this conceptualisation of processes as objects. Abstract thought is thus built up out of schematisations deriving from our embodied condition.

(15)   The US's decision to release 30m barrels from its strategic petroleum
        reserve helped to push oil prices back from a peak of $34 a barrel
        (Financial Times 1/10/2000).

(16)   The US government decided to release 30m barrels from its strategic
        reserve. Thus, the US government helped to push oil prices back from a
        peak of $34 a barrel.

Sentence (16) above is a congruent reading of (15) above. The direct
cause-and-effect relationship is no longer expressed. Instead, a linking adjunct is
used to underscore the cause-and-effect relationship of the two sentences. Yet,
the linking adjunct does not properly render the strength of this cause-and-effect
relationship. I would argue, even, that it makes the relationship more remote and
difficult to grasp. It may be that the use of the grammatical metaphor clarifies
the cause-and-effect relationship by grounding it in a physical event, in this case
the impact of objects. In Langacker's (1990) analysis the metaphor could be
construed as the energy-charged 'head' of the sentence. It achieves its meaning
by expressing a cause and its effect as the impact of one object upon another
with a resultant transfer of energy.

Adjuncts that express 'cause' may also be derived from words expressing
spatial relations. 'Cause' itself employs the idea of physical linkage or the 'path'
schema (Lakoff 1987) as can still be seen in how the Latin word 'causa' retained
the meaning of an abstract 'link' in sense of a family connection. 'The path' or
connection schema shapes such expressions as 'make a logical connection, or
'one thing leads to another'. Yet English linking adjuncts have long lost the
meanings from which they are derived. They are an abstract entity pointing up
an abstract relationship. The problems caused by grammatical metaphor for
apprentice academic writers are a subject of well-documented concern (see
Ravelli this volume). However, one might wonder if the problems posed by
linking adjuncts are not as great or greater. It might therefore be the case that a
nominalised expression of cause-and-effect such as that found in sentence (15)
above is not difficult to process because of its metaphorical nature but because
of the highly abstract relationship that it expresses. The grammatical metaphor
evokes the impact of objects upon each other and as such it may ground that
abstract relationship in the type of physical event from which it has been
derived. A linking adjunct, on the other hand, signals the existence of a causal
relationship between two clauses as existing on an entirely abstract level.

John Robert Ross (e.g.1973) has demonstrated what are called prototype
effects in syntax. Prototype effects build upon the work of Rosch (1973, 1975,
1978) who suggested that a given category may have a member that is somehow

more central to it than other examples. In her most famous example, she showed how Americans will treat a robin as best representing the qualities of a bird while an ostrich will be a marginal category member. By a similar token, Ross holds that a word such as 'toe' will be treated as a better exemplar of a noun than a word such as 'time' in sentences where the syntax is the same as in: 'to stub one's toe' and 'to take one's time' (Lakoff 1987).

An interesting possibility is that in example (15) the sentence is meaningful because it has been established around a prototypical noun structure where nouns are objects, and the verb an action that represents the impact of one such object upon another. Congruent language would be meaningful in this case, not as a rewording that somehow brings the sentence into line with the lexico-grammar but as the underlying expression of the observable impact of visible phenomena upon each other. Congruent language could be reformulated as an expression of everyday events through which an abstract relationship of cause and effect is being conceptualised.

To the cognitivist then, a nominalisation or grammatical metaphor such as (15) shows how we use normal physical events to conceptualise abstract ideas. Grammatical metaphor may therefore emerge, not as a departure from congruent language but as an exploitation of the natural or direct relationships from which it is held to evolve.

3.   Grammatical metaphor as a cognitive construct

3.1.   Image schema, primary metaphor and conceptual metaphor and the problem of how these take a given textual form

My intention is now to take the example of grammatical metaphor and to explore how far we can treat its textual form as having emerged from an interplay of conceptualisations that are universal, culturally specific and specific to a given configuration of genre and register. At this point, I can only set out a framework of analysis that could look at the hypothetical interplay of these elements and I will take as my examples two cases of grammatical metaphor in a genre of event-appraisal.

3.1.1. Culture and conceptualisation
Cognitive accounts of metaphor stress the cultural organisation of conceptual metaphor, thus giving a hierarchy of metaphors as they emerge into text. Lakoff and Johnson (1999: 61) give as an example, (17) below:

(17)   People are supposed to have purposes in life, and they are supposed to act
        so as to achieve those purposes.

Using Grady's (1997) analysis, this statement is read as being composed of
two primary metaphors (Lakoff & Johnson 1999: 61):

(18)   Purposes are destinations

(19)   Actions are Motions

Culture uses these schemata to transmit the value of a purposeful existence
(Lakoff & Johnson 1999: 61): "people are supposed to have destinations in life,
and they are supposed to move so as to reach those destinations".
        (18) and (19), above, will in turn entail the mappings:

Journey ➔ purposeful life
Traveller ➔ person living a life
Destinations ➔ life goals
Itinerary ➔ Life Plan (ibid.)

These can in turn be developed as guidelines for life of the kind that are
familiar in many cultures.
        The cognitive analysis of metaphor thus sets up a hierarchy of conceptual
entailments. This hierarchy presupposes a movement from schemata that are
more general in the sense of being productive of a wider range of textual
examples in different languages to ones that are more specific to a language or
even a context and, therefore, less productive. I will now explore this idea of a
hierarchy, treating it as an emergence from the most general or reductive
conceptualisation towards one that is more ideationally or interpersonally
specific. I will do this by looking at the types of conceptualisation that might
underlie a grammatical metaphor.

3.1.2. Grammatical metaphor as the product of a conceptual hierarchy:
        Process as actor
In order to show how we might plot a process of emergence of grammatical
metaphor into text, I will take example (20) below:

(20)   Default would in turn deal another damaging perhaps fatal blow to the
        IMF's credibility (*Financial Times:* January 29, 1999)

'Default' in this sentence is a Repetition that creates cohesion by referring back to the previous sentence, (21) below:

(21)   Russia might default on a large chunk of 150 billion external debt, including, perhaps, the $4.5 bn it must repay the IMF this year – and turn itself into a financial *pariah.*

Arguably, there are two main reasons why a grammatical metaphor has been used here. First, if we made a congruent wording of (20) where the verb was a Process, 'default', this would begin: 'if Russian defaulted on its debt.' Such a wording would create a repetitive structure that might be at odds with the stylistic demands of the genre. Second, the genre is one which appraises or explains the events that it unfolds. It therefore recounts the events inside a cause and effect structure that tends to reduce human actors to a hypothetical presence. The action of default is one that directly impacts on events without the presence of human actors. 'Default' therefore requires a verb that will express its directness of impact. 'Default' and 'the IMF's credibility' are personified as two prize-fighters, with the first dealing a damaging blow to the other.

In Figure 1, we can see how one might plot the emergence of a grammatical metaphor from a cognitive or image-schematic perspective, using example (20). The diagram does not so much examine the idiom 'deal a blow' and its incorporation of the object. It looks at the subject, or Process as Actor and at the Receiver which is arguably the personification of an attribute, 'credibility'.

The fundamental feature of this construction as a grammatical metaphor is:

Process → actor

This requires the nominalisation of the verb, 'default'. From a cognitive perspective, the nominalisation requires the conceptualisation of a Process as a person or thing capable of causing an action. In the example under discussion, the reference to 'fighting' with the idiom 'deal another damaging blow' clearly places us in the domain of people and not of objects. Therefore personification, as a capacity to perceive 'a Process' as an Actor, is given as a primary schematisation here. This in turn yields the general and highly reductive conceptual metaphor, 'processes are people', which takes grammatical form as 'processes are actors.'

Thompson (1996) speaks of a knock-on effect in grammatical metaphor, where the metaphor is not confined to a single part of a clause. For example, in

becoming a noun, a verb will acquire the capacity to have Attributes. In this case
'the subject as Process requires that an Attribute, 'credibility', function as a
'receiver' (to the IMF's credibility).

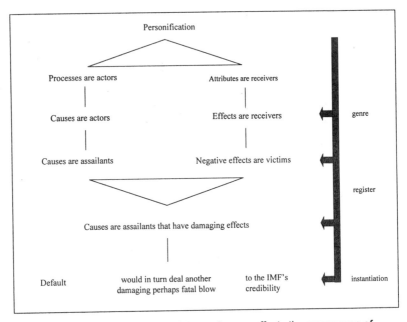

Figure 1: How context as register and genre affects the emergence of
grammatical metaphor from an image schema towards a textual form

In the next stage of proximity of concept to text, one might anticipate a
generic effect. We are dealing here with an event appraisal and hence a cause-
and-effect assessment. Therefore the personified Process expresses a cause-and-
effect relationship, with a cause an Actor and the effect a Receiver.

At the next stage one can perceive effects that are textual, interpersonal
and ideational. An ideational effect starts to emerge in the conceptualisation of
causes as aggressors or assailants and effects as a victim. The 'business is war'
metaphor (Lakoff & Johnson 1980) will commonly skew economic or business
appraisal towards this type of conceptualisation. However, there may be a
stronger interpersonal effect here, arising from the need to augment the power of
an argument by creating stronger reader identification with an effect by
expressing it as an injured person. (22), (23), and (24) are examples of the same:

(22)   Oil price rises may inflict some damage on the prospects of economic revival in the Far East

(23)   The 'No' vote struck a blow against the process of economic growth and monetary union

(24)   The regime's actions forced back the desire for change

The above analysis is a somewhat tentative framework for how one might treat an Actor-to-Process grammatical metaphor as emerging from a conceptual hierarchy that is selected by the objective of appraising financial events.

4.   Conclusions

The SFL concept of grammatical metaphor shows how social context operating through genre can structure text according to its representational purposes and not those of the facts of the world in which the text's elements were primarily grounded. The concept of grammatical metaphor suffers, however, from the contradiction of any analysis of metaphor that depends on linguistic description. This is that the metaphoricity of any given item or statement is finally determined by how far its representation is treated as conventional by the community in which it occurs. Thus, a discussion as to whether something is metaphorical or not must finally be the somewhat fruitless debate about whether a given language community holds it to be so.

Doubts about where metaphor ends must also affect how we determine where congruency begins. The risk in this is that without a notion of congruent usage, the larger SFL framework starts to unravel because there are no longer categories of meaning which given linguistic categories typically instantiate. Here, we should perhaps stress two ideas. One idea is revisiting congruent language as natural or direct. The other is that of stressing a difference between whether we choose to explore language as a key to its underlying conceptualisations or as a system of meaning representation.

I will take the issue of naturalness first. The issue here is that we may want to qualify the idea of congruent language as being more natural and direct. Metaphor is natural to the mind and there is abundant evidence (e.g. Gibbs 1994) to show that we access its meaning in a direct and effective manner. Instead, we should stress how congruent language suggests a greater stability in sign-meaning relationships. Congruent wordings represent the preferences of a given linguistic system, setting out what is typical and by default, less typical of the system. Any language is finally a zone of conflict between its need to stabilise as an agreed symbolic system and its need to represent novelty or the perceived uniqueness of individual experience. Metaphor, as a response to the strangeness of experience, threatens the congruency of the linguistic system that efficient communication requires.

Thus we could treat congruent language as a construction that has evolved as a representation of observable, common events. Such events, would normally dictate, for example, that a subject is more likely to be an Actor than a Process. This is because Processes are not observable, independent entities capable of instigating actions. They have to be conceptualised as such. The conceptualisation is achieved when the identity of an Actor is mapped onto that of a Process. Processes are better perceived as Actors in this case because Actors are an expression of embodied, physical experience. According to this, admittedly controversial reading, congruent language could also be characterised as the trace language through which the metaphor is expressed. It sets up a trace of the physical experience through which the abstract idea is conceptualised. From this it could follow that a grammatical metaphor does not in fact make language harder to understand because it is not congruent. We need to consider how it helps us to conceptualise an abstract set of relationships through a grammatical structure that has evolved out of a primary need to express a physical set of relationships. For example, it is as if a cause and effect structure contains within it the trace of an impact between concrete phenomena. This impact is a prototypical physical event that will in turn become a template able to conceptualise and structure the interaction of abstract ideas. In sum, a clash of objects will yield the lexico-grammar that makes it possible to conceptualise the clash of ideas.

The above assertion leads me straight to my second point about how we explore language. This is that SFL is looking at how a given linguistic system instantiates meanings and thus at that system's existence as a stable entity, at least as it emerges from a given context. The cognitive view, on the other hand, is concerned with the conceptualisation of the meanings themselves, and thus with our need to remodel the linguistic system according to the novelty of the conceptualisations that result.

Further, the cognitive analysis accounts for the linguistic instantiation of a given context without a proper understanding of the cultural or generic effect that brings this into being as a particular form of words. Culture is perceived as a homogeneous and historical influence upon language. Less thought is given to the effects of a given context, as a largely socio-cultural construct, upon the text that actually unfolds.

The SFL notion of grammatical metaphor is of a construction formed by contextual pressures as they are or are not manifest in genre. According to my analysis, a grammatical metaphor may, at the same time, exemplify how abstract language can be an instantiation of a set of conceptualisations that are formed out of image schemata. These schemata are fundamental to cognition but when context is taken into account they must, at some higher level, be skewed by genre or register. This is not to suggest that the hierarchies represented above are actually an attempt to chart a conceptual process that precedes the use of language. They are rather an attempt to show the resources, both cognitive and contextual, which a given item in text may employ. If, how or when these are combined by their users is a different issue altogether.

References

Albritton, D. (1992) *The use of metaphor to structure text representations: Evidence from metaphor-based schemas.* Ph.D. Dissertation, Yale University.

Alverson, H. (1995) *Universal metaphors of time in English, Mandarin, Hindi and Sesotho.* Baltimore: The Johns Hopkins UP.

Asch, S. & Nerlove, H. (1960) The development of double function terms in children: An exploratory investigation. In: B. Kaplan & S. Wapner (eds.) *Perspectives in Psychological Theory: Essays in honour of Heinz Werner.* New York International UP. 46–60.

Coffin, C. (1997) Constructing and giving value to the past: An investigation into secondary school history. In: F. Christie & J.R. Martin (eds.) *Genre and Institutions: Social processes in the workplace and school.* London: Cassell. 196–230.

Cooper, D. (1986) *Metaphor.* Oxford: Basil Blackwell.

Cometa, M. & M. Eson (1978) Logical operations and metaphor interpretation: A Piagetian model. *Child Development* 49: 649–659.

Davidson, D. (1978) What metaphors mean. *Critical Enquiry* 5: 31–47

Downing, A. & P. Locke (1992) *A University Course in English Grammar.* Hemel Hempstead: Prentice Hall International.

Elgin, C.Z. (1983) *With Reference to Reference.* Indianapolis & Cambridge: Hackett Publishing Company.

Gibbs, R. (1994) *The Poetics of Mind.* Cambridge: Cambridge UP.

Goatly, A. (1998) *The Language of Metaphors.* London: Routledge.

Goodman, N. (1993) *Ways of World Making.* Hassocks, Sussex: The Harvester Press.

Grady, J. (1997) *Foundations of Meaning: Primary metaphors and primary scenes.* Ph.D. Thesis, University of California, Berkley.

Halliday, M.A.K (1985) *An Introduction to Functional Grammar.* London: Edward Arnold.

Halliday, M.A.K (1993) Some grammatical problems in scientific English. In: Halliday & Martin (1993). 69–85.

Halliday, M.A.K & J.R. Martin (1993) *Writing Science*. Pittsburg Pa: University of Pittsburg Press.

Heine, B. (1993) *Auxiliaries. Cognitive Forces and Grammaticalization*. New York: Oxford UP.

Heine, B. (1997) *Cognitive Foundations of Grammar*. Oxford: Oxford UP.

Hopper, P. & E. Traugott (1993) *Grammaticalization*. Cambridge: Cambridge UP.

Johnson, M. (1987) *The Body in the Mind: The bodily basis of meaning imagination and reason*. Chicago: University of Chicago Press.

Johnson, M. (1989) Image-schematic basis of meaning. *RSSI* 9: 109–118.

Johnson, M. (1991) Knowing through the body. *Philosophical Psychology* 4: 3–18.

Johnson, M. (1992) Philososphical implications of cognitive semantics. *Cognitive Linguistics* 3: 345–366.

Johnson, M. (1993) Conceptual metaphor and embodied structures of meaning: A reply to Kennedy and Vervaeke. *Philosophical Psychology* 6: 413–422.

Lakoff, G. (1987) *Women, Fire and Dangerous Things*. Chicago: University of Chicago Press.

Lakoff, G. (1993/1979) The contemporary theory of metaphor. In: A. Ortony (ed.) *Metaphor and Thought*. Cambridge: Cambridge UP. 202–252.

Lakoff, G. & M. Johnson. (1980) *Metaphors We Live By*. Chicago: University of Chicago Press.

Lakoff, G. & M. Johnson (1999) *Philosophy in the Flesh*. New York: Basic Books.

Langacker, R. (1986/1991) *Foundations of Cognitive Grammar* (2 vols). Stanford: Stanford UP.

Langacker, R. (1990) *Concept, Image , Symbol: The cognitive basis of grammar*. Berlin: Mouton de Gruyter.

Langacker, R.W. (1994) *Foundations of Cognitive Grammar*. Stanford, California: Stanford UP.

Martin, J.R. (1985) Process and text: Two aspects of human semiosis. Benson & Greaves (eds.) *Systemic Perspectives on Discourse*. Vol 1. Norwood, NJ: Ablex. 248–74.

Martin, J.R. (1993) Life as a noun: Arresting the universe in science and the humanities. In: Halliday & Martin (1993). 221–267.

Martin, J. R. (1997) Analysing Genre: functional parameters. In: F. Christie & J. R. Martin (eds.) *Genre and Institutions: social processes in the workplace and school*. London and New York: Continuum. 3–39.

Rosch, E. (1973) Natural categories. *Cognitive Psychology* 4: 328–50.

Rosch, E. (1975) Cognitive reference points. *Cognitive Psychology* 7: 532–547.

Rosch, E. (1978) Principles of categorisation. In: Rosch & Lloyd (eds.) *Cognition and Categorisation*. Hillsdale, N.J.: Lawrence Erbaum Associates. 27–48.

Ross, J.R. (1973) Nouniness. In: O. Fujimura (ed.) *Three Dimensions of Linguistic Theory*. Tokyo: TEC Corporation. 137–258.

Sadock, J. (1993) [1979] Figurative speech and linguistics. In: A. Ortony (ed.) *Metaphor and Thought*. Cambridge: Cambridge UP. 42–57.

Searle, J.R. (1978) Literal meaning. *Erkenntnis* 13: 207–24.

Searle, J.R. (1993) [1979] Metaphor. In: A. Ortony (ed.) *Metaphor and Thought.* Cambridge: Cambridge UP. 83–111.

Tannen, D. (ed.) (1993) *Framing in Discourse.* New York: Oxford UP.

Thompson, E. (1995) *Colour Vision: A study in cognitive science and the philosophy of perception.* London: Routledge.

Thompson, G. (1996) *Introducing Functional Grammar.* London: Arnold.

Thompson, S.A. & A. Mulac (1991) A quantitative perspective on the grammaticalization of epistemic parentheticals in English. In: Traugott & Heine (eds.) *Approaches to Grammaticalization.* Amsterdam: Benjamins.

Thompson, G. & P. Thetela (1995) The sound of one hand clapping: The management of interaction in spoken and written discourse. *Text* 15.1: 58–75.

Ullman, S. (1962) *Semantics: An introduction to the science of meaning.* Oxford: Blackwell.

Winner, E. (1988) *The Point of Words: Children's understanding of metaphor and irony.* Cambridge, Massachusetts: Harvard UP.

Yu, N. (1998) *The Contemporary Theory of Metaphor: A perspective from Chinese.* Amsterdam: Benjamins.

'Having things both ways'
Grammatical metaphor in a systemic-functional model of language

Robin Melrose
South East Essex College, Southend-on-Sea

1. Introduction

In a recently published work, Halliday and Mathiessen (1999: 271) make the following point about grammatical metaphor (the example they give relates to the nominal group *engine failure*):

> The grammatical metaphor is a means of having things both ways [...] An element that is metaphorized does not lose its original status. Its construction is not triggered by being associated with any new semantic feature [...] So *failure* is both process and thing

In what follows I will be focusing mainly (though not exclusively) on the type of grammatical metaphor known as nominalization, and I will be arguing that this most *crystalline* of grammatical features (see Halliday 1987: 148–149 and 1994: 224) can also be seen as field- or wave-like (see Halliday 1978: 139, and Halliday 1994: 190), and that this "dual" aspect of metaphor can give us a crucial insight into the nature of semiosis. The argument that I will be advancing depends crucially on my interpretation of three key areas in SFL, namely semantics, genre and ideology, and this is where my discussion will begin.

2. Semantics, genre and ideology

The nature of *semantics* in systemic-functional linguistics (SFL) has always been somewhat indeterminate: Halliday sometimes seems to argue that it is a

separate stratum (e.g. the "context-specific semantics" of parental control
strategies presented in Halliday 1978: 82), but sometimes seems to suggest that
systems like transitivity and modality constitute semantic systems. An early
definition of the semantic system (Halliday 1978: 79) throws some light on this:

> the semantic system can be defined as a functional or function-oriented
> meaning potential; a network of options for the encoding of some
> extralinguistic semiotic system or systems in terms of the two basic
> components of meaning that we have called the ideational and the
> interpersonal. In principle this higher-level semiotic may be viewed [...] as
> a conceptual or cognitive system [...] But it may equally be viewed as a
> semiotic of some other type, logical, ideological, aesthetic or social. Here it
> is the social perspective that is relevant.

Two points can be made. The first point is that since the semantic system
encodes "some extralinguistic semiotic system or systems", then it does seem
possible to argue that there is "something" between the extralinguistic semiotic
system and the lexicogrammar that could be called a semantic system (and
indeed, the semantic systems that Halliday constructed for parental control
strategies and for Nigel's speech (1978: 82–83, 118–120) seem to support this
argument). The second point is that although Halliday opts for language as social
semiotic, he leaves open the possibility that language could also encode other
extralinguistic semiotic systems, including the "conceptual or cognitive [...],
logical, ideological [or] aesthetic".

In recent years Martin (e.g. 1992: 1) has argued that the semantic stratum
(or discourse stratum, as he calls it) is made up of discourse systems like
identification, conjunction and ideation. In arguing that semantics should in fact
be seen as a discourse stratum, he is clearly rejecting the "rather fluid
boundaries" between semantics and lexicogrammar that Halliday favours (1978:
43), but he does appear to be following Halliday's suggestion that semantics can
encode an extralinguistic semiotic system other than the social.

As far as *genre* is concerned, Halliday sees it as an aspect of mode –
though he also notes (1978: 145) that a genre "may have implications for other
components of meaning" – whereas Martin sees it (1992: 495) as a connotative
semiotic whose expression form is register. In the early 1990s Martin also
argued for a separate higher level that he called *ideology*: ideology, he says, is
the content form of genre, register and language, which are the expression form
of ideology. This level is required, says Martin (1992: 495) because "meaning
potential is not evenly distributed across a culture", given that "[a]ccess to genre,
register and language as semiotic resources is mediated through discourses of

ethnicity, class, gender and generation". Halliday does not often use the word *ideology*, but he does use an equivalent term, Bernstein's *code* or 'sociolinguistic coding orientation', the "particular subcultural angle on the social system" which "controls the semantic styles of the culture" (1978: 111, 123). Interestingly, in the last few years, Martin (1997: 7, 9–10) has abandoned the notion of ideology as a separate level, and is now arguing for an approach to ideology which takes into account logogenesis (how subjects engage dynamically with texts), ontogenesis (the development of social subjectivity), and phylogenesis (the ways in which a culture reworks hegemony across generations). This is a fruitful way to approach ideology, and I will be returning to it presently.

3.   Ideology, discourse and text semantics

I will return to the question of genre later, but for now I'd like to focus on ideology and semantics. Like a number of linguists, I have tried to approach ideology through the work of Michel Foucault. This poses certain problems: Norman Fairclough, who gives an excellent account of discursive formations (1992: 39–49), is pessimistic about the direct value of Foucault's work to the text analyst, saying (1992: 38):

> given that Foucault's approach to discourse and the intellectual context in which it developed are so different from my own, one cannot simply 'apply' Foucault's work in discourse analysis; it is [...] a matter of 'putting Foucault's perspective to work'

A view which Jay Lemke seems to share when he remarks (1995: 29) that "[i]t is not possible to know in terms of linguistic features of texts exactly how to interpret many of Foucault's theoretical principles".

But at the risk of oversimplifying Foucault's analysis of discourse, I believe that some useful parallels can be drawn between Foucault's work and SFL which will permit us to 'apply' (admittedly in a rather crude way) Foucault's insights to a linguistic analysis of ideology. First, though, I need to give a brief outline of what Foucault means by *discursive formation*.

Discursive formations are discussed at some length in Chapters 2–6 of *The Archaeology of Knowledge* (Foucault 1972). Foucault sees discourse analysis as concerned with analysing *statements* (in French, 'énoncés', perhaps best translated as 'utterances'), that is, with specifying sociohistorically variable *discursive formations*, systems of rules which make it possible for certain statements and not others to occur at particular times, places and institutional locations. A discursive formation consists of 'rules of formation' for the particular set of statements which belong to it, in particular rules for the formation of *objects*, rules for the formation of *enunciative modalities* and *subject positions*, and rules for the formation of *concepts* and *strategies*. The set of statements is dispersed over a multitude of texts which are related in a systematic way by the rules of formation, and can therefore be recognised by the following features:

1. All the texts discuss the same *discursive objects*: for example, since the 19th century, the branch of psychiatry called psychopathology has dealt with 'objects' such as motor disturbances, hallucinations, speech disorders, minor behavioural disorders, and sexual aberrations and disturbances (the list is not exhaustive).

2. All the texts have the same *enunciative modalities* and *subject positions*. In other words they all involve an authority who has the 'right to speak' (medical texts can only be enunciated by a doctor); an institutional site from which the discourse emanates (doctors speak from hospitals); and a subject position assumed by the speaking subject (a doctor who is diagnosing a patient's illness is assuming a different subject position from a doctor reporting on the case to his colleagues).

3. All the texts have the same *concepts* and *strategies* (themes or theories), which are organised in the same way – that is, by using the same rhetorical devices to set forth an argument, the same rhetorical schemata according to which different groups of statements may be combined, the same way of presenting information discursively and non-discursively (e.g. in tables).

How do we link discursive formations to SFL? The answer lies in the work of Jay Lemke on what he calls variously *intertextual thematic systems* or *intertextual thematic formations*. The key to the intertextual thematic system, as set out in Lemke (1983), is the *thematic item*, which may be explained as follows.

If we look at a number of related texts, we may eventually notice that certain so-called **thematic items** (for example, key participants or concepts) may regularly fulfil certain roles in the texts studied – or to put it in more linguistic terms, certain thematic items may frequently be assigned certain participant functions (e.g. Actor, Goal, Senser, Sayer) in a significant number of clauses. At the same time, we may discover that certain thematic items regularly collocate with certain other thematic items. And it is thematic items that provide the link, for they have some important features in common with Foucault's discursive objects: thematic items are distributed across a range of texts, they are discrete yet defined partly by their relationship with other thematic items, and above all they signal where power lies through the transitivity relations into which they enter.

This early paper concentrated almost exclusively on experiential meanings, with only passing reference made to interpersonal or textual meanings. This gap has been filled by Lemke (1995), which also looks at intertextual thematics in a broader perspective. His main concern, he says (1995: 40) is with *text semantics*, which, he says, "deals specifically with [...] patterns of continuity and change in clause-level meaning across texts". In order to "describe what I see happening most typically in text semantics", he says (1995: 41), Lemke takes Halliday's three metafunctions (experiential, interpersonal and textual), and "somewhat generalize[s]" them to produce three kinds of meaning in text semantics, the **presentational, orientational** and **organizational**. These three kinds of meaning are in some ways a formalisation of what many systemic-functional linguists have been doing for some time, except possibly that they operate not only "across meaningful stretches of text", but also "from text to text" (that is, intertextually). Thus presentational meaning is "the construction of how things are in the natural and social worlds by their explicit description as participants, processes, relations and circumstances standing in particular semantic relations to one another"; orientational meaning is "the construction of our orientational stance toward present and potential addressees and audiences, and toward the presentational content of our discourse, in respect of social relations and evaluations from a particular viewpoint"; while organizational meaning is "the construction of relations between elements of the discourse itself, so that it is interpretable as having structure [...], texture [...] and informational organization and relative prominence" (1995: 41).

What Lemke says here suggests that it is possible to 'apply' Foucault's concept of discursive formations to a linguistic analysis of ideology. However, first some modifications need to be made to Foucault's terminology: *discursive objects* is unproblematic, but I would prefer to drop *enunciative modalities* and simply use the term *subject positions*, and likewise dispense with the somewhat confusing *concepts*, using instead a new term, *textual strategies*. With that done, I believe that Foucault's discursive objects can be linked to Lemke's thematic items, or presentational meaning; subject position can be linked to orientational meaning; and textual strategies can be linked to organizational meaning.

What we now have in principle is a way of approaching ideology and semantics – and, therefore, grammatical metaphor – through the twin perspectives of Michel Foucault's discursive formations and Jay Lemke's text semantics. I would like to illustrate this approach by analysing a piece of academic discourse – an extract from a book by Edward M. Hundert called

Philosophy, Psychiatry and Neuroscience: Three Approaches to the Mind (see Appendix 1). In this extract (pp. 246–248), Hundert has been explaining what a theory of brain functioning should be able to achieve.

The first question to answer in this analysis of ideology and semantics is: what are the discursive objects (thematic items) in this text? The answer to this lies in determining the main word-chains (see Appendix 2), which unsurprisingly turn out to be BRAIN and THEORY. On the basis of these word-chains, it can be inferred that two discursive objects are at work in this extract:
• the object of study
• the theory used to explain the object of study

Presentational meaning can now be explored by examining the participant roles played by the discursive objects. This obviously requires an analysis of transitivity, showing process types, participants and circumstances. Such an analysis (see Appendix 3) shows that there are eleven material processes, ten relational processes, five verbal processes, one mental and one behavioural process. One or other of the discursive objects is a participant in all of the material processes, either as Actor (six times), Goal (five times), or Range (three times); the brain also appears four times as a Circumstance. As regards the relational processes, one or both of the discursive objects is a participant in every process, either as Carrier (five times), Attribute (four times), Identified (three times), and Identifier (four times). As far as the remaining processes are concerned, the only ones worth mentioning are the verbal processes, most of which involve some sort of explanation or definition with the author or Edelman as Sayer. The number of relational processes is to be expected: much classifying and identifying goes on in academic writing. More surprising, perhaps, is the number of material processes. However, if we focus on the Actor role, it is not difficult to see why material processes are so common: the role of Actor is realised five times by the discursive object 'brain' because Edelman's theory is one in which groups of neurons are given a very active role; and the Actor function is realised three times by the discursive object 'theory', because the writer, Edward M. Hundert, assigns an active role to Edelman's model of higher brain function.

Next I will consider the subject position (orientational meaning) in this extract (see Appendix 4). An analysis of appraisal (see Martin 1997: 18–26, Coffin 1997: 206) shows that there are a variety of appraisal devices, with engagement (9 items) as the most frequent type, followed by amplification (5 items), and appreciation and judgement (5 items each). It is not within the scope of this paper to deal with interpersonal meaning in any detail; however, given the fact that all the clauses are declarative, we might say that the interpersonal elements, when considered in conjunction with the appraisal choices, indicate a writer who has few doubts, and is happy to express fairly strong convictions about his subject. He is, after all, writing as a respected academic, from a position within one of the most prestigious institutions in the country (the Harvard Medical School).

4.   Grammatical metaphor in the MIND text

That leaves only textual strategies (organizational meaning) to explore. From what I have said so far about textual strategies, and from what Lemke says about organizational meaning, it would seem that textual strategies might be best explored by analysing options chosen in systems of the textual metafunction. However, for reasons which I'll explain later, I will instead be looking at grammatical metaphor, in the form of two related types of ideational metaphor, nominalisation, a metaphor of transitivity in which a process is encoded as a thing, and metaphors of transitivity proper, in which a semantic configuration that would be congruently encoded as one type of process is encoded as a different type of process – see below for a fuller explanation. Nominalisation is very much in evidence in this text, as the following analysis shows – in each case I have taken the nominalisation and "unpacked" it to reconstruct the process or property of which the noun phrase is a rewording:

(1)   the sheer complexity of neural organization

(1a)	neurons	are organised,	and	this	is done	in a very complex way
	Goal	Material		Range	Material	Manner

The noun phrase has been unpacked into a clause complex, but one which remains a metaphor, in the sense that 'neurons' is encoded as Goal in a material process:passive whose Actor is unknown, and in which the phenomenon is encoded by a process ('organised') that implies agency. The most natural role for 'neurons' is as Actor, which is achieved in the following:

(1b)	neurons	work	together	to perform	a single function
	Actor	Material	Manner	Material	Range

But even this interpretation implies that the neurons are purposeful actors, and still leaves us in the realm of metaphor (probably the only non-metaphorical encoding would be one which described in detail the biochemical and electrical pathways which allow groups of neurons to "communicate"). And this concept of neurons as purposeful actors is only reinforced by the next noun phrase, *repertoires of behaviours*, which I think refers to 'interacting networks within the brain'.

(2)   repertoires of behaviours

they	can follow	one of a number of possible different repertoires
Behaver	Behavioural	Range

when	they	behave
	Behaver	Behavioural

Of course only animate beings can behave, so this is also a metaphor for something like 'operate'; and 'repertoire' is also a metaphor, apparently meaning something like 'pattern':

The next metaphor to be considered comes in the second paragraph:

(3)   the necessary conditions for self-conscious experience

the brain	requires	certain conditions		so	it/ people	can ex- perience	things
Senser	Mental	Phenomenon			Senser	Mental	Pheno- menon

and	know	that	it/they	is/are experiencing	these things
	Mental	Phenomenon			
			Senser	Mental	Phenomenon

This is a complex metaphor to unravel, and when it is unravelled, it is not difficult to see why it has been used: it leaves it open as to whether the brain or people do the experiencing, and avoids two equally difficult problems (can the brain experience things, or how can people be aware that they are experiencing something?).

The next metaphor, *group selection and phasic re-entrant signalling*, is one that demonstrates very clearly how nominalisation can be used as a device to show that the writer has power over the reader, and also as a device to exclude all those who are not 'experts' or, at least, aspiring 'experts'. It packs a huge amount of information into one short noun phrase, but after reading a section of the work, I think it can be analysed as follows:

(4) group selection and phasic re-entrant signalling

groups of neurons	are selected	and	stabilised
Goal	Material		Material

then	used	to recognise	external signals;
	Material	Mental	Phenomenon

other unselected goups of neurons	recognise	internal signals	from the selected groups of neurons
Senser	Mental	Phenomenon	Place

then	send	them	to other groups of neurons –
	Material	Goal	Place

and	this	happens	repeatedly	between groups of neurons
	Actor	Material	Manner	Place

Again a number of questions are suggested by this analysis: Who selects and stabilises? In what sense can neurons be said to be animate beings capable of recognising something? And in what sense can a neuron be said to be an Actor? The unravelling of one complex metaphor has brought to light a number of simpler metaphors that are undoubtedly more powerful than the metaphor which obscured them.

Moving on to the third paragraph, we find something a little more accessible:

(5) competition between pre-existing neural connections

neurons	once	connected	with each other,	and now
Actor	Time	Material	Accompaniment	

compete	with other neurons	that	previous-ly	connected	with each other
Material	Accompaniment				
			Time	Material	Accompaniment

Again it appears from this that neurons are active, purposeful social beings like animals or humans.

The next grammatical metaphor follows direcly on from the previous one:

(6) those which are functional will be selected and stabilized, those which are less functional will drop out

some neural connections	operate	frequently,	and	these	will survive,
Actor	Material			Actor	Material

while	others	don't operate	very often	so	they	will probably not survive
	Actor	Material			Actor	Material

The most notable feature of this grammatical metaphor (not a nominal-isation here, but an example of an effective clause replacing a middle clause) is that, as in the first "unpacked" version of (1), neurons are encoded as Goal in material process:passive clauses in which the Actor is unknown, and in which at least one phenomenon is encoded by a process ('selected') which implies agency – at least in commonsense discourse. It is probably more natural for neurons to be encoded as Actor, which is achieved in the congruent version.

The next grammatical metaphor occurs in the fourth paragraph. Here we have a clause with high lexical density (9) and a very dense nominalisation:

(7)   the fundamental requirement for successful selective adaptation to an unknown future is pre-existing diversity

organisms	don't know	what	's going to happen	in the future
Senser	Mental	Phenomenon		
		Actor	Material	Time

so if	they	want	to be able to change	so that
	Senser	Mental	Pheno....	
		Material		

they	can survive	when	something in their environment	changes
...menon				
Actor	Material		Actor	Material

they	need to come	in all shapes, sizes and colours
Carrier	Relational	Attribute

It is no doubt quite apparent that I struggled to unravel this metaphor and express it as something meaningful in the spoken mode. This clause is another good example of a grammatical metaphor which excludes those who do not understand the basic principles of natural selection.

The next metaphor I want to comment on is in the fifth paragraph:

(8)   cells form groups of cells

cells	collect	to-gether	and	these collections of cells	are called	groups
Actor	Material	Manner		Indentified	Relational	Identifier

In the metaphorical realisation the cells are Actor in a 2-participant material process (they "create" something); in the congruent realisation the cells are Actor in a 1-participant material process (they act only on themselves), and Identified in a relational process (their only interest lies in their identity).

Nominalisation is, as suggested above, an example of ideational metaphor. Ideational metaphor occurs when something in the field (ongoing social situation and subject matter) is not encoded congruently (see Halliday 1994: 342), that is, in the most direct and "natural" way, but metaphorically , drawing on lexico-grammatical resources that "de-naturalise" then "re-naturalise" the social situation and subject matter. In the case of nominalisation, this metaphorisation takes a world swarming with activity and freezes it so that it can become the object of scientific scrutiny. However, as the previous analysis has shown, nominalisation is not the only type of ideational metaphor used in the text – there are several examples, actual or implied, of metaphors of transitivity proper, in which, as indicated above, a semantic configuration that would be congruently encoded as one type of process is encoded as a different type of process. Almost all the nominalisations, when unpacked, seem to imply metaphors of transitivity of this type, and a number of the material processes (e.g. 4, 5, 7, 8, 9, 10, 11) seem equally to be metaphoric. In general these metaphoric realisations present the brain or its neurons as purposeful actors involved in processes which would normally be attributed only to humans or other sentient beings. Interestingly, as a textual strategy such metaphors of transitivity appear to work in the opposite way from nominalisation: whereas the nominalisations in this text arguably seek to exclude those outside the discipline, the metaphors of transitivity used in the extract attempt to naturalise the brain and its operation, and make it accessible to those not "in the know".

5. Grammatical metaphor and everyday practices

I began this paper with the claim that nominalisation, that most crystalline of grammatical features, can also be seen as field- or wave-like, and it is now time to investigate this claim in some detail. Now the idea of language as particle, field and wave, first outlined by Halliday 1978: 139, and further developed in Halliday 1994: 190, states that there are three ways of looking at meaning: as particles (the "nucleus" and "electrons" of transitivity), as fields (the "electromagnetic fields" of modality and attitude), and waves (the "peaks" and "troughs" of theme, information focus and conjunction). So on one level, to say that nominalisation is both crystalline and field- or wave-like is to state the obvious: nominalisation is a thing, and therefore a particle, but it also has a role to play as a textual strategy, and is therefore wave-like (see Halliday 1994: 353, Halliday & Martin 1993: 241, Rose 1997: 50–52, Coffin 1997: 218, Halliday & Matthiessen 1999: 238 for discussion of the role played by nominalisation in theme and information focus).

However, this is not precisely what I had in mind when I said that nominalisation is both crystalline and field- or wave-like. In a clause like "the fundamental requirement for successful selective adaptation to an unknown future is pre-existing diversity", a standard analysis might specify that the crystalline meaning is at the rank of the nominal group, while the wave-like meaning is at the rank of clause. But this is not what I am claiming: what I am saying is that the the *nominal group* is simultaneously crystalline and field- or wave-like, that information in a nominalisation has been condensed into a 'crystal', but at the same time the information has been so condensed that it seems to come at you like a series of waves, or attract you like a magnet without ever quite catching hold of you.

How can we account for the dual nature of nominalisation? The answer lies in placing textual strategies (organizational meaning) in a larger framework, that is, in relating text semantics to context of situation and context of culture on the one hand, and to language on the other hand. At this point it is necessary to refer to our initial discussion of genre, and to note Lemke's observation that genres are grounded in "*activity formations* (*action genres*), the typical doings of a community which are repeatable, repeated, and recognized as being of the same type from one instance or occurrence to another"; speech genres and written genres are simply "special cases of action genres", which are "clearly definable as the products of the activities that produce them" (1995: 31–32).

These comments on genre can also be applied to grammatical metaphor, in that we can see grammatical metaphor as a product of everyday practices. Nominalisation, for example, can be readily seen as a means of showing that you have gained mastery over a discipline (I use the word 'mastery' advisedly – the echo of gender ideology is quite deliberate), and you have therefore appropriated some power for yourself. Nominalisation is a technique for taking a chunk of information, or even large body of knowledge, that you assume will be shared by your reader, and referring to it by a kind of shorthand. It shows that you and the reader belong to the same in-group – but it can also exclude those who do not belong to the in-group. As such, it is no different from the practices of inclusion and exclusion that mark any social group, from the smallest to the largest.

6. Topological meaning, systems of interpretance and the two-faced grammatical metaphor

What help is it to know that genre and grammatical metaphor are grounded in everyday practices? Earlier in this paper I was discussing ideology, and noted that in recent years Martin has abandoned ideology as a separate level, and is now arguing for an approach to ideology which takes into account, among other things, logogenesis, or how subjects engage dynamically with texts. How subjects engage dynamically with texts is obviously central to the ideological function of grammatical metaphor, and is therefore an area that needs further exploration. To do this, I turn to the recent work by Jay Lemke on *systems of interpretance*, which, while not explicitly addressing the question of how subjects engage dynamically with texts, does offer some useful pointers to the processes involved.

To understand systems of interpretance, we need first to discuss Lemke's distinction between typological and topological meaning. This distinction is referred to briefly in Lemke (1995: 180), where typological is equated with Halliday's particle-like meaning (experiential meaning), and topological with Halliday's field- or wave-like meaning (interpersonal and textual meanings). Lemke uses the distinction rather differently from Halliday, however, since he is applying it not just to language, but to semiotic systems in general. So he makes the point that what he calls 'verbal-semantic meaning systems' are 'predominantly typological', while those he calls 'visual-motor meaning systems' are predominantly 'topological'. Although some aspects of verbal meaning (e.g. the gradable semantics of evaluations) may be thought of as "more topological in character", says Lemke, "most of the topological meaning in speech is considered "paralinguistic" (presumably because paralinguistic features can never be "completely and exhaustively described by a typological code").

Lemke (1999) develops this discussion by offering some criteria for distinguishing between topological and typological semiosis (1999: 6):

Topological	Typological
Meaning by degree	Meaning by kind
Quantitative difference	Qualitative distinction
Gradients	Categories
Continuous variation	Discrete variants

He also gives examples of typological and topological semiosis:

Topological	Typological
size,shape, position	spoken word
color spectrum	written word
visual intensity	mathematical symbol
pitch, loudness	chemical species

It appears from this that topological semiosis cannot readily be equated with field- and wave-like meanings, except in certain limited areas such as intonation and the gradable semantics of evaluations, which of course are aspects of interpersonal (field-like) meaning. Yet the examples that Lemke gives of topological semiosis – quantitative-X represented as colour spectrum, as visual intensity, as pitch or loudness – do leave room for further speculation. Clearly when Lemke refers to colour spectrum, visual intensity, pitch or loudness, he is speaking as a physicist and using the terms as a physicist would use them, but it is possible to see them in a different light.

This can be illustrated by the grammatical metaphor I have been exploring, both the complex nominalisation and the metaphors of transitivity. As I read the Hundert text, I found that my understanding of the nominalisation in the text varied considerably: I could interpret a word like 'organisation' without much difficulty; however, words or phrases like 'selection' and 'successful selective adaptation', which required some familiarity with the theory of evolution, were more difficult to interpret, and other phrases like 'phasic re-entrant signalling' and 'gene flow' I found virtually impenetrable. To use Lemke's terminology, some of the nominalisations were fairly "intense" or "loud" (for example, 1, 5), while other were rather "pale", "blurred", "soft" (for instance, 3, 4). The metaphors of transitivity work slightly differently: whereas the nominalisations vary constantly in "intensity" or "loudness", the metaphors of transitivity carry a message of neurons as purposeful actors which is at first "soft", "pale", "blurred", but gradually become more strongly defined as the reader progresses, until it is almost impossible not to "hear"or "see" it.

But it *is* possible not to hear it or see it, and that is where systems of interpretance become sigificant. Lemke's "Opening Up Closure" paper is a fairly complex one which shifts between Peircean semiotics and biology, but I will attempt to summarise it. Lemke starts with biology, but for a linguist it is easier to start with Lemke's later discussion of semiosis (Lemke 1999: 4). The first point he makes in this discussion, which derives from the principle set out by Peirce that "a sign is something, A, which denotes some fact or object, B, to some interpretant thought, C" (Buchler 1955: 93), is that in any act of decoding meaning, "there is work of interpretation to be done, there are principles or codes by which this interpreting is done, and so there must be, in my terms, *a system of interpretance* (SI)".

But what, in Lemke's terms, is 'a system of interpretance'? The answer to this question lies in understanding a phenomenon that Lemke (1999) calls *hierarchies of scale in complex systems*, and considering this in the light of an earlier discussion by Lemke (1995) on *dynamic open systems*. First hierarchies of scale in complex systems. In complex systems, says Lemke and the example used here is biological systems – the richness of their complexity derives in part from a strategy of organizing smaller units into larger ones, and these in turn into still larger ones, and so on. This strategy works in such a way that on any given level of the hierarchy (level N),

> units on level N are constituted by interactions at level (N-1) among the units at that lower level, but [...] of all the possible configurations which such interactions might produce at level N, only those actually occur which are allowed by boundary conditions set at level (N+1) (Lemke 1999: 1–2).

By putting together the Peircean notion of interpretation, and the biological concept of hierarchies of scale, Lemke advances a hypothesis about what he calls *semiotics across scales*, with his so-called Principle of Alternation (1999: 10):

> The Principle of Alternation:
> Each new, emergent intermediate level N in a complex, hierarchical, self organizing system functions semiotically to re-organize the continuous quantitative (topological) variety of units and interactions at level (N-1) as discrete, categorial (typological) meaning for level (N+1), and/or to re-organize the discrete, categorial (typological) variety of level (N-1) as continuously variable (topological) meaning for level (N+1).
> In each case, level (N+1) functions as the system of interpretance which construes entities and phenomena at level N as signs of microstates at the level (N-1).

Lemke illustrates the Principle of Alternation (1999: 19–20) by turning to the field of neuroscience, and showing the transformations from discrete to continuous and from continuous to discrete as we move up the scale from quantum variety to neuro-transmitter threshold effects to smooth motor behaviour. The final transformation (p.20) is the one that is most accessible to the non-scientist, and of most interest to the linguist:

Smooth motor behavior (topo) organized as visual and verbal signs (typo): "gestures" "words" in an ecosocial supersystem functioning as the meta-system of interpretance.

Finally, I will end here with the last step of the link from physics to language and human social semiotics that I promised, namely the smooth motor actions (topological) are re-organized by learned processes of organisms in communities to be produced and interpreted as signs, such as word-utterances and gesture-productions, which are classic instances of typological signs. The SI here is not just the organism, but the organism in a community, and not just a community of other persons, but an ecosocial system that includes all the relevant nonhuman agents or actants as well (e.g. written texts).

If I understand Lemke correctly, the lower level here (N-1) is smooth motor actions, among which Lemke identifies "gesticulating" and "enunciating", the level-in-focus (N) is words and gestures (signs), and the higher level where the boundary conditions are set (N+1) is the community, the ecosocial system. If this is the case, then we could reformulate the last transformation as: signs (words and gestures) are constituted by the relevant smooth motor actions at the level below, but of all the possible configurations which such interactions might produce, only those actually occur which are allowed by boundary conditions set at the level above, the level of the community, the ecosocial system.

What are these 'boundary conditions' that Lemke refers to? On one level we could view the 'boundary conditions' as the phonological, lexicogrammatical and semantic rules that constitute the language, but on another level we could construe them as something much broader – and this is where the concept of *dynamic open system* becomes important. In the "Making Meaning, Making Trouble" paper I referred to earlier, Lemke comes up with some fascinating insights into meaning-making by seeing the meaning system as precisely a dynamic open system. Dynamic open systems, says Lemke (1995: 162) "are those which survive only by continuous interaction with their environments through processes that exchange matter, energy and information with those environments". A good example of a dynamic open system is a flame, which "must be *open* to its environment to survive; if we close off the flame from its source of fuel or oxygen, it dies". A flame is only one example of a dynamic open system – a person, a community, a city is also a dynamic open system. One important feature of dynamic open systems is that they survive at the expense of the environment, and are therefore "caught in a paradox of survival: to continue to live they must disturb and degrade the environment that sustains their lives". This problem is solved by the integration of dynamic open systems into larger *supersystems* (p.164) (it is here that we can see a possible link between dynamic open systems and hierarchies of scale, in biological supersystems like *homo sapiens*). Supersystems are still dynamic open systems, and as such they must be able to change and respond to changes in the environments with which they have to interact to survive. As Lemke points out (p.165), supersystems cannot become perfectly self-regulating, because then they would be unable to respond to change; for this reason "[t]hey must leave themselves room to maneuver; they build into their subsystem processes *contradictions, processes that run counter* to one another, and counter to self-regulation".

What can be said of human communities can also be said of the meaning system of a community, what we have been calling the context of culture. Meaning systems "operate so as to limit change, to narrow the range of behaviours that people might meaningfully imagine doing"; but at the same time they "must also incorporate gaps and contradictions" (p.175). Meaning systems hide their limits from us by what Lemke calls "the *absence* of certain contextualisations", "gaps in the system of contextualizing relations".

Thus when Lemke refers to 'boundary conditions' at level N+1 in hierarchies of scale, he may be thinking not only of language, but also of the meaning system, a dynamic open system, which operates so as to "limit change", to "narrow the range of behaviours that people might meaningfully imagine doing". Interestingly, Martin has used a somewhat similar formulation in an early characterisation of genre: the function of genre, he says (1982: 3, my italics) is to "*constrain* the possible combinations of field, tenor and mode". This has two implications that need to be considered: firstly, it suggests that Lemke's system of interpretance may be linked to genre as Martin uses the term, or rather, to genre plus register and language. Secondly, it implies that while there can be only one global system of interpretance, only one meaning system, it may be that there can also be numerous local systems of interpretance. Indeed, in "Making Trouble" (1995: 168), the equivalent of system of interpretance is meaning system, which is always regarded as a *local* meaning system; but here the meaning system does not 'construe' entities and phenomena at the level below – rather it *contextualises* them through a 'hierarchy of *meta-redundancy relations*' (a network of meanings that tend to co-occur in particular contexts). Seen from this perspective, a local system of interpretance would function in effect as the highest contextualising level for a network of meanings, the top of the hierarchy of a restricted set of meta-redundancy relations.

Let us suppose that there are such local systems of interpretance, and that they can in fact be linked to genre as hypothesised above. In that case, the system of interpretance at work in the *Mind* text is that 'genre' we call academic discourse, more specifically academic discourse focusing on that area where philosophy, psychiatry and neuroscience converge. The role of this system of interpretance is to transform the topological into the discrete, to ensure that the fluctuations of "intensity" or "loudness" in the nominalisations and metaphors of transitivity (the wave-like "face" of meaning) are smoothed over and converted into a set of discrete propositions (the particle-like or crystalline "face" of meaning). The system of interpretance is in Lemke's terminology level (N+1), and the text is level N. As for level (N-1), in the case of the nominalisations, this is presumably the discrete propositions (processes) that have been nominalised, and in the case of the metaphors of transitivity, it is presumably the congruent versions that have been passed over in favour of the metaphorical variants.

7. Conclusion

It may be argued at this point that I am trying to make systems of interpretance perform a trick they were never designed to perform. After all, Lemke is saying that the system of interpretance known as the meaning system permits us to transform something topological – bodily movements and vocalisations – into gestures, words, grammatical structures and meanings, and as far as the principle of alternation goes, that is the end of the process. Lemke of course is talking about the biological production of language – if, however, we move away from the biological, we can look at other processes involved in language production and interpretation. And this brings me back to four questions that have arisen in the course of this paper:

1.   How can nominalisation be seen as both crystalline and field- or wave-like ("have things both ways")?

2.   What role does ideology play in the model?

3.   How can text semantics be linked to context of situation, context of culture (the meaning system) and language?

4.   What are the implications of saying that genre and grammatical metaphor are grounded in everyday practices?

Let us first focus on context of culture, which for most of this paper we have been calling the meaning system. In the process of making academic meanings, our starting point is of course the meaning system, and in particular the set of options that constitute the system of interpretance (the 'genre') that "guides" the making of academic meanings. The local system of interpretance, like the meaning system as a whole, "guides" not only verbal meaning-making, but also non-verbal meaning-making, and the redundancy relations between the two types of meaning (that is, their tendency to co-occur in the same context). The choices made in this local system of interpretance determine the context of situation, or field, tenor and mode, (the social situation, subject matter, social role, discourse role, and role of the text), and the text semantics, or configuration of presentational, orientational and organizational meanings (the ideological positioning of the speaking or writing subject). The context of situation and text semantics, linked by a complex web of meta-redundancy relations, then jointly determine the linguistic realisations, plus what we might call the situationally and ideologically significant non-verbal realisations (this applies mostly to spoken discourse, though not exclusively – think of an academic paper with sub-headings, versus an academic paper without sub-headings). It is in this complex web of meta-redundancy relations that we find nominalisation and metaphors of transitivity: as everyday practices they are redundant with other academic practices and contextualised by the local system of interpretance (the "meaning" of nominalisation is not the same in an academic work as in, say, a legal or political document, just as the metaphors of transitivity in the *Mind* text have a "meaning" peculiar to this particular discipline).

This is an account of producing academic discourse, and it might seem to be a case of taking what is largely typological, namely a body of knowledge, and reproducing something equally typological. But it is my contention that a different process is at work here, something that is close to that aspect of ideology that Martin calls logogenesis (how subjects engage dynamically with texts): for in transforming people's words and deeds into our own words and deeds, we are engaging dynamically with a text, transforming topological into typological, a "spectrum" of knowledge and activities of varying degrees of "loudness" into a discrete well-ordered argument. However, once this discrete well-ordered argument has to be interpreted by somebody else, then our typological becomes their topological, and the process must be repeated, even if the typological version exists only in the mind of the interpreter.

It seems that grammatical metaphor, in the shape of nominalisation, can tell us something fundamental about semiosis. Nominalisation is crystalline because somebody has crystallised it – changed something topological into something typological. But nominalisation is also field- or wave-like because to the reader it has become topological, and must be once more rendered typological. I am reminded here of the French philosopher Jacques Derrida, who once said, in a critique of Austin's speech act theory, that all speech acts are quotations (Derrida 1982: 326). Arguably, a metaphor of transitivity is a quotation, or rather a *mis*quotation, since it is a "rewording" of the congruent version of the same experience and carries within it a *trace* (as Derrida might say) of the congruent version. But a metaphor of transitivity is only a slight misquotation which adult listeners or readers have little difficulty in interpreting. A nominalisation, on the other hand, is a flagrant misquotation since when nominalisation occurs, a number of elements get lost – most notably, participants, location in time and personal evaluation – and accordingly poses more interpretive problems for adult listeners or readers. Text semantics, of course, makes extensive use of quotations: for example, discursive objects (thematic items) and participant roles are "borrowed" from other relevant texts.

I said earlier that according to Lemke, the meaning system is a dynamic open system. Like all dynamic open systems, says Lemke, meaning systems "operate so as to limit change, to narrow the range of behaviours that people might meaningfully imagine doing"; but at the same time they "must also incorporate gaps and contradictions" (1995: 175). In a way grammatical metaphor in the form of nominalisation seems like a good illustration of this phenomenon: on the one hand, it tightly controls the way we behave in academic discourse (and in many other types of highly favoured formal discourses as well); on the other hand there is something so bald, so nakedly authoritarian about some examples of nominalisation, that they almost invite us to challenge them. Perhaps nominalisation is at times so contradictory to some contemporary modes of viewing the world that we want to revolt against it, or, as Lemke says, "make trouble". It is perhaps no accident that one metaphorical encoding of the phenomenon construed by the non-finite clause "having things both ways" is "having a foot in both camps" – "having things both ways" is a risky business which implies not pleasing either "camp" or, even worse, being attacked by one or both "camps". In that way grammatical metaphor, as represented by nominalisation, instead of being a device for maintaining the ideological status quo, becomes a weapon for challenging it.

References

Buchler, Justus (1955) *Philosophical Writings of Peirce*. New York: Dover Publications.

Christie, F. & J.R. Martin (eds.) (1997) *Genre and Institutions: Social processes in the workplace and school.* London: Cassell.

Coffin, C. (1997) Constructing and giving value to the past: An investigation into secondary school history. In: Christie & Martin (eds.) (1997). 196–230.

Derrida, J. (1982) *Margins of Philosophy* (trans. by Alan Bass). Chicago: University of Chicago Press

Fabb, N., D. Attridge, A. Durant, & C. McCabe (eds.) (1987) *The Linguistics of Writing.* Manchester: Manchester UP

Fairclough, N. (1992) *Discourse and Social Change.* Cambridge: Polity Press.

Foucault, M. (1972) *Archaeology of Knowledge.* London: Tavistock.

Halliday, M.A.K. (1978) *Language as Social Semiotic.* London: Arnold.

Halliday, M.A.K. (1987) Language and the order of nature. In: Fabb et al. (eds.) (1987). 135–154.

Halliday, M.A.K. (1994) *Introduction to Functional Grammar.* 2nd edition. London: Arnold.

Halliday, M.A.K. & J.R. Martin (1993) *Writing Science: Literacy and discursive power.* London: Falmer.

Halliday, M.A.K. & Matthiessen, C.M.I.M. (1999) *Construing Experience Through Meaning: A language-based approach to cognition.* London: Cassell.

Hundert, E.M. (1991) *Philosophy, Psychiatry and Neuroscience: Three approaches to the mind.* Oxford: Clarendon Press.

Lemke, J.L. (1983) Thematic analysis: Systems, structures and strategies. *Semiotic Enquiry* 3.2: 159–87.

Lemke, J.L. (1995) *Textual Politics: Discourse and social dynamics.* London: Taylor & Francis.

Lemke, J.L. (1999) Opening up closure: Semiotics across scales. URL: http://academic.brooklyn.cuny.edu/jlemke/papers/gent.htm. 23/03/1999

Martin, J.R. (1982) Process and text: Two aspects of human semiosis. Paper presented at the 9th International Systemic Workshop, Toronto, Canada. Published, 1985 in: J.D. Benson & W.S. Greaves (eds.) *Systemic Perspectives on Discourse.* Vol. 1. Norwood, NJ: Ablex. 248–274.

Martin, J.R. (1992) *English Text: System and structure.* Amsterdam: Benjamins.

Martin, J.R. (1997) Life as a noun: Arresting the universe in science and humanities. In: Halliday & Martin. (eds.) (1997). 221–267.

Rose, D. (1997) Science, technology and technical literacies. In: Christie & Martin. (eds.) (1997). 40–72.

Appendices

Appendix 1

Edward M. Hundert, *Philosophy, Psychiatry and Neuroscience: Three approaches to the mind* (1991: 246–248).

A theory such as the one I am describing is a tall order. Certainly no current theory gives us all of these things in relation to the detailed anatomy of all of the complex, interacting networks within the brain. The sheer complexity of neural organization, repertoires of behaviours, and possibilities of experiences makes such a detailed and precise theory impossible at this time (and possibly, even, at any time).

It is, however, not premature to look for a more general theory of higher brain functioning whose unifying neuroscientific principles would provide the necessary conditions for self-conscious experience, while meeting all of the (high!) expectations outlined above. Such a general theory is provided by Nobel laureate Gerald Edelman (1978), whose theory of 'group selection and phasic re-entrant signalling' offers an excellent starting-point for this final step of our journey.

Edelman's theory of higher brain function is an ingenious elaboration of the idea of selection as applied to neuronal networks [...] Edelman defines 'selection' to mean more or less the same as it does in evolutionary theory. That is, through some sort of competition between pre-existing neural connections, those which are functional will be selected and stabilized, while less functional connections will tend to drop out. The term 'connections' is used loosely for good reason. Edelman considers the basic unit of interest to be groups (e.g. 'columns') of neurons rather than individual neurons, and so two broad classes of 'connections' may be defined. Extrinsic connections between the cells in one group and the cells in another will typically (though not exclusively) be of the 'synaptic type. Intrinsic connections within a neuronal group, on the other hand, may involve all sorts of synaptic and nonsynaptic interaction (including various local neuromodulations that can act on a time-scale of minutes to hours, consistent with the formation of short- and long-term memories-see Stevens 1985).

As in evolutionary theory, the fundamental requirement for successful selective adaptation to an unknown future is pre-existing diversity. As Edelman (1978: 56) explains, this is achieved in evolution by mutation and gene flow. For the nervous system, it is achieved by the formation through embryogenesis and early development of a massive number of diverse collections of neuronal groups, which he defines as the primary repertoire.

Edelman's model of the hierarchy within the nervous system is that cells form groups of cells (the basic unit of interest) and that groups of these groups form 'repertoires. As just mentioned, the 'primary repertoires' are specified during embryogenesis and development. Each repertoire is essentially a collection of groups of cells wherein each group has similar extrinsic connectivities, but where each group can have enormously diverse intrinsic connectivities.

Appendix 2: Main lexical chains

BRAIN lexical chain

networks; brain; neural organization; higher brain function; neuro-scientific principles; higher brain function; neuronal networks; neural connections; connections; 'connection'; neurons; neurons; 'connections'; Extrinsic connections; cells; cells; 'synaptic' type; Intrinsic connections; neuronal group; synaptic and nonsynaptic interaction; local neuromodulations; memories; nervous system; neuronal groups; nervous sytem; groups of cells; groups of cells

THEORY lexical chain

theory; no current theory; detailed and precise theory; general theory; general theory; theory of 'group selection and phasic re-entrant signalling'; theory of higher brain function; evolutionary theory; evolutionary theory; evolution; model of the hierarchy within the nervous system

Appendix 3: Analysis of transitivity

Material Processes

1.

Certainly no current theory	gives	us	all of these things	in relation to the detailed anatomy of all of the complex, interacting networks within the brain.
Actor	Mat	Beneficiary	Range	Matter

2.

Such a general theory	is provided by	Nobel laureate Gerald Edelman
Goal	Material	Actor

3.

whose theory of 'group selection and phasic re-entrant signalling'	offers	an excellent starting-point for this final step of our journey.
Actor	Mat	Beneficiary

4.

That is,	through some sort of competition between pre-existing neural connections,	those which are functional	will be selected	and stabilized.
	Manner	Goal	Mat	Mat

5.

while	less functional connections	will tend to drop out.
	Actor	Material

6.

The term 'connections'	is used	loosely	for good reason
Goal	Material	Manner	Cause

7.

this	is achieved	in evolution	by mutation and gene flow.
Range	Material	Place	Actor

8.

For the nervous system,	it	is achieved	by the formation through embryogenesis and early development of a massive number of diverse collections of neuronal groups.
Matter	Range	Material	Means

9.

cells	form	groups of cells (the basic unit of interest)
Actor	Mat	Goal

10.

groups of these groups	form	'repertoires'
Actor	Mat	Goal

11.

the 'primary repertoires'	are specified	during embryogenesis and development
Goal	Material	Time

Relational Processes

1.

A theory such as the one I am describing	is	a tall order.
Carrier	Relational	Attribute

2.

The sheer complexity of neural organization, repertoires of behaviours, and possibilities of experiences	makes	such a detailed and precise theory	impossible	at this thime (and possibly, even, at any time).
Attributor	Relational	Carrier	Attribute	Time

3.

It	is,	however,	not premature	to look for	a more general theory of higher brain functioning whose unifying principles would provide the necessary conditions for self-conscious experience, while meeting all of the (high!) expectations outlined above.
Carrier -	Rel		Attribute	– Carrier	
				Behavioural	Range

4.

Edelman's theory of higher brain function	is	an ingenious elaboration of the idea of 'selection' as applied to neuronal networks.
Carrier	Relational	Attribute

5.

(Edelman defines selection)	to mean	more or less the same as it does in evolutionary theory.
	Relational	Identifier

6.

Extrinsic connections between the cells in one group and cells in another	will typically (nouth not exclusively) be	of the 'synaptic' type.
Carrier	Relational	Attribute

7.	Intrinsic connections within a neuronal group, on the other hand,	may involve	all sorts of synaptic and nonsynaptic interaction (including various local neuromodulations that can act on a time-scale of minutes to hours, consistent with the formation of short- and long-term memories …)
	Identified	Rel:possessive	Identifier

8.	As in evolutionary theory,	the fundamental requirement for successful selective adaptation to an unknown future		is	pre-existing diversity.
	Comparison	Identified		Rel	Identifier

9.	Edelman's model of the hierary within the nervous system	is	that cells form groups of cells (the basic unit of interest) and that groups of these groups form 'repertoires'.
	Identified	Relational	Identifier

10.	Each repertoire	is	essentially	a collection of groups of cells wherein each group has similar extrinsic connectivities, but where each group can have enormously diverse intrinsic connectivities.
	Carrier	Relational		Attribute

Verbal Processes

1.	Edelman	defines	'selection'	(to mean more or less the same as it does in evolutionary theory)
	Sayer	Verbal	Verbiage	

2.	and so	two broad classes of 'connections'	may be defined.
		Verbiage	Verbal

3.	As	Edelman	…	explains
		Sayer		Verbal

4.	which	he	defines	as the primary repertoire.
		Sayer	Verbal	Role

5.	as just	mentioned
		Verbal

Mental Processes

1.	Edelman	considers	the basic unit of interest	to be	groups (e.g. 'columns') of neurons rather than individual neurons.
	Senser	Mental	Phenomenon		
			Carrier	Relational	Attribute

Behavioural Processes

1. (It is, however, not premature)	to look for	a more general theory of higher brain functioning.
	Behavioural	Range

Appendix 4: Analysis of interpersonal elements

a tall order – amplification
Certainly (no current theory) – engagement
sheer (complexity) – amplification + appreciation
(makes) such a detailed and precise theory impossible – amplification + appreciation + engagement
possibly (... at any time) – engagement
not premature – appreciation
high! (expectations) – judgement
excellent (starting-point) – judgement
ingenious (elaboration) – judgement
more or less (the same) – engagement
(for) good (reason) – judgement
(two broad classes ...) may (be defined) – engagement
(will) typically (be) – engagement
(though not) exclusively – engagement
(Intrinsic connections ...) may (involve) – engagement
the fundamental (requirement) – appreciation
a massive (number) – amplification
essentially (a collection) – engagement
enormously (diverse) – amplification

Subject index

CURRENT ISSUES IN LINGUISTIC THEORY

E. F. K. Koerner
Zentrum für Allgemeine Sprachwissenschaft, Typologie
und Universalienforschung, Berlin

The *Current Issues in Linguistic Theory* (CILT) series is a theory-oriented series which welcomes contributions from scholars who have significant proposals to make towards the advancement of our understanding of language, its structure, functioning and development. CILT has been established in order to provide a forum for the presentation and discussion of linguistic opinions of scholars who do not necessarily accept the prevailing mode of thought in linguistic science. It offers an alternative outlet for meaningful contributions to the current linguistic debate, and furnishes the diversity of opinion which a healthy discipline must have. A complete list of titles in this series can be found on the publishers website, **www.benjamins.com/jbp**

Compostela, 7-11 September 2000. 2002.

224. FANEGO, Teresa, Belén MÉNDEZ-NAYA and Elena SEOANE (eds.): *Sounds, Words, Texts and Change. Selected papers from 11 ICEHL, Santiago de Compostela, 7-11 September 2000.* 2002.

225. SHAHIN, Kimary N.: *Postvelar Harmony.* 2002.

226. LEVIN, Saul: *Semitic and Indo-European. Volume II: comparative morphology, syntax and phonetics; with observations on Afro-Asiatic.* 2002.

227. FAVA, Elisabetta (ed.): *Clinical Linguistics. Theory and applications in speech pathology and therapy.* 2002.

228. NEVIN, Bruce E. (ed.): *The Legacy of Zellig Harris. Language and information into the 21st century. Volume 1: philosophy of science, syntax and semantics.* n.y.p.

229. NEVIN, Bruce E. and Stephen JOHNSON (eds.): *The Legacy of Zellig Harris. Language and information into the 21st century. Volume 2: computability of language and computer applications.* 2002.

230. PARKINSON, Dilworth B. and Elabbas BENMAMOUN (eds.): *Perspectives on Arabic Linguistics XIII-XIV. Papers from the Thirteenth and Fourteenth Annual Symposia on Arabice Linguistics.* 2002.

231. CRAVENS, Thomas D.: *Comparative Historical Dialectology. Italo-Romance clues to Ibero-Romance sound change.* 2002.

232. BEYSSADE, Claire, Reineke BOK-BENNEMA, Frank DRIJKONINGEN and Paola MONACHESI (eds.): *Romance Languages and Linguistic Theory 2000. Selected papers from 'Going Romance' 2000, Utrecht, 30 November - 2 December.* 2002.

233. WEIJER, Jeroen van de, Vincent J. van HEUVEN and Harry van der HULST (eds.): *The Phonological Spectrum. Part I: Segmental structure.* 2003.

234. WEIJER, Jeroen van de, Vincent J. van HEUVEN and Harry van der HULST (eds.): *The Phonological Spectrum. Part II: Suprasegmental structure.* 2003.

235. LINN, Andrew R. and Nicola MCLELLAND (eds): *Standardization. Studies from the Germanic languages.* 2002.

236. SIMON-VANDENBERGEN, Anne-Marie, Miriam TAVERNIERS and Louise RAVELLI: *Grammatical Metaphor. Views from systematic functional linguistics.* 2003.

237. BLAKE, Barry J. and Kate BURRIDGE (eds.): *Historical Linguistics 2001.Selected papers from the 15th International Conference on Historical Linguistics, Melbourne, 13–17 August 2001.* 2003.

238. NÚÑEZ-CEDENO, Rafael, Luis LÓPEZ and Richard CAMERON (eds.): *A Romance Perspective in Language Knowledge and Use. Selected papers from the 31st Linguistic Symposium on Romance Languages (LRSL), Chicago, 19–22 April 2001.* 2003.

239. ANDERSEN, Henning (ed.): *Language Contacts in Prehistory. Studies in Stratigraphy. Papers from the Workshop on Linguistic Stratigraphy and Prehistory at the Fifteenth International Conference on Historical Linguistics, Melbourne, 17 August 2001.* 2003.

240. JANSE, Mark and Sijmen TOL (eds.): *Language Death and Language Maintenance. Theoretical, practical and descriptive approaches.* 2003.

241. LECARME, Jacqueline (ed.): *Research in Afroasiatic Grammar II. Selected papers from the Fifth Conference on Afroasiatic Languages, Paris, 2000.* 2003.

242. SEUREN, Pieter A.M. and G. KEMPEN (eds.): *Verb Constructions in German and Dutch.* 2003.

243. CUYCKENS, Hubert, Thomas BERG, René DIRVEN and Klaus-Uwe PANTHER (eds.): *Motivation in Language. Studies in honor of Günter Radden.* 2003.

244. PÉREZ-LEROUX, Ana Teresa and Yves ROBERGE (eds.): *Romance Linguistics. Theory and acquisition.* 2003.

245. QUER, Josep, Jan SCHROTEN, M. SCORRETTI, Petra SLEEMAN and Els VERHEUGD (eds.): *Romance Languages and Linguistic Theory 2001. Selected papers from 'Going Romance' 2001, Amsterdam, 6–8 December.* 2003.

246. HOLISKY, Dee Ann and Kevin TUITE (eds.): *Current Trends in Caucasian, East European and Inner Asian Linguistics. Papers in honor of Howard I. Aronson.* 2003.